REV wright
     material with
        Indigen
        labor day

(m) p 22 vmwp

136: limits of amivityb

Distrib 22

CARBON COUNTY
USA

CARBON COUNTY
USA

Miners for Democracy in Utah and the West

CHRISTIAN L. WRIGHT

THE UNIVERSITY OF UTAH PRESS
SALT LAKE CITY

Copyright © 2020 by The University of Utah Press. All rights reserved.

The Defiance House Man colophon is a registered trademark of The University of Utah Press. It is based on a four-foot-tall Ancient Puebloan pictograph (late PIII) near Glen Canyon, Utah.

Library of Congress Cataloging-in-Publication Data

Names: Wright, Christian L., author.
Title: Carbon County USA: Miners for Democracy in Utah and the West / Christian L. Wright.
Description: Salt Lake City : The University of Utah Press, [2019] | Includes bibliographical references and index. |
Identifiers: LCCN 2019008128 (print) | LCCN 2019009616 (ebook) | ISBN 9781607817246 () | ISBN 9781607817239 (pbk. : alk. paper)
Subjects: LCSH: United Mine Workers of America—History—20th century. | Coal miners—Labor unions—Utah—Carbon County. | Coal miners—Labor unions—Utah—Emery County. | Labor movement—Utah—Carbon County. | Labor
movement—Utah—Emery County. | Labor unions—Utah.
Classification: LCC HD6515.M7 (ebook) | LCC HD6515.M7 W75 2019 (print) | DDC
331.88/12233409792566—dc23
LC record available at https://lccn.loc.gov/2019008128

Errata and further information on this and other titles available online at UofUpress.com

Printed and bound in the United States of America.

CONTENTS

Preface — vii
Acknowledgments — ix
Abbreviations — xvi
Prologue: Deer Creek — xvii
Introduction — xxvii

Part I

CHAPTER 1: The UMWA at High Tide — 3
CHAPTER 2: Twilight of the New Deal — 39
CHAPTER 3: Collapse — 59

Part II [1960s REVIVAL]

CHAPTER 4: Prophets — 99
CHAPTER 5: Carbon County, USA — 134
CHAPTER 6: Hell or High Water — 174

Part III [race, gender, age + unionism]

CHAPTER 7: El Movimiento — 201
CHAPTER 8: A Quiet Revolution ♀ — 224
CHAPTER 9: Unbridled — 253

EPILOGUE	276
APPENDIX A: Chronology	290
APPENDIX B: Locals of District 22 Locals, ca. 1983	305
APPENDIX C: Historic UMWA Locals in Utah	307
Abbreviations Used in the Bibliography and Notes	308
Bibliography	310
Notes	326
Index	384

PREFACE

CARBON COUNTY USA IS A NARRATIVE of rank-and-file power within America's premier industrial labor union at the height of its historic strength in the American West. Centered on the events of the great intermountain energy boom that lasted from about 1970 to its stunning 1982 collapse, it explores the origins of organized labor's long retreat within the failure of the decade's most inspiring bid for grassroots union reform: the Miners for Democracy movement within the United Mine Workers of America. To contextualize this movement, this book reaches back to the organization's Utah origins within the stormy 1930s and employs lenses of demography to examine how miners' racial, gender, and generational identities shaped their relationships to unions and inspired visions for their potential.

Instead of presenting an institutional history in the traditional sense, I have prioritized the experiences of those whose identities and needs imperfectly match the moral archetypes of class-struggle heroes and villains. By taking mine owners, nonunion miners, the unemployed, and dissident unionists seriously, I have endeavored to create a product that is sensitive as well as relevant to contemporary readers' most difficult questions about the potential for transformation within American workplaces today. In some ways, this book is an epitaph for a world that no longer exists. In others, it is an organizing manual for the future.

By the late 1960s, the structural contradictions at the heart of American coal mining's postwar peace began to unravel. While those who ruled from union offices and corporate boardrooms could no longer do so in the old ways, neither could those who labored underground depend upon traditional champions to address their most pressing concerns. As coal recovered from its long recession, miners gravitated towards one of two conclusions: For the union to survive, a revolt of working miners, widows, and retirees endeavored to restore responsive leadership through militant action, whistleblowing, and internal electoral campaigns. Alternately, a small yet vocal antiunion coalition assembled new sources of capital, the latest technology, comparable benefit packages, and flexible work rules to provide alternative employment frameworks at radical odds with established collective practices. From the same crisis in organizing, safety, and benefits, Miners for Democracy and nonunion mining operations raced against each other to determine coal's future. And it was here in the thick-seam, highly productive mines of the West that the most decisive battles would be fought.

ACKNOWLEDGMENTS

WRITING A BOOK IS A SOCIAL PROCESS, and in the course of this project's development I have incurred more debts than I have the capacity to ever repay. An initial word of thanks is undoubtedly due to historian Nancy Taniguchi and the staff of the Western History Reading Room of the Denver Public Library, where in 2008 I mistakenly picked up a copy of *Castle Valley, America* expecting to learn about the obscure village of that name near my adopted home of Moab, Utah. Instead, I discovered in Utah's "other" Castle Valley the historical questions I had long pondered in other contexts. Taniguchi herself extended to me the courtesy of reviewing an earlier version of this manuscript, and for her comments, encouragement, and extensive oral history work I am eternally grateful. I have similarly benefited from the pioneering work of a generation of scholars with ties to Carbon and Emery Counties. For their construction of archives and manuscripts, as well as their review and support of this one, I am among the thousands of students forever indebted to Floyd A. O'Neil and Allan Kent Powell.

For the opportunity to pursue historical study at a graduate level, I must thank Northern Arizona University's History Department—and Leilah Danielson, Eric Meeks, Michael Amundsen, and Karen Underhill in particular. Beyond their shepherding of this project in its early stages and the financial assistance that enabled its research, their presence as mentors, scholars, and members of a creative intellectual community continues to inspire. Likewise, I must thank Lance Newman of Westminster College, Jim Bullington of Adams State College, Andrew Gulliford of Ft. Lewis College, Tom Martin of Vishnu Temple Press, and Marty Genereux of Centennial Canoe as friends and mentors who each, in their own way, bear a share of the blame for my development as a historian. To Karen Garthwait of the National Park Service I owe immeasurable thanks for the opportunity to discover the challenges and rewards of an interpretive career in public service.

For their stewardship of our collective memory and assistance in my research, I must thank Jim Boyd and Lenise Peterman of the Western Mining and Railroad Museum in Helper, Utah; James Quigel Jr. and Alexandra Bainbridge of Penn State's Paterno Library; Erik Nordberg of Wayne State's Walter P. Reuther Library; and Selena Harmon of East Tennessee State University's Archives of Appalachia. Similarly, the special collections staff at Brigham Young University's Harold B. Lee Library, the University of Utah's J. Willard Marriott Library, and Utah State University–Eastern's library in Price have been instrumental to this project. Whitney Miller of Detroit and Caleb Bailey and Chase Price of Johnson City, Tennessee, made research financially possible as well as personally and politically illuminating. Friend and GIS specialist Zachary Rothwell assisted expertly with maps, and graphic designer Amie Shaw skillfully reconstructed several illuminating historic graphs. Archeologist and life partner Jessica Delbozque supported this project in innumerable ways, from creative family management to her passion for regional history.

If archives have captured only the fragments of our past, memory remains a resource of incomparable corrective and clarifying power. I am indebted to numerous residents of Carbon and Emery Counties in Utah who patiently encouraged and oriented a young historian. Among those who lived the events described in this book, I must thank Frank Markosek, Dennis Ardohain, Robert Trapanier, Duane Preston, John Palacios, Jon Passic, and Jim and Ramona Valdez for sharing their memories with me in depth. Similarly, Lee Bennett and Jim Mattingly of the Utah Division of Oil, Gas, and Mining's Abandoned Mine Reclamation Program have set the standard for twenty-first-century oral history and their outreach, videography, and transcription have been of tremendous benefit.

Personally, I must thank my family for supporting this project in countless ways through the years over which it has developed, and for teaching me at a young age the joy of reading and the value of history. I am also indebted to my coworkers among the service, guiding, and historical communities of five states who have taught me not only the skills necessary to thrive in today's economy but the meaning of solidarity in the practical sense. As collaborators and mentors, I owe much to Zachary Lown, Dave Zirin, Laya Monarez, Isaac Silver, Josh Brand, and Howard Zinn.

Lastly, I must thank my editors, John Alley, Tom Krause, and Ginny Hoffman with the University of Utah Press, whose patience and professionalism have brought this manuscript to life.

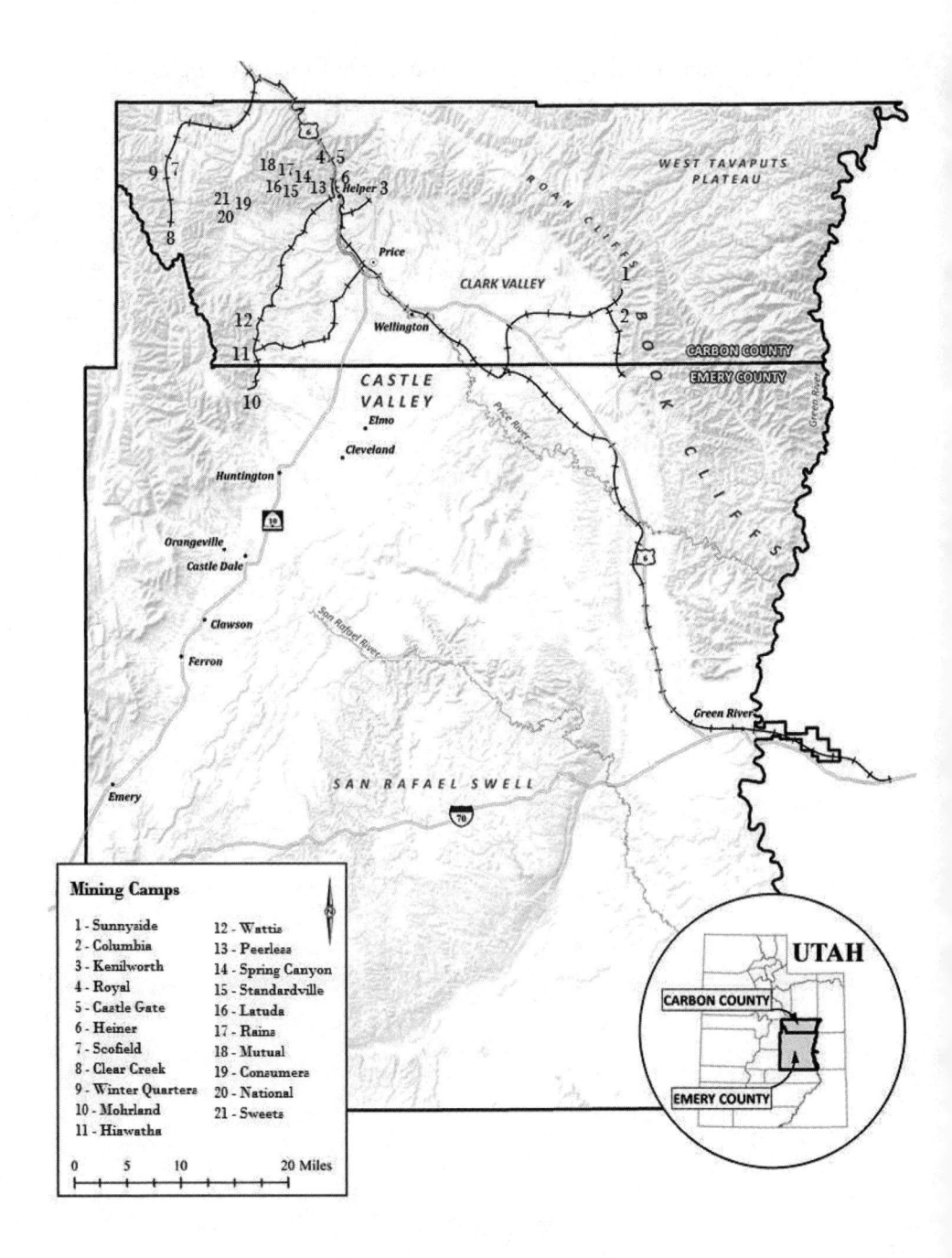

FIGURE 0.1. Utah mining camps, ca. 1930s–1940s.

Coal Mines

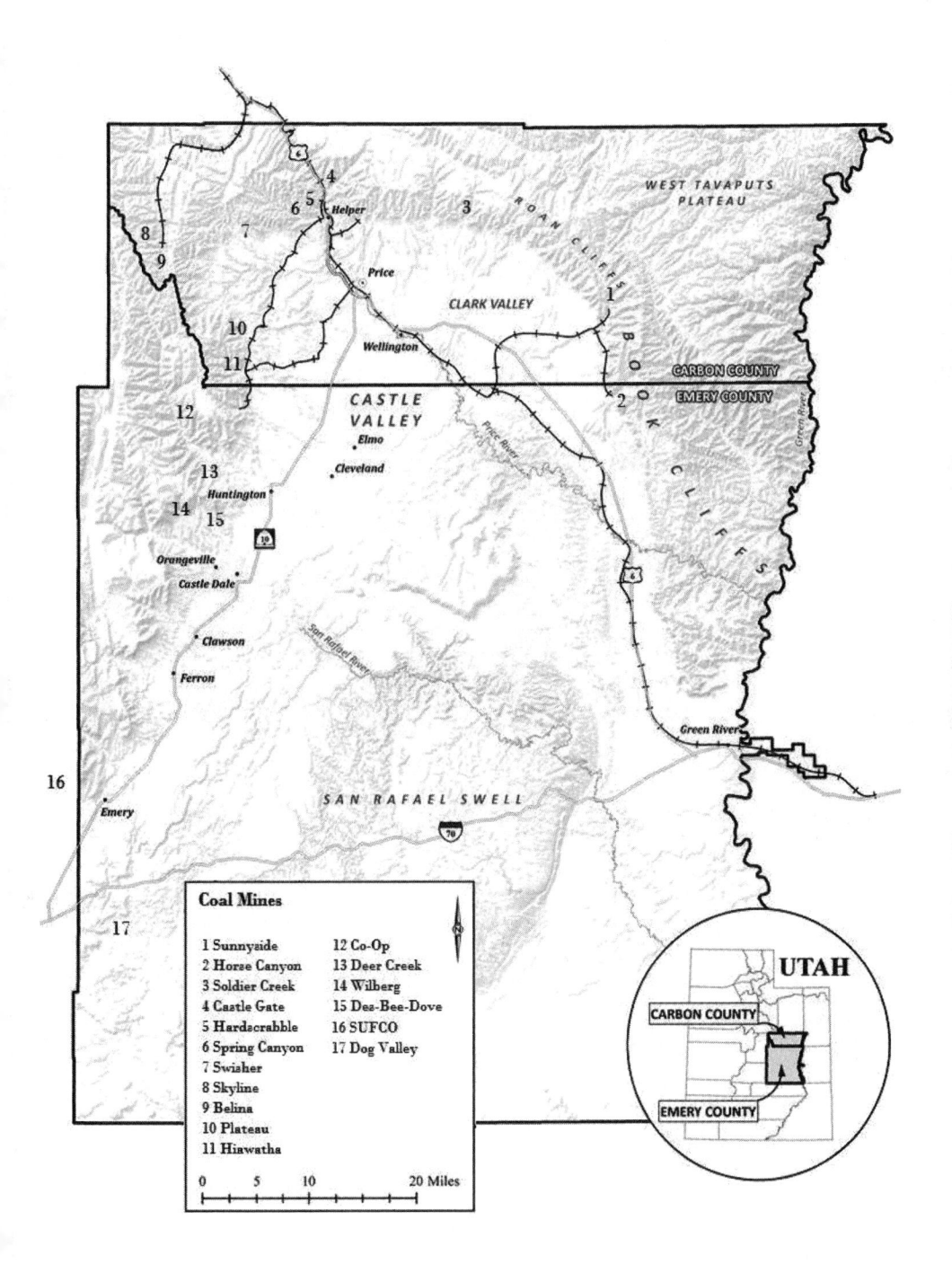

1 Sunnyside
2 Horse Canyon
3 Soldier Creek
4 Castle Gate
5 Hardscrabble
6 Spring Canyon
7 Swisher
8 Skyline
9 Belina
10 Plateau
11 Hiawatha
12 Co-Op
13 Deer Creek
14 Wilberg
15 Des-Bee-Dove
16 SUFCO
17 Dog Valley

FIGURE 0.2. Utah coal mines, ca. 1970s–1980s.

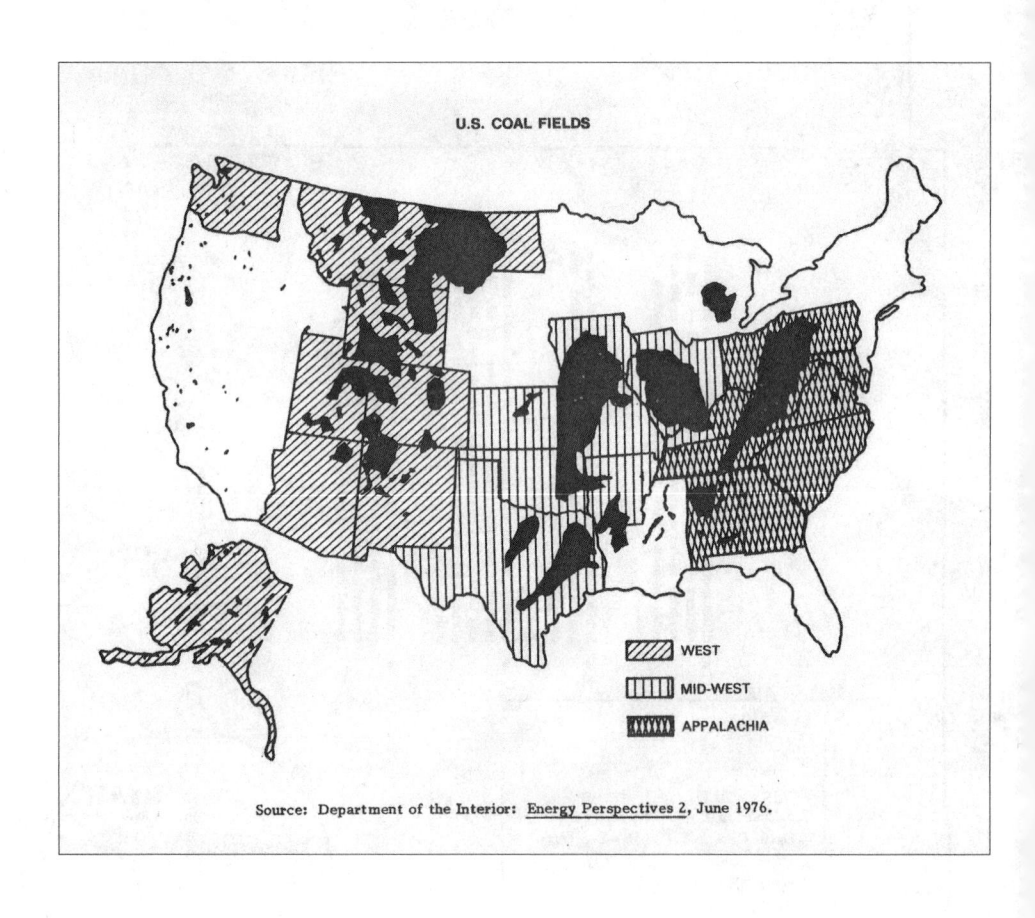

FIGURE 0.3. U.S. coal fields. From the President's Commission on Coal, *Coal Data Book*, 1980.

Production and Employment in Utah's Coal Industry, 1960-2016

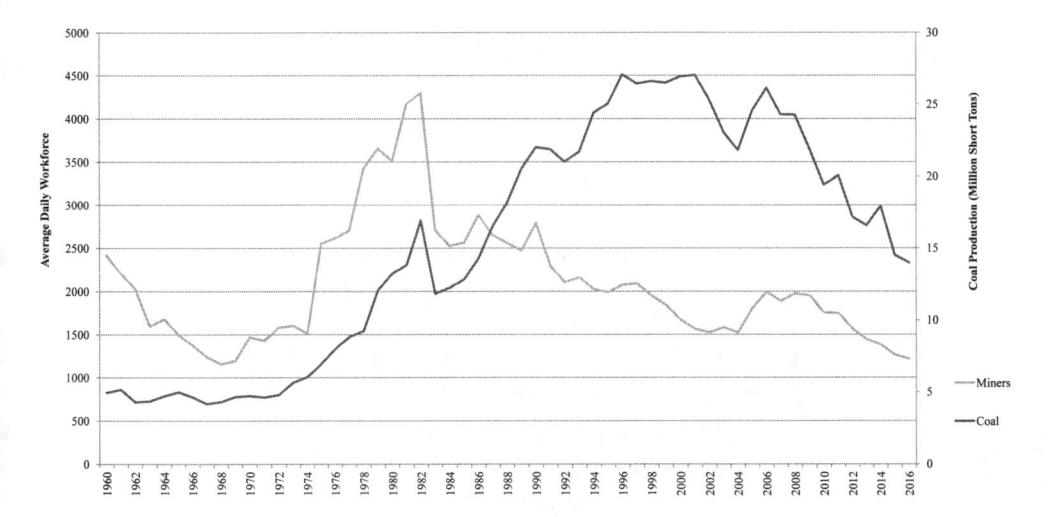

FIGURE 0.4. From 1950 to 1968, operators facing declining markets rapidly mechanized, which accelerated unemployment. After 1969, new safety regulations and utility development increased employment, which boomed after 1974. With high oil prices and federal support, coal peaked in early 1982 before falling prices and overcapacity led to mass layoffs. As Utah's underground mines increasingly depended on longwall systems and nonunion labor to stay competitive, the correlation between employment and production reversed after 1983. The 2008 recession ended a decade of revival. At the time of publication, new EPA regulations on power plant emissions and several regional power plants' conversion to natural gas have left many anxious for the industry's future. Source: Utah Geological Survey.

ABBREVIATIONS

AFL—American Federation of Labor
BCOA—Bituminous Coal Operators Association
CEP—Coal Employment Project
CIO—Congress of Industrial Organizations
CVWA—Castle Valley Workers' Association
D&RGW—Denver & Rio Grande Western Railroad
EMC—Emery Mining Corporation
ERA—Equal Rights Amendment
IEB—International Executive Board (of the United Mine Workers of America)
International—The UMWA's Washington, DC–based leadership
LDS—Latter-day Saints
LMU—Lady Miners of Utah
MFD—Miners for Democracy
NBCWA—National Bituminous Coal Wage Agreement
NLRB—National Labor Relations Board
NMU—National Miners' Union
SOCIO—Spanish-Speaking Organization for Community, Integrity, and Opportunity
SUFCO—Southern Utah Fuel Company
SWP—Socialist Workers Party
TVA—Tennessee Valley Authority
UP&L—Utah Power and Light
UMWA—United Mine Workers of America
WPA—Works Progress Administration

PROLOGUE

Deer Creek

With labor completely gone, little guerrilla actions may pop out of nowhere, with acts of sabotage that have nothing to do with unions or even in pursuit of a rational goal. All that will be left is rage.

—Thomas Geoghegan, *Only One Thing Can Save Us*

AS AVERAGE AMERICANS TRAVEL—whether running errands, going on vacation, taking a business trip, or relocating—they are often not even aware that they are in the vicinity of a modern coal-fired power plant. While in eastern regions forests and rolling hills allow most of these plants to operate with little scrutiny from the customers they serve, western aridity and geography have conspired to announce coal's architecture, infrastructure, and impacts in ways that are more visible. With their ubiquitous box architecture, prominent smokestacks, conveyor belts, and outdoor stockpiles, these industrial behemoths tower provocatively over the country's landscape. On I-80 in Nebraska they appear as distant aberrations upon an otherwise featureless horizon. On I-40 in Arizona the Cholla Generating Station interrupts an endless vantage of red rock and desert scrub near Petrified Forest National Park. On I-15 the Reid Gardner Generating Station defies the Basin and Range's apparent emptiness. And, until recently, the Cameo power plant on I-70 near Grand Junction, Colorado, and the Castle Gate plant along Highway 6/50 near Helper, Utah, cryptically suggested the Book Cliffs' vast mineral wealth to millions of travelers passing through those areas. On quieter roads like Highway 40 near Craig, Colorado; Highway 6-50 near Delta, Utah; and Highway 10 in Emery County, Utah, such a plant's sudden appearance amid otherwise pastoral settings challenges our preconceptions about the West, its sustainability, and its future.

While during the 1950s regional utilities experimented cautiously with "coal-by-wire," twenty years later accelerating urbanization and a national energy crisis drove their rapid proliferation across the western states. With railroads' adoption of dedicated unit trains and an increasingly integrated high-voltage energy grid, investors built coal-fired power plants nearer to fuel sources and farther from population centers. While urban centers got cleaner air and cheaper electricity, the rural West got mercury, nitrous oxides, fly ash, reduced air quality, and thousands of enthusiastically welcomed, high-paying jobs. Whether as monuments to progress and a better life, aesthetic curiosities jarringly imposed upon expansive landscapes, or anxiety-inducing reminders of our continued dependence on fossil fuels, encounters with coal-fired power plants inspire a breadth of emotion-

FIGURE 0.5. The Hunter Power Plant near Castle Dale further transformed Emery County into an industrial boomtown. Photograph by author.

al reactions that tell us as much about ourselves as the regions whose fates we ponder.

Just over half a century ago, motorists passing through coal country might have recognized its architecture with a greater familiarity. Known to most travelers, industrial society's essential fuel had not had its transportation, storage, and consumptive infrastructure cordoned off like an embarrassing secret in the nation's peripheral hinterlands. For urban and rural residents alike, smoke from domestic coal-burning stoves and decentralized commercial boilers was ubiquitous, unavoidable, and almost noxiously inescapable. In December 1952, over four thousand London residents literally choked to death from the exponentially increasing quantities of pollutants daily ejected into the aerial "pea soup" that since Shakespeare's time had periodically enveloped the city.

Unparalleled in its strategic value, coal dominated global energy markets. Despite gasoline and diesel fuel's increasing utility, coal still made the steel, ran the factories, and powered merchant shipping and railroads that supplied and transported the soldiers who won (and lost) World War II. It also kept the lights on, the house warm, and the breakfasts cooked for hundreds of millions of people whose children skidded across chilly floors each morning to shovel ash and kindle fires. In the United States, coal mining employed nearly 500,000 and was—for a few years still, at least—of equivalent importance to economic health as retail giants, fast food chains, software developers, and online shopping are for us today. Mesmerized by the wonders the black mineral had made possible, even the industry's sharpest critics bowed linguistically to its magic. As future radical strategist Saul Alisnky glowingly opened his 1949 biography of coal miners' leader John L. Lewis:

> Coal is the prime mover of our life. In these black chunks of the earth's history is the energy that pours power into our gigantic industrial empire. Beyond the conjuring of any imagination is the awesome vastness of man's industrial procession. Just a small segment of this Gargantuan industrial scene reveals interlaced speeding railroads, giant whirring dynamos lighting up the nation, and overwhelming surges of power spun from steam. For within coal is man's industrial holy trinity of light, heat, and power.... If steel provides the skeleton for our cities and towns, then coal provides the heart. It also yields infinite products to

our chemical industry. Break up this jet black nugget, and its by-products burst into more than ten thousand hues and colors, shaming the rainbow with its most delicate tints; for coal is basic to our making of dyes and colors. This black chunk, which murders men underground, is the base for that lifesaving miracle of modern times, the sulfa drugs. From nylon to plastic, from aspirin to perfume, the list of products is as great as our supply. It is estimated that in America alone we have enough coal to last twenty-five hundred years.[1]

Like the primordial tropical deltas where tens of millions of years' worth of slowly decaying plants and animals deposited the carbon that would one day release its energy into an iPhone, an air conditioner, or an automatic emergency defibrillator, the process of mining coal accelerated mankind's diffusion into social classes through the accumulation of hitherto-unimagined stores of want-dispelling energy, security, and profits. At the cost of traumatized childhoods, mangled limbs, crushed brains, and suffocated lungs, coal's jumpstarting of the Industrial Revolution exacerbated the complexities of decision-making, sharing, and sacrifice for human beings whose mental capacity to negotiate conflict had developed over hundreds of thousands of years of wandering the earth in familial clans.

From the Gilded-Age abuses of child labor, wage theft, and mass causality disasters, those who mined coal eventually established durable frameworks of self-advocacy, coordination, and resistance to exploitation. These were not casual associations, but brotherhoods of loyalty forged in the kiln of shared oppression, self-sacrifice, and survival. Vilified, outlawed, and marginalized for generations, labor unions won small victories while often learning harder lessons through failure. Explored through libraries of books (though largely forgotten in the popular imagination), places like Ludlow, Harlan, and Matewan evoke pitched battles between working-class Americans, private armies, sheriff's deputies, and state national guards. By the early twentieth century, unions like the United Mine Workers of America (UMWA) represented a growing power for which fathers and mothers were willing to face eviction, imprisonment, blacklisting, tear gas, police batons, martyrdom, murder raps, and unheralded death.

Outbreaks of violence, however, most often characterized periods of miners' organizational weakness and defensive confrontations that usually ended in defeat. It was not until the economic and political chaos of the Great Depression's darkest year that labor leaders, their political sympathizers, and far-sighted industrial planners negotiated a truce, rewrote law to legalize unions' existence, engineered the regulatory machinery that ensured their rapid proliferation, and gave their leaders seats at the table as negotiators and arbitrators in a national project of saving their industry from perpetual crisis. Haunted by generations of injustices, workers given their first chance to freely join a union did so by the millions. Discovering their power, they were not modest in deploying it. For five years in the late 1940s, half a million coal miners annually tightened the valve over their country's principle energy supply. Defying their employers, congressmen, judges, and even the president they had voted for, they won dramatic improvements for their families' health care as well as the first pensions most had ever known.

Transitioning from an afternoon of deep archival digging through organized labor's New Deal triumphs to a walk through any coal-mining community today is an exercise in historical trauma and spiritual revelation I invite every reader of this book to experience for themselves. Since the 2016 election, the trickle of journalists and social planners who periodically remind us that coal mining still exists has increased to some degree, yet the masses of ordinary citizens who might have the most to gain from embracing the heartland's tougher questions are more likely to pass right through it in favor of the less contentious mountains, forests, deserts, and rivers that not coincidentally overlap with coal mining's historic geography. Here in southeast Utah, we can hide behind our rocks. We can contain the world's explorers, seekers, and yearners within corrals of national monuments, high-speed interstates, and officially designated scenic byways carefully routed to minimize anxiety. But we don't have to, and we probably shouldn't.

Southeast Utah's more than two million annual tourists don't visit East Carbon–Sunnyside. It would be like intentionally dead-ending into Telluride or Park City if no one had ever invented skiing, film festivals, or real-estate speculation. Highway 10, with equal tragedy, remains decidedly off the beaten path despite its proximity to the principle routes of Utah's overwhelmingly successful "Mighty Five" National Parks campaign. This might be for the best, as the twenty-four-hour clockwork of double-trailered coal trucks, steaming thousand-megawatt power plants, boarded-up small-town storefronts, and retirees wheeling around oxygen canisters might be more than the average person seeking a relaxing recreational experience is willing to put up with.

For better or for worse, ever since Interstate 70's 1972 completion, small-town boosters, public lands managers, friendly museum directors, and capable historical societies have promoted historical tourism with some success. Most notably, five museums now interpret local history in Helper, Price, East Carbon-Sunnyside, Castle Dale, and Green River. Some time ago, local tourism bureaus and the state of Utah were even brave enough to draw a trans-Wasatch scenic "Energy Loop" on highway maps. Yet, coal country's efforts to rebrand itself appear mired in an uphill battle. Maybe industrial geography is just too socially disconcerting, and that's a regional assumption we've yet to seriously challenge. Maybe it's one we shouldn't. Who wants to jeopardize peace and quiet to get discovered by tourists anyway?

Putting regional cynicism aside, I will argue passionately in defense of crossing personal and conceptual boundaries. We grow—spiritually and intellectually—when we push our comfort levels to embrace the questions and emotions that we know are hard. So, I am thankful for downtown Price, with the closed K-Mart and historic J. C. Penney, where a little piece of me dies inside each time I walk or drive by. And I am thankful for Standardville and Kenilworth and Hiawatha, which rot along so beautifully in the sun of a hundred years. And I am thankful for the March 2015 closure of the Deer Creek coal mine up the fork of Huntington Canyon. Not because it laid off 182 miners who made nearly the best wages of anyone in the state; or because it tore $60,000 per month of mineral leasing money out of Emery County's budget; or because it was the last UMWA-organized coal mine in the state (Kentucky's closed that year, too); or because it felt like, and probably was, the New Deal's last stand in eastern Utah. I am thankful because—for whatever reason—I know it often takes a loss before we realize the value of things that we have long taken for granted.

Directly connected to the Huntington power plant with its two-mile-long conveyor belt that had operated nearly continuously since 1974, Deer Creek was a safe, efficient, and profitable coal mine for Rocky Mountain Power's Energy West/PacifiCorp subsidiary to operate. At the time of its closure it had about five years' worth of minable coal left, although it had run into higher ash and sulfur content that made its processing more expensive. While Rocky Mountain Power cited its obligation to consumers as a reason to sign new contracts with other coal mines, local residents largely interpreted the closure as an evil corporation's woeful insensitivity to the large number of workers, retirees, and pensioners Deer Creek supported.

Exactly one month and five days before the closure announcement was made, Deer Creek Local 1769's members voted in the last UMWA contract to have since been signed in Utah's coalfields. Over the preceding *two years*, District 22 president Mike Dalpiaz estimated he had spent literally thousands of hours in negotiations, and at the time of its signing miners had worked nearly a year without a strike since the old contract's expiration. Conceding to company concerns with rapidly escalating pension liabilities, it contained language that would have given future operators a major concession if Energy West had been successful in its final attempts to sell the mine. As the *Emery County Progress* summarized,

> Once the mine is sold, all those still working would have their retirement benefits frozen. While they would keep everything they had earned up to that point, Energy West would no longer be responsible to continue any investment into their retirement fund. The new owner would then be required to start a 401K account in the name of all current employees.[2]

If few outside of coal seemed to notice Deer Creek's closure at the time, during the 2016 election coal miners affected by increasing layoffs and the proposed elimination of their communities' principle economic activity helped create a political crisis that has succeeded, to no small degree, in bringing national attention to their plight. Far from inexplicable, the signs were plainly visible for years. Historically the most strident Democratic voters in the state, Carbon County went Republican back in 2008. By the summer of 2014, proposals to decommission power plants or convert them to natural gas had generated palpable senses of regional dread that festered for two years with little hint of comparable redevelopment or transitional compensation. By September 2016, signs of resentment weren't limited to names on mass-produced campaign paraphernalia, but included outlandish, homemade lawn displays, effigies, and puppets rarely seen outside of leftist marches on Washington or distant, social-democratically inclined European capital cities. How shocking the rejection was to party insiders and political commentators spoke volumes to just how marginalized working-class communities feel their existential needs have become.

If environmental concerns have polarized the way we talk to each other about coal, approaching our communication problems in isolation from the collapse of the American labor movement may condemn us to circular arguments and endlessly talking past each other. We can have a rational conversation about climate change. But we can't do it if our best alternative to making over $70,000 a year mining coal with a high school diploma and a mining certificate is to make $9 an hour folding sheets in a motel, to turn every quiet rural community of lifelong friends and neighbors into a Park City or a Moab (two Utah cities that have made the complete transition from mining to tourism), or to tell fifty-year-old homeowners to move across the country and/or go back to college.

The UMWA's vice president, Cecil Roberts, is exactly right that debating science is not the point. Mining economies have always disrupted their participants' lives with the swings of wild boom-and-bust cycles. In 1960, Appalachian coal's postwar collapse appalled a campaigning John F. Kennedy with its human toll and inspired a series of government programs collectively referred to as the "War on Poverty." The resources might exist for workable transitions to some other energy alternative. But a political program based on a toxic merger of Russian conspiracy theories, Wall Street financial backing, identity politics, and denial about the extent of political alienation within the traditionally unionized industrial working class is not a substitute coal miners—or anyone—should be willing to accept.

America needs to know Deer Creek. Not just the Deer Creek underground coal mine that fueled the Huntington power plant in Emery County, Utah, but the thousand-odd other Deer Creeks stalking the heartland with the chronic pain of a loved one's steady decline, frantic rumors of miracle cures, and quiet lifetimes spent with the ever-present specter of professional insecurity. We are right to mourn, and fight to defend, the last well-compensated jobs left anywhere. That doesn't have anything to do with telling electrical engineers, underground diesel mechanics, or power-plant operators that they need to start believing in science. It does have everything to do with understanding what labor unions were, why they were once allowed to freely organize, and how the most idealistic, principled, and sincere leaders, given a chance to rethink their operation at any time since World War II, failed to revive them into usable, sustainable tools.

Countless generations ago, it was through the light and heat of coal that humans learned to read, experiment, and work together in hitherto unprecedented ways. During the Great Depression, coal miners shook organized labor from a seemingly moribund lethargy to provide models of industrial democracy that by midcentury had transformed innumerable professions into desirable careers so unrecognizable from their origins that millions of wage-laborers referred to themselves for the first time as "middle class." In the late 1960s, coal miners' activism around Black Lung disease inspired reforms that culminated in the Occupational Safety and Health Act of 1970 which has since saved countless lives. Within the broader labor movement, miners' willingness to confront executive corruption inspired a number of similar democratization movements elsewhere.

If history is any guide, one may hope that coal mining's latest crisis could inspire a rethinking about energy, politics, power, and class, as it has on multiple occasions throughout the industry's past. Coal's recent decline has left many postwar multiemployer health care and pension funds financially insolvent, prompting miners to lobby for the Coal Miners' Health Care Act of 2017 and the yet-to-be-passed Miners' Pension Protection Act. These efforts have inspired a broader rethinking of relationships between the state, private industry, and society's obligations to meet miners and retired miners' basic needs.

With spiraling wealth inequality driving our political stability over a cliff, labor history in 2019 is not an esoteric tribute to bygone worlds or an academic subculture speaking an obscure language and trading union memorabilia like pogs or baseball cards. Industrial democracy can be whatever we make it. If we are today so clearly confronted with the fact of its collapse, perhaps we might also begin to start rethinking its origins, its orthodoxy, and its future.

INTRODUCTION

> Yes, and the day that the LABOR UNIONS passes out then woe be to the people in this great COUNTRY of OURS, for it shall really cease to exist and the COUNTRY will be just a GHOST of its former self. Mark that and well.
>
> —William Dalrymple, 1951

THE STORY OF THE AMERICAN labor movement's decline—to the extent that it is talked about at all—has to date suffered in its telling from a fairly one-sided point of view. This assertion is not intended to be partisan or imply any barbs against conservative individualists who may have greeted the signs of its disappearance with sighs of relief. Labor's sins—one might say—mattered, and there is much in disillusionment that can and ought to be forgiven. Similarly, academic scholars who are more sympathetic to organized labor in general must be thanked for their accomplishments but not overlooked for their assumptions. If the organizations that rapidly dwindled in membership and influence after the 1970s may be mourned with a well-founded sense of loss, it should not be forgotten that by that time most American unions were deeply flawed, conflicted, and misanthropic creatures. Today's armies of often involuntarily "nonunion" workers can be forgiven for avoiding unions, not because so many workers are greedy, shortsighted, selfish, or unintelligent—but because so many tried everything they could to revive these institutions and were still fired, blacklisted, shut down, sold out, strung along, or otherwise instructively convinced that unions' historic stature had by the 1970s come to stand at drastic odds to their usability as practical tools.

Narratives highlighting legal restrictions on labor's ability to organize, the National Labor Relations Board's (NLRB) pro-employer politicization and operational lethargy, globalization, outsourcing, and corporate consolidation are well known—and not at all without consequence. This history matters, matters powerfully, and has been ably documented by many, from Mike Davis's *Prisoners of the American Dream* (1986) and Michael Goldfield's *The Decline of Organized Labor in the United States* (1987) to Nelson Lichtenstein's *State of the Union* (2002, 2013).[1] Constrained within these limits, American collective bargaining's internationally unique complexity has required unions to adopt high levels of legal expertise and frequently deemphasize potentially costly membership activism. This in turn has encouraged the development of what Goldfield and many others have called "business unionism," or "the literal running of a union as a business . . . to preserve its income, not deplete its resources unnecessarily. . . . [At worst] such a stance may mean . . . bureaucratic domination of the membership [and] the submergence of the rights of the rank-and-file whose desires and goals might present organizational risks." Right-to-work laws do not, in fact, prevent anyone who wants to from exercising their legal right to voluntarily join a union. Within the context of the high legal costs of organizing a union, however, such laws have condemned most unions to a fatally pessimistic financial logic: Organizing in the traditional way now costs unions more money than they can probably hope to recoup from dues paid by new members.

In Goldfield's analysis, such a bleak outlook may explain why few unions appropriated substantial expenditures for new organizing during the defensive 1980s and beyond. Where major confrontations did occur—such as the 1981 Professional Air Traffic Controllers Organization strike, the 1983 Phelps-Dodge copper strike, or the 1985 Hormel meatpackers' strike—business unionists' inability to mobilize mass support for embattled striking workers led to their isolation and defeat in most instances. Unable to grow substantially through new organizing campaigns and anticipating a future of defensive battles to protect their historic bases, traditions of self-organization have become increasingly distant to most American workers since the early eighties. Assessing the long-term legacy of these failures, Goldfield was among the first of many scholars to gloomily note "a long-term decline in the image of labor unions" unmatched in any other industrialized capitalist country.²

Until recently, a major historical gap within deunionization narratives has been exceedingly light treatments of the rank-and-file rebellions that occurred within many unions throughout what historian Jefferson Cowie has persuasively identified as the "long seventies." As Mike Davis briefly noted, "Every major ex-CIO union (with the sole exception of the democratic and militant packinghouse workers), as well as the miners, teamsters, and postal workers, was eventually challenged at some time between 1963 and 1973 by a major internal insurgency."³ Limiting his exploration of these movements' potential to two pages is a major shortcoming of his otherwise extremely illuminating work. Did viable alternatives exist to unions' fantastic decline since the 1980s? Maybe. Were these also doomed to failure? Perhaps. Why do we so rarely hear about them? That's a good question.

Maybe the stories we want to tell and the stories we want to hear are more likely to be those about heroic leaders, strong organizations, and victories over injustice than they are to be about dissident movements, shortchanged members, anticorruption campaigns, or defeated strikes. This imbalance, however, is not without consequence. In a world of diminishing expectations, growing economic inequality, fragmented labor movements, and a global rise in political authoritarianism, we probably have more to gain from a critical analysis of New Deal–style industrial democracy's origins, transformation, and decline than any mountains of praise for the accomplishments of forgotten times.

Selective storytelling may serve partisan and professional interests as well. By understating the importance of internal power dynamics, the world is more easily divided into "union" and "nonunion" camps to which moral binaries of "good" and "bad" may be easily assigned depending on the writer's point of view. This may serve a short-term interest in flattering unions, or employers, as more heroic and less conflicted than they may have ever actually been. In the long term, however, such mythologies may be better at assigning blame than they are at helping us understand how our present worlds came to be.

Filling in these gaps by historicizing such movements as the UMWA's Miners for Democracy, the United Steelworkers' Steel Workers Fight Back, the Teamsters' Teamsters for a Democratic Union, and rank-and-file activists' efforts within the United Autoworkers has been an exciting and, perhaps, somewhat more optimistic project of multiple scholars over the past decade. In addition to historicizing these movements' potential and ultimate limitations, rank-and-file activity also expanded during the late sixties, seventies, and early eighties among racial and gender minorities, who merged civil rights and union activism to confront unique workplace injustices with profound relevance for the present. Excellent introductions to several of these movements can be found in Jefferson Cowie's *Stayin' Alive: The 1970s and the Last Days of the Working Class* (2010); Aaron Brenner, Robert Brenner, and Cal Winslow's *Rebel Rank and File: Labor Militancy and Revolt From Below During the Long 1970s* (2010); Steve Early's *Save Our Unions* (2013); Curtis Seltzer's earlier *Fire in the Hole: Miners and Managers in the American Coal Industry* (1985); and Dorothy Sue Cobble's *The Other Women's Movement: Workplace Justice and Social Rights in Modern America* (2004).

Broadening labor's story to include these actors is a crucial endeavor that gets us away from moral language lionizing heroes and demonizing villains, and closer to understanding the complexity and imperfection of those on both sides of labor-management and union-nonunion divides. From the institutional center, there is a tendency to ignore glaring defects in order to mythologize the past may excuse internal corruption and weak strategy while blaming workers for failing to triumph over circumstances, laws, and power structures it may have been impossible for anyone to surmount. From the left, critics who may feel comfortable denouncing union officers' conservatism without understanding the legally restrictive confines they functioned under run the risk of overidealizing the practicality of dramatic or militant actions that may have failed repeatedly in the past. And from the right, in celebrating the decline of unions altogether it is possible that far greater threats to our political democracy have been unleashed. Without an effective counterweight to the fantastic energies of profit, millions of Americans' working and living conditions have inarguably and precipitously declined since the late 1970s. The extreme polarization of wealth that has resulted bodes ill for the integrity of any democratic society.

Politically, our sympathies all too often compound our ignorance. Maybe the stories we want to hear are tales of worlds we haven't known.

Should we dare to inspect them more closely and critically, our personal heroes and villains might appear more complex and contradictory than any moral boxes we might wish to put them in. Perhaps, therefore, an exploration of labor unions' decline, a rethinking of their origins, and a careful cultivation of those lessons rank-and-file reformers learned as they struggled to articulate alternatives has a significance beyond any academic project. Labor history is the history of most Americans. It is a past we risk forgetting at our peril.

Within this conversation, coal mining matters not just because UMWA members led the most successful reform effort within any American union during the 1970s, or because earlier during the 1930s they established the Congress of Industrial Organizations (CIO) model through which most other industrial unions organized. Coal mining's deunionization timeline uniquely bucks the narratives of economic globalization, permanent striker replacements, and Reaganite intervention that dominates memories (and conversations) about the 1980s and beyond. While once-powerful unions in manufacturing industries such as auto, steel, and rubber suffered greatly from international restructuring in the late 1970s and early 1980s, Utah's coal industry boomed from 1974 to 1982. And although mechanization had eliminated three hundred thousand coal mining jobs nationally from 1948 to 1970, employment in the following decade rose alongside tonnage. While corporate mergers and industrial consolidation reduced national contract strikes' effectiveness, it was plucky entrepreneurs rather than large corporations who pioneered union-avoidance strategies from the late 1940s to the early 1970s. When, during the subsequent boom in coal development, union power fragmented at an accelerated rate, it did so over long-contentious disagreements, through predictably effective union-avoidance strategies, and along recognizably familiar timelines.

As the system of collective bargaining established by John L. Lewis during the New Deal broke down, union reformers and antiunion advocates competed to influence the workforces at newly opened mines across the western coal-producing states. While high unemployment reduced miners' willingness to organize after energy markets' 1982 collapse, union support declined, and organizing drives failed, during years of rapid growth amid a national miner shortage. How, then, could nonunion mines open within the heart of UMWA support and keep the union from organizing their employees? Did organizers simply make mistakes, or was the organization they had known for over thirty years in the midst of a systemic crisis? Who were the coal miners of the 1970s, and to what degree did their identities, worldviews, and social environments affect their attitudes toward unionization? And if the stakes really were the reversal of gains hard won through generations of struggle, what could rank-and-file unionists do to revitalize an organization so crucial to their lives?

Nowhere was the answer to these questions more important for the UMWA than in District 22, the administrative jurisdiction encompassing Arizona, Utah, and Wyoming. While the 1970 Clean Air Act's original sulfur-content provisions gave the region a natural competitive advantage, and OPEC nations' 1973 oil embargo nudged utilities toward conversion to coal-fired power plants, longer-term shifts in energy production set the stage for coal's recovery well before that year. As western urban growth demanded new sources of electricity, utility planners' eyes increasingly turned to the vast deposits of coal scattered across the rural hinterlands of seven states. From Montana and the Dakotas to Arizona and New Mexico, the continental compression that created the Rocky Mountains drained a vast interior seaway that for millions of years had nourished lush deltas at the mouths of ancient rivers. Charismatically indicated by Iguanodon footprints and Plesiosaur skeletons, layers of stream and ocean deposits compressed thousands of feet of rotting vegetation to form peat—and eventually, North America's largest deposits of bituminous coal. As urban centers expanded over the first two postwar decades, advances in rail transportation and high-voltage electrical transmission allowed this energy source to be tapped ever further from consumers and ever nearer to its geologic source. As increasingly diversified energy conglomerates recognized this potential, they mobilized capital on the scale of hundreds of millions of dollars to finance new coal mine development and power plant construction.

By the mid-1970s, boomtown conditions exploded across the Intermountain West, with dramatic implications for community transformation as well as work-process restructuring. On the periphery of unionized coalfields, new investors transformed marginal operations into commercial mines employing hundreds. In Montana and Wyoming's Powder River Basin, lightly unionized surface miners developed the nation's largest deposits of thick-seam, low-depth coal, with dire implications for underground miners who produced less tonnage at higher cost. In Arizona the UMWA had its greatest success, where it won predominantly Navajo miners' support at a pair of massive strip mines newly opened on Black Mesa. In Utah, environmentalist opposition to strip-mining near national parks nixed plans for similar operations on the Kaiparowits Plateau and confined the industry's growth to underground mines within the Book Cliffs and Wasatch coalfields in Carbon and Emery Counties. Here, new owners revived dormant and formerly unionized properties at Wattis, Gordon Creek, and Soldier Creek as nonunion operations. Their successful resistance to organization and subsequent high productivity transformed coal's price and reliability at union mines' expense.

While nonunion production's rise coincided with a shift in statewide output from Carbon and Emery Counties, the UMWA's decline cannot be explained by any historical religious divisions between Mormon agriculturalists and religiously diverse coal miners. In 1933, LDS miners in several "coal camps" overcame their church's historical coolness toward unions to help organize new UMWA locals. At Castle Gate and Hiawatha, Utah, large LDS populations erected the only physical churches in town and incorporated Latter-day Saints' theology into a pro-union, working-class culture that produced numerous local and district union leaders.[4] In fact, organizers during the late 1960s and early 1970s had their greatest success in Emery County, and in 1972 signed contracts that covered three properties poised for rapid growth. Managed by Huntington miner, politician, booster, and entrepreneur Shirl McArthur, American Coal Company and Castle Valley Mining's Des-Bee-Dove, Deer Creek, and Wilberg mines expanded quickly to supply coal to Utah Power and Light (UP&L)'s newly constructed mine-mouth Huntington (1974) and Hunter (1978) power plants. While tensions between Mormons and non-Mormons persisted well into the twentieth century—and periodically influenced union politics—these cannot explain the union's difficulties in this period.

More compelling than religious or geographic divisions, demographic change along racial, gender, and generational lines may have caused the greatest social friction underground. Initially excluded from full participation as unionists, Chicano and women miners' community infrastructure and activism enriched reform efforts within the UMWA and provide a crucial lens through which to view the changes that affected all miners at the time. Conversely, the arrival of several thousand young workers new to mining substantially diluted union identification. Many of these did not come from mining families, were unattached to the UMWA, and had not experienced the deference to authority older miners had accepted in the years of precarious employment. Furthermore, these miners' increasingly mobile, decentralized, and individualistic lifestyles contrasted notably with the tight-knit, interwoven community-workforce linkages of the company town era. Unlike prior campaigns, organizers now faced the difficult task of "selling" union traditions across a generational divide.[5]

Aware of the UMWA's needs to organize new mines in order to maintain bargaining strength and benefit programs, personnel managers carefully screened new hires. At newly opened Swisher Coal in the late 1960s, owner Ura Swisher imported antiunion miners from as far as away as his former home in Ohio. At Plateau Mining during the same period, Wyoming-born entrepreneur Wayne Baker hired several former employees of the Knight Ideal mine—a small, nonunion operation closed in 1965 which had for years operated as a thorn in the UMWA's side. After 1978, selective hiring became easier as layoffs at eastern mines increased the pool of experienced miners willing to relocate. Four years later, with almost one-third of Utah's coal miners idle, managers planning the next round of layoffs had a powerful tool to purge suspected activists. As production slowly recovered, employers' use of subcontracting, probationary hiring periods, and sophisticated interviewing of new hires further separated union loyalists from the active mining workforce.[6]

Locally, some expressed a hitherto exceptional (if not heretical) skepticism about the UMWA and other unions' usefulness with an escalating tenor and frequency as these organizations' setbacks became increasingly apparent. By the late 1970s, disillusioned by benefits cutbacks, corruption scandals, lengthy national strikes, and failed organizing drives, antiunion miners began purchasing assertive ads under their own names, writing hostile letters to the editor, and even carrying guns while crossing picket lines.[7] Cumulatively, this nascent ideological antiunionism evolved into another obstacle just as threatening to the

UMWA's future as the structural changes in ownership, geography, and technology that transformed coal mining materially.

While some rejected the UMWA entirely, most may have done so reluctantly—recognizing the union's historic accomplishments while lamenting its current limitations. At several nonunion properties, some miners appear to have intentionally feigned interest in unionizing in order to extract concessions from alarmed employers without having to pay union dues, risk a contract strike, punitive layoffs, or any of the other uncertainties that increasingly appeared to characterize traditional union organizing. And with few exceptions, nonunion miners' working conditions increasingly transcended traditional stereotypes of substandard pay and exceptional danger. With massive investment from large energy companies and without the burdens of strikes, union work rules, safety committee objections, or fixed royalties to shared union benefit funds, nonunion mines now provided higher wages and competitive health and fringe benefits. Though coal operators may have gained the most from such paternalism, antiunionism's power lay in the convergence of managerial priorities with employees' needs and worldviews.

With union power weakened, a new generation of aggressively antiunion operators with unprecedented access to capital ultimately outmaneuvered union reformers. While those who organized a nationally coordinated rebellion of the UMWA's rank-and-file did so with abundant justification, by broadening this study beyond the events of one decade to consider the unions' historical weaknesses and long postwar decline it is difficult to see how leadership changes alone could have reversed American unions' overall trajectory by the late 1970s. While it was not until that decade's end that unionization rates and strike frequency entered a period of long-term decline, a critical perspective on industrial unionism's emergence during the 1930s and 1940s suggests that the options available to any group of union leaders in later decades were severely circumscribed by a number of deep-seated fault lines within the systems they sought to reform.

The history of coal mining, like most history, does not fit neatly into decades. While the questions this book asks have focused on events that occurred from about 1966 to 1984, those seeking to understand the historical constructions of power within American workplaces—and the alternatives to them that exist or have existed—would do well to consider labor's story as interrelated with the social and institutional evolutions that unfolded across the entire twentieth century. Class struggle is intergenerational. By the late 1960s, twenty years of economic restructuring, benefit-program management, and administrative bureaucratization had transformed most unions into institutions vastly different from what young workers' fathers and grandfathers had earlier experienced and fought to build. Thus, asking why or how labor unions declined during the long seventies begins with a set of big assumptions about what labor unions (and their adversaries) are or were.

This book's initial section, which examines coalfield unionism's heyday and postwar struggles, is included for multiple reasons. With private sector American union membership down to 11.1 percent in 2015, the experience of life and work as a labor union member is perhaps as distant to most readers today as the social worlds of the New Deal itself.[8] A review of this experience allows one to understand the UMWA's accomplishments through much earlier struggles to articulate industrial democracy's meaning. A critical perspective also allows one to identify the limitations built into John L. Lewis's model of collective bargaining and membership participation.

Taking such scope into consideration, many of the UMWA's challenges during the 1970s appear related to changes that occurred over the preceding two decades. In 1950, John L. Lewis and Consolidation Coal Company's George H. Love brought the industry's largest employers into the Bituminous Coal Operators Association (BCOA) to negotiate a National Bituminous Coal Wage Agreement (NBCWA). Faced with the loss of key markets in transportation and home heating, both Lewis and his traditional opponents feared the return of ruinous competition that had sapped profits, bankrupted companies, and haphazardly laid off miners throughout the 1920s and 1930s. A uniform national agreement was palatable to both sides, who hoped to retain the union sector's competitive advantage through economies of scale over the many capital-poor, nonunion entrants who had always dotted the margins of coal-producing areas. Of course, such "pattern bargaining" favored the largest employers who had the capital to afford the newest machinery (and not coincidentally owned the mines where most UMWA members worked). While Lewis's support for mechanization resulted in the rapid elimination of hundreds of thousands of coal mining jobs, it was the tradeoff BCOA members demanded to restore profitability to the point that they could afford higher wages and benefits. These in turn served the institutional needs of Lewis's administrative machine, which had co-opted or expelled most of its political rivals, yet ultimately had to answer to a membership it could not totally control.

While stressful to smaller companies, biannual wage increases and hitherto unimagined health and pension benefits perpetuated Lewis's nearly messianic image. Despite an increasingly problematic funding structure, to their credit these programs had dramatically increased living standards for several hundred thousand miners and their families. While western European nations confronted the same problems with nationalization, subsidies, and an expanded welfare state for all citizens, within the political constellation of American postwar politics a single-industry benefit plan and rapid mechanization seemed the most realistic option to capital as well as labor.[9]

Despite its inflated numbers, there is logic to Lewis's argument that "it's better to have half a million men working in the industry at good wages, high standards of living than it is to have a million working in the industry in poverty and degradation."[10] Similarly, one can justify the UMWA-BCOA campaign for oligopoly, which endeavored to reduce costs with machines faster than capital-poor, smaller mines could by reducing wages. Until 1970, small mines were exempt from many safety regulations, and by putting them out of business some of the industry's worst conditions were eliminated. Yet, while obviously an impalpable argument for small-mine owners, this policy also alienated thousands of ex-UMWA members who worked at nonunion mines where no other employment was available.[11]

While for almost twenty years the UMWA-BCOA partnership appeared to work, organizers in the 1950s encountered the arrangement's limitations firsthand. In its earliest days the union had negotiated diverse wage rates to suit individual mines' circumstances, but pattern bargaining protected established union mines while it enraged small and newer operators.[12] Few small-mine owners realized profit margins high enough to comfortably afford the national contract's provisions, and many accused union organizers of intentionally attempting to put them out of business. Nationally, the UMWA experienced its greatest setbacks at this time in southern Appalachia, where the Tennessee Valley Authority (TVA)'s new coal-fired power plants purchased coal based on cost alone. In east Tennessee and east Kentucky, violence flourished as nonunion mines proliferated and stonewalled union organizers. Amid these struggles, one small operator sued the nation's largest producer, Consolidation Coal Company, and the UMWA together for violating the Sherman Antitrust Act. In a significant but quietly reported 1970 decision, a federal judge in Lexington, Kentucky, found the defendants guilty of attempting to create a monopoly. After a month of testimony, a jury decided the conspiracy had existed since 1950 and awarded the South East Coal Company of Eastern Kentucky $7.3 million in damages—half to be paid by the company and half by the union.[13]

As echoes of these conflicts reverberated across the West, nonunion operators pioneered a number of strategies to outmaneuver union organizers. Taking this experience into consideration, the comparatively slower pace of economic development appears to have been a determining factor in postponing a showdown here until the 1970s. While there was no TVA in Utah, as early as the mid-1950s western utilities experimented with the construction of mine-mouth, coal-fired power plants. Built in 1951 by Utah Power & Light and controversially demolished for failing to meet revised EPA requirements in 2016, the Castle Gate power plant north of Helper, Utah, embodied electric utilities' abandonment of urban power plant construction in favor of investment in "coal-by-wire." While such projects provided the greatest hope for coal's revival, it took over a decade for regional growth, fuel shortages, and capital mobilization to develop the model on a larger scale.

Thus, coal mining's revival during the mid-1960s provides the setting for Part II of this book. As demand increased, UMWA organizers engaged a growing number of operators in a struggle for industrial control. As chapter four demonstrates, union hegemony within coal mining communities can be gauged from the fact that at all seven Utah organizing drives in the late 1960s and early 1970s, majorities of nonunion miners signed union-authorization cards and, where able, selected the UMWA as their bargaining representative in NLRB or Utah Labor Board elections. These miners were not convinced of their employer's antiunion rhetoric, nor were they totally satisfied with concessions of higher wages. However, at five of these mines employer retaliation, regulatory inaction, and negotiators' tactical mistakes transformed organizing successes into collective-bargaining failures. Subsequently, benefit cutbacks and the increased length and bitterness of national contract strikes incubated antiunion sentiments, allowing employers to shift tactics from reactive union busting to preventative union avoidance.

By this time, nonunion coal mining's ownership structure and working conditions began to change dramatically from the "dog-hole" stereotype of years past. As diversified energy conglomerates invested in coal, corporate capital's marriage with small operators' antiunionism proved formidable. Mines with only a handful of employees could now afford the most modern machinery, which they operated more efficiently than their BCOA competitors. Mechanization also provided a rhetorical basis for antiunionists, who cited productivity disparities in attacks

FIGURE 0.6. On December 16, 1963, nine men died in Utah's Carbon Fuel mine explosion. While disasters generated headlines, smaller accidents killed 284 miners nationally the same year. Also unreported, mechanization increased coal-dust inhalation, which has killed at least 78,000 miners since record-keeping started in 1969. Used with permission from the Eberly Family Special Collections Library, Pennsylvania State University Libraries.

on union benefit systems. Under the NBCWA contract, a mine that used a longwall system and produced ten thousand tons a day with a few dozen workers paid the same per-tonnage royalty rate into the UMWA Welfare and Retirement Fund as a mine that produced a third as much with continuous mining machines and two or three times as many employees. In the days of conventional mining when the Fund was established, productive disparities had never been so high.

While technological changes could undermine miners' industry-wide solidarity, mechanization's dark side inspired an unprecedented rank-and-file revolt. Newly invented cutting and loading machines dramatically increased the amount of coal dust miners inhaled. State and federal requirements for ventilation standards lagged far behind these changes to facilitate an epidemic of "coal miner's pneumoconiosis," or "Black Lung" disease. While doctors in England had long viewed coal dust as harmful, Black Lung remained medically unrecognized, unregulated, and uncompensated in the United States until 1969. Simultaneously, mechanical equipment's increased noise could deafen even experienced miners to the signals of impending roof collapses. Throughout the 1960s, two to three hundred coal miners died annually from workplace accidents, while tens of thousands of retirees spent the last years of their lives literally gasping for air.

Such a toll was not an inevitable consequence of mechanization but was exacerbated by union policy. The UMWA's belated support for Black Lung compensation and prevention can be understood as one of several policies that endeavored to stabilize the union sector in ways detrimental to miners' long-term interests. In November 1968, John L. Lewis's appointed successor, W. A. "Tony" Boyle, revealed a troubling and apparently indifferent attitude toward safety in his response to an explosion at Consolidation Coal Company's No. 9 mine in Farmington, West Virginia. After a visit to the mine, Boyle enraged much of his membership when he characterized the explosion responsible for the deaths of seventy-eight union miners as an "inherent danger" and praised Consolidation's record as "one of the better companies to work with."[14] Similarly unacceptable to members, Boyle signed a growing number of "sweetheart" contracts to reduce or excuse royalty payments for union mines threatened by non-union competition. While this can be understood as a defensive response to organizing setbacks, such arrangements cost the Fund millions in lost revenues and excluded thousands from health care and pension benefits they felt entitled to receive.¹⁵

While a united and stable union may have had better success at the bargaining table, by the late 1960s the leadership structure John L. Lewis established and his successor inherited increasingly proved so antagonistic to miners' interests that for many the union's institutional future appeared inseparable from a revival of internal democracy—an issue that had not been seriously contested since the 1920s. Authoritarian unionism's costs were paid in organizing, where nonunion miners began to ask questions even the most sympathetic UMWA representatives could not answer. And as more tonnage evaded UMWA control, Boyle's increased reliance on sweetheart contracts failed to restore the union sector's competitiveness or adequately fund its programs. They did, however, allow the union leader to save face, paper over expanding fault lines, and outwardly project an image of control. While censorship and posturing hid a deteriorating strategic position from most members' understanding, International officials and district leaders—particularly those few who still had independent bases of support—increasingly wrestled with a guilty conscience.

Throughout the years of compromise, it was easier to make excuses for John L. Lewis. He spoke the miners' language, understood their needs, and inarguably had delivered them from the worst days of company-town serfdom. Now, despite the many years he spent by the elder labor statesman's side, Boyle reflected little of his charm, tact, or charisma. Housed comfortably in the best hotels, chauffeured conveniently in Cadillac limousines, spendthrift with expense accounts, and—as age approached—well insulated from benefit cutbacks with secretly organized retirement accounts, the "Payrollers" and "Porkchoppers" of Boyle's inner circle lived high on the hog, basked passionately in the limelight, embezzled millions, rigged elections, and deployed paid thugs against their opponents while in 1969 the men and women who had gone on strike to win the union retired on a $115-per-month pension. The tenor of this corruption, and the heroism of those who risked firings, beatings, and even murder to overthrow it, is suggested by the titles of national narratives constructed by able historians. Brit Hume's *Death and the Mines* (1971), Joseph Finley's *The Corrupt Kingdom* (1972), Curtis Seltzer's *Fire in the Hole* (1985), Paul Clark's *The Miners' Fight for*

Democracy (1981), and Shaunna Scott's *Two Sides to Everything* (1995) provide ample introductions to the story of escalating corruption and underdogged reform as it unfolded on a national (if disproportionately Appalachian) scale.

While some responded to revelations of corruption with increasingly antiunion attitudes, more coal miners supported campaigns to democratize and reform the UMWA's functioning. Starting in the 1960s, members protested their leaders' performance in NBCWA negotiations with unauthorized, or "wildcat," strikes and protests against proposed contracts. Affected by benefit cutbacks and suspicious of internal fraud, disabled miners and widows led strikes against the fund itself and filed the successful *Blankenship v. Boyle* (1972) lawsuit against its managers. In January 1969, West Virginia miners affected by Black Lung Disease stopped deferring to International leaders' timid approach to prevention and compensation. For over three weeks in February, forty thousand miners shut down nearly every mine in the state and sat in on the steps of the capital building while legislators drafted and passed a compensation bill. Giving expression to these movements, the insurgent candidacies of Joseph A. "Jock" Yablonski in 1969 and Arnold Miller's Miners for Democracy (MFD) slate in 1972 challenged and ultimately defeated Tony Boyle. This victory, and Miller's enduring democratic reforms, remain unequaled to this day within the American labor movement.

As chapter five demonstrates, Utah miner Frank J. Sacco's concern over these issues led him to leave a well-paid position as an international representative to become the leading MFD organizer in the state. While an analysis of this moment is centered in Utah, western coal markets' integration and District 22's administrative structure makes it prudent to consider their experience within a regional context. Here the movement encountered a number of unique difficulties after MFD's 1973 decision to dissolve itself in the name of unity. Over the next four years, rank-and-file advocates struggled to work alongside district officers hostile to their movement, whom they viewed as unfairly reelected and whose organizing competency they strongly doubted. If the union was to retain its members' allegiance, counter offensives by large energy conglomerates and steel producers, *and* organize the unorganized, reformers had to do more than critique their predecessors' failings. Limiting their effectiveness, district and International officers conspired against each other while officially engaged in collaborative organizing projects. While MFD's electoral victory inspired many, getting cost-conscious entrepreneurs to accept a rigid system of national bargaining and shared benefit obligations proved far more difficult. Unable or unwilling to modify nationally standardized agreements, union reformers struggled to improve on recent organizing records. By decade's end, a growing east-west rift in coal markets, productivity, and beneficiary populations challenged the UMWA to maintain the national unity that had historically served coal miners so well.

As Miller's limitations became apparent, the length and tenacity of national contract strikes increased as members bore the burden of defending historic gains. Losing key provisions of their national contract as well as months of pay from lost work, unionization's appeal declined among many new to mining and thankful for any stable, well-paying job. Meanwhile, resignations, purges, and suspicion wracked an overworked and stressed International staff. While MFD veterans won election to District 22's top offices in 1977, a string of national setbacks and that winter's lengthy and divisive contract strike substantially limited their potential. The membership's experience during these strikes, as well as the erosion of militant unionism in the years that followed, provides a useful bookend to this section.

Historically, union campaigns in Utah's coalfields have been powerfully influenced by divisions and connections across demographically distinct identity groups. Where organizing drives succeeded in the early decades of the twentieth century, sympathetic community infrastructure developed among immigrant and ethnic populations proved vital to their success. Elsewhere, defeats have often been attributed to the inability of ethnically and religiously diverse miners to come together.[16] This book's final section uses race, gender, and age to explore demography's impact upon miners' experiences with unionism and the UMWA. Amid energy boomtowns' sociological upheavals, historically marginalized groups of workers often embraced and applied the politics that remade American society nationally. In Utah, Chicano and women miners exerted their own demands for equal opportunity and representation, within coal mining and within the UMWA. Their stories—in triumph and defeat—provide more than missing links between the labor and civil rights movements. Lenses of race and gender also provide essential windows into history. Exemplifying what one historian has called the "forgotten heyday of American Activism in the 1970s and 1980s," the organizational records and personal memories of Utah's Spanish-Speaking Organization for Community, Integrity, and Opportunity (SOCIO) and the Coal Employment Project (CEP)–affiliated Lady Miners of Utah preserve expansive visions of an inclusive labor movement at the twilight of its influence.[17] While these groups carried miners' struggles for democracy the farthest into the 1980s, a new generation of younger miners—many new to Carbon and Emery Counties and of diverse backgrounds—encountered unionism's limitations without the benefit of historic attachment. While in some ways the "generation gap" that arose in American coal mining in these years contributed to MFD's early success, militancy's increasingly punitive consequences, along with most migrants' desires for stable employment, substantially diluted union identification.

While the UMWA increasingly recognized the threat posed by non-union western coal, the organization's subsequent decline appeared far

FIGURE 0.7. Kaiser Steel Miners celebrate after breaking a world productivity record in 1982. In addition to pioneering longwall mining, Kaiser's large workforce was a center of UMWA strength and produced many of the union's district leaders from the 1940s through the 1980s. Courtesy, *Sun Advocate*.

from certain in 1979. As a second energy crisis began that year, the Carter administration committed to a long-term investment in coal as a reliable domestic energy source.[18] This support extended beyond the resumption of federal coal land leasing to include subsidies for coal liquefaction and gasification as alternatives to imported oil. While residents of small, traditionally agricultural hamlets in western Emery County considered tentative proposals for a *third* massive coal-fired powerplant, a coal liquefaction plant, two unprecedented strip mines, and associated quality-of-life impacts to already overcrowded infrastructure, coal operators projected similarly increased production figures for existing mines as well. Now an obscure and forgotten artifact of the rural West's hyperindustrialization at the height of coal mining's slightly longer western boom, one 1981 survey of Utah's underground coal mines revealed plans to create 128 percent more mining jobs by 1990. State coal employment had already grown from a historic low of 1,155 in 1968 to 4,166—a figure not seen since coal employment's twentieth-century peak during the mid-1940s.[19]

As Miller retired in 1979 to be succeeded by his conciliatory vice president, Sam Church, some anticipated relief at the passage of a tumultuous decade. In addition to hope for executive stability, the frequency of injunction-inspiring wildcat strikes so disruptive in eastern coalfields had fallen sharply, largely as a result of the lengthy 1977–1978 coal strike that depleted miners' savings and combativeness. In December 1979, delegates to the union's International convention reflected this mood, and brought fewer proposals for aggressive contract demands. The assembled delegates agreed upon the urgency of organizing the West and passed motions to double the union's initiation fee and raise monthly dues in order to fund additional organizers' hiring and training.[20]

Representing miners in three booming states, District 22 officers saw their workloads grow and predicted this trend would continue. In March 1981, they announced plans to construct a new, 9,760-square-foot office building in downtown Price. Completed at a cost of $500,000 and opened in April 1982, the building continues to serve a reduced union membership today. Along with Emery County's mine-mouth Huntington (1974) and Hunter (1978) power plants, Huntington Canyon's Electric Lake, the West Price Shopping Center, and numerous apartment buildings and housing subdivisions scattered across the region, the UMWA building at 525 East 100 South remains a part of the intermountain energy boom's architectural legacy. Historically, it represents organized labor's contributions to America's energy crisis, as well as the optimism its officers felt for their organization's future at that time.[21]

After 1982, the historical window in which union reformers and antiunionists competed suddenly and dramatically closed. By the following year thousands of coal miners had lost their jobs, and in the fiercely competitive environment that followed underground coal mines increased their use of highly efficient longwall mining systems which could be operated with a fraction of the workforce required under previous methods. Unlike the post-1968 recovery, coal production now increased while employment continued to shrink. Fearful for their jobs and observing disproportionate closures of union mines, even those unsatisfied with management felt discouraged from joining a union. For union miners, organizing the unorganized was the only possible alternative to a future of demands for givebacks and lost market share. Yet the combination of high unemployment, contractual givebacks, and reactive worker antiunionism provided the UMWA with an insurmountable paradox: Even if more organizers were hired and more campaigns were initiated, would "the unorganized" be responsive?

PART I

CHAPTER 1

The UMWA at High Tide

> Whole mining communities, operators, miners and merchants alike are pauperized; salt pork and calico are living standards in the more fortunate sectors of the non-union outlaw areas.... [M]anagement in bituminous coal was incapable of industrial leadership essential to a stabilized industry, functioning on American standards.
>
> —John L. Lewis, 1933

JUST BEFORE NOON ONE DAY IN 1939, twenty-eight-year-old miner Howard Browne found himself a member of a crew assigned to pull pillars from a worked-out area of the Peerless mine near Helper, Utah. Here, in 1917, entrepreneurs Arthur and Fredrick Sweet exploited a boom in coal demand to develop a property earlier companies had passed by. While seams thickened steadily to the west, here the coal rose only four feet high—uncommonly low and uncomfortable to work in for a mine in Carbon County. Employed here since 1936, Browne's experience as a miner engaged in "conventional" methods of coal extraction was typical of the time. While many lived at the camp of Peerless itself, Browne commuted to work in his own automobile from Helper. After they rode an electric tram of mine cars up a steeply graded canyon to a portal several hundred feet above the valley floor, miners crouched low while the "man trip" delivered them to their underground working locations. Here, skilled operators prepared coal for extraction with electric

FIGURE 1.1. The layout of Independent Coal and Coke's Kenilworth mine was typical of the 1910s–1950s. From high in the cliffs above, a tramway carried loaded cars to the tipple where the coal was cleaned and loaded. Nearby, a powerhouse supplied electricity and steam heat. Used with permission, Utah State Historical Society.

cutting machines that undercut the working "face." Next, miners drilled into the seam and placed explosive charges. After being blasted down into a pile of rubble, miners shoveled coal by hand into a conveyor that transported it to tracked coal cars for delivery to the tipple. Here the coal was cleaned, sorted, and loaded into railroad cars for delivery to commercial customers.

At every step of this process, coal mining contained a multitude of dangers. Personally, Browne carried the memory of one coworker earlier crushed to death after he failed to evade a runaway train of coal cars. And, like many of his peers, he observed a number of superstitions to ease the tensions of an unpredictable work environment. As noon approached, he feared the implications of the moon's gravitational influence upon the hundreds of feet of sandstone towering above his head. Browne well knew that to pull pillars—large supports of coal left in place between worked-out "rooms"—was perhaps the most dangerous task in a mine. Only undertaken if an area was to be abandoned, it ensured a roof collapse was no longer a matter of "if," but when. Interviewed in 1983, Browne remembered that day:

> We . . . had gotten almost to the main entrance. And the superintendent of mine, he was an Englishman. . . . And he was sitting, he was back behind us and I was up front throwing this coal back to the other guys [who were loading it]. . . . I worked in the mine long enough to know something. . . . And I knew that around noon and around 12 o'clock at night is the most dangerous time in a mine. . . . I kept watching the roof and the floor. And cracks start coming in the roof, in the rock. . . . And then cracks started coming in the floor and that's what they call "working." The mountain was working. And you can tell by the sound and by the way it's popping and everything, so pretty soon, why I grabbed my shovel and started out towards the main haulage way and so, superintendent says, "what's the matter?" And I said, "Well, I'm coming out of there because this thing's coming in pretty quick." And he says, "Oh, that won't come in before tomorrow." And I said, "Well tomorrow I ain't going to be up there. I'm coming on out of here now." And so the other guys that were around there, they said, "Well we're coming out too. If Howard's coming out, we're coming out." He said, "Okay, let's break it off, let's go eat our lunch then." And while we were sitting there eating our lunch, that whole thing came in, covered up all the machinery, the mine and the drills. And everything. And I said, "You son of a bitch, you tried to get me killed." I said, "You can have your mine. This is the last day." He might not have, but I still think that son of a gun tried to get me killed. Either that or he was just so greedy for coal, that he wanted to take the chance, you know, just take the chance.[1]

As illuminated by Browne's near-death experience, underground coal mining's inherent hazards lead the list of reasons that explain the conflict that has always characterized employment in the industry. In 1900 and 1924, Utah experienced two of America's worst mine disasters—explosions of methane and coal dust that killed 200 and 173 men, respectively. Additional explosions killed 25 miners at Peerless and Standardville in 1930, another 30 at Sunnyside and Kenilworth in 1945, and nine at Carbon Fuel in 1963.

In 2014, retired miner Frank Markosek of the Miners' Memorial Project compiled a list of 1,352 men and women who died in all known

Utah coal mine accidents since 1884. Erected at the Peace Gardens in downtown Price that year, a memorial of granite and bronze now identifies every one of them by name. Markosek's list itself, however, notes the causes of these accidents in terms more viscerally familiar than the relatively difficult-to-imagine experiences of century-old mine explosions. Mining coal has always, and will always, require that someone's brother, father, son, mother, uncle, friend, or daughter will one day be remembered by an epitaph such as "crushed chest, head almost severed"; "electrocution"; "shock from hemorrhage amputation of thigh"; "drug by loaded trip forty feet up a slope"; "entangled in belt"; "leg was drug into cutter machine"; "caught in the chain picks of the mining machine"; "fell while unhooking a choker cable from a tube 35 feet above ground"; "crushed between protective cab and raising conveyor"; or the endless variations of "roof fall skull fracture"; "crushed head and chest"; "crushing injuries"; "struck by falling rock"; and otherwise "crushed by several tons of coal." Uncommonly matched in other industries, innumerable bonds of tragedy, loss, and hope have always anchored cultures of solidarity throughout coal mining communities.[2]

Despite such risks, mining remains a devil's bargain millions of workers have always been willing to make. For those who live within or near the nation's coalfields, mining has always offered a higher wage than most other available forms of employment. Coal miners are fiercely proud of their work and contributions to the larger economy and are well aware that their labor supplies much of the world's electrical demand. "Coked" coal, concentrated by slow burning in controlled ovens, is an industrial fuel essential to the steel that has built American skyscrapers, bridges, ships, and schools. In national emergencies—including world wars and the energy crisis of the 1970s—coal miners have given their labor and their lives to keep America a free, mobile, and productive nation.

For as long as anyone has mined coal, decisions to boost productivity require negotiations with workplace safety. To prevent potentially catastrophic explosions, mines must maintain adequate ventilation and pipe pressurized water to the face where it reduces the quantity of flammable (and breathable) coal dust. Miners not directly engaged in the physical removal of coal must be hired and paid to apply nonflammable rock dust to the inside walls of mined-out areas, hang brattice cloth and build cement walls to channel ventilation, shovel loose coal from passages where it spills off conveyor belts, and repair underground electrical systems and multimillion-dollar mining machines. Roof integrity must be maintained, either through wooden supports and metal archways or by injecting steel bolts into roofs to bind successive sandstone and shale layers together. If the sounds and signs of danger are detected, miners must decide whether to keep working, or to withdraw from the area until conditions improve. Even in the safest mines, rescue teams must be regularly trained and drilled.

Yet every minute of lost production, call to a safety inspector, or reminder of regulatory fine print carries inherent risks of retribution. As a cyclical industry plagued by chronic overcapacity and periods of high unemployment, owners as well as miners face strong incentives to maintain production as consistently as possible. As miners and managers have endeavored to protect their interests, each developed associative networks to a higher degree than is commonly found elsewhere in American industry. On January 25, 1890, delegates representing coal miners from the United States and Canada came together in Columbus, Ohio, to form what would become the most effective advocate for miners' health and safety in the twentieth century: the UMWA.

While coal miners today enjoy wages, pensions, health care, and benefits unknown to many employed in other sectors, these conditions do not flow from coal operators' benevolence or their shareholders' disinterest. Rather, they are the direct results of miners' historical association with unions, which transformed an extremely dangerous and brutally exploitative industry into one of the best-compensated industrial jobs. In 2010, the average annual pay for a Utah coal miner was approximately $70,000—nearly double the state's average.[3] After the UMWA organized all of Utah's major coal mines in 1933, miners gained not only wage increases but control over housing and purchasing decisions, a definition of job classifications with set pay scales, and a system of grievance handling that curtailed punitive firings and work assignments.[4] Later contracts added portal to portal pay, stronger seniority language, parental leave protections, and fringe benefits such as vacations and paid days off. In a series of national strikes in the late 1940s, the UMWA won its most endearing victory: a multiemployer healthcare system and a pension plan funded by royalties on union-mined coal. And while harder to measure from newspaper headlines or statistics, being a union member—as Howard Brown knew in 1939—let miners question authority without necessarily risking their jobs.

In many ways, coal miners' historic solidarity has transcended their industry's borders to provide models and direct assistance for other groups of workers. Through the UMWA's treasury and its offshoot, the CIO, miners provided the funding and the framework for industrial unionism nationally. The decline of coal mining unions then, appears paradoxical. How could such an important institution vanish from so many centers of historic strength? And as the most prominent host of the rank-and-file upsurge that ran through many American unions in the 1970s, why were the reformers who came to power within the UMWA unable to reverse their organization's decline?

If internal democracy, health care, organizing, and labor law became the central questions for the union in the decade of its fracture, a return to the New Deal and immediate postwar period provides an essential comparative experience. Not only can this period tell us why miners were willing to join unions, it also reveals why they were able to do so with an ease and a success rate subsequently unmatched. By extending an analysis of organizing and the limitations of a distinctly American "contract unionism" through the 1950s, one discovers the limitations of the UMWA model, as well as a window into the motivations of union leaders that later proved so controversial.

Within the lofty cretaceous deposits of the Wasatch Plateau and Book Cliffs, Utah's coal industry has historically been distributed along a wide semi-circle surrounding Carbon County's capital city of Price. From commercial mining's 1875 beginnings until the late 1940s, Utah Fuel—a subsidiary of the Denver & Rio Grande Western Railroad (D&RGW)—and a number of independent producers constructed two dozen company towns that housed most coal miners and their families. In 1879, the Pleasant Valley railroad connected mines near Scofield, Utah to Wasatch Front cities' home heating markets and smelters. As the D&RGW connected this line to Colorado via Grand Junction, it discovered additional seams of coal where it established the communities of Castle Gate and Sunnyside, the later notable for multiple seams of metallurgical coal uniquely suited to steel production. Located at the base of the Book Cliffs approximately thirty miles east of Price, Utah's steel producers later built the adjacent towns of Columbia and Dragerton to provide a "captive" source of fuel for their own operations. From Helper to the Emery County line along the Wasatch Plateau's eastern slope, independent companies proliferated to compete with Utah Fuel and to take advantage of World War I's heavy fuel demands. From north to south, these include the six adjacent towns of Peerless, Spring Canyon, Standardville, Latuda, Rains, and Mutual along the geographic Spring Canyon's winding floor; the towns of Consumers, National, and Sweets along the Gordon Creek drainage; and further south the towns of Wattis, Hiawatha, and Mohrland. Thus distributed, miners lived in close proximity; organized a multitude of ethnic, social, and professional organizations; shared recreational and consumptive activities with their coworkers; and enjoyed multiple opportunities for informal

FIGURE 1.2. At Spring Canyon, tight geography forced miners to live in close proximity to their workplace and each other. Community and ethnic organizations dominated social life and provided a basis for union power. Photo courtesy of the Western Mining and Railroad Museum.

discussions of common concerns. Although ethnic and racial divisions between European, Asian, and Mexican immigrants (along with and a smaller number of black Americans) were consciously integrated into each camp's construction, miners' solidarity had innumerable foundations of social and material support.

Underground hazards and company towns' power disparities led miners to periodic expressions of militancy well before joining a union was legally permissible. During strikes in 1901, 1903–1904, 1919, 1922, and 1933, demands for pay raises and protests of pay cuts led the list of miners' grievances. Alongside them, other challenges to managerial control linked economic concerns to broader questions of fairness, discrimination, and citizenship.[5] First sought in 1901 and repeated in each successive confrontation, miners demanded bimonthly paydays, lower prices at company stores, and the right to elect checkweighmen to ensure accurate measurements of loaded coal. During World War I's coal boom, miners without a recognized union struck the Spring Canyon, Sego, and Peerless mines where they demanded an end to payment at the company store, the firing of a resented superintendent, and the reinstatement of two arbitrarily dismissed miners. Over two-thirds of Utah's miners walked out in 1922 to protest a 30 percent wage cut, a raise in housing prices, and favoritism in work assignments.

In 1933, the communist-led National Miners' Union (NMU) organized strikes at five Utah coal mines, where the key demands were hardly radical. In addition to addressing earlier grievances, they asked for pay for "dead work" such as timbering and track laying, fifteen hours' notice before frequently idle mines would be worked, the right to select a doctor of their own choosing, and the right to live outside of a company town if they so chose. To ensure the permanence of such concessions, union recognition demands accompanied every strike. Miners understood that it was only through a legally binding contract that any gains could be protected. Furthermore, only union recognition could protect their leaders from punitive dismissals.[6]

In former miners' recollections, personal experiences breathe life into such generalized demands. Having begun mining in 1925, Val Turri described in stark terms the deference supervisors expected: "When we had no union they used to treat us like slaves.... The boss came in and if you didn't talk just right to him he would say, 'Take your bucket and get outside, you're fired.' . . . If they found a piece of rock in the car when you dumped it they used to take a ton off. . . . The third time they used to say, 'Take your bucket and go outside, we don't need no rock.'" Louis Pestotnick Jr. remembered his father's punishment after he attempted to check official measures: "They'd give him the worst place they had. . . . They had him working in the water up to his knees, where he couldn't make hardly any money at all." At Castle Gate, Willard Craig incurred managerial wrath after he refused to donate a day's worth of labor to purchase Christmas presents for supervisors because "I had children that needed a Christmas and a wife that needed a Christmas a lot more than that superintendent needed one." Though he worked a skilled, higher-paying job operating machinery at the time, his comment landed him a punitive transfer to a pick-and-shovel position where he worked harder for less pay.[7]

Others experienced transfers or firing for far less. Antonio Guadagnoli, a married miner, recalled a supervisor's blunt instructions after he introduced him to a new employee, as well as the ensuing high cost of his own personal rebellion in 1922: "The boss he told me, he says, 'I'll

FIGURE 1.3. Handloading coal at Castle Gate was dangerous and dirty work. To get to such working "rooms," miners relied upon unique industrial and social infrastructure. Photo courtesy of the Western Mining and Railroad Museum.

let you work three or four [more] days and teach this fellow what he got to do on this job. . . .' So I told the boss, when he told me I had to give my job to this other guy—I had my oil can in my hand. I put it down and say, 'Tell your man to get oil can and start right now. I'm going home.' . . . I told him, I says, 'Teach the guy yourself.' He's the boss, teach him. I go home now. So I left."

While not all mine managers are so remembered with disdain, some appear to have experienced particular delight in their ability to take advantage of those under their control. When in 1924 Carbon Fuel Company hired Stanley Harvey as a temporary foreman and future superintendent of its mine at Rains, he quit after ninety days "when I saw the way things were going and the way the company officials were acting toward the labor. . . . The superintendent was there bragging about how he beat this man out of so much money. I don't like that kind of business

FIGURE 1.4. While riding a "mantrip," miners shared lives, hopes, politics, and concerns. Used with permission, Utah State Historical Society.

and I could see that it was being encouraged I thought by top management or near top." As the son of a mine inspector and sympathetic to working miners, Harvey's resignation mirrored Guadagnoli's defiance from the opposite end of class experience. While both desired meaningful changes, at this time symbolic and personal protest—not practical and organized activity—remained the most accessible option.[8]

While those who worked by hand enjoyed a degree of autonomy to set the pace at which they worked, the amount of effort put forth over the course of a working day varied greatly. As Tommy Hilton recalled of a time at Castle Gate when "we were supposed to have been on eight-hour shifts," working late was not an option after "the boss would say, 'You guys stay until all those empty cars are loaded.' We used to have to stay or lose our job. If we didn't like our job, there was always somebody else outside waiting to take it from us. So we stayed in." On other occasions, he suspected paycheck irregularities: "When it came payday, a lot of times I would think I would go down to the boss and would tell him, 'Say, you short changed me five or six hours or a couple of shifts,'" and anticipated the likely reply: "'We did not. How can you prove it? We haven't got it booked down.'" Estimating the extent of wage theft, he suspected that "we worked for the company sometimes maybe forty or fifty hours a month. We couldn't do anything about it."[9]

Where companies weighed coal cars to pay miners on the basis of tonnage loaded, many regularly underreported weights. In 1933, Tony Frungi noticed that the first time his employer allowed a union-elected checkweighman to monitor scales, the reported tonnages jumped by over 20 percent. At Mohrland, Tony Pestotnick estimated, "The company would steal maybe a ton or half a ton from every car." Sometimes, even getting enough coal cars to be able to work productively was a struggle. At Castle Gate, Fay Thacker recalled how Japanese miners bribed their superintendent with cash and gifts in exchange for a reliable number of cars. And as Albert Vogrenic remembered at Little Standard, miners incurred a litany of expenses for equipment and services essential to the company's operation: "You used to have to buy your powder, and buy your [blasting] caps and you'd have to pay to get your pick sharpened, you'd have to pay to get your bits, all your grill bits sharpened, you had to pay for the lamp, pay for the bath house."[10]

Managerial control extended beyond the workplace into a variety of situations where miners' vulnerability could be manipulated. At Columbia, one manager partnered with an auto dealer in Price to force employees' purchasing decisions. As Albert Robles remembered, "If you wanted to buy a car, you had to buy a Studebaker from him. If you didn't buy Studebaker, they fired you." While individual companies exerted control over their employees' purchasing decisions, prices in many company-operated general stores reflected mining families' limited options. Common in periods of idle work, those who accepted an advance on future earnings in the form of store-specific "scrip" found it easy to rapidly accumulate debt. While rents for company houses varied significantly from camp to camp, some companies reclaimed a higher share of wages when they charged as much as twice regional standards. And at all mines, those who resided in company towns risked eviction if they lost their jobs. Inconvenient enough for single men, married miners with families had the most to lose. While a 1919 coal strike idled mines nationally but not in unorganized Utah, United States Fuel felt threatened enough that it evicted eight Hiawatha miners with wives and children, along with a number of single miners, whom they accused of joining the union.[11]

Among those whose lives spanned both eras, it is not technical language, dollar amounts, or fringe benefits that set the tone for most retired miners' memories. It is a deeper sense of liberation and relief from what had been life under a pervasively unjust system. In 1974, Castle Gate resident Tommy Hilton spoke for many when he argued that the UMWA's arrival in Utah "was one of the best things that ever happened to working men around here." Two years later Manson Huff reflected, "When the United Mine Workers came in . . . I would say we began to live. We were practically living under dictatorship up until that period of time. I remember one of the superintendents saying 'this is a one man town and I'm the man.' That was the way it went. You just couldn't call your life your own."[12] Also at Castle Gate, Pete Tabone summarized a number of tangible and intangible changes:

> It really made a big difference to us that worked before. A lot of people didn't realize that. Before you didn't dare say anything because they could fire you for no reason at all. You didn't have anything to back you up. As the union got stronger, we had more backing so that they had to have a reason to fire you. . . . Then after seniority come in, they

couldn't lay you off unless you were down on your seniority. But if you had enough you could stay on.

Tabone served on Castle Gate's pit committee, which was

> more or less a safety committee.... If anybody has any complaints they would come to the pit committee man. He would go check and then he would talk to the boss. And if the boss wouldn't fix it he would turn it to the local president and the union took care of it.... There was always a lot of things that would come up that weren't exactly safe the men would turn in.... That was really the biggest change. To know that if you had any complaint you could talk to the boss and you could get something done. I don't say you were always right, but at least they had to listen to you and consider what was going on. Also safety conditions and wages improved.... In the coal mines—mostly in the winter time—men were killed and quite a few of them got hurt with broken backs and lost arms and legs. That safety feature alone was worth the union coming in.[13]

In 1947, Welsh immigrant and Columbia mine Local 6089 recording secretary Arthur Biggs lobbied Congress against several antilabor bills then under consideration. In his letter to Utah's Republican senator Arthur V. Watkins, he summarized, "Our Union means everything to us. It is the means of our livelyhood [sic]. We never enjoyed any freedom of speech; a right to live where we wanted to or to spend what little money we made where we wanted to; not mentioning working conditions which have improved 100%.... We have a hard enough time having the coal companies comply with present mining rules.... If we are weakened I am afraid they are going to have to find some more miners to mine the nation's coal."[14]

Miners were not the only Carbon County residents who organized unions at this time. Over the course of the 1930s and 1940s, steam laundry workers in Price and Helper, retail workers in Price, and Wellington dry ice plant employees obtained signed contracts with their employers. Auto mechanics, gas station attendants, tailors, cooks, waiters, bartenders, musicians, butchers, and county road department employees also organized unions.[15] With the onset of fall weather in 1939, fifteen students at Spring Canyon demonstrated community support for organized labor's tactics when, dissatisfied with conditions on an old and poorly heated school bus, they refused to board and asked the driver to negotiate with school officials in Price for a newer vehicle. This protest, however, appears to have been unsuccessful.¹⁶

In 1936, the UMWA and various craft unions within the American Federation of Labor (AFL) formed the Carbon County Central Labor Union as a body to coordinate activity and charter locals in new industries. Later that year, Wyoming miner and former District 22 sec-

FIGURE 1.5. Union power on display at the 1935 Labor Day parade through Price, Utah. Photo courtesy of the Western Mining and Railroad Museum.

retary-treasurer James Morgan followed the coal miners' split from the AFL to form the CIO, which he served in the late 1930s as regional director for Utah and neighboring states. Utah miner and longtime UMWA organizer Frank Bonacci assisted him as field representative, and the CIO's statewide achievements included the organization of construction workers, furniture makers, and cannery workers in Salt Lake City and Ogden; three hundred cast-iron–pipe makers in Provo; and several thousand metal miners, mill workers, and smelter workers under the International Union of Mine, Mill, & Smelter Workers in western Utah and along the Wasatch front.[17]

Along with miners' revelations of conditions in the preunion days, unionism's spread to other industries allows us to understand a holiday almost totally divorced today from its origins in this period. While by the latter part of the twentieth century Labor Day became known more for retail sales and backyard barbecues than any official relationship to unions, beginning in 1933 and extending well into the 1980s UMWA locals in Carbon and Emery Counties celebrated a multitude of hitherto unknown freedoms over several days of activities. Perennially, the main event was a parade that alternated annually through the streets of downtown Helper and Price. Coworkers and residents of company towns built floats that competed for cash prizes. While coal-shoveling, mine-timbering, and drill-hammering contests demonstrated pride and lent visibility to miners' skills, their wives and daughters competed in beauty contests and for a chance to lead the ceremonies as "Labor Day Queen." In later years, organizers incorporated children's carnivals and rodeos. Regularly, state governors and congressmen traveled to Carbon County as parade speakers where they recognized labor's achievements and reinforced electoral alliances. For a largely immigrant workforce long subjected to epithets and treatment as outsiders, Labor Day ritualized miners' inclusion as citizens. Summarizing the meaning of the 1937 celebration, which "approximately 4,000 organized workers participated in," the Price *Sun Advocate* used two words almost entirely absent from political discourse today to recognize "the annual holiday set aside for the nation to pay homage to the working class."[18]

While injustices proliferated in early twentieth-century coal mines, discontent alone failed to ensure collective-bargaining success. In contrast to most organizing drives the UMWA launched in later decades, the 1933 organization of Utah's mines occurred amid a unique set of circumstances. The union did not, for instance, depend upon the professional competency (or procedural lethargy) of a NLRB election to certify the UMWA as sole bargaining agent by a majority vote of employees. The Wagner Act, which created this institution, was still two years away from being signed into law. While in 1933 section 7(A) of the National Industrial Recovery Act gave workers the legal right to form a union for the purposes of collective bargaining, this bill was not signed until June 16—three weeks after John L. Lewis optimistically dispatched an organizer to Utah. While organizing drives after the 1940s commonly dragged on for years and involved heavy reliance on attorneys and courts, unions' early independence from state control allowed events to move much faster. Within five months, the UMWA had organized and signed contracts with every commercial mine in the state.[19]

Central to the breakthrough were two unique conditions that led Utah's coal operators to recognize the UMWA simultaneously and voluntarily. Perhaps most important, by 1933 few of these coal operators envisioned a path to prosperity—or even profitability—through the mechanisms of a competitive free market alone. While the Great Depression further reduced coal demand, a decade of ruinous competition preceded the emergency. During World War I, operators invested in new mines and equipment only to see coal markets decline quickly after 1920. Now, after four years of depression, many mines operated only one or two days a week. Several intermittently produced at a loss in order to keep any stream of revenue from going to their competitors. In a series of Roosevelt–initiated negotiations during the summer and fall of 1933, Utah operators adopted a uniform code to standardize mining conditions. All remained wary of unions philosophically, and steel producers particularly feared that recognizing a union at their coal mines would set a precedent for their employees at mills and smelters. Yet all eventually agreed that uniform wage rates and collective bargaining would standardize operating costs and help stabilize the industry.[20]

The second factor that disposed operators to accept the UMWA was a competing radical union's growing traction. In 1928, communist miners and their supporters founded the NMU in Pennsylvania. Organized to some degree in many states, in 1933 it was particularly active in

Utah and New Mexico, where it gained sympathy for the charge that the UMWA had abandoned unorganized miners after the massive if inconclusive 1922 national coal strike. Through its paper, the *Carbon County Miner*, NMU leaders criticized their rivals for negotiating away miners' rights to strike, denying miners the right to vote to approve the contracts they were to work under, and negotiating dues-checkoff systems that strengthened union finances before more immediate problems, such as unpaid dead work, had been addressed.[21]

While the *Miner*'s incendiary rhetoric and sweeping generalizations about complicated economic problems is easier to dismiss, it also preserves more historically significant visions of what Staughton Lynd has called "the alternative unionism of the early 1930s."[22] Among them, the National Miners' Union raised funds, boosted morale, and strengthened community linkages with regular Saturday night dances at the Helper roller rink. A youth section integrated students' civic and academic concerns with their parents' economic struggles and organized its members' children into a dramatic club that broadened the scope (and content) of entertainment available at coal camps. Supporting then-arrested members in two states who had contested the boundaries of free speech and labor union legality, in late October the union organized a branch of the International Labor Defense, which fifty people reportedly joined at one Helper meeting. In parallel with its workplace organizing, the union also organized unemployed workers into self-advocacy groups that studied unmet needs, appealed on behalf of denied relief claimants, and erected a grievance committee to study their problems systematically. By November it had established at least two branches for this purpose in Spring Glen and Helper. Perhaps most divergent from the UMWA, the National Miners promoted independent political campaigns, and supported the Progressive Party ticket in Helper's 1933 election for city offices.[23]

To the detriment of its activists' quest for legitimacy and durable organization, the NMU suffered greatly for its subservience to the Communist Party's "ultra-left" stance in this period. Predicting capitalism's imminent demise, and glowingly optimistic about the prospects for impending world revolution, the party's international theoretical advisors encouraged radical activists around the world to sever links with center-left moderates who might have otherwise formed valuable allies in common projects. It also disparaged long-term base building in favor of loud rhetoric and splashy actions. As Germany's spiraling unemployment discredited its political center, this attitude contributed to a global catastrophe after that country's large Communist Party was forbidden from working collaboratively, or running joint electoral slates, with its closest allies in the larger Social-Democratic Party. In American coal mining, the same sectarianism had the unfortunate result of ensuring that many of the strongest advocates for rank-and-file power were unable to influence the dominant labor union in directions that might have counteracted some of John L. Lewis's more problematic tendencies.

After miners at Mutual pressured their owners to sign a contract with the NMU in the spring of 1933, the organization attracted the growing interest of miners throughout Carbon County. With its strongest bases of support in the Spring Canyon and Gordon Creek areas, the NMU's optimistic leaders hoped a strike for recognition at Spring Canyon, National, Consumers, and Sweets would inspire miners elsewhere where it

FIGURE 1.6. With miners' political rights strictly controlled, a rare, privately owned store gave Mutual's miners and their families space to organize under the NMU in 1933. Photo courtesy of the Western Mining and Railroad Museum.

FIGURE 1.7. On September 11, 1933, approximately two hundred NMU supporters marched through downtown Price, Utah, to protest their leaders' imprisonment. Shortly after this photo was taken, they were dispersed by tear gas and armed deputies. Photo Credit: Special Collections, J. Willard Marriott Library, University of Utah.

had a weaker following. Noting the rival federation's growing traction, John L. Lewis sent organizer Nicholas Fontecchio to Utah, where he worked with local supporter Frank Bonacci to defend the UMWA's reputation. The two organizers also re-established previously hostile lines of communication with Carbon County's coal operators and political leaders, impressing upon them their organization's comparative professionalism, moderation, and contractual reliability.[24]

As the two unions' rivalry peaked in August and September, the NMU initiated what it hoped would become "the Carbon County Strike." While specifically the union hoped to win a signed labor agreement for its largest memberships at the Sweets, National, Consumers, and Spring Canyon mines, it also hoped the action would inspire undecided miners, perhaps bringing them out on strike as well.

In response, UMWA members controversially joined forces with local police to break NMU-led strikes through physical force and mass arrest. After radical hopes for a county-wide general strike fizzled, on September 11 several hundred NMU supporters marched through downtown Price to protest their leaders' arrests. Shortly after starting, they were dispersed by tear gas and police batons.[25]

Despite its intensity, those eager for representation by any union appear to have benefited the most from the intensity of partisan competition, which allowed the UMWA to present itself as a reasonable and responsible alternative. Thus, organizer Nicholas Fontecchio described his presence in Utah that year as one "for the purpose of establishing ... cordial relationship between the miners and operators ... to assist in the establishment of mutual relations with peace and prosperity." Rather than communist militancy, Fontecchio promised, "You can rest assured that there will be no strikes nor turmoils [sic] in the conduct of our work. The miners are asked to join our Union and to remain at work until a joint contract is consummated. . . . The UMWA is purely an American institution, working under American ideals and believing in solving problems in line with the American laws and policies." Inspired by presidential support for the National Industrial Recovery Act, Fontecchio balanced his attacks on "the trumpets of discord" blown by the "menace" of the Moscow-instructed NMU with a vision of unionism wrapped in the flag. Privately, however, he recognized his adversaries' presence "will do our union a great amount of good instead of harm."[26]

Many miners drew similar conclusions. While late summer's violence left lasting divisions, Carbon County folklore preserves an alternate memory of this struggle for control. In at least ten interviews conducted over an eleven-year period by five different oral historians, respondents suggested a conspiracy whereby John L. Lewis "sent" the NMU as "a trick on purpose," "so they would start a lot of trouble . . . so that United Mine Workers would look good."[27] While this study has found no archival evidence to substantiate the claim, the UMWA's position as a lesser-evil alternative definitely softened operator hostility. Ironically, as this union and its contract changed in later decades, rivals including the International Union of Operating Engineers, the International Brotherhood of Electrical Workers, the Progressive Mine Workers, and the International Brotherhood of Teamsters periodically positioned themselves as a "reliable" alternative in a number of raids upon the UMWA's jurisdiction.[28]

Unlike its latter modifications, which by the 2000s had grown into an indexed, spiral-bound booklet well over two hundred pages in length, fifteen pages sufficed to spell out the initial agreement Utah's coal operators signed.[29] The contract recognized wages for seventy-six different classifications of work ranging from $3.52 per day for "boney" pickers who removed waste rock from mined coal and "trappers" who operated doorways as needed, to $6.80 per day for mechanical loading and cutting machine operators. While coal production's seasonal nature complicates efforts to estimate yearly incomes, adjusted for inflation these wages ranged from $66.55 to $128.56 per day in 2018 dollars. In addition to wage standardization, classification protected miners from many of the strategies formerly associated with favoritism and wage theft, such as arbitrary transfers. Additional gains included a prohibition on house rental increases, miners' right to elect checkweighmen, bimonthly paydays, excuses or reductions of fees for essential equipment purchases, prohibition on employment for miners under seventeen years of age, automatic dues check-off, and nine holidays throughout the year.[30]

Notable limitations of the 1933 agreement modified in later contracts included the definition of an eight-hour day and seniority language. At the time, coal operators defined eight hours of work as those spent "at the usual working places" and not the time miners spent riding trams or walking to arrive at working locations. Used in many mines, horse and mule drivers also worked late because of returning their animals to stables. Seniority particularly mattered in the event of layoffs, where miners had long felt it unjust for newer employees to be kept on while those who had worked longer, and therefore earned a higher wage, were dismissed. While negotiators improved language in later years, at this time seniority only protected older employees within their own classification of work. While operators had long used layoffs to remove men with pro-union sympathies, in 1933 miners secured a promise that operators would not intentionally "encourage the discharge of [union members], or [refuse] employment to applicants because of personal prejudice or activity in matters affecting the United Mine Workers of America." In later years, however, many sharply debated their employers' commitment to the spirit of this clause.[31]

To resolve disputes over the course of a working day, each mine's workforce elected a committee of three men who served as arbitrators at the second level of a four-part grievance procedure, with the initial disagreement between a worker and his supervisor serving as the first step. If the committee was unable to negotiate a satisfactory agreement with managers, a miner could appeal to a board of four men, with two designated by the union and two by operators. Failing here, a fourth step allowed a miner to appeal the board's decision to an umpire designated by the National Recovery Administration. In the event of serious contention, a "district conference" could also be established as an intermediate board consisting of one operator and one mine worker representative.

While in many ways a powerful foundation of economic democracy, coal operators secured language that clearly limited the power of the mine committees. This body, it explained, "shall have no other authority or exercise any other control, nor in any way interfere with the operation of the mine," and "for violation of this clause the Committee or any member thereof may be removed from the Committee." Furthermore, the contract clearly demanded that in the case of any grievance "there shall be no suspension of work." Philosophically, comanagement between workers and operators was deliberately circumscribed, as the contract explained: "The management of the mine, the direction of the working force, and the right to hire and discharge are vested exclusively in the Operator, and the [UMWA] shall not abridge these rights." Reiterating the point again, an illegal suspension-of-work clause rigidly asserted that "a strike or stoppage of work on the part of the Mine Workers shall be a violation of this Agreement. Under no circumstances shall the Operator discuss the matter under dispute with the Mine Committee or any representative of the United Mine Workers of America during suspension of work in violation of this agreement."[32] Evident in such language, operators' acceptance of unions as bargaining agents—and strong opposition to cooperative management—shaped American unions' internationally distinct form and structure.

The debatable fairness of layoffs and transfers, classification for different types of work, underground and bath-house conditions, or dissatisfaction with specific supervisors constituted most grievances. However, periodically an issue arose of such seriousness that miners felt justified to bypass the grievance procedure in favor of a strike to force an immediate resolution. While those who filed a grievance for back pay or reinstatement generally waited weeks, if not months, for their cases to work through successive hearings, safety concerns most commonly led miners to violate the contract and stage an unauthorized, or "wildcat," strike. This tool was so powerful that often only a suggestion of its deployment was needed. As John Houghton of Castle Gate summarized, "When the union came in, [it] organized a safety committee. When these unsafe practices would start, then they would have this safety committee go and inspect it along with the company. They would show that there wasn't the safety thing there that it should be. A lot of times they had to threaten them with a strike unless it was taken care of."[33] However, miners' periodic flexing of their ultimate economic power exposed contract unionism's limits. To actually initiate such a strike invited a number of penalties. While all who participated lost the day's wages, those who organized such strikes could potentially be fired. Further damage resulted from a heightened perception of instability among unorganized workers, as well as stiffened operator resistance to the union.

Prior to World War II, Utah's coal miners initiated very few such strikes. Two in 1940, however, set a pattern for subsequent conflicts. At Sweets in early February, 160 miners stopped work for three days to protest the accumulation of twenty-five grievances the company had not yet settled. While the company blamed the strike on a radical minority of its workforce, Richard Murray, a Kenilworth miner and subdistrict board member sent to investigate, concluded that the "men were justified in their demands," and noted the strike's effectiveness in winning the miners "full satisfaction and settlement of these grievances."[34] At neighboring Grand County's single coal camp of Sego that October, miners struck for twenty-two days after a foreman's questionable safety policies led to two men's hospitalization. Sego Local 6597 president Adolph Pyantil supported the strike, and felt the acute threat posed to miners' lives was more important than contract language. District president Alfred Carey lamented the local's "refusal to comply with the instructions of this district office" and appealed to John L. Lewis directly to send a back-to-work order. He did, which the miners also ignored. With most other district officers out of town, CIO regional director James Morgan traveled from Cheyenne, Wyoming, to Utah where, "after several meetings and conferences and many trips from Price to Sego, the men finally returned to work."³⁵

In both cases, appeals from struck companies and district officers reached John L. Lewis's desk, who insisted that the miners return to work immediately and only afterwards "take up any grievances which may be in existence through the proper channels provided in our contract." While Pyantil and his fellow miners were well aware that their strike "was in plain violation of the joint agreement and was doing a great deal of harm in our relationship with the Operators' Association," their position as working miners gave them a different appreciation of the issues involved. Throughout its history, such gaps in perspective and consequences periodically led to differences of opinion between the UMWA's officers and its working rank-and-file.³⁶

The other major cause of strikes—flexing of economic muscle during contract negotiations—imposed little into miners' lives during the 1930s. Upon its termination, labor and management harmoniously renewed the six-month contract signed on November 8, 1933. In 1935, an uncertain future for federal coal regulation inspired operator coolness to union proposals. Initiated on September 23, an eight-day national strike revived negotiations and secured a swift agreement.³⁷ In 1937, negotiators signed another two-year contract with minor alterations without any work stoppage. As talks stalled in 1939, Lewis called the miners out on April 3. After an eight-week national strike, which affected Utah mines for only the final three weeks, Lewis won his key demand for a closed-shop clause with commercial mines though not with steel producers.³⁸ In both years, the principal negotiating took place far from District 22. In a 1935 letter to International vice president Thomas Kennedy, Columbia's recording secretary, Orwel Peterson, described strikers' experiences in Utah:

> In behalf of the strike or holliday [sic] as we might call it I can say that there was never more peace and harmony than was shown in those few days we were off work, the sherrif [sic] of this county (Carbon) stated he had not received as much as a single phone call to settle any disorders, however we were successful in gaining the co-operation of the employes [sic] of the so called Wagon-Truck coal mine operators, who promised to refrain from work until our strike was settled, and these small Wagon-Truck mines produce in the neighborhood of 500,000

tons annually, we were also able to organize most of these employees and place charters in their locals, which they will greatly benefit by in wages, as they were only receiving $3.00 per day as compared to the minimum of 5.44 in the mines of the organized field.[39]

In light of subsequent difficulties organizing smaller mines in Utah, nonunion miners' cooperation in this strike is remarkable. So too is Peterson's faith in the durability of the locals chartered at this time, few of which managed to secure signed contracts. In light of later tensions, his view of the UMWA as a vehicle for all coal miners exemplifies labor's optimism during the mid-1930s.

While miners benefited from unionization's elimination of the most egregious abuses, the persistence of Depression conditions until the advent of World War II ensured that daily life around the coal camps remained a struggle. Mining continued to be a precarious profession, characterized by irregular work, general poverty, and periodic mine closures. In the summer of 1936, Standardville's recording secretary, Theo Reese, explained his coworkers' struggles to meet a minimum suggested contribution of $1 for Roosevelt's re-election: "A large number of our members have been laid off at the Mine here and have been idle nearly all spring and summer. Many of them are on relief, some are working on W.P.A. projects, those who are working at the mine are just getting a small amount of work each month but each member is quite willing to contribute the amount they feel they are able to give to this very worthy cause."[40] After a quiet summer and six months of waiting for a Reconstruction Finance Corporation loan that failed to materialize, by November 1936 National's miners had gone eight months without pay. Unable to find jobs elsewhere, they struck for approximately $2,000 in back pay and appealed to Lewis to use his political influence to look into their company's loan.[41] Two years later, Spring Canyon miners reported that "the men who still have work only get 1 and 2 days a week, in which event their entire earnings, in many cases, are being checked off for this or the other, leaving very little for them to live on." Similarly, those at Wattis lamented, "Our men are hardly making enough to meet their living expenses." By early 1939, six mines in District 22 had closed. After Standardville admitted it couldn't meet its payroll for January, 265 employees—some of whom had lived at the company town for as long as twenty-five years—voted unanimously to work for food alone to keep the mine open.⁴²

Following their success in organizing all of Utah's larger, commercial, and railroad-connected mines, UMWA organizers quickly encountered what became perennial difficulties in their attempts to unionize the smaller truck and wagon mines that proliferated throughout Carbon, Emery, and Sevier Counties. Organizer Frank Bonacci and his successors made a few breakthroughs, such as at the Willow Creek Coal Company's mine near Castle Gate. By October 1934, he had organized the thirty men who worked there and convinced the company to sign an agreement "covering wages and working conditions in the same lines as the agreement between the Utah Coal Operators and District 22." Similarly, Bonacci chartered a union at the smaller Maple Creek mine in Spring Canyon, although its owner's discriminatory discharge of three union members necessitated a strike to win their reinstatement. Twenty men employed at the Twelve Mile Coal Company of Salina, Utah, also joined the union, though it is unclear whether a contract was signed. Nearby, economic difficulties encountered by the recently organized Sevier Valley Coal Company illustrated the continued havoc the Depression inflicted upon such small producers. By October, its workforce had been on strike for three months in protest of their owners' inability to pay them. Though Bonacci supported the strike, he doubted whether the mine would be able to reopen.⁴³

Such mixed results characterized coal-mine organizing during the rest of the 1930s. In 1936, district officers levied an assessment upon their members "due to the expense the District has been put to in the last few years, organizing new fields." As secretary-treasurer Virgil Wright and president John Ross wrote Lewis, "The strikes that have been in progress in the last 18 months [include] Coalville, Salina, Mutual and Maple Creek . . . Huntington Canyon which has several mines located there, also Carleon mine, Hardscrabble mine, Heiner and a lot of others." In contrast to larger operators' willingness to sign contracts two and a half years before, proliferating strikes at newly organized mines indicates an apparent hardening in small producers' attitudes.⁴⁴

A well-preserved correspondence from officer J. D. DeFries of the Deer Creek mine's newly organized Local 7142 in Huntington Canyon provides insight into the difficulties small-mine organizers faced. In December 1935, he reported that operator B. O. Howard "refuses to give the union any recognition at all and threatens to discharge all union agitators working in the mine." As at many smaller operations, Deer Creek's miners worked amid inferior conditions: "We are only receiving about 40 cents per tone [sic] for pick mining—a 4,500 lbs car of coal for the first half of December only brought 83 cent per car straight throo [sic]. . . . [W]e have no mine scales, and no check weighman." Out of twenty-eight men employed that winter, twelve joined the UMWA and appealed to district officers for negotiating assistance. Yet Howard maintained his opposition: "He says that he will not recognize the union, that he will shrink down to 4 men first. He says that Huntington Coal Co. got by without recognizing the union and so he won't either." By late March, DeFries had been laid off for sixty days, and appeared pessimistic about his coworkers' prospects: "We are not organized yet, and possibly will not be. It seems that the district officers has quit us. We do not hear from them anymore. . . . The majority of the men in the mine are scabs."[45] Along with smaller workforces, family operation, Emery County's religious homogeneity, and seasonal production, Howard's willingness to reduce output by laying off pro-union employees may have been a decisive factor that defeated the union.

In addition to their miners' grievances, small mines also threatened miners' standards at unionized producers through their widespread failure to observe the bituminous coal industry's Code of Fair Competition, as written and adopted by commercial operators in September 1933. This attempt to standardize operating conditions and prices suffered greatly for National Recovery Administration officials' weak enforcement, and by late 1934 supporters of the code opened a series of hearings, legislative revisions, and court battles over its interpretation.[46] While in later decades several top UMWA officials drew sharp criticism for inappropriately close employer collaboration, union officials' and unionized producers' interests appear fundamentally united against a nonunion periphery as early as this time. Thus, in October 1934, Virgil Wright identified "The Operator's Association in both [Wyoming and Utah]," rather than unorganized miners themselves, who "are requiring the officers to do considerable traveling around to line up the wagon mines and to bring them under the Code of Fair Competition."[47]

Periodically, small mines' resistance to organization and threats to price stability disposed some unionists to prefer their shutdown altogether. In early 1935 District 22's newly elected president, John Ross, noted that "father and son and trucking mines" had produced approximately three hundred thousand tons district-wide over the past year, and communicated an alternative proposal to A. D. Lewis, a UMWA official and brother of John L. Lewis. Taking into consideration many western mines' dependence upon land leased from the federal government, he suggested that "if every mine opened on Governmental land large or small were compelled to observe such regulations of the Bureau of Mines as may be set up covering safety, conservation of natural resources and good mining practices observed in the mining of such coal ... it would materially assist in curbing the evil of the small mines, largely truck mines, that usually operate in violation of all laws." Subsequently, "supervision by the Bureau of Mines in enforcing their regulations would assist very materially in eliminating them as destroyers of wage and decent price levels. I also believe that the Government should refuse permits that would allow any more mines to be opened on Government land, where production of going mines, can supply all the coal required in that territory at Code prices."[48]

In June, Columbia's recording secretary, Orvel Peterson, requested that the International clarify federal mine inspectors' jurisdiction "as there are a number of so-called Wagon–Truck coal mines in this state who are persistently violating the state mine orders and safety laws and it seems that we cannot get the matter adjusted." Peterson suspected that local and state politicians limited the Utah Industrial Commission's effectiveness and concluded that "it seems they are hand in hand with the state mine inspector." It is unclear, however, whether he was as interested as his district president in shutting down small mines altogether. Rather, his objections to lax regulation appear to have flowed from a number of specific practices that threatened miners' safety, which he noted included "blasting with black powder, shooting coal on the solid, wearing open lights, no ventilating system, no sprinkler system and many others ... in violation of our state mine orders and safety laws."[49] In 1936, Frank Bonacci noted similar conditions at Huntington Canyon's Stump Flat Coal Company, which had "no scales installed at the mine for the weighing of coal mined and produced by miners ... [and] very few safety laws adopted for the protection of men. ... [Did] not carry out the maximum daily and weekly hours of labor, [nor] pay the wage scale adopted in this District." After regional Civilian Conservation Corps camps contracted with the company to furnish their fuel needs, Bonacci unsuccessfully tried to halt its operations when he filed a complaint with the federal government.[50]

Assigned in 1938 to devote himself exclusively to organizing, International Executive Board (IEB) member Tony Radalj noted how most small mines' ownership structures and seasonal nature posed substantial barriers. From a total of forty-six nonunion mines scattered across the state, Carbon, Emery, and Sevier Counties contained thirteen, twenty-one, and two mines, respectively. Of these, owners or lessees operated twelve mines personally with no employees. With the rest largely owned and staffed by family members, acquaintances, and seasonal farmers whose production met winter home-heating demand, their workforces fluctuated from a high average of eleven employees during the winter to a low of five by May. Radalj concluded his report in mid-May, at which time he noted, "All the mines named in this report were visited and efforts made to organize employees of the same. In my opinion, this is not a precipitous time to attempt to organize the miners. Little progress can be made at this time for the number of men employed is decreasing." In his opinion, which future organizers echoed over the next thirty years, "it would probably be advisable, therefore, to post-pone endeavors to organize these small mines until the latter part of August or early September when the mines are working to capacity and employing the maximum number of workers."[51]

By September 1938, district officers noted only one organizing success in a report to the membership: Miners at the Vail mine in Wyoming's Blind Bull District joined the UMWA and obtained a contract with their employer. Adding to organizers' woes and reversing established unions' previous advance, the "Roosevelt Recession" of 1937–1938 slowed union gains to a trickle. While they remained hopeful for additional successes, mines within District 22's jurisdiction now produced 28.6 percent less than they had the year before, and "many mines, large and small, have closed down, many of them permanently. Among the larger operations being Gebo, Megeath, Susie, National, Consumers, Mohrland, and No. 3 mine, Castle Gate." Nearly 1,600 miners, a significant part of District 22's entire membership, were unemployed.[52] Across the West and the nation, the apparent return to depression conditions stalled organized labor's advance. As regional CIO director James Morgan summarized:

> The depression has made it extremely difficult to get men interested in organization. They are fearful of their jobs and directly and indirectly pressure seems to be exerted to keep them out of organizations. Pressure is exerted usually in such a manner that it isn't possible to charge violation of the Labor Act and it is becoming harder and harder to obtain the necessary members so that we can insist on collective bargaining rights. . . . [W]e believe that should employment pick up when the weather becomes better, we will obtain results again. At least we hope to maintain the organizations that have already been established.[53]

Similarly, Bonacci's CIO activism shifted from organizing the unorganized and chartering new locals to "covering the territory as thoroughly as possible in order to allow the interest not to lapse."[54] Though short-lived, this recession's effects are worth noting for two reasons. First, they anticipated future economic cycles which had highly negative effects on the willingness of many groups of workers to join a union. And second, while postwar legislative changes limited the tools available to organizers, it is notable that as early as 1938 employers found the National Labor Relations Act flexible enough to discourage organizing campaigns without technically violating its letter.

While throughout the 1930s and 1940s John L. Lewis enjoyed unrivaled control over his union at the national level, Utah's miners attentively exercised their freedoms as members of a nominally democratic organization. In this sense, their experience was somewhat exceptional within the UMWA, which had revoked most districts' autonomy during factional battles in the 1920s. To put it mildly, John L. Lewis was not above elevating close family members and sycophantic followers to influential and highly paid union posts. Nor was he inexperienced in the arts of parliamentary manipulation, political purges, and force. If Lewis retired an icon while his inheritors retired in scandal, it can be said that his gauge of political winds and his sense of membership moods were outstanding personal traits his successors failed to master. Lewis also led his union during a fortuitous historical epoch. Here, his conception of "guided" democracy persisted through the 1930s largely because his opponents had been driven out of the organization or co-opted into its structure. In Utah, most members recruited in the 1930s were unfamiliar with past debates and were joining a union for the first time. To Lewis—who in the past had seen a number of incompetent or otherwise overwhelmed elected officials fail—faithful contract observance, not principled autonomy, guaranteed miners' protection. Perennially, he painted autonomy's advocates as communists or pawns of mine owners who would elevate popular yet inexperienced leaders with predictably negative results.[55]

Politically, union structure began with the local organization, chartered by the International Union to represent a specific mine. The new local union then held monthly meetings where any member in good standing could attend, make a proposal, and vote. While some positions were merged or forgone at smaller mines, locals elected a president, vice president, up to three secretaries (financial secretary, treasurer, and recording secretary), and a doorkeeper. These officers conducted union meetings, maintained finances, passed working miners' concerns on to district and International officers, and represented members in the lower stages of grievance processing and in discussions with company management. Locals also served as schools for administrative and legal training, where rank-and-file miners developed skills necessary to serve at higher levels.[56]

Periodically elected district officers consisted of a president, vice president, secretary-treasurer, and IEB member. These men negotiated contracts, led organizing, managed finances, processed grievances, and met with state political leaders and employers' associations. In each geographic region, miners also elected a subdistrict board member who worked part-time as needed. IEB members frequently served as organizers, and periodically traveled to UMWA headquarters where they collectively served as a legislative body to develop policy and rule on membership appeals. Elections for these positions, held in 1934, 1937, 1939, 1941, 1945, and 1949, remained competitive well into the 1950s, with incumbents periodically upset and run-offs held for close races.[57]

At the international level—so named for a number of UMWA locals organized in Canada—a president, vice president, and secretary-treasurer carried the most operational power, negotiating responsibility, and defined the organization's public image. To supplement individual districts' needs, the president's office had the power to appoint salaried international representatives, or "international commissions" consisting of two or more representatives and/or IEB members to assist in organizing, grievance handling, and investigating membership appeals. While international officers were periodically reelected, Lewis's prestige and competency, his successful baiting of "outsiders," and restrictive nomination requirements ensured these contests were more ritualistic than genuinely competitive.

As applied in District 22, some limitations are notable within this structure. Above all, a wide geographic spread limited centralized administration's effectiveness. From Salina, Utah, to Sundance, Wyoming, these states' coal-mining regions spanned a distance of nearly seven hundred miles. A pair of tragic accidents in 1944 and 1945 illustrated the hazards of frequent travel when within eight months of each other two district presidents, Alfred Carey and William McPhie, died in car accidents.[58] The persistence for many years of separate headquarters buildings in Rock Springs, Wyoming, and Price, Utah, served both states' miners at the expense of isolating officers from each other. Geography also limited rank-and-file candidates' chances in district elections, where incumbents' expense accounts and frequent travel gave them natural advantages. Yet officers who took their responsibilities seriously could also find themselves isolated for weeks or months during organizing campaigns in remote locales. In 1961, perhaps one of District 22's most farsighted and capable presidents, former Rains miner Harry Mangus, lost his bid for reelection under such circumstances. Rather than campaign on his own behalf, he remained for months in Kemmerer, Wyoming, where he successfully negotiated a contract at a newly organized major producer.[59]

As many discovered through experience, to become a district officer was to embark upon a precarious professional career. After losing an election, these men faced daunting changes in lifestyle. To return to the uncertainties of mining coal underground was to give up the glamour and security of private offices, expense accounts, national and international travel, public speaking, and intellectually stimulating quasilegal work. In periods of industrial contraction, former officers could not even be sure of returning to their old jobs. Illustrative of these pitfalls is George Cole, District 22's president who led effectively during the UMWA's Utah expansion. In 1934 he lost his post to challenger John Ross. As Cole encountered difficulty finding work again in the mines, his supporters appealed to the International union to retain his expertise and reward his service by hiring him as an organizer. Unsuccessful in this appeal, Cole moved to Michigan's Upper Peninsula where he organized steel companies for the International Union of Mine, Mill, and Smelter Workers. While he found this work rewarding, in an October letter to John L. Lewis, Cole lamented that life in Michigan "is like living in someone else's home," and hopefully concluded, "if you should think of me at any time and there is any service that I could perform in my own home I would be very glad to get back."[60]

Thirty years later, District 22's capable IEB member Malio Pecorelli similarly lost his seat in a period of comparable coalfield unemployment. Like Mangus, amid a time of bitter setbacks his leadership won a contract with the T and K Coal Company where "under almost unbearable conditions . . . he personally conducted an eighteen-day picket line at Kirby, Wyoming during temperatures in excess of twenty-five below zero." With few mines hiring, the UMWA lost Pecorelli's skills as he transitioned into a career as a car and life insurance salesman.[61] While several deposed officers similarly left mining entirely, organizing appointments offered an attractive alternative to unemployment. In 1958, 1961, and 1983, three former district presidents sought such a position after an electoral defeat. Two of them, J. E. Brinley and Frank M. Stevenson, succeeded. While the union retained these men's uncommonly rich experience, many rank-and-file miners resented the continued influence of men they had just voted to replace.[62]

Unlike later generations, those who brought the UMWA to Utah had not grown up in the shadow of any leader's personal charisma, nor did their union's bureaucracy exert as much control over its members' lives through the management of complex benefit systems. In their correspondence with International officers, rank-and-file miners' letters suggest little of the conformity or personality cults that permeated such communications in later years. In late 1934, miners at Sweets and Spring Canyon reviewed their unions' structure and communicated to International vice president Thomas Kennedy their suspicions that "the salaries and expenses of our district officer[s] are far too high and unreasonable." Kennedy, however, responded with the revelation that their salaries were in fact "very much lower" than those of other districts.[63] In 1938, officers and delegates of the Carbon County Industrial Union Council, which represented approximately three thousand UMWA members in Utah, protested organizing's slow pace in truck and wagon mines. Suspicious of IEB member Tony Radalj's effectiveness, they charged that he "be instructed to give the membership some service for the Salary and Expenses he is receiving. Or be removed from office at once."[64]

While largely appreciative of his competency and achievements, membership dissatisfaction with Lewis peaked in the summer and fall of 1940 when the labor leader and lifelong Republican broke his political alliance with President Roosevelt to endorse his opponent, Wendell Willkie, who at the time campaigned aggressively against American involvement in World War II. District 22 president Alfred Carey publicly criticized Lewis, called his charges against Roosevelt "a deliberate lie," and pledged continued support for the popular Democrat. One Wyoming local published its resolution in the Rock Springs *Rocket*, which charged "that the speech made by International President John L. Lewis on behalf of Mr. Willkie's candidacy was a brazen betrayal.... We ask [Lewis] not to await the outcome of the Presidential Election to resign but request you do it immediately."[65] In Utah, Standardville's resolutions committee probably sent the most strongly worded protest:

> You, John L. Lewis, have turned traitor to organized labor.... We are of the opinion, and have been for some time; that you are a communist at heart and in spite of the fact that you have dictated to us for a number of years there is no reason why you should have sold us out to the Republican Party.... [W]e... are asking you to withdraw from these apparently traitorous aspirations and stand up on your own feet as an organized labor leader should and live up to the principles and standards of unionism instead of trying to be a corrupt politician.... [W]e will go on record as being ashamed that we ever paid into a campaign fund and we will fight this appropriation of our paychecks because we feel that it is a fund that we can hardly afford to keep replenished so that through it somebody may bite us in the back.[66]

From their critique of his position in national politics, these miners also questioned Lewis's manipulation of internal democracy when they demanded, "Also, that you submit to having another name alongside of yours this coming [UMWA] election so that we may exercise some choice and practice of our liberty as United States citizens." Clear Creek miners felt the same way, and in November communicated an identical protest.⁶⁷

Wattis miners raised another concern when they asked Lewis to explain some of his quieter financial projects with the UMWA treasury. Alerted by a *Salt Lake Tribune* article that investigated a secret loan given to the Rocky Mountain Fuel Company—then under the ownership of Lewis's friend and collaborator Josephine Roche—Wattis's recording secretary Harold Olsen asked Lewis to "give us a satisfactory answer to the charges . . . circulating among our members and caus[ing] considerable comment." Lewis responded evasively and suggested that "the *Tribune* story is, of course, filled with misrepresentation." Without a forthright explanation, Lewis asked Wattis's miners to place their faith in higher levels of institutional checks and balances. In his view, "the whole question is one to which the officers of the International Union, and members of the International Executive Board will give consideration."⁶⁸ Given the large number of appointees then serving on the board, Lewis's response appears disingenuous, and reveals a major weakness in the UMWA's accountability mechanisms.

Political winds, rather, suggest the enigma of Lewis's survival through his broader isolation in 1940. While he had purged or otherwise silenced left-wing critics within the union during in the early 1930s, his isolationism in 1940 mirrored that of his largest radical adversary: the American Communist Party. Within the UMWA, rank-and-file miners who might have scrutinized union functioning for financial or democratic irregularities lacked an organizational vehicle to synthesize protests beyond the local level. And for those who tried, few had a reputation accomplished enough to rival Lewis's image. Thus, in December when John L. Lewis, vice president Philip Murray, and secretary-treasurer Thomas Kennedy all ran for re-election unopposed, membership dissatisfaction registered only through a twenty-thousand-vote discrepancy between ballots cast for Lewis and his slightly more popular lieutenants. Outside of the UMWA, however, Lewis faced stronger criticism he could not so easily contain. Bowing to political pressure, he resigned as president of the CIO.⁶⁹

While the New Deal was not the first or last time that American workers attempted to organize unions, as an era it is unique for the exceptionally fair chance they were given to do so. During this time a distinctly American model of unionization emerged, which contained within it a number of contradictions that would be tested as political and economic winds changed. From 1938 to 1940, every subsequent nemesis encountered by the UMWA appeared as clouds on the horizon: an unstable price and wage gap between union and nonunion sectors, small mine owners' successful resistance to organization, limitations of NLRB protections, and membership concerns over internal accountability. As early as December 1936, miners at Latuda, Spring Canyon, and Standardville anticipated the central competitive dilemma of the 1950s when they alarmingly noted neighboring mines' installation of new machines that "have reduced the price of coal through the mechanization . . . to a point where the Independent operators will be forced out of business."[70]

International conditions, however, intervened to alter the trajectory of United States—and labor—history. As America entered World War II, full employment and industrial expansion reversed unions' 1938 organizational setbacks. Eager to secure lucrative government contracts, businessmen throughout basic industry rapidly recognized labor unions to ensure steady production and curry favor with liberal purchasing agents faithful to New Deal ideology. These conditions also allowed John L. Lewis to break out of his 1940 isolation and place himself back at the head of labor militancy. From an increase in unauthorized strikes that resisted worsening safety conditions to a coordinated postwar strike wave that allowed the UMWA to win its most significant victories in healthcare and pension coverage, the late 1940s marked coal miners' peak of national influence. While the war allowed unions to embark upon on a second major wave of growth that raised nonagricultural workers' unionization rate from 26 to 36 percent, the contradictions of the late 1930s were not so much resolved as postponed for another decade.

CHAPTER 2

Twilight of the New Deal

We feel that our organization is built around honesty and fairness. If the rank-and-file know they have been fairly dealt with they will go through hell and high water to back up their leaders.

—Officers of Local 6511, Sweet Mine, 1949

IT WAS JUST AFTER THREE PM on Wednesday, May 8, 1945, when a half-mile underground in the third left entry of Utah Fuel's Sunnyside mine, eighteen men's thoughts drifted from work routines to hot showers, clean clothes, and the relaxation of a hard-earned evening. Many looked forward to shortly greeting their wives and children in the nearby communities of Sunnyside, Columbia, and Dragerton. Those whose families waited farther away knew it took a little longer for their husbands and fathers to come home from work. Each morning, many who commuted from elsewhere in Carbon County ate breakfast under electric lights before they shared a ride to work. Few expected anything other than a normal routine, though the memories of the deaths of seven men just two months prior in an explosion at Kenilworth may have uncomfortably clouded some men's thoughts. Miles apart, in the optimism of a Utah spring or amid the noise of whirring machinery, men and women shared personal uncertainties in an era of global catastrophe. As the battle for Okinawa raged into its second month, some thought less of themselves than of sons and brothers stationed overseas. One or two fretted over the impending shift change and pondered the next round in an ongoing domestic argument. Others relieved tension with a curse or dirty joke, shared fluently in Spanish or passed along a crew through a tapestry of English in a half-dozen accents.[1]

Already the mine's evening shift had arrived and begun to make their way underground. At 3:15 pm the earliest—a crew of eleven working in first right—had just reached the main entry when the world exploded. Four died quickly, while the rest were later hospitalized for burns. According to witnesses, ventilation fans spewed flames and dust as far as the tipple two miles distant. Three hundred feet from its point of origin the explosion's force knocked men to the ground. Somewhere in third left, something had ignited methane, which the miners failed to notice had exceeded tolerable levels. As word spread, Castle Gate, Columbia, Horse Canyon, and Kenilworth's rescue teams arrived to fight fires and help the injured. Yet their capacities were limited as mechanics and electricians scrambled to revive a damaged ventilation system. For most of the night, families of the missing waited outside the mine. As dead miners' bodies arrived one by one at the surface, coroners looked on as frantic wives attempted to identify their husbands by the color of burnt clothing. By noon the next day, one woman remained torn between two agonies: Had she failed to recognize her husband at the mortuary in Price, or was he alone still missing somewhere underground?[2]

Most of the eighty-seven men working at the time escaped with only minor burns, largely thanks to rock dusting which had coated flammable walls of coal with a veneer of pulverized limestone. Standardized after deadlier explosions in 1900 and 1924, in the opinion of state mine inspector S. C. Harvey this probably prevented the entire mine from blowing up. In total, the Sunnyside mine disaster took the lives of twenty-three men and hospitalized seven more. For forty years, it remained the worst in recent memory. More important than any contract's wording, or any supervisor's instructions, such potentially catastrophic mine explosions were the ultimate nightmare every miner knew they had a personal responsibility and collective obligation to prevent.

As repair work neared completion ten days later, Local 6244's membership voted to strike with the demand that Utah Fuel replace three managers they claimed had operated the mine in unsafe conditions. Aware of the threat of such insurgencies to their contract's integrity,

District 22 president William McPhie and vice president Joe Dowd reminded them that "contracts provide selection of personnel and management of mine is company responsibility and strike hence is violation of contract. Therefore [the] men should return to work." This appeal, however, swayed few. Equally unconvincing was Utah Fuel vice president Claude Heiner's praises of his managers' long experience. Even John L. Lewis deviated from his standard denunciation of wildcat strikes and reminded Heiner: "[The] record of recent explosion just does not justify your representatives as to competency of management. Can appreciate reluctance of men to work under unsafe conditions in view of recent catastrophe. I am telegraphing president McPhie at Rock Springs, suggesting that he work with your company and men to secure adjustment of the situation."[3]

After five days, Utah Industrial Commission chairman E. M. Royle met the miners to hear out their demands. Potentially, his organization could affect management changes if it threatened to revoke the mine's operating licenses. Joseph S. Mayer, of the War Manpower Commission, also traveled to Sunnyside to meet with union officials. His presence as representative of a national command economy may have been decisive in brokering a compromise. Under the arrangement, the managers in question retained their positions for the time being, pending the outcome of an official investigation. Yet their decisions now faced the scrutiny of state mine inspector S. C. Harvey, who accepted temporary employment as Sunnyside's safety engineer.[4]

On June 9, the commission released its report on the explosion, which supported miners' claims to find the company negligent in its application of safety measures. While they had conducted a routine methane inspection on the morning of the accident, and as late as noon had reported the face in third left as adequately "free of gas," Utah Fuel had allowed electrical equipment capable of igniting gas to operate in an area known to liberate methane in variable and unpredictable quantities. Furthermore, management had been lax in routine searches of employees for smoking materials, with no inspection conducted for six months prior to the accident. Concluding its hearing, the commission mirrored miners' original demands when it revoked the licenses of superintendent Arch Morrison and mine foreman Frank Markosek for six months.[5]

FIGURE 2.1. Sunnyside area, ca. 1950s. Newly constructed homes in foreground, Dragerton in upper-right background. Used with permission from the Eberly Family Special Collections Library, Pennsylvania State University Libraries.

At Sunnyside, industrial conflict simmered throughout 1945 as miners initiated at least five unauthorized strikes that cost a total of twenty-six lost working days. Five days after work resumed, miners walked out again when Utah Fuel attempted to reopen the explosion area in violation of state mine inspectors' orders. Later, miners struck to protest a unit foreman's firing for abandoning his official duties when he helped bring an injured employee out of the mine. Over the summer and fall, management decisions that questioned miners' need for adequate safety equipment attracted the greatest wrath. As the local's executive board summarized, "On one occasion, the miners were refused brattice until the superintendent made an investigation as to whether or not the brattice was necessary, on another occasion, the man that loads up material on the outside was stopped for loading timber up for use in the mine that had been ordered by the Unit Foreman. . . . [He] was sent to clean railroad cars for a couple of days whilst the need for props were ignored." Not all of these strikes gained International support, however. In March, after miners had struck to force Utah Fuel to provide adequate space for a doctor's office, Lewis requested that they abandon the endeavor, as "the question of a doctor's office is one which should not interfere with the production of coal at this time."[6]

In December, a final wildcat drew a now-familiar rebuke, as Lewis suggested to Local 6244's president William Cox "that your membership return to work [as] any grievance you may have can be adjudicated while the mine is in operation." The men, however, ignored this request. In their view, at stake were fundamental issues of safety and control. At their new superintendent's orders, two rooms were driven in the mine's second left entry in a manner that allowed the ventilation system to blow air from an area known to be actively releasing methane to another where electric motors were running. While the mine's safety engineer

FIGURE 2.2. Dispute negotiation, unknown Utah coal mine, ca. 1940s–1950s. After decades of bitter conflict, the UMWA framework let miners question management, defend their rights, and enforce safety through democratic discussions alongside coworkers and legal experts. Photo courtesy of the Western Mining and Railroad Museum.

maintained the action was acceptable, the union maintained it violated state mining laws and could potentially trigger another explosion. As the local appealed to the state industrial commission, Superintendent Walter Odendahl escalated tensions when he fired twelve men who had worked in the now-closed area of the mine—including a member of the safety committee that first identified the problem. On December 19, the men unanimously voted to strike until Odendahl was removed.[7]

While the conflict began as a safety dispute, it escalated into a deeper clash over each party's right to control the workplace. On December 28, Utah Fuel took its case to the court of public opinion when it placed a full-page ad in the *Sun Advocate*. After citing the no-strike clause in the 1945 National Wage Agreement, noting the official steps of the grievance procedure written into District 22's constitution, and asserting perhaps obliquely that its commitment to safety "is in line with the best coal mining practice, either within Utah or the nation," Utah Fuel defended its prerogative to manage and asked, "Has labor the right, under this agreement, to resort to strike tactics in order to bring about the removal of a mine superintendent or any other mine official? We say NO. If that right were conceded, then all operators of coal mines would have virtually relinquished their right to manage their own properties—a right clearly recognized by labor itself." Perhaps most objectionable to strike supporters, the company's attempt to quantify stakes failed to account for human dimensions. While the 425 employees idled by the strike no doubt missed the collective loss of $4,800 per day in wages, and perhaps recognized the value of an additional 3,500 tons of coal per day going to warm homes and power industry, they rejected the argument that such numbers totaled "too much here at stake to justify a sudden and unauthorized strike."[8]

The following week, Local 6244 responded with its own full-page advertisement. The first paragraph elaborated on the safety issue and cited industrial commissioner R. H. Dalrymple's support for union claims. Clarifying their demand for Odendahl's removal, and recalling the previous disaster, the miners mocked Utah Fuel's assessment and defended their right to intervene:

> We are doing now what we did months prior to the May 9th explosion, fighting for the safety of life and limb. What is $4800 per day in comparison with the scorching of 23 of our members? Human lives are above any

working agreement or property rights. . . . You stated that the strike was unwarranted on either moral or legal grounds. We still claim that human lives come first, last, and all times. . . . We cannot surrender our rights for safety by the disregard of laws and safe practices by your management. . . . The first man layed [sic] off in the recent controversy was a member of the safety committee, also a member of our L. U. Executive Board. . . . Why the discrimination? . . . Yes, miners need wages, but not in the Great Beyond."[9]

The miners also published supportive correspondence, including the explanation of its actions Local 6244's executive board had written John L. Lewis on December 23. Here, the board identified the limitations at the heart of contract unionism:

Brother Lewis,

Do the membership have to forfeit safety of life and limbs of our members whilst the management hides behind contract to force us to work under said conditions? Do we have to jeopardize our lives to live up to contract whilst the management disregards safety where expense is their excuse? Brother Lewis, we are sure that on your past record of militancy in fighting for the rights of our membership as our leader, you would not tolerate for one moment, the actions of the management of Utah Fuel hiding behind our working agreement to force us to work under such conditions, [where] nothing was done hastily in our action as there was a lapse of ten days from first taking up the matter until the work stoppage. . . . We look forward to your support in our fight for the safety of the lives and limbs of our membership.[10]

While the contradiction between management's legal right to manage and these decisions' potential consequences for miners existed in UMWA contracts since their inception, the 1940s stand out as exceptional years for the aggressiveness with which each party tested the boundaries of their power.

Through its tragedy and aftermath, the Sunnyside mine disaster exemplifies the convergence of several trends that reshaped coal mining during the tumultuous 1940s. Up a side canyon just a few miles south of Sunnyside, a United States Steel subsidiary had operated the Columbia mine since 1924 to fuel its smelter at Ironton, Utah. As America mobilized for war in 1942, the federal government's Defense Plant

Corporation loaned United States Steel $200 million to construct a brand new, state-of-the-art smelter near Provo to be managed by another subsidiary, Geneva. Nine miles south of Columbia, Geneva opened a new mine at Horse Canyon to fuel the Provo plant. Meanwhile, in California the government similarly gave industrialist Henry Kaiser a $112 million loan to construct another large steel mill in the quiet community of Fontana, an agricultural area forty miles east of Los Angeles. Now the largest steel producer on the west coast, Kaiser leased Utah Fuel's Sunnyside mines which it purchased after the war. By 1945, Geneva Steel employed 4,100 workers directly with 900 more working at its coal mine and limestone quarries. Kaiser employed 2,500 steel workers and over 400 Utah miners.[11]

To house the new miners and their families, Defense Plant Corporation also funded construction of the Dragerton subdivision adjacent to Sunnyside. Together, these properties employed several hundred relatively consistently for the next forty years. As postwar commercial mining declined, Dragerton, Columbia, and Sunnyside's ties to the comparatively robust steel industry allowed them to retain a greater share of their populations. With the largest and most concentrated number of coal miners, what is today known as the East Carbon–Sunnyside area recentered union power to give the UMWA its greatest concentration of regional support.

While by far Utah's worst coal-mining accident during the war, the Sunnyside disaster tragically highlighted declining safety records as productivity increased. From 500 million tons in 1940, American coal mines produced a record 684 million tons in 1944. Yet this came at a tremendous cost. From 1942 to 1943, nearly 3,000 American miners died on the job. Each week an average of 500 men reported disabling injuries, and by May 1943 over 34,000 miners had been injured since the war began. Locally, during the war 87 men from Carbon and Emery Counties died fighting in uniform, while 119 died working underground. From a 1939 low of 0.76 miners killed per one thousand employed, the Sunnyside explosion tilted Utah's average from 4.8 in 1944 to 12.79 in 1945.[12] With Sunnyside's mines long recognized as particularly prone to releases of flammable gas, wetter conditions that prevailed in most properties along the eastern Wasatch Plateau reduced the likelihood of explosions there. Still, rock falls, haulage incidents, and heavy machinery led to a number of fatalities. In 1943, the last wartime year for which injury statistics were recorded, accidents affected 1,661 Utah miners—39 percent of the state's coal-mining workforce and a 50 percent increase from the year before.[13]

Throughout the war, labor scarcity overshadowed every aspect of coal mining. From the poverty and property closures of the 1930s, operators now scrambled to fill coal orders with limited manpower and an overburdened transportation infrastructure. While by the summer of 1943 some 3,200 coal miners worked in Utah, the US Employment Office in Price estimated a need for an additional 1,395.[14] As smaller companies' managers canvassed the countryside to entice farmers to accept mine employment, larger organizations placed ads for experienced miners in distant states. Commonly, both accepted applicants new to mining. As Horse Canyon started from scratch and Sunnyside boomed alongside it, approximately 2,000 new residents had moved to these communities by 1944. While some had traveled from as far away as Alabama, ethnic Mexicans who relocated mainly from Colorado and New Mexico shifted Carbon County's demographics and constituted approximately half the new arrivals.[15]

Fully aware of their irreplaceability, experienced miners no longer accepted inferior conditions they had tolerated in earlier years. For all the dangers they faced underground, a miner who earned seven dollars per day in 1943 chafed at the knowledge that an unskilled worker at an urban defense plant now made double the pay amid far safer conditions. With the prewar pattern of collective bargaining subsumed beneath a command economy directed by Roosevelt's National War Labor Board, coal miners' wages lagged behind inflation while the prices of food and other consumer products rose.[16]

By May 1943, John L. Lewis concluded that federal regulators and coal operators had failed to uphold their end of the agreement, and abandoned the wartime no-strike pledge he had taken along with most labor leaders in the AFL and CIO. That year he led 416,000 bituminous coal miners through four short if demonstrative strikes that ranged from forty-eight hours' to six days' duration. Vilified in the national press as an irresponsible, dictatorial manipulator of his members, Lewis in many ways directed, rather than prompted, miners' militancy. The national strike he tacitly supported during contract negotiations in the first days of May 1943 actually began the previous week, as 60,000 to 75,000 men had stopped work at eastern mines on their own initiative by April 28. Earlier in the year, nearly half of Pennsylvania's 40,000 struggling anthracite miners struck to protest a fifty-cent dues increase passed over their objections by the UMWA's national convention. While union officials quickly quelled the revolt, Lewis seized upon these miners' other demand—for a two-dollar-per-day wage increase—to channel dissatisfaction away from union policy and into national negotiations.[17] As War Labor Board formulas attempted to limit inflation by moderating wage increases, Lewis's other proposals focused on tangential issues that increased miners' share of earnings through other avenues, such as portal-to-portal pay, increases in vacation pay, and elimination of paycheck deductions.

Berated by the national press as "unpatriotic" for refusing to endure longer hours and deteriorating conditions, miners identified with their leader's defiant posture, who in these years cemented his nearly religious persona as their hero and champion. In March 1945, some 2,700 out of 3,551 eligible Utah miners voted on whether to authorize a strike should national negotiations fail to reach an agreement at the conclusion of the two-year 1943 agreement. The vote was 2,040 in favor. While a last-minute agreement avoided a national work stoppage, by Monday, April 2, a communications delay led several hundred miners to strike three Utah properties.[18]

While some aspects of militant unionism appeared locally, Utah's miners weathered the war with comparative moderation. Although unauthorized strikes proliferated nationally in coal, this study has only located nine that occurred in Utah during the war years. Seven of these took place at Sunnyside where, in addition to safety issues, miners struck in 1944 over their employer's failure to abide by an umpire's decision in a grievance case. Other strikes stemmed from one Gordon Creek company's failure to issue vacation pay, and excessively wet conditions at Hiawatha. Such an unbalanced record suggests the centrality of local

TABLE 2.1. *Opposite*, no record was kept by Utah's Industrial Commission on nonfatal injuries from 1944 through 1948 inclusive, also 1952. Adapted from J. E. Brinley and Arthur Biggs, "Joint Report of the Officers of District 22 to the Nineteenth Consecutive Constitutional Convention of the United Mine Workers of America," 1957.

Table 2.1: Mine Accidents in Utah 1925–1955

Year	Killed	No. of Men Employed	Tons of Coal Produced	Killed Per 1,000 Employed
1925	34	4,707	4,690,342	7.22
1926	20	4,798	4,373,793	4.16
1927	28	3,792	4,781,480	7.38
1928	17	3,828	4,842,544	4.44
1929	25	4,207	5,160,521	5.94
1930	64	3,615	4,257,541	17.70
1931	21	3,184	3,350,044	6.59
1932	12	2,568	2,852,127	4.67
1933	5	2,093	2,674,986	2.38
1934	13	2,570	2,418,000	5.05
1935	12	2,531	2,918,047	4.74
1936	9	2,758	3,129,116	3.26
1937	12	2,998	3,651,727	3.60
1938	9	2,926	2,759,047	2.50
1939	2	2,626	3,075,100	0.76
1940	8	2,393	3,313,826	3.34
1941	16	2,866	4,032,879	5.58
1942	14	3,476	5,478,591	4.02
1943	19	4,164	6,781,298	4.46
1944	19	3,760	7,206,107	4.80
1945	51	3,872	6,728,462	12.79
1946	15	4,073	6,116,410	3.56
1947	12	4,327	7,619,378	3.60
1948	10	4,462	6,978,803	2.24
1949	11	4,443	6,090,040	2.48
1950	8	4,467	6,464,007	1.79
1951	12	3,932	5,803,357	3.05
1952	5	3,789	6,129,109	1.32
1953	10	3,918	6,550,070	2.55
1954	7	2,833	5,008,347	2.47
1955	6	2,912	6,223,986	2.06

Source: Adapted from J. E. Brinley and Arthur Biggs, "Joint Report of the Officers of District 22 to the Nineteenth Consecutive Constitutional Convention of the United Mine Workers of America," 1957. No record was kept by Utah's Industrial Commission on nonfatal injuries from 1944 through 1948 or for 1952.

conditions and personalities to the escalation of industrial conflict.[19]

In February 1945, District 22's president William McPhie summarized miners' wartime experiences in a speech to the body's annual convention in Salt Lake City. At a high human cost, and despite many younger miners' induction into the armed forces, coal production in Utah and Wyoming had increased by 50 percent over the previous year alone. Though the war still raged across two continents, American industrial power had helped decisively to tilt its direction. Yet in national opinion, coal miners carried the stigma of what McPhie identified as "one of the most misunderstood groups of workers in essential industry." As an attending reporter summarized, "While strikes are publicized, the sacrifices of miners are not."[20]

If the 1930s provided the conditions that allowed coalfield unionism to gain a foothold, the immediate postwar period may be understood as an era of transition. In a series of nearly annual national contract strikes from late 1945 to early 1950, John L. Lewis defied federal injunctions to win unprecedented gains, particularly in miners' health care and retirement. With mines still under federal control in the spring of 1946, Interior Secretary Julius Krug signed off on the creation of a multiemployer Welfare and Retirement Fund financed by a royalty on each ton of union coal produced. A 1947 strike secured operator acceptance for the program, and in 1948 a new contract raised the fund's royalty from 10 to 20 cents. That September, John L. Lewis personally presented Rock Springs, Wyoming, miner Horace Ainscough with the first $100 monthly pension check issued by the fund. To be eligible, a miner had to be sixty-two years old or older, have mined coal for a total of twenty years, have been a member of the UMWA, and have retired after May 26, 1946. For hundreds of thousands of working and retired miners, widows, and children, this program quickly symbolized the benefits of union membership and cemented Lewis's legacy.[21]

These strikes, however, came at a high cost. In spring 1946, some 3,500 Utah miners remained idle for six weeks. After operators refused to abide by the contract signed at this strike's conclusion, another lengthy shutdown in November cost the state's miners approximately $25,000 per day in lost wages. As their savings dwindled and local grocers refused to extend credit, many miners petitioned for relief. In 1946 and 1948, the International's financial health endured heavy blows as it paid millions in fines after federal courts found it in contempt for having continued strikes despite injunctions. In 1950, this series of postwar contract strikes concluded under a shadow of picket violence, while miners' families got by on surplus potatoes, dried milk, and donations from other unions.[22]

While an extremely popular achievement, it is important to note that the fund also arrived as an imperfect creation. From its earliest days, thousands fell between the cracks of eligibility requirements as its ruling body of one union, one neutral, and one operator-appointed trustee grappled with revenue streams chronically insufficient to pay all potentially deserving beneficiaries. While the union hoped that coverage could be improved and extended in future contracts, over the long term rising healthcare costs, the Fund's tonnage-based funding structure, and its opaque management and investment record frustrated many miners while it increased nonunion operators' resistance—particularly as mining technology became more efficient at producing large tonnages. The strikes that enabled the Fund's creation also weakened consumer confidence in coal's reliability at the same time natural gas, oil, and diesel made new inroads into coal's core markets in home heating and transportation. While much change was inevitable, industrial conflict hastened the abruptness of these shifts in energy markets.[23]

While few miners long familiar with company doctors' limitations or the experience of growing old with little or no savings questioned the wisdom of fighting for the strongest single-industry benefits program they could get, a number of independent observers perceptively noted coal's weakening position. By October 1945, few considered the fuel's long-term future optimistically besides a handful of dreamers who followed coal derivative research and conversion to cleaner fuels through as-yet commercially unviable gasification and liquefaction proposals. While some journalists rallied hopes at the latest rumors of new coal uses, others used the word "dying" to describe the plight of a "competitive commodity of decreasing utility." Signs of transition increasingly appeared, as in 1946 when Brigham Young University converted its heating system from coal to oil. While in 1945 the Denver Rio Grande & Western railroad owned 320 coal-burning engines, had consumed 1.5 million tons of coal, and hauled 125,000 coal cars over its rails for commercial customers, a year later miners and their families who lived in

Helper, Wellington, and Price looked out of their windows to see freight pulled behind the latest diesel locomotives.[24]

Well aware of these new challenges, in 1945 Utah coal magnate Moroni Heiner urged "determined action to bring about a sane and practical attitude on the part of labor." The following November, the *Sun Advocate* reprinted a pointed editorial from the Grand Junction *Sentinel*—perhaps a calculated decision to deflect readers' disagreements from punishing the coalfield paper itself—in which the writer suggested that those "who so unquestioningly obey the edicts of Czar Lewis might profitably begin to do a little questioning. Is he really promoting their welfare as he leads them into actions that turn the public against them, or is he hastening the day when there will be no coal industry to furnish them their livelihoods?"[25]

Coal was not the only industry to experience the pangs of peacetime reconversion, GI and veteran reintegration, and strong unions eager to defend (if not expand) recent gains. In the immediate postwar years there was a surge in American workers' willingness to strike. As the war in Europe drew to a close, labor and management both anticipated the war in the Pacific would last another year and allow more time for the twelve million men and women in uniform and the eight million directly engaged in war production to adjust to a peacetime economy. President Truman's decision to drop atomic bombs on Hiroshima and Nagasaki ended the war almost immediately and with no notice for economic planners. Unsurprisingly, this escalated popular anxieties about inflation and full employment's impending halt. Subsequently, the fall of 1945 marked the biggest strike wave in American history, as over five million workers stopped production in core industrial sectors that at one point simultaneously included auto manufacturing, steel, electrical production, and meat packing.[26]

Politically, contesting the postwar order involved more than quantitative debates over wages and working conditions. Within the largest businesses (and the largest unions), managers and executives debated the meaning of collective bargaining and the direction future negotiations would take. Summarizing the outcome of Truman's National Labor-Management Conference in October 1945, historian Mike Davis observes,

> The business delegation, while accepting the utility of collective bargaining in the abstract, "laced managerial inviolability at the center

of its program for postwar labor relations." . . . Rejecting the CIO's warmed-over pleas for more "industrial democracy," the front-line corporations in auto, steel, and electrical manufacture adopted a plan of battle which, by maintaining a hard position on wages, aimed purposefully to provoke long, draining strikes to deflate grass roots militancy. Ultimately, the corporations hoped to force the unions to accept a tough trade-off between wage increases and control over working conditions. In particular they wanted strong curbs on the role of rank-and-file leadership, and the restriction of the right to strike, and long, multi-year contracts. . . . In contrast to 1936–37 or even 1941, however, there was minimal rank-and-file initiative in the organization of the strikes. The corporations generally did not attempt to run scabs, and the CIO bureaucracy was in firm control of day to day tactics. Indeed . . . there was a deliberate strategy to use the strikes to let off steam in the ranks while centralizing further the power of the national union leaderships.[27]

As Truman failed to control inflation and attempted to corral strikes, much of the Democratic Party's base in unions expressed dissatisfaction by abstaining from voting during the 1946 congressional elections. Nationally, only 30 percent of the electorate participated. This allowed a conservative backlash of those most alienated by the New Deal, organized labor's flexing of its wartime muscle, and fourteen years of government domination by a single party to retake Congress. This reversal allowed the new Republican majority to craft unprecedented restrictions on labor's ability to organize. Most significant among them, in 1947 it passed the Taft-Hartley Act over President Truman's veto. In the South, these restrictions as well as escalating antiunion sentiments doomed the CIO's "Operation Dixie"—a massive seven-year, twelve-state organizing drive that endeavored to transform the lightly unionized region—to flounder on the rocks of regional race and politics and geographically isolate many industries' union sectors within their northern and midwestern cores. In other workplaces across the country, employers and conservative unionists also used rising fears of Soviet-style communism to purge militant employees of diverse political backgrounds. So soon after union members reached their peak of twentieth-century power, they encountered new shackles of legality as well as circumstance. Nationally, labor movements and labor unions would never be the same.[28]

As energy consumers converted to alternative fuels and operators rapidly mechanized, layoffs and mine closures transformed coal communities with particularly devastating results. While western European democracies nationalized their coal mines and eased the pain of reduced markets and mechanization with subsidies, Lewis and the coal operators' commitment to free enterprise provided fewer safety nets to those who fell between the cracks. Here, in the twilight of the New Deal, these challenges to job security, organizing, and membership democracy transformed union politics and culture for the following twenty years.

By 1949, even Lewis acknowledged the fact of coal's decline, and the UMWA *Journal* warned of "a repetition of the disastrous cut-throat competition of the 20's and early 30's." In a temporary stop-gap measure, Lewis supported the establishment of a three-day work week, to reduce both the speed of layoffs and the accumulation of stockpiles that undermined the power of miners' strikes. Operators, however, chafed at these restrictions. Steel producers who transformed metallurgical coal into coke complained that a three-day week failed to ensure an adequate supply to keep their furnaces burning. Managers of all mines also complained that they could only keep their mines competitive by maximizing the time expensive machinery spent in operation. In a final winter of contentious bargaining, 4,500 Utahns joined 480,000 coal miners nationwide to halt production after the nationally negotiated contract expired in September. Alarmed, idled miners and mine owners looked on as nonunion properties continued to operate and ship coal by truck up Highway 6-50 through Price Canyon. While concurrent organizing campaigns still hoped to win over these men, idled union members established their own picket lines to stop the passage of coal trucks and prevent these mines from operating at all.[29]

At first, the *Sun Advocate* reported pickets' nearly 100 percent success in turning back nonunion coal trucks, many of which came from Emery County. In late September, Emery County sheriff Bryant Nelson may have thought he had deescalated a situation when, at strikers' request, he confiscated one nonunion trucker's pistol before he escorted him through a picket line near Huntington Canyon. The pickets, however, later attempted to flip the sheriff's car until he flashed his badge and unholstered his revolver. In February and March, increased patrols un-

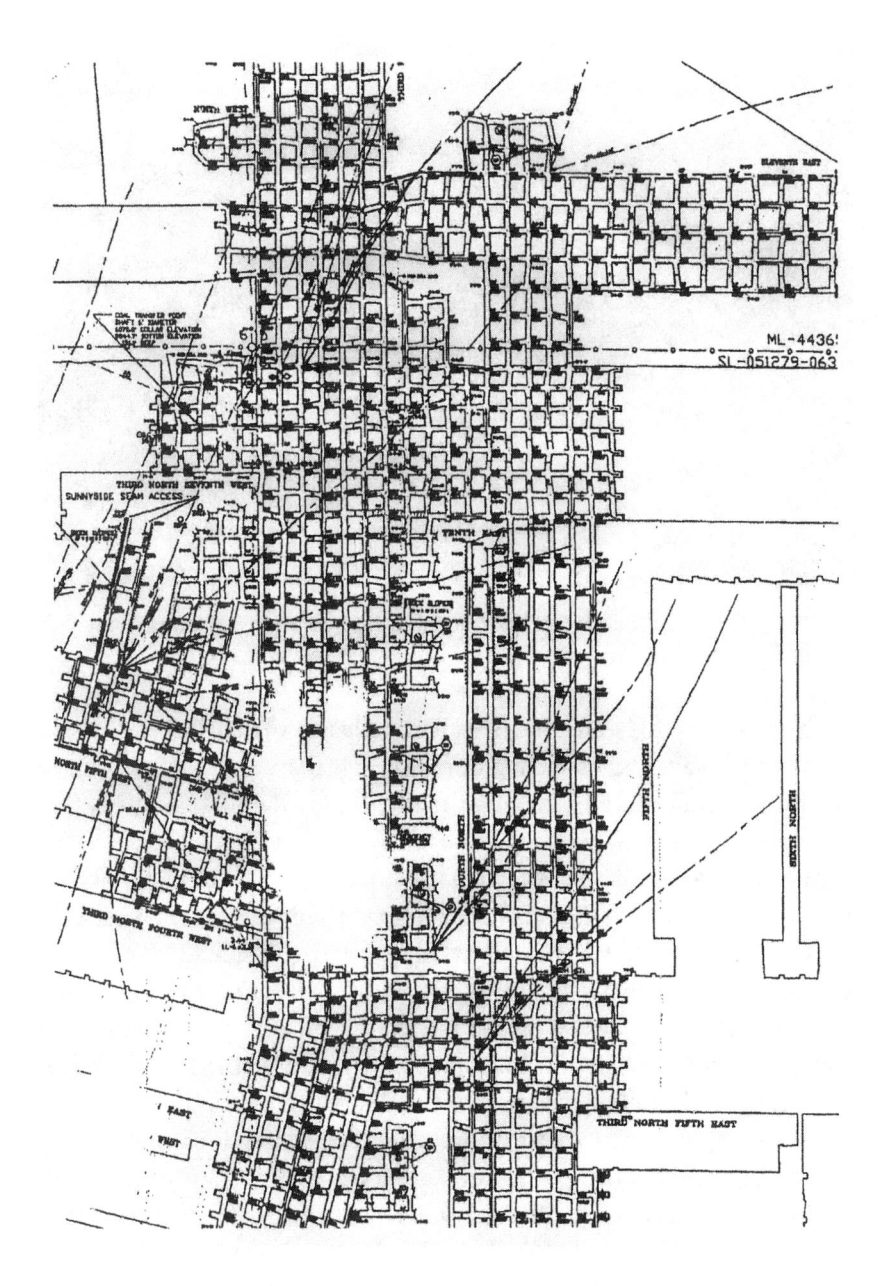

FIGURE 2.3. Part of the layout of the Soldier Creek–Soldier Canyon Mine, demonstrating the room-and-pillar method. Continuous miners extract coal in a gridlike pattern, leaving square pillars of coal to support the roof. Courtesy of the Utah Geological Survey.

FIGURE 2.4. A continuous mining machine at Kaiser-Sunnyside. Image courtesy of John Palacios.

dermined picketing's effectiveness, with only a few trucks stopped along county highways and obliged to dump their loads. As the strike dragged on, miners' mounting frustrations found expression in a handful of violent incidents. One February night, as driver Steve West began the ascent up Price Canyon with a load of nonunion coal, he was flagged down by a group of pickets near the Carbon County line. After their discussion escalated into a fistfight, West broke away, got back to his cab, and drove off. Suddenly, two bullets shattered the driver's side window, with one passing through his wrist. At the Book Cliff coal mine in northern Emery County, three trucks belonging to a nonunion firm similarly had their cylinder heads cracked by rifle fire. Rather than helping to advance coal miners' cause, these escalations undermined public support.[30]

The year 1950 ended with a reversal of the UMWA's attitude toward national negotiations. In March, under a threat by President Truman to once again place mines under federal control, Lewis and northern operators' representative George Love led the industry to sign a two-and-a-half-year contract that promised a reprieve. While union wins included a seventy-cent daily pay raise, an increase in Fund royalties from twenty to thirty cents a ton, and operators' acceptance of Lewis's ally Josephine Roche as the Fund's "neutral" trustee, both parties benefited from the stability this contract symbolized. As Lewis's biographers Dubofsky and Van Tine summarized, "The warring parties settled their differences when they realized that while they fought, outside powers were weakening the kingdom of coal. The rise of competitive fuels, the threat of intensified and continuous government intervention . . . and the increase in small 'gopher hole' nonunion mines led the combatants to rapidly become allies."[31] For the next twenty-three years, collective bargaining ceased to become a drawn-out, public spectacle. Rather, Love organized industry representatives into the BCOA, which negotiated new contracts with John L. Lewis quietly and in secret. In exchange for modest wage increases every two to three years, the UMWA promised labor stability. While by the late 1960s members increasingly chafed at this arrangement, the union did not authorize a single national contract strike until 1971.

The way out of coal's dilemma, Lewis and Love decided, lay in peace with the largest producers and rapid mine mechanization. As manager L. E. Adams of the Spring Canyon Coal Company had predicted in 1945: "It would seem, therefore, that the price of coal eventually must be reduced. Labor will exert itself to retain present wages or perhaps tend to increase per-ton costs. Since the price of coal must be reduced . . . the solution of the problem appears to be the complete mechanization of coal mining."[32] With wartime rationing and a priority system for new equipment purchasing abolished, technology and capital promised a way forward for those with access to them. Of all the machines invented to ease various aspects of mining, undoubtedly the most significant at this time was the continuous mining machine, introduced in Utah in 1948. Now, the work of several men who had undercut, drilled, blasted, and hand-loaded coal could be accomplished by a single operator of an electric, wheeled vehicle whose rotating drum ripped coal from the face and loaded it automatically. While mechanization insured a sharp rise in coalfield unemployment, it allowed those who retained their jobs to enjoy favorable pay and benefits. For younger miners able to relocate, urban manufacturing promised a number of high-paying industrial jobs with comparable benefits and transferrable skillsets. While not ideal, relocation provided a relief valve from the tensions of a contracting industry.

In the breech, the smaller, independent, and unionized firms who produced for commercial markets faced the greatest pressure. Unable to invest as easily in new machinery, or to match nonunion firms' prices, these properties gradually found themselves priced out of the market. Prophetically, as the *Sun Advocate* surveyed recent mining technologies in late 1947, it asked, "Will small and medium sized coal companies be able to scrap existing equipment and purchase this highly expensive machinery? If not, will it lead to heavy consolidation of producers, with a tendency towards monopoly in the coal industry?"[33] Two years later, the sixty members of Sweet mine Local 6511 faced exactly this situation, and appealed to Utah's Republican senator Arthur Watkins for legislative relief. Unemployed after their company lost a contract to a lower bid from a large producer, these men hoped that if Congress passed an act to stabilize coal's price, "the evil of the large operators squeezing out the smaller fry would be eliminated and the whole industry could profit."[34]

Congress, however, had no stomach for price controls on coal by 1949. Similarly, collective bargaining failed to regulate coal prices, or the pace at which mine owners were allowed to mechanize. Year by year, managers of Utah's commercial mines found themselves slowly edging toward the red. While larger properties such as Utah Fuel's Castle Gate, Independent Coal and Coke's Kenilworth, U.S. Fuel's Hiawatha, Geneva's Horse Canyon, and Kaiser's Sunnyside mines weathered the storm comparatively well, by the 1960s a dozen regional ghost towns now marked the era's passing.

While in many ways postwar militancy improved the standard of living for hundreds of thousands of miners and their families, coal mining's subsequent decline had radical implications for the UMWA's health as an organization. Faced with layoffs and mine closures, survival politics—rather than aggressive demands—now dominated miners' thinking. As payrolls shrank, few could balance the probable costs of militant activity with the certainty of reemployment in a neighboring mine. Organizing also stalled as traditional obstacles and new pressures isolated the union sector. Increasingly, those who defended membership democracy lost ground before the forces of bureaucracy and compromise.

CHAPTER 3

Collapse

Miners and their families have been angered at the incompetence and irresponsibility of their leaders, but they didn't know that there were broader causes for the union's policies in the 1950s and 1960s—and they didn't know there were alternatives to the way things were running. We need to explode the myths that the leaders have built there over the years—myths about the issues and myths about their own power.

—Frank Sacco, 1972

IN DECEMBER 1951, Carlo Balducchi rested his bags in a room of the Lincoln Hotel in downtown Price, Utah. Since 1910, he had worked in Iowa's coal mines, many of which had recently closed. Over the previous year, he had wandered across the western coalfields looking for work. After another day of fruitless inquiries, he sat down to share his predicament in a letter directly penned to John L. Lewis. "In Colorado," he summarized, "a man over 45 is not hired.... [I]n Utah they have the age limited at 50.... I am still in good standing and am 57 years old willing to work for a living." Along with thousands, he wondered, "if a coal miner has to work one year before retaring [*sic*] just how can he get back in coal mines to work up to the age where he can get the pension? Seems like when a man gets 50 years old they might as well take him to the chopping block." While Lewis forwarded the inquiry to District 22's officers, by the time they received it Balducchi had moved on, headed out of state or out of coal altogether, with no forwarding address beyond "Albuquerque, New Mexico."¹

As an organizer in regular contact between district officers, nonunion miners, and rank-and-file UMWA members, International representative William Dalrymple occupied a unique position to understand miners' anxieties. While in previous years many had struck and picketed for aggressive contract demands, few now felt willing to even bother filing a grievance: "Desire to say, that so many things has taken place lo these many years out here that the real UNION MEN felt that they had been for gotten, for they had seen so much going the coal operators way instead of coming towards the coal miners, they just felt that it was not worthwhile to even take the case up as they felt that the cases were lost before they went up to the officials to handle."² At Kaiser, local officer Frank Sacco agreed: "We have members . . . who are afraid, at times, that if they attempt to make a grievance that they are jeopardizing their job."³

Perhaps better than any statistics, such personal and private reflections provide windows into miners' challenges during coal's steady postwar contraction. Unlike Balducchi, those lucky enough to keep their jobs experienced sea changes in fortune and outlook. As layoffs targeted the most militant and outspoken unionists, those who saw the writing on the wall steadily lowered their expectations. At higher levels, the UMWA's steady substitution of technocratic management for rank-and-file activity transformed relationships between officers and the rank-and-file, while in organizing the union struggled to extend a hard-won contract to peripheral mines. While the industrial democracy of the 1930s and 1940s was not demobilized without resistance, membership activism and control steadily eroded. While some of the union's decisions may be sympathetically understood as necessary adaptations, economic decline and organizational bureaucratization provided a powerful material basis for corruption. Without

FIGURES 3.1 AND 3.2. *Opposite*, Sunnyside Mine yards, ca. 1950s *(top)*, and Drew Richards's Seagull mine near Huntington, ca. 1940s *(bottom)*. The divergent scale, capital, and social relationships of these two operations challenged the UMWA to develop contracts and membership requirements equally workable for both. Used with permission from the Eberly Family Special Collections Library, Pennsylvania State University Libraries and the Emery County Archives.

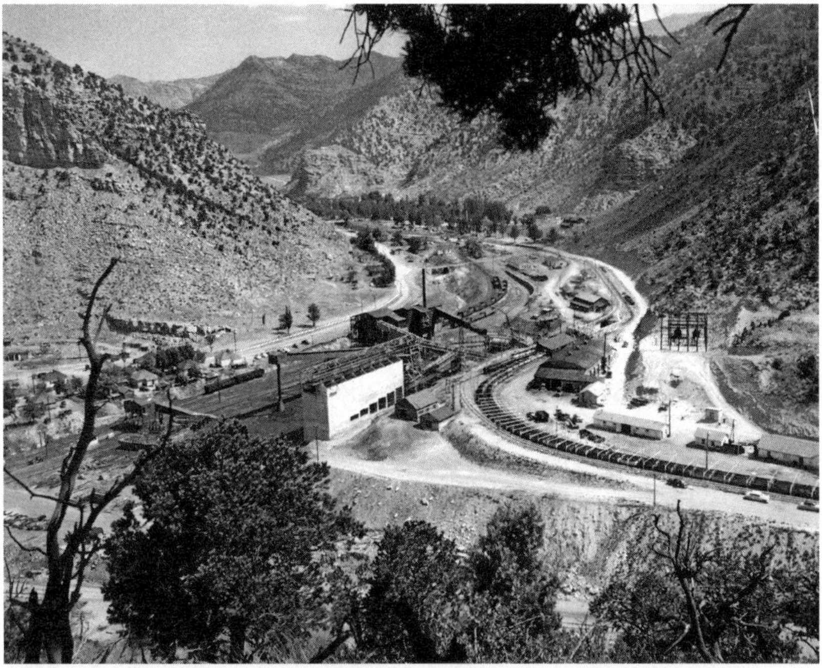

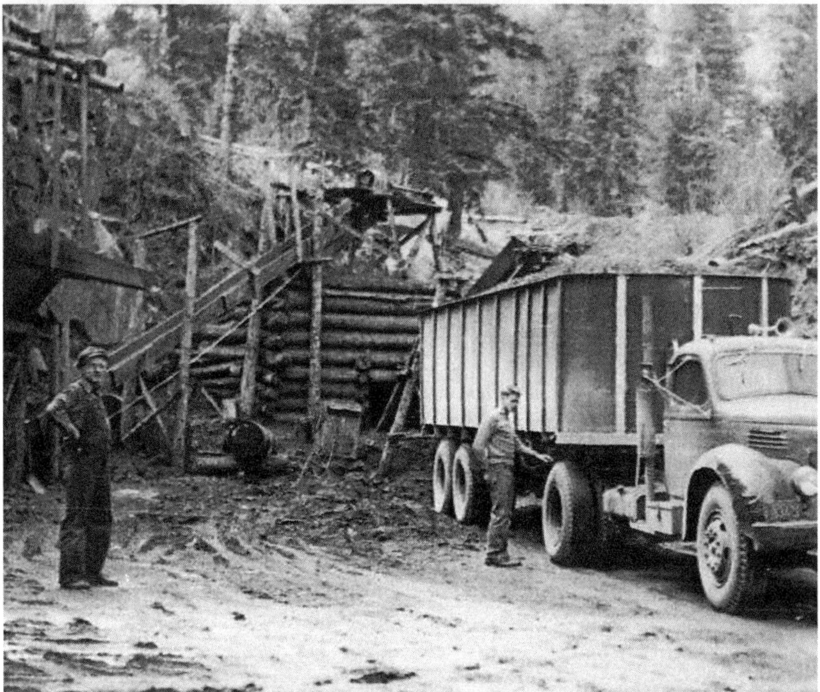

the corrective of democratic control, this transformation ultimately proved disastrous.

As competition returned, on every coalfield's periphery a number of small and nonunion operators experimented with ways to outcompete the union sector. Simultaneously, organizers motivated by coal miners' historic solidarity, nonunion miners' dissatisfaction with inferior conditions, and a practical desire to prevent nonunion mines from undercutting coal prices struggled to extend union coverage. As District 22 engaged with traditional adversaries at small truck mines and newer strip mines, rare successes were increasingly overshadowed by defeats. Although too capital-poor to existentially challenge the UMWA at this time, nonunion operators pioneered a number of strategies applied with greater consequence in later years.

While a few local unions were chartered at small mines in Emery County in 1940 or 1941, none appear to have secured contracts or to have persisted for more than a year. As one of the larger nonunion producers, American Fuel Company's Deer Creek mine in Huntington Canyon strategically mirrored union miners' pay and contracts while its employees avoided paying dues. While royalties to the UMWA Welfare and Retirement Fund significantly raised organized producers' costs after 1946, when miners asked Deer Creek's manager Malcolm McKinnon to sign a UMWA contract in August 1945, he countered that to do so would not only "reduce . . . employees' amount of take-home pay [as] you will have to pay union dues," it would ultimately "create conditions under which a mine in our circumstances cannot exist."[4]

During the national contract strike that winter, nonunion mines in Carbon and Emery Counties produced and shipped approximately three thousand tons of coal per day. In a letter to John L. Lewis, Columbia's Arthur Biggs—then a young, ambitious local officer and member of Carbon County Miners' Central Union Council—noted the implications:

> This has a tendency to hurt the morale of Carbon Miners and as it grows becomes worse. These wagon mines have been on the increase steadily. We understand the workers in most of these mines receive the wages we do and are given increases that are gained by the UMWA. . . . Other rumors are some of these miners have asked to be organized and have signed a petition for an election to be held. The petition for a bargain-

ing agency is now in the hands of Frank Fox, District V.P. stationed in Price. The Carbon County Miners Central Union Council . . . has requested that I write you of the above-mentioned facts due to the fact that District Officials . . . [have] been contacted and no action has been taken to the organizing of these mines. . . . Therefore President Lewis we are asking your consideration of this problem which confronts us and ask that steps be taken immediately to have Board Member Malcolm Condie take care of this situation.[5]

District 22 officials were not indifferent to the threat nonunion mines posed. However, at this time their attention seems to have been pulled toward other projects. Stationed in Price, Frank Fox spent much of that fall organizing culinary workers into the UMWA's District 50—a catch-

FIGURE 3.3. Officers, delegates, and guests attending District 22's 1953 convention in Salt Lake City. A new generation of younger miners entered leadership positions at this time. Note Harry Mangus, kneeling, *far left*, and Frank Stevenson, standing, *seventh from left*. Used with permission from the Eberly Family Special Collections Library, Pennsylvania State University Libraries.

all administrative unit for workers beyond its traditional base in coal mining. And perhaps unknown to Biggs, the UMWA's International Executive Board had launched a major push to organize strip mines, with District 22 devoting considerable resources to organize the Big Horn Coal Company's property near Sheridan, Wyoming.

While miners' maintenance of a central, executive union council composed of delegates from each local gave District 22 another measure of accountability, Biggs's letter suggests a disconnect between professionalized organizing work and rank-and-file miners' knowledge or involvement. While the *Sun Advocate* periodically mentioned organizing campaigns, it was beyond this paper's mission to publish detailed updates. Rather, as the responsibility for organizing rested in individual officers' hands, historic perspective, progress reports, and strategic discussions rarely involved membership participation. Not surprisingly, 1945 was neither the first nor last time that a minor union official or

FIGURE 3.4. Officers, delegates, and guests attending District 22's 1957 convention in Salt Lake City. *Bottom row, right to left*, key figures in Utah's coal industry included Malio Pecorelli, Arthur Biggs, Frank J. Sacco, and J. E. Brinley. Used with permission from the Eberly Family Special Collections Library, Pennsylvania State University Libraries.

rank-and-file miner initiated direct correspondence with an International president over concerns of nonunion proliferation, apparently unaware of perennial difficulties or already ongoing efforts.[6]

In 1946, relations warmed somewhat between American Fuel's miners and the UMWA, and the latter chartered Local 8282 on February 6.[7] During that spring or summer, these men struck to win a contract. At the top of their list of grievances was an unkept promise for back pay and the persisting lack of vacation pay. Those who loaded coal by hand further resented that while the mine sold all of its output under contract to the US government, time spent loading finely grained "slack" coal was uncompensated. It is unclear, however, exactly why District 22 vice president Joe Dowd failed to secure a contract. In August, the miners asked for an update and charged that when "we were out on strike to get the union . . . Dowd . . . come over and we had a few meetings and [he] told us if we go back to work he would fix it up and see if he couldn't get us in the union. But he was bought off. And never did come back and even see us. . . . [H]e didn't do a thing about it." However, their letter to district president Houston Martin remained cautiously optimistic: "We would sure like to see why we can't get him to sign up with the union. . . . We would sure like to get a little information on what to do and how to go about it."[8]

While Martin and Fox picked up where Dowd left off, Martin questioned the depth of miners' support. By September, he noted it was not McKinnon's opposition but the difficulty in getting a majority of men to sign up that proved the greatest hurdle. As Fox continued outreach, Martin noted "that the former district officers have tried on several occasions to hold a Local Union in this canyon and during our recent trouble when we negotiated a [national] contract, the men in Utah had to picket this mine to keep them from operating. They would promise the men not to work and as soon as these men returned back to Helper they would open their mines and go to work again." Possibly, mishandling of the original recognition strike or seasonal hiring shifts had marginalized union supporters by this time. Similarly inconclusive, another organizing drive over the same period established a charter for Local 8444 at a small nonunion mine near Scofield. By March 1946, the nine miners then employed noted their mine's closure in a final communication.[9]

In February 1947, veteran UMWA and CIO official James Morgan joined IEB member Malcolm Condie to investigate truck mines near Salina, Utah, approximately 130 miles from Price. They returned with an unfavorable assessment, which predicted these properties' seasonal nature as the toughest barrier to overcome: "They are very largely in isolated sections, widely scattered and with a constant labor turnover, a difficult problem and hard to handle, the labor in most of the above mines seem to be recruited from the farming forces, who seek this work only temporarily for the winter months and they are not very much interested in any organizational program."[10]

After Biggs raised the subject again in January 1948, Lewis's prodding revived organizing once more. However, these exchanges also reveal the extent to which organizing had become politicized. As Biggs concluded his letter, he asked that his "name not be used, although I know these District Officers will know where [this letter] came from anyway because they know how I feel about the situation. . . . They are still angry with me for carrying out my duties as secretary of the union when I wrote you about the unorganized mines of Carbon and Emery Counties some time back." Perhaps correctly sensing Biggs's ambitions for district office, incumbent officers probably interpreted these letters as personal threats.[11]

Lewis's follow-up request for an organizing update received two detailed responses. In the view of long-serving secretary-treasurer Virgil Wright:

> The organizing of the truck mines in Carbon and Emery County, Utah . . . is a problem that has been facing this Organization for a good many years. There has been a lot of money spent in this effort to organize these outfits, and establish Locals, at different times at different truck mines throughout Carbon and Emery County sometimes failing to get contracts for the operators. In many cases where we were successful in organizing according to contract, they would be worked by very few men and some of these men being old and decrepit, and former members of our Organization that were thrown out of employment because of old age.
>
> Many of these mines are worked by farmers who own little tracts of land, and work on them in the summer time and in the winter time work in the mines. It is a serious problem trying to keep them in our Organization once we have them. However, this matter was also dis-

cussed at our recent board meeting at which time we agreed to do what we could trying to bring these mines back in line again. I am sure we will do whatever is humanly possible.

Beyond such conditions' inherent obstacles, he noted:

One thing that does get in the way of the District was in policing these truck mines. This District has only three Officers who are on the job all the time. Our Board Members do not work continuously, and . . . when they are called upon to handle cases . . . when the district officers cannot . . . with the vast amount of area in this District there is a lot of time put in travel from place to place. You know with the membership, it handicaps us in trying to meet all ends with the amount of tax received by the District, and try to keep the financial end of our District in good condition.[12]

In a separate letter, Condie added:

To the best of my knowledge there are only a few mines left to organize with probably less than one hundred men employed in all of them. The two largest operations employ approximately twenty men each during their peak periods. Many of these men are farmers who seek employment only in the winter months. We have contacted them many times, endeavoring to get them into the Organization. We were successful recently in securing bargaining rates whereby the State Industrial Commission conducted an election at one of the larger mines. Since the election [District 22] President Martin and Vice President Fox met with the operator to secure a working agreement. President Martin informed me that the operator complained that he could not pay the same wage rates in effect at the union mines because the additional cost of trucking coal more than twenty miles to the railroad made it prohibitive. . . . I do not know if any further discussions with the operator are contemplated.

Despite his concerns, Condie appeared cautiously hopeful, and concluded with the opinion that "by applying a little concentrated effort, I believe these mines can be organized."[13]

As Lewis urged the district to devote more resources to organizing, he also sent a talented organizer, International representative William

Dalrymple. In June, Dalrymple and Fox, aided by Biggs and Rains local president Harry Mangus, kicked off the new drive with a pair of well-publicized mass meetings at Hiawatha and Huntington that explained unionism's benefits. At the July 8 meeting in Huntington, every wagon miner present reportedly joined the UMWA on the spot. By August, enough interest revived among Deer Creek's miners to reissue the charter for Local 8282, with Local 9528 chartered for miners near Salina. Despite this initial enthusiasm, that summer Houston Martin soberly predicted, "I do not believe that is going to be the hardest part of the work. The hardest task attached to the organization work in Utah is going to be in securing contracts with the companies. . . . It is my belief that they will fight us on every move that they can make under the National and State labor laws and even go to the extent of shutting down their mines and rehiring other men."[14]

By February 1949, seven members remained at Local 8282, with no contract signed either here or at Salina. That fall, the number of paid-up members at American Fuel increased to ten, yet the chances for victory at either property appear to have been lost. By October, American Fuel's minority of union supporters had been fired, and the twenty-seven who remained signed their names to an anti-UMWA letter delivered to the Utah Industrial Commission and printed in local papers. Here, miners' fluid allegiances are indicated by three men's signatures who had, six months earlier, been elected to the new local's positions of vice president, financial secretary, and recording secretary. Local president Jack Smodey, however, had either been fired or simply not rehired after work slacked off over the summer.[15] At Salina, geography may have posed greater difficulties, as organizer Richard Murray noted: "The [Sevier Valley Coal Company and Convulsion Canyon] MINES are anywhere from 18 to 58 miles DISTANT from Salina, Utah. [While] the men working in these mines live on farms, and in the little towns scattered all over the DESERT and the Valleys, and it is quite a chore to get them together."[16]

The connection between organizing gridlock and factional unrest expanded further during these years in a pattern that repeated itself in subsequent decades and, indeed, continues to guide attitudes toward union organizing campaigns today. During the summer of 1948, a feud between Frank Fox and William Dalrymple began after the latter "blistered" Fox for a derogatory remark about John L. Lewis's control over subordinate officers.[17] Memory of this event may have influenced Fox's subsequently curt dealings with the well-recommended organizer. Whether he sought to undermine his popular rival for political advantage or, more simply, sought to cut financial commitments to marginal mines after negotiations deadlocked, Fox ordered organizers to cut ties with still-hopeful miners on alarmingly short notice. While defeat may have been inevitable, Murray and Darlymple sharply criticized such actions at Deer Creek and the nearby Howard mine. In a heated letter to Lewis, they summarized:

> After we had organized the men in HUNTINGTON CANYON, we sent a letter to District President Houston Martin, asking him to proceed to try and get the OPERATORS, to sign a CONTRACT.... [L]ater we received a somewhat LOCONIC letter from President Martin, saying that someone else could NEGOTIATE the CONTRACT, and we find that some time previous to this, that a Mr. Reed Arnold, of Huntington, Utah, had received a letter from one of the officials of District No. 22 to the affect [sic] that the District Union had decided not to go any further with the ORGANIZING of the TRUCK MINES. Now, the question naturally arises, are we working at CROSS PURPOSES with the District Union, or is the District Union so DESIROUS of making it impossible to ever organize these PEOPLE[?], if so they are sure following the right POLICY.[18]

In late January 1949, Murray reported being in conference with recently unionized operators when for unclear reasons he was informed to drop the matter and return home. On March 7, just a few hours before a mass meeting with Salina miners that he had spent the previous week putting together, Murray received another instruction to return at once or face the canceling of his expense account. The following month, two Salina miners sharply rebuked Fox, although their letter's unusual syntax suggests Dalrymple may have typed it on their behalf. As failure became apparent, many became demoralized. While in October ten laid-off miners from American Fuel voted in District 22's 1949 election, Salina miners returned no ballot sheet at all. While some paid dues for another year, communications ceased after September 1950.[19]

While World War II's influence upon American coal mining is most commonly remembered for its fantastic boom followed by a debilitating bust, signs of qualitative transformations into alternate growth trajectories—with dramatic implications for the UMWA—appeared quietly during these years as well. As Manhattan Project scientists working in Dupont's Hanford Engineering Works in Washington State unlocked the secrets of atomic power, they did so in laboratories heated and electrified by coal strip-mined near Sheridan, Wyoming. Here, two coal seams—twenty-five and thirty feet thick, respectively—lay buried only twenty to sixty feet below the surface. While the state's underground mines had fueled western industrialization for seventy years, the new methodology undercut their price by as much as $1.60 per ton, with obvious implications. After Peter Kiewitz & Sons Construction Company won the Hanford Contract for their experimental Big Horn Coal subsidiary, they expanded from supplying a Montana sugar refinery with 30 to 40 thousand tons of coal per year to more than doubling their output for 1944. In 1945, their mine produced 250,000 tons, with strip operations statewide producing 800,000.[20] For the Kiewitzs, their venture's continued expansion appeared exciting and inevitable. But for the UMWA, the company's growth evoked far more contradictory and unsettled responses. While it officially pledged to seek signed contracts for all coal miners, many underground workers considered strip operations a greater threat to their jobs and preferred to see them prevented from operating at all. As these reservations fueled distrust, organizing campaigns at such properties were difficult and complicated affairs from the beginning.

Given Wyoming strip mines' later significance, the timeline of organization at Big Horn Coal is worth exploring in detail. In September 1945, the union began intently studying the company's growth. By mid-November, the men of UMWA Local 230 in Monarch, Wyoming, along with District 22 officers speaking for over 5,000 underground coalminers, began protesting Big Horn's public land leasing to state and federal officials. With the mine having extracted most of the easiest coal to get to on its present lease, the union combined conservationist and job-protectionist arguments to oppose granting any new leases until the company first mined deeper, more expensive, and harder-to-access coal within the lease areas it had already disturbed. In a November 14 letter to Wyoming's Democratic senator Joseph O'Mahoney, former Wyoming miner and longtime UMWA and CIO official James Morgan summarized:

To encourage stripping only parts of a lease with the smallest amount of over-burden and then moving on to new land where the over-burden is light, is destructive to one of our state and nation's greatest resources and robs our permanent school fund of a substantial source of revenue, makes for most unfair competition in a limited market, and most assuredly would have a damaging effect on employment in the deep mines. Deep mines in this field furnish the maximum in number of employed, pay good wages, and furnish coal at a very reasonable cost to the consumer. Strip mines, with extremely large production per man, provide work for a minimum number of men, and, if all the saving in production costs were passed on to the consumer—which is not done— it would not materially reduce the annual coal bill . . . enough to compensate for the loss of some 50% or more of the man power presently employed in the deep mines. . . . New strip mines, cheap production, few employees, mean unfair and disastrous competition for deep mines where there are large numbers of employees and a large investment of capital. It spells unemployment and misery for the worker and loss of investment for the stock holders.[21]

While they seemed to have been able to do little to assist, Wyoming politicians do appear to have been sympathetic. While O'Mahoney's response has not been located, Wyoming's Republican congressman Frank Barrett responded to a similar appeal by "promising any assistance he could render on the lease question."[22]

Numerous additional expressions of an overall preference for strip mining's elimination run through District 22 correspondence at this time. During a November meeting with Wyoming governor Lester Hunt, district officers "pointed out to him that if these strip pits continued unabated a large number of miners would be displaced in deep mines, and there would be a consequent loss of capital." Specifically, union officer John Ghizzoni reportedly proposed "the question of cancelling the lease with the Peter Kiewitz Coal Company. Governor Hunt replied that it was a legally and properly drawn lease and could not be amended or cancelled before its termination without entailing long legal proceedings." Ghizzoni personified the union's contradictory position by reporting to John L. Lewis within the same letter that "I impressed the district [22] organization with the necessity of immediately organizing this strip operation [where] all agreed to tackle the problem immediately," while concluding that "the district is also interesting itself in protesting to [Department of Interior] Secretary Ickes of granting any federal coal leases to this same company."²³

Similarly, International vice president John O'Leary responded to one update from James Morgan with an initial congratulation for getting contracts signed at three strip mines near Hanna, Wyoming, before moving on to assure him that "we will continue to do what we can to have the Department of Interior withhold granting leases to the Big Horn Coal Company or any other company when it means that our members in the deep mines will be deprived of work within the future by the granting of such leases." Alerting him to an upcoming meeting of Wyoming's Board of Land Commissioners, he urged Morgan to attend and "do what you can to have this menace eliminated in the interest of the men who work in the deep mines."²⁴

Despite these reservations and active lobbying to prevent strip mines' expansion, a December 1945 meeting of the UMWA's International Executive Board revealed, as none other than John L. Lewis summarized, "the consensus of opinion . . . that each district having [strip] operations should go forward with the work of organization."²⁵ While continuing to lobby against Big Horn's expansion, Morgan began an organizing campaign among its employees. By January 11, 1946, he managed to establish a functioning local, and a week later expressed the hope that "we can within a day or two have signed up a good majority of the employees." However, majority support appeared much harder to win than at underground mines, and by early February still appeared to be elusive.²⁶

Superficially, the principle reason for delay was a jurisdictional dispute. With a maximum workforce that winter of approximately fifty-six employees, as many as twenty-four were already members of the AFL-affiliated International Union of Operating Engineers. Among them, "shovel and cat operators, patrol men and control men on the tipple" occupied the most skilled positions. While the UMWA's wage rates for these positions were higher than Big Horn was currently paying, and Morgan could easily critique the rival union which "has never asked for a conference to adopt an agreement for the Strip Mine, has never submitted a wage scale for the Mine, and have worked months at a lower scale," more than wages were at stake for many of the company's employees. As Morgan noted in late February:

> We have been informed by both the members of the Operating Engineers and the Company and a considerable number of men employed at the Strip pit, largely Cat Operators, but also some Shovel Operators, and possibly some mechanics, are on their job only until Road Construction opens up, perhaps in a few weeks, and may not return to their strip mine job for months, if at all.... This number is estimated anywhere from 12 to 15 or more ... nearly one-fourth of all employees working on jobs that could properly come under Union Wage Rates. It would mean that men who expect to be employed only temporarily at the Mine could determine the organization that the men permanently employed at the tipple and on coal haulage, would have to yield bargaining rights.[27]

Although by this time "a large majority of production men" had joined the UMWA, strip mines' work-process, equipment, and labor needs ensured that their employees' backgrounds, affiliations, identities, aspirations, and career paths could not so easily be predicted, nor taken for granted.

Unsurprisingly, Big Horn strongly resisted Morgan's overtures to negotiate. Keenly aware of ongoing efforts to prevent their operation's expansion, at their first meeting in January Morgan noted, "The Company officials ... spent a great deal of time in discussing not any proposed contract, but the mine workers opposition to them." Repeatedly, management did their best to delay negotiations, while exploiting divisions among their workforce's loyalties. After their initial meeting, the company requested thirty days to study demands and wage agreements effective across the state. Attempting to exploit the jurisdictional question, Big Horn "further complicated matters" when it insisted on a secret ballot election supervised by the NLRB to ensure a majority of its employees supported the UMWA before committing to a contract. While in recent decades union organizing has usually meant a predictable chronology of base building, union authorization card collection, an NLRB election, negotiations, and maybe, if necessary, a strike, in 1946 James Morgan was so used to axiomatic majority support and contracts' speedy negotiation that he chafed at an actual election's formality and delay.[28]

While Big Horn's anti-UMWA resistance suggested a pioneering new trend, its managerial staff appeared relatively unsophisticated at union avoidance at this time. While today it is exceedingly rare for employers to begin any negotiations prior to an NLRB election, James Morgan and Big Horn's management had been in frequent communication for almost two months prior to the February 28, 1946, election date. Furthermore, they appeared unwilling to defy Morgan when, sure of majority support, he threw down the gauntlet even earlier: "We notified the Company that so far as the wages were concerned, our members would refuse to work Monday morning, February 25, 1946, unless the Mine Workers' scale was paid and made retroactive to February 1, 1946. . . . After almost continuous session, lasting until 11 P. M. . . . the company agreed. . . . This gives our members an increase averaging $2.00 per day and the retroactive pay to all men will be between $1,200 and $1,500." Days later, Morgan met with the Operating Engineers' representatives, whom he compelled to recognize the UMWA's jurisdiction. Finally able to negotiate with Big Horn for an agreement, Morgan met with management in an all-day session on March 2, at which time a union contract was signed.[29]

Intellectually, Big Horn Coal's management never accepted collective bargaining's theoretical principles, nor did they forgive the UMWA for its machinations against their growth. Under contract, its managers made it clear to John L. Lewis that their tolerance of his union required an end to these activities. During national contract strikes in 1947 and 1948, it was one of the last district operators to sign. In the former year, it did so only reluctantly after "they tried to recruit men in South Dakota, and they also placed a full page advertisement in the Sheridan Press stating that they were being forced to operate without a Contract." Malcolm Condie noted the effectiveness of responding with equal militancy: "We increased our picket line from day to day. . . . [T]he Coal Company realized that they were licked."[30]

In 1948, Big Horn tried to shake the union again. Two months prior to the contract's expiration, general manager Geo. A. Nugent clarified his company's intention not to renew or renegotiate it.[31] As president of its local union, employee Gene Bondi observed,

> The company has been working on the weaker minded employees, to rid themselves of the mine union. Since they have layed off a lot of the stronger union men, there is now better than half of the weaker members on the payroll, thus putting them in a good position to call for an N.L.R.B. vote. . . . I have notified the District officials that our

local was slipping some time ago, that we would be needing help if we expect to stay here.... The big talk is that the men want to go operating engineers.[32]

UMWA officers and supporters suspected that Operating Engineers' representative O. D. Kinnman had established an unethical, "more than cordial" relationship with Big Horn management and was petitioning again to represent its employees more as a favor to them than out of any sense of concern for their staff. However, an attentive response by competent district officers, and the cooperative assistance of sympathetic NLRB administrators ended the attempt. As Malcolm Condie summarized,

> It can be said that the company and representatives of the Operating Engineers were working together to push the United Mine Workers out. They were so confident that they would not be disturbed that a contract had been agreed upon.... It provided for a reduction in wages and longer hours and they were busy telling the men that they could work all they wanted without any threat of a strike. Other provisions were uniformly bad. Both parties were striving for a quick consent election on a petition filed by the Big Horn Coal Co. naming the Operating Engineers as the bargaining unit. We put a stop to that in a hurry.
>
> The key to the problem rests with Mr. O. D. Kinnman, State Supervisor for the Engineers. We met with him several times and applied the pressure. It had a good effect and the fellow is now afraid to go any further. We forced him to state to a field agent for the Denver Office of the [NLRB] that he would not consent to an election naming his group as the bargaining unit.... The field agent for the Board whom I have known from the early C.I.O. days privately assured me that he would co-operate with us and he expressed the opinion that the petition would be tabled and in any event he would delay action on it.... It seems to me that we have them on the run and we intend to keep [it] that way....
>
> At the present time the local is rent [sic] with dissension and we have put in a lot of our time meeting with various groups endeavoring to create a degree of harmony among them. We have also attended two local meetings and put some of the dissenters in their place. We are glad that we got here in time to put a stop to the conspiracy. It can be said that had we not been here our local would have been lost.[33]

The 1948 contract signing at Big Horn did not end contentious bargaining at this property. Of the five total strip mines operating within District 22's jurisdiction, Big Horn's wages were the highest in 1949, and reflected the labor shortage of the war years better than the increasingly competitive markets it struggled against even now.[34] Creating a uniform strip-mine wage agreement without lowering wages here, or putting its two other unionized competitors out of business, presented negotiators a formidable task they struggled for years to resolve. Unfortunately for Wyoming strip miners, in future years the kinds of militant assertiveness that worked so well in 1948 became increasingly difficult to replicate.

While Utah's geology and rail networks ensured that little strip development was likely to occur, one entrepreneur who tried to develop a strip mine near Scofield revived the intradistrict theoretical clash over their existence. With their relations already strained, District 22's vice president Frank Fox tried "everything possible to stop [it] from operating" to the chagrin of organizers William Darlymple and Richard Murray. The property's owner had no interest in taking on the UMWA and reached out to district officers to negotiate a contract. Faithful to his coworkers, friends, and neighbors among Utah's underground mines who had the most to lose from competing against strip mines, Fox drug his feet, stonewalled, and refused to draft anything in language appropriate to strip-mining conditions. Before dropping markets led to the project's abandonment, its owner contacted John L. Lewis directly for help arranging a meeting to negotiate with other officers. Lewis responded promptly, and sent his righthand assistant, Tony Boyle, to sign a contract.[35]

At underground Utah mines, organizers won a few victories at a handful of smaller properties. Among them, ten employees at the McAlpine Coal Company near Scofield, and thirteen employees of the Hardscrabble Coal Company near Helper, successfully unionized.[36] However, as tightening coal markets stiffened operator resistance, nonunion miners who joined the UMWA encountered a growing number of obstacles. Illustrative of these difficulties is a long drawn-out campaign at Grant Powell's Coal Creek Coal Company, a small mine north of Wellington that operated in the postwar years.

During the September 1949 national contract strike, pickets won over several of this property's miners, who supported the strike and joined the UMWA. For respecting the picket line most of them were soon after fired. One of them, Alvin Blackburn, found new employment at Wattis, where a rigid policy designed to discourage union members from working at nonunion mines presented him with a fifty-dollar penalty fee for having earlier accepted nonunion employment, as well as a new fifty-dollar initiation fee to the union of which he had formerly been a member. Supporting Blackburn, Dalrymple protested, "There must be some leeway to cover the cases in QUESTION, and we just cannot double cross men who join the UNION, then expect them to come in and remain LOYAL." While a "dispensation" or exception to the fine appears to have been granted in this case, these policies were not repealed, and continued to strain relations between the union and those who accepted nonunion work when no other unemployment could be found.[37]

Despite these layoffs, several of Coal Creek's miners continued to support the union, and in March 1950 the International chartered Local 9750. As before, to secure a contract proved more difficult. On March 27, after the company refused to negotiate with and then fired union supporters, the miners struck. This effort, however, did not win a contract, and after the strike was abandoned up to eleven men were quickly terminated. In a hotly worded letter to John L. Lewis, Dalrymple summarized:

> This I am going to say, when the picket lines was ordered off by the former District President, [who] claimed that you had demanded that they all by all means should return to work[,] those same open shop coal miners said that they had been sold down the RIVER[.] I told all of them that you by no chance had ordered them to return to work as you had no jurisdiction over them, that was [Houston] Martin and [Malcolm] Condie, that done same, without even consulting myself, and that is the barrier that confronts us today with these same men.
>
> You can be assured that I have resorted to everything that I know of to try and get these same men back into the UNION, but, it just seems as if it will take more than words to get results with them.[38]

While the laid-off miners quickly filed unfair labor practice charges, they waited a year for the NLRB to award them back pay and reinstatement. As the conflict resumed, a retaliatory lockout idled the mine until

What do you receive under NON-UNION CODITIONS, do tell us.

You best know the answers only, what the powers who are desire you to and just as little as they can let you get by with. Yes open shopisim only allowed you so much and so little, still today you will see some who call's themselves yes, men, why, GOD alone knows for the facts are they will do everything a REAL MEN, will not do.

Sure, under NON-UNION CONDITIONS men can hardly call their SOULS there own, still those same CREATURES, will pat themselves on their chest and say they are FREE BORN AMERICANS, why no one can tell, but, they and for the simple reason real men will not do what they the open shop COAL MINERS will do. Yes, when you see open SHOP MINERS going into COAL COMPANIES STORES, to get their daily supplies and take what is ever thrown down in front of them, why ? all because while they like the GOOD BOSSES, they also fear them.

Sure, fear is one awful thing to be POSSESSED with, but, then when working in an OPEN SHOP MINE, one can never exercise that FREEDOM of SPEECH, why ? because they the NON-UNION COAL MINERS are FEARFUL of LOSING their SCABBING JOBS.

Are, the UNION COAL MINERS fearful of loseing their jobs, NO, and the reason why they are not is all because they have A LABOR UNION, to protect them always, so to be in a UNION is one of the best PROTECTORS known to a real MAN KIND.

So we say, to every man WORKING in any kind of a MINE, join a real LABOR ORGANIZATION, yes, a real LABOR UNION for it is ever your GREATEST PROTECTOR and one that goes all out for you, the GOOD BOSSES will fail you when you need assistance and PROTECTION, the most, mark that for it has been proven to many times to be at least REALLY 'DENIED.

Whom, was it that went out and got the COAL MINERS, the INCREASES in WAGES, no not the NON-UNION COAL OPERATORS, it was the United Mine Workers of AMERICA, with its GREAT LEADERS John L. Lewis, the National President, and Vice President Thomas Kennedy, and the other out standing LEADERS, yes the OPEN SHOP COAL OPERATORS, only fell in line when they had to and no SOONER,

Today, you will hear some BRAINLESS CREATURE, saying the OPEN SHOP MINERS have received BIGGER and BETTER INCREASES than have the UNION COAL MINERS, the STATEMENTS as alleged are as FALSE as HELL and contain not one word of TRUTH and the person so making them well knows he or they are lieing from their hearts and SOUL, and such CONTAINING no TRUTH what so EVER.

So to all of you Non-Union Men we say, JOIN the United Mine Workers of America,, and try to become MEN, join up now dont DELAY, for life is not at the best of it to long, and you just cannot be keeping it off just to long. See the International Representative of the U.M.W of A., at Hotel Savoy, Price, Utah.

FIGURE 3.5. Organizing leaflet authored by William Dalrymple, ca. 1948. Note the characterization of inferior conditions, confidence in International leaders, moral language, optimism, and typos. While today advanced degrees are common among union officers, men and women with manual typewriters and high school educations or less built the UMWA and CIO. Used with permission from the Eberly Family Special Collections Library, Pennsylvania State University Libraries.

Industrial Commission of the State of Utah
State Capitol,
Salt Lake City, Utah

Gentlemen:

We the undersigned, being employees of the American Fuel Company, located in Deer Creek Canyon, Emery County, Utah, do hereby formally petition you to use your influence with the United Mine Workers of America, and ask them to discontinue their efforts to organize us for the following reasons:

1. The wage scale paid by the American Fuel Company is higher than the union scale. For example: the minimum underground rate in the American Fuel mine is $14.40 and the maximum scale is $19.20 for an eight-hour day, portal to portal. The union scale in comparison carries a minimum of $14.05 and a maximum of $17.21 for the same type of work and same number of hours.

2. The underground working conditions in the American Fuel mine are as good or better than any mine in the entire coal producing areas of our state.

3. We employees at the American Fuel Company mine have always had employment six days per week, compared to the union mines two to five day work week. This makes our take home pay considerably higher than it would be if we were subject to unionized conditions.

4. We are conscious of the fact, and want herewith to acquaint you with the fact that this mine lies 22 miles from the nearest railroad, therefore all the coal that is produced at this property has to be moved by truck either to the market area or to the railhead. This results in a much lower net realization to the owner than is enjoyed by the owners of the unionized properties.

5. We as a group desire to make it known that we have been fairly dealt with by the American Fuel Company, and are satisfied with our wage scale and our working conditions.

In view of the above facts we petition your body to take whatever steps possible to assure us the right, as citizens of the State of Utah and the United States of America, to be able to work in peace and harmony at the American Fuel Company mine, without being intimidated or coerced by the organizers of the United Mine Workers.

We feel that we will have better jobs and more harmonious working conditions along with a larger income by maintaining the status quo rather than by joing the union...

1. Samuel I Teagarden
2. Kay Wadsworth
3. Elmer A. Johnson
4. Archie M. Blackham
5. Lyman Binkerhoff
6. Glen C. Johnson
7. Dell R. Sherman
8. Lavon Powell
9. Earl Christensen
10. Joe Jeffs
11. Karl Burnside
12. Jack Brinkerhoff
13. Joe Piccolo
14. Milton Roper
15. Blain Collard
16. Clearon Christensen
17. Stanley Cowley
18. Don B. Kofford
19. Reid Arnold
20. Lealend Collard
21. Grant Childs
22. Clifford Collard
23. Volmer Oviott
24. S. A. Nielsen
25. James P. Heaton
26. James H. Potter
27. E. James Grange

This represents 100 per cent of the employees at the American Fuel Company with the exception of those who are active in management.

AMERICAN FUEL CO.
Malcolm N. McKinnon, Mgr.

FIGURE 3.6. Anti-UMWA letter signed by American Fuel employees and published locally, ca. 1949. Note the predominance of economic considerations' and the relative absence of ideology. Used with permission from the Eberly Family Special Collections Library, Pennsylvania State University Libraries.

mid-April 1952, when the company finally signed a contract. This victory proved pyrrhic, however, as by 1954 the mine closed.[39]

In characteristically colorful language, Dalrymple described Grant Powell as a man of moral weakness: "about the lowest individual I have ever come in contact with, nothing to [sic] low for him to do or say. . . . [H]is word is just not worth a DAM." Economics, however, may paint a clearer picture of his motivation. While Dalrymple's leaflets cited the Welfare and Retirement Fund as one of the strongest reasons to join the union, Coal Creek's abstention from the program allowed it to undercut union competitors—even as far away as Washington State where in 1951 it won a government contract to supply Camp Lewis's fuel needs. Had organization succeeded at this and other mines, price disparities could have been reduced, allowing miners to face retirement with greater security even as marginal producers saw their own opportunities diminish. The struggle for survival, however, pushed such operators to spare no tool in union busting.[40]

Five years later, another initially promising effort ended in defeat at the Star Point Coal Company's mine near Price. Around 1953, former Sunnyside superintendent Walter Odendahl and his son, Thurston, opened the small operation to produce for regional home-heating markets.[41] In January 1956, the mine's eight employees joined the union. As the UMWA-BCOA contract now set fund royalties at 40 cents per ton, Odendahl countered that to sign it would put his company out of business. To nullify the union's progress, Odendahl successfully experimented with corporate reorganization, and leased the mine to a new partner who operated it with three former employees as the Blue Flame Coal Company. After the UMWA unsuccessfully challenged the arrangement in court, on February 2 two former employees and allied union members picketed the road leading to the mine. Unable to halt production, anonymous actors temporarily stopped coal trucks after they distributed sixty pounds of roofing nails and dynamited a bridge along the mine's access road. After these actions allowed the owners to get a temporary injunction against picketing, an unknown rifleman further escalated tensions by shooting out two coal trucks' radiators. While the union's appeal to a higher court prevented a permanent injunction from being issued, Arthur Biggs later noted that it lost its jurisdiction at the mine "through the element of time in litigation."[42]

Elsewhere, rising unemployment allowed nonunion operators to strategically hire men with ambivalent or hostile attitudes to unions, which organizing's spotty record did little to improve.[43] By August 1950, Harry Mangus summarized the legacy of organizing's increasingly diminishing returns: While "the members of our Organization and the Local Unions have made spasmodic attempts to organize . . . their time was limited, their funds were limited, and they have been led on so many wild goose chases that to ask a man to go out on a picket line is like asking him for his right arm anymore."[44] Four years later, Malio Pecorelli, District 22's recently elected IEB member and a longtime advocate of expanded organizing, noted the impact of coal markets' continued evaporation:

> Some of our mines have closed down for the season and the others had large lay-offs [while] the men fortunate enough to still have employment have been working from two to three days per week. The unorganized mines have been also curtailing production in most cases even though they have a better chance to compete for the available coal business because of lower wage rates, smaller inside mine transportation, no Welfare Fund Royalty payments and not complying with . . . Safety standards.[45]

That year the Knight-Ideal property near Wellington employed thirty-eight men to produce 160,360 tons as Carbon County's largest nonunion mine. Using the NLRB framework to its advantage, this company created a private, company-controlled "union" with a signed contract that prevented the UMWA from petitioning for a certification as bargaining representative. Perennial organizing, however, never won over a majority.[46]

It is difficult to imagine that organizers' appeals to class solidarity, local grievances, and expanded healthcare and pension benefits failed entirely to resonate among these men, whose communities largely benefited from and supported the many reforms unions had accomplished over the previous twenty years. Yet a now familiar pattern of enthusiastic conversion, contractual deadlock, strikes and/or layoffs, and mine closures in place of signed contracts appeared difficult to get beyond. While scholars might debate the exact blame attributable each to disunited officers, contractual rigidity, lethargic regulators, or managerial conniving, these factors cumulatively inspired a growing weariness about the utility of traditional union-organizing approaches. In deciding to operate as a nonunion workplace, Knight-Ideal's miners did not see themselves so much as useful idiots to unethical managers, or as the acolytes of superior frameworks for labor-management relations. Rather, they compromised between altruism, precarious operating conditions, and the limited likelihood of getting a UMWA contract signed. While no one at the time would have claimed the arrangement to be the best of all possible worlds, or the most ethical type of pressure to exert upon fellow miners employed elsewhere, in an age of mass layoffs, mine closures, and outmigration these men could assert the inarguably significant advantage of still having a job at all.

While ideological antiunionists remained a fringe minority in coal country, organizing failures and nonunion mines' competitive advantages stiffened operator attitudes and inspired them to experiment with increasingly vigorous union-avoidance strategies. At Wyoming's Roncco coal mine in 1961, Mangus noted, "The operator has convinced [the employees] that if he continues to operate under Union contract, it will be necessary to close operation . . . as two or three other mines in the area . . . have ceased operations. . . . [T]hese men are indeed fearful of losing their jobs, regardless of the circumstances or their feelings toward our Union." Meanwhile, Pacific Power & Light developed a one-million-ton-per-year coal mine to fuel a new power plant at Glenrock, Wyoming, "with forethought for the purpose of preventing the [UMWA] from obtaining a contract." To limit organizers' access to employees, the company constructed a twelve-foot fence around the property and paid Burns Detective Agency to guard it. They also hired employees "hand picked . . . from various parts of the West Coast." Largely young men with new families, their desire for steady employment was further "financially entangled" as they took out mortgages on newly constructed homes. Not surprisingly, Mangus noted, "They are very reluctant to chance their present security by joining and assisting the Organizing."⁴⁷

For operators across District 22, the pressure of coal markets' continued decline is perhaps best preserved in a flurry of December 1958 telegrams unionized coal companies dispatched to John L. Lewis on the eve of national contract negotiations. With a major regional natural gas pipeline recently completed, higher railroad freight rates, and an unseasonably warm winter, U.S. Fuel president Oscar A. Glaeser recalled, "No period when the coal markets available to our business have been beset and threatened by so many economic factors and where the outlook for survival gave as much concern." W. J. O'Connor, president of Independent Coal and Coke—then the largest commercial coal operation west of the Mississippi River—noted a profit that year of only thirteen cents per ton of coal mined. Regionally, he noted, "there is practically no commercial coal mining left in Colorado, Wyoming, Montana, and Washington and Utah seems to be heading to the same end" and summarized, "We have spent $1,300,000 in three years for new equipment and our Castle Gate, Kenilworth, and Clear Creek Mines are mechanically and efficiently operated. A two dollar wage increase is twenty five cents a ton on costs and we must get an additional ton per man to equalize." Given the stronger position of steel operators' captive mines, he asked, "Is there any way you can except our commercial mines from the same wage scale as the coking coal mines? We know this is a difficult problem but from an economic standpoint commercial coal and coking coal are not the same products with regard to value and we can't pass a wage increase on to our customers.... Our situation is becoming desperate."[48]

Recognizing coal's weakening position, Lewis's stance shifted in this year toward greater accommodation. In addition to the customary two-dollar-per-day wage hike miners expected, Lewis and BCOA negotiators inserted a "protective-wage clause," designed to insulate the union sector by forcing BCOA companies to sever links to hundreds of small operators who mined coal under lease or used larger companies' coal-washing plants and sales departments to clean and market their output. In 1963, however, the NLRB found the clause illegal and prevented the union from enforcing it. More enduring were Lewis's May 1958 overtures to his former opponents gathered at the coal convention of the American Mining Congress. Addressing the body, Lewis outlined what would (in a year) become the National Coal Policy Conference—a united public relations and lobbying front of the largest coal producers, thirty-two coal-supplying railroads, seven power companies, the UMWA, and several mine equipment manufacturers.[49] Indicative of this shift toward market protectionism, officers in western states lobbied against hydroelectric projects and municipal hookups to natural gas pipelines. They also experimented with the "catchall" District 50 administrative framework to organize workers in industries beyond the union's traditional strength in coal. By late 1961, these proceeded—with limited success—among uranium and trona miners in Riverton and Green River, Wyoming, and among potash miners in Moab.[50]

Internally, coal's decline provided a material basis for further bureaucratization. Not only were union officers seduced by staff positions' perks and lifestyles, operators' acceptance of union contracts required a stability that translated into increasingly circumscribed roles for working union members. One by one, organizations and traditions that supported accountability, transparency, and independence faded or were dismantled. Where membership apathy proved insufficient, some incumbents preserved their rule through fraud. And where instability persisted, International officers retained an ultimate power to place locals—and even entire districts—under "provisional" control. While some officers went to great lengths to defend membership democracy, others whose careers began in the postwar era increasingly learned to look above, rather than below, for guidance and support. With apologies for exercising some minor chronological license, it is through thematic examinations of union membership's evolving meanings that the steadily narrowing trajectory of membership activity most clearly emerges from the records of these years.

As rank-and-file miners' most direct expression of power, unauthorized strikes occurred periodically into the early 1950s. While in December 1945 Sunnyside's miners returned to work under the same superintendent, they struck briefly again in 1949 and twice in 1952. In January of 1952, a twenty-one-day wildcat targeted Dr. Frank V. Colombo, owner and operator of the thirty-bed Dragerton Hospital, whom the UMWA Welfare and Retirement Fund's administrators had found guilty of charging inflated prices and providing inferior services. While illegal, the strike hastened Colombo's replacement.[51] Two months later, a minor underground explosion burned two men. The local of seven hundred blamed mine foreman Howard Kissel, whom they had cited for four prior safety violations and further resented for not reporting the accident until ten hours after it happened. Six days later, state and federal inspectors identified numerous deficiencies related to timbering, roof bolting, and ventilation. While International leaders noted the walkout's illegality and the potential for a retaliatory lawsuit, District

22 president J. E. Brinley felt the shutdown was justified. Thirteen days later, the mine reopened after he convinced the men to drop their key demand and return to work once the mine was declared safe. In 1953, as Kaiser merged management of its No. 2 and No. 3 Sunnyside mines with the No. 1 recently purchased from Utah Fuel, miners struck again over a seniority interpretation that disadvantaged some of the longest-serving employees.[52]

Nearby, on two occasions a decade apart, Horse Canyon miners struck to protest a requirement that those on the mine's layoff panel submit to physical examinations prior to reemployment. As Biggs summarized, many felt this requirement "provided the company with a deadly weapon to discriminate against any undesirable or union men." These strikes won reinstatement for those who had protested the practice. At Kenilworth, miners struck for two weeks in 1949 after local president William Byrge interceded to help a miner paid below the standard union wage. After management demoted him from blacksmith to tool dresser, he initiated the walkout. Seven years later, Kenilworth miners again resorted to the tactic to resist unfair and arbitrary layoffs. After their employer laid off 72 men with improper regard for seniority, the 167 remaining miners struck for one day, which led the company to revise its order. As Hiawatha restructured its operations in 1955, one wildcat occurred as miners and managers debated U.S. Fuel's obligation to bus employees to its newly opened South Fork Portal. This dispute ended with bus service's elimination in exchange for a company promise to maintain the road.[53]

The effectiveness of wildcats, however, declined as unemployment and competition increased. In March 1951, then-district vice president J. E. Brinley met with the Utah Coal Operators' Association to streamline a layoff procedure. Previously, he had charged, "the various coal companies have discriminate[d] against certain members of our Organization.... [They] have switched these employees around on different shifts and have then laid off the entire shift in order to eliminate the older employees who have in many instances been active with the organization." However, he now found himself in a difficult position to threaten miners' ultimate weapon: "They have challenged me to shut their mines down in preference to making a fair settlement, and of which I realize I do not have that authority, and furthermore our members are not in a position to stand a shutdown."⁵⁴ By the lead-up to contract negotiations the following year, however, industry's desire to fight had similarly eroded. As Independent Coal and Coke's president noted: "A work stoppage here would be disastrous for everyone. The commercial mines in Utah have practically no stocks. Dealers and consumers are short because of a car shortage curtailing operations and shipments since August 15. To stop production would only provide a harvest for the non-union mines, the gas and oil competition. . . . [N]either the miners nor the companies are financial[ly] able to stand a strike."⁵⁵

In February 1953, a series of local union resolutions presented to District 22's constitutional convention indicate miners' defensive orientation by this time. Four resolutions sought additional fines for members who worked at nonunion properties during slack periods. Two sought to limit mechanization's impacts, while one cited safety concerns to ban production bonuses and another asked for a guaranteed two hundred days of work per year and an annual minimum wage.⁵⁶ Yet as layoffs continued, survival became more relevant than aggressive contract demands. In 1953, Sunnyside Local 9958's recording secretary Pratt Lindsey asked Lewis if local union funds could be used to assist recently laid-off men—a request that Lewis denied.⁵⁷ At Reliance, Wyoming, miners erected storage facilities for the surplus commodities they depended on and asked if their local could buy lunches for malnourished children at their school. Less grimly, other locals that anticipated shutdowns seemed eager to expend accumulated treasuries while they still had control over them. While Rock Springs miners had long celebrated Labor Day, in 1955 district officers expressed dismay when Local 2282 generously spent its funds on "intoxicating liquors."⁵⁸

Politically, many miners aggressively defended membership control over internal decision making even as the UMWA's overall position weakened. When District 22 president William McPhie's unexpected death complicated a district election scheduled for September 4, 1945, Sunnyside, Kenilworth, and Columbia miners protested the election's postponement to their district board and to John L. Lewis.⁵⁹ Two years later, as Frank Fox urged the Carbon County Miners' Executive Council to moderate its criticisms, the council responded that "they had a perfect right to backbite, harass, and interfere with District Officers, and it should be regarded as normal."⁶⁰ And in 1949, three locals' officers protested Lewis's temporary appointment of a district officer. As Sunnyside's officers warned, "It seems like dictatorship is creeping into our District by such action. Our constitution has been by-passed. . . . We believe a great unjustice [sic] has been done to our District Vice-President."[61]

At the membership level, other sources of miners' power ebbed, though not without resistance. In 1948, an International commission composed of Henry Allai and Charlie Funcannon had ordered miners to abolish the Carbon County Miners' Executive Council. Two years later, Frank Fox charged that at this meeting, "the members of the council demanded Allai, Board member Condie, President Houston Martin, and myself to leave the meeting so they could decide whether or not to go underground with the council." Fox suspected that the body still functioned, and later led a campaign for his ouster.[62] Also at the International's recommendation, district officers trimmed expenses when they ceased printing verbatim reports of executive board meetings, as well as summaries of grievance settlements that had formerly been distributed to all locals. In 1950, Wattis recording secretary Lloyd Noyes shared his members' resolution that "went on record protesting this action because we feel the dues paying members of this organization have a right to know what is going on. . . . [We] can learn from those reports, also Local Officers can learn from the district labor case report how to handle similar cases and whether or not they should push them to the limit."[63] Similarly, a year later Local 2282 communicated a resolution to District 22's board that "request[ed] the minutes of the board meeting to be transcribed and submitted to each Local Union." Rather than fulfill this request, the district secretary communicated the International's new policy that had eliminated this measure. While these changes saved slightly on printing costs, they significantly undermined members' awareness of regional developments, ended a basic avenue through which rank-and-file members could learn grievance processing and contractual interpretation, and placed working miners and local officers in positions of greater dependency upon district officers' individual talents.[64]

While many complained of membership apathy during this period, the 1948 International Convention contributed to this problem with a constitutional revision that ended local unions' traditions of assessing small fines for nonattendance of meetings.[65] In district union elections, working members' chances of successfully running for office also weakened. By 1956, an International commission composed of Henry Allai and John Kmetz recognized that "the Constitution of District 22 is now outmoded and should be changed to meet the conditions that now exist." Their recommendations focused on ways to lower expenses, and they kept in place a requirement that to run for district office a candidate must be nominated by five local unions.⁶⁶ As the number of active locals shrank and operating mines became farther isolated geographically, campaigning for nominations became increasingly difficult, expensive, and time consuming for newer candidates. This gave a heavy advantage to incumbents and institutionally loyal candidates whose reliability earned glamorous and profile-raising appointments. Thus did Arthur Biggs thank John L. Lewis in 1962 for his election to the IEB:

> To put it pure and simple, you were the deciding factor that contributed to my good fortunate [sic] and success when you branded the former International Executive Board Member of District 22 back in 1957, who, incidentally, stayed branded. . . . In addition, my assignment by your office to the Ludlow Ceremony in 1959 and President Kennedy's assignment for me to participate in the Congressional Hearings of 1960 affecting the Burns Creek Legislation were also contributing factors which influenced my election in 1961. . . . [T]he then incumbent International Board Member . . . Malio Pecorelli failed to garner enough nominations to gain a place on the ballot because he only received three nominations when the District constitution required five.⁶⁷

As membership steadily shrank, District 22 eliminated other positions, such as doormen and conductors whose responsibilities merged or disappeared in most locals. In 1963, the district secretary-treasurer position also disappeared, which its occupant Paul James protested as personally retaliatory and detrimental to membership services.⁶⁸

At small and seasonal properties, rigid dues structures and Fund requirements imposed disproportionate hardships. As local officers at Gebo, Wyoming, protested the IEB's decision to levy a twenty-dollar tax upon each member during February and March 1951, they explained:

> We all feel that this levy is entirely uncalled for in view of the wage situation at present time. We are morally certain that no such sum was necessary to obtain the one dollar and sixty cent raise which we recently

obtained and we can see no necessity for the expenditure of such a vast sum in the near future.... We are all certain that all members not presently employed in the Coal Industry will be lost to the Organization through this levy and many more struggling to remain financially solvent will have to look elsewhere for employment.... Most of the mines in this area will close for the summer March 1st.... In this field, our members were employed an average of less than two days per week during the past year.... [M]any of our members are not now even eligible for Unemployment Compensation. All of our members have to take jobs outside the Coal Industry to make ends meet between periods of work at the mines. While thus employed outside the Industry they are not eligible for any benefits whatsoever from the [UMWA] Welfare and Retirement Fund.... They have paid their Four Dollars Dues to keep their Cards in good standing in case the work should ever pick up because they have belonged to the Organization all their working lives and are vitally interested in its continuation for the good of all organized labor.[69]

To consolidate benefit management, International officers instructed local and district organizations to abolish supplemental death and hardship funds that had previously been independently maintained. While these programs never reached the levels of coverage the Fund provided, their elimination left miners increasingly vulnerable where they slipped between eligibility criteria. In 1948, District 22's annual convention had even passed a resolution that applauded its death benefit fund's successful operation and asked the IEB to allow it to continue. However, the International convention that year disagreed, and ordered the abolition of all such funds.[70] Now, Gebo's miners noted:

Very few members under the age of fifty have any hope whatever of becoming eligible for a Pension under our present Welfare and Retirement set-up; neither can they qualify for enough Assistance to keep body and soul together in case of disability. We have in our midst pitiful cases of men who gave their all in the Coal Industry and yet cannot qualify even for the necessities of life so the future holds no rosy glow for those of us who are able at the present time.... We were forced in District 22 to discontinue the greatest insurance program of the Organization when the International insisted that we liquidate our District Insurance set-up. We cannot locally ask the Coal Operators to check off twenty cents to buy flowers for the grave of a deceased Brother, yet the International can ask them to check off Twenty Dollars from each man!⁷¹

While Houston Martin questioned the wisdom of forcing these men to pay the assessment that had inspired their protest, International secretary-treasurer Thomas Kennedy appeared tone-deaf in his response: "Through [increased financial reserves], a campaign to organize the small truck mines, stripping operations, and other non-union production can be conducted. We are sure you want to participate in such a program, as well as to improve the benefits already attained."⁷² At Castle Gate, Sweets, and Wattis, miners similarly protested the 1951 assessment,⁷³ and at least six other District 22 locals formally protested local benefit funds' liquidation in these years.⁷⁴

The dwindling coal market left union members fearful for their jobs, former members willing to accept work at nonunion mines, and others doubtful of finding any future at all in coal mining—all of which provided a material basis for internal union corruption. On three separate occasions in the mid- to late 1950s, investigators found individual local officers at Sunnyside, Rains, and Kenilworth guilty of embezzlement.⁷⁵ The most divisive and contested usurpation of democracy, however, arose after the District 22 election on October 11, 1949. The timing of this controversy is not coincidental, and contrasts with members' relative passivity in later years. While dark clouds brewed on the horizon, the miners of '49 were still relatively confident, boosted by wartime savings, aware of their power, and fresh from major victories in national contract strikes. As the last great postwar strike began, miners voted—and contested—the same type of internal election which in prior years had proceeded with little controversy. This time, however, incumbents refused to accept the results. Across the district, miners wrote, argued, and fought for their candidates with passion unseen in prior District 22 elections. Possibly, many of them sensed the uncertainty of years ahead. As before, they fought as if their union, and their lives, depended on it.

With president Houston Martin reelected by a wide margin, incumbent vice president Frank Fox and secretary-treasurer Virgil Wright retained their seats from Utah challengers J. E. Brinley and Arthur Biggs through creative campaigning, ballot review, and fraud. This began during the nominating election on September 6, when incumbents reportedly paid supporters to pass out campaign materials outside of polling places. In October, the district's tellers—whom Brinley and Biggs felt "served as a Gestapo"—cited spurious technicalities to disqualify four locals' votes. Fox may have also tried to get an additional 258 votes for Brinley thrown out from Sunnyside Local 6244, where only two miners had voted for him. According to Brinley and Biggs, who in parked cars one morning observed a secret liaison at the First National Bank in Price, Fox offered $100 bribes to three black miners whom he encouraged to sign affidavits claiming their votes had not been counted. Two of these men kept the money but refused to sign, and tipped Brinley off.[76] Already, the election had been heated, with many angry at Virgil Wright for having signed a secret agreement with Union Pacific Coal Company that eliminated time-and-a-half pay for Sunday work.[77] Now, revelations of fraud fueled outrage, and eighteen locals asked the International to designate a commission to investigate. In December, ten anonymous local officers sought to remedy the situation directly through a "Vigilante Committee," which issued a call to arms:

> We believe all members interested in the best interests of the organization and in seeing that justice prevails should assemble at the [UMWA] office . . . in Price, Utah, on January 5, 1950 at 10:00 AM and be prepared to use manual force if necessary to remove incumbent Frank Fox from office and to preserve all records by having the Price office securely locked until such time as duly elected officers are placed in office to conduct the affairs of the membership.[78]

Ultimately, the crisis ended after the International supervised a new election, where on May 31 the Utah challengers won their seats.[79] However, in July District 22's board met at the union's Rock Springs office where they heard two locals' charges against President Martin. Martin had recently signed a contract with Union Pacific Coal Company that standardized, and thereby raised, house rents at three Wyoming locals. After being found guilty by a four-to-two vote, suspended, and replaced by new vice president Brinley, Martin denounced the decision and ran outside the building to a crowd of supporters whom he invited to physically take over the district office. They were repelled, however, by board members wielding lead pipes. Four months after police dispersed the crowds, the International union upheld the district board.[80]

While miners and officers at local and district levels passionately contested internal democracy, such sentiments did not necessarily coalesce into a principled movement—which would have necessarily placed it in sharp opposition to John L. Lewis. In the 1940s the closest thing to a democratically minded faction mobilized behind Illinois miner Ray Edmundson. As District 12's provisional president and a loyal officer for years, he perhaps had never entirely abandoned the principles that led him to support an autonomy movement back in 1931. While for years he emulated Lewis as a faithful protégé, by 1944 differences of opinion strained their relations. As he interpreted the beginning of retaliatory measures, Edmundson resigned from his position and returned to the mines where he issued calls for autonomy as a rank-and-file miner. At the 1944 convention, his supporters presented a total of 198 resolutions that favored returning self-government to the membership.[81] Lewis, however, remained the superior parliamentarian. As he arrived at the convention, Edmundson found his credentials denied and his ability to speak silenced. With his supporters harangued and outmaneuvered, District 22's officers condemned his movement while an internal investigation revealed that his active support was confined to two smaller locals at Reliance and Winton, Wyoming. More politically astute than vain, Lewis soon after co-opted Edmundson back into the organization through appointment as a regional director to District 50.[82]

Probably the most poignant denunciation of union authoritarianism written by a UMWA official to appear in a Utah newspaper during the 1940s was the parting shot of an anonymous ex-organizer, written to nationally syndicated columnist Drew Pearson and printed in the *Salt Lake Telegram*:

> My home is in Indiana. I was transferred to Pennsylvania mainly because I disapproved of beating up or murdering a Negro organizer of the rival CIO. [UMWA officer] George F. Rice . . . was nearly framed in the standard way because he couldn't see his way clear to holding up an employer for the last outside cent during contract negotiations. . . . [H]e was ruthlessly fired. The list of Lewis ex-employees is large and growing daily. You can readily see why. The pay doesn't attract the higher type of men, and when it does the treatment soon sickens them. When I say sickens, I mean that you fight like hell for a leave-of-absence clause

or seniority in a contract, only to find that the union you represent wouldn't think of allowing these benefits to its own employees.

We little fellows are just waking up to the fact that the good old days of union for union's sake are about gone; replaced by the $1,000,000 treasury and a dictatorial attitude that makes the meanest employer of the dark ages of labor look like a piker. I came into the work of union organizing with the conviction that there was no more noble occupation than trying to better the condition of my fellow men. That is still my honest conviction. What I didn't know, however is that the top brass refused to recognize the signs of the times and sat right down astride their multimillion dollar treasuries and in effect said: "From now on all you can do is pour it in here while we dictate your politics, your privilege of earning a living, and generally become more paternalistic than any employer ever dreamed of being in his palmist days."[83]

Unfortunately, those most alienated by authoritarianism within the UMWA frequently found themselves pushed out of the coal miners' movement entirely. Unable to imagine constructive avenues for internal reform, some found themselves shooting parting arrows in public forums at the organizations they had once lionized. Here, their words were as likely to have been used by antiunionists to undermine—rather than improve—the union movement as a whole. Reading this letter, the Utah local union officer who forwarded it to Lewis did not question its authenticity, but took the opportunity to demonstrate his own loyalty, and added, "a union official that will make such remarks . . . should be dropped from the payroll and suspended. He did not have guts enough to sign his name to it. I believe you can identify him anyway."[84]

Unwilling to challenge the man who brought unionism to their state, many of those who advocated the strongest for rank-and-file miners were more likely to view Lewis as a potential advocate and ally. During heated district politics from 1949 to 1951, personalities on both sides wrote to Lewis as a confidante and courted his support.[85] During this controversy, Richard Murray concluded the most sharply worded denunciation of incumbent district officers with this observation: "Desire to say, I have met several of the OFFICERS you have put in PROVISIONAL DISTRICTS, and all of these men have proven their COMPETENCY, and in comparing what we elect time after time, I have come to the CONCLUSION that AUTONOMY is a real curse rather than a BLESS-

ING." Similarly, Latuda miner and former officer Joe Dowd thought the best way out of an electoral crisis that year was "to place District 22 under provisional government." While International leaders and a personal rival later conspired to remove Malio Pecorelli from his IEB position, in 1954 he considered Lewis's executive leadership so highly that, after Sunnyside miners "criticized and condemned" Thomas Kennedy during a local meeting for his interpretation of a seniority rule, he visited the local to remind them that "unjustified remarks made against our International Vice President would not be taken lightly by the UMW of A and it was the duty of the presiding officer at any meeting to see that only constructive criticism be allowed."[86] Rather than consider the relationship between Lewis, his political machine, and the UMWA's difficulties systematically, most critical miners considered the aging labor statesman as unfortunately outmaneuvered by lesser enemies. Shared in passing during a frank report upon the district's difficulties that year, Harry Mangus poignantly summarized that "as most of the miners have a great deal of faith in you . . . I have repeatedly heard them remark, 'If only President Lewis knew what was going on!'"[87]

While by 1969, District 22 was among only four of twenty-three UMWA districts that retained autonomy, its democratic culture steadily eroded as its officers increasingly viewed the International, rather than active members, as the basis of their power.[88] Perhaps no personality better illustrates this transformation than Arthur Biggs, who first won district office in the 1949 election which he described at the time as a campaign "to get District 22 cleansed of the parasites that infest it."[89] In a postelection exchange with a former local officer who recently resigned with sharp criticisms of the union, Biggs argued for the power of corrective democracy, pleading, "I am very sorry to see you take this attitude inasmuch as if there is something wrong in the Local Union it is your responsibility as a member to see that things are run right and are worked out. . . . If things are as you say, the membership there should demand an audit and should elect them a new Officer if what you have stated is found out to be true."[90]

Like many of his peers, Biggs fell deeply under Lewis's spell, and in the years that followed carefully developed his relationship with International officers. Periodically dispatched to resolve western issues since the early 1950s, Montana native, appointed staffer, and ambitious technocrat W. A. "Tony" Boyle emerged as Lewis's heir to serve as UMWA president from 1963 to 1972. Two years before his elevation to the union's top office, Biggs reached out to Boyle for help undermining his rival for District 22's IEB seat: "[Malio] Pecorelli's cronies in the Utah Labor Day Committee have named Pecorelli as Master of Ceremonies for the celebration. It will be greatly appreciated if you will arrange for him to be sent out for Labor Day to some dog hole where he can address a half dozen miners or so, about the same as occurred last labor day."[91] After his victory, Biggs thanked not the miners whose confidence he had won, but president emeritus Lewis, to whom he pledged, "I will do everything I know how in order to be worthy of the honor bestowed upon me."[92]

Kaiser Steel, where industrial conflict raged hottest in District 22 during the war years, transformed politically through its loss of local autonomy in 1954. Alerted by reports of membership dissatisfaction, Commissioners Henry Allai and John Kmetz traveled to Sunnyside to defend International policy and investigate. Citing "innumerable wildcat strikes," "no respect for contracts, laws or policies of our organization," "[no] regard for law and order," and apparent embezzlement by its financial secretary, they recommended that John L. Lewis place Local 9958 under provisional administration, which he did effective June 21.[93] Four of the local's officers—Ben A. Fermon, H. A. Brownfield, Garth Frandsen, and Frank M. Stevenson—claimed they had no knowledge of any financial irregularities and appealed the decision a year later. Pennsylvania IEB member Joseph A. Yablonski chaired the commission that heard this appeal and favorably concluded, "They have assured [us] that if they are reinstated to good standing in the Organization with all rights and privileges, that in the future, they will be diligent members of our Organization in insisting that the constitution of our Organization and contract be complied with." Perhaps in a nod of recognition to the International's power, Stevenson noted in his appeal that "if . . . my record will be cleared . . . I will be in a much better position to do my part in aiding my Local Union in any task that I may be called upon to perform. . . . It will also . . . permit me to seek any office I desire when atonamy [sic] is restored." For the young local officer, the ordeal must have left a lasting impression and undoubtedly contributed to his understandings of militancy, loyalty, and power.[94]

While for two decades capital shortages and transportation limitations allowed union coal to dominate through economies of scale, nonunion operators persisted as perennial thorns in union miners' sides—and potential threats should industry recover. Prophetically, the strategies developed in this period—selective hiring, workforce purges during slack periods, company unions, lockouts, and threats of shutdowns—provided frameworks for union avoidance used successfully by later entrants. Internally, the union's bureaucratization also left a tragic legacy. While those who fought against this tendency did not last as union officers without substantial compromises to their values, the generation that entered district politics at this time preserved living connections between the militancy of the 1940s and the upheavals of the 1970s. Unfortunately for organized labor, by the time the best of them found themselves in a position to advocate for new leadership, the UMWA stood upon shakier foundations than at any time since 1933.

PART II

CHAPTER 4

Prophets

I have heard you state that a Union can be destroyed from within, by officers failing to perform their duties and the membership losing faith in its officers. . . . I do not have any malice against the Organization as a whole and I believe that time and facts will disclose that I was right and recognized the enemies of our Union to a greater extent than the average member.

—Harry Mangus, 1954

INTO THE EARLY 1970S, the UMWA outwardly maintained an image of historic strength throughout its traditional core of influence in Carbon County, Utah. In 1969 its members mined 85 percent, or 3,976,309 of 4,658,743 tons of coal produced statewide. In Carbon, Emery, and Sevier Counties, 952 out of 1,017 miners belonged to the union and produced 98 percent of state output. For decades, union news provided headlines for local papers. Labor Day celebrations lasted three days, and regularly featured high-profile guest speakers such as Utah's Democratic governor Calvin Rampton and Democratic senator Frank Moss. Each year, union miners alternately marched through downtown Price and Helper, led by school bands and carefully decorated miners' floats. While a nonunion periphery of small, family-owned "truck" or "wagon" mines quietly produced as it always had, casual observers had little sense of the changes to rock the industry—and the union—over the following decade.[1]

FIGURE 4.1. Union power reflected in local coverage of Labor Day 1972, with a guest speech by Utah's governor and a parade of union miners marching down Helper's Main Street. Courtesy, *Sun Advocate*.

Beneath the surface, District 22 struggled mightily to maintain its hegemonic position. In January 1969, International representative Frank J. Sacco and district president, International Executive Board member, and secretary-treasurer Frank M. Stevenson divided their attention between five organizing drives and kept tabs on two temporarily suspended ones. In Emery County, Shirl McArthur's Castle Valley Mining Company continued its speculative nonunion development work for Peabody Coal, while the Mormon Church's "welfare" mine at the Deseret-Beehive complex (Des-Bee-Dove) attracted the labor of unemployed and Mormon miners. Along the Emery–Sevier County border, collective bargaining inched along at Southern Utah Fuel Company (SUFCO) and Sun Valley, where enthusiasm had all but disintegrated among those who joined the UMWA nearly two years prior. In western Carbon County, pro-union majorities appeared more solid at the newly opened Plateau and Swisher Coal mines, yet their outspokenly antiunion owners responded with tenacious and aggressive resistance. And in Soldier Canyon north of Wellington, new interest expressed by miners at Premium Coal inspired cautious optimism after years of coolness to union overtures.

FIGURE 4.2. UMWA organizing in Utah, 1966–1973.

While each of these mines employed less than twenty men, all threatened to imminently undercut established producers' markets. In 1968, Plateau underbid union mines for a contract with Kennecott Copper's McGill, Nevada, power plant; Swisher Coal won a five-thousand-ton order for Carbon County's School District; and Premium signed a contract with Anaconda Copper formerly filled by Bear Coal Company of Somerset, Colorado. In response, Bear Coal's general manager predicted imminent bankruptcy and urged the UMWA that "every consideration and effort should be given to eliminate the vast differential" between the costs of each sector.[2]

In a 1962 report—well before any of these conflicts had come to a head—Stevenson and then–secretary-treasurer Paul James recognized a trio of organizing obstacles that later appeared prominently in many narratives of American union decline. When former IEB member Malio Pecorelli and International representative J. E. Brinley had picketed a nonunion mine in Utah, a district judge had responded with a permanent injunction. While the union won in its appeal to the Utah State Supreme Court, "all the individuals whose jobs had been taken by scabs had left the area . . . and again, the court litigation in this case . . . involved several thousand dollars." At the Nugget mine in Hanna, Wyoming, the owner "manipulated law to form a 'partnership' with employees" which exempted the company from collective bargaining. Elsewhere, nonunion employers' "bitter opposition" included "influence, threats, and employees . . . paid higher hourly rates than provided in our contract. . . . Insurance is furnished to provide for hospital and medical benefits, also death benefits, which procedure is followed to offset the UMWA organizing drive and to avoid the forty-cent royalty payments into the . . . Welfare and Retirement Fund."[3] Through such avenues, operators during the period of coal's decline had pioneered multiple strategies for union resistance.

Specifically, the 1947 Taft-Hartley Act had undermined coal miners' power in several ways. By eliminating supervisors' right to join a union, it fragmented solidarity among the most experienced and skilled workers who might have otherwise moved between skilled wage and supervisory jobs. Historically, those with longer coal careers had formed the core of union supporters. Now, to accept supervisory work meant the loss of union health care and pensions and a total reliance on the employer for comparable benefits. More than the financial cost of lost dues, this statute undermined working miners' capacity for teamwork and conflict resolution while it polarized class tensions. Of his refusal to accept such a promotion in 1950, Hiawatha miner Kendell Barnett recalled, "I would have to quit the union to be supervisor. I ain't got a foot to stand on. They could fire me the next week. That is the reason they didn't want John L. Lewis to have those salary people. Since then it's showed . . . all the guys on salary. . . . They . . . beat those guys all out of their pensions."⁴ Where antagonisms prevailed over cooperation, the law gave employers another weapon: a clarified right to sue labor unions over unauthorized strikes. By the 1950s the UMWA faced millions of dollars a year in such fines, which cumulatively encouraged union leaders to consider any form of militant activism carefully.⁵

Taft-Hartley also denied union members the right to picket nonunion operations. By differentiating between employees and nonemployees, this empowered operators who temporarily reduced operations in order to purge union supporters—a strategy successful at Wyoming's Nugget Coal and Timber Company in 1959 and upheld by a Wyoming court later that year. Union members could also no longer boycott other enterprises owned by a union resister. In 1961, District 22 considered this as members of a fundamentalist LDS sect moved into Carbon and Emery Counties to invest in a number of collectively owned enterprises. These included the "Co-Op" mine in Huntington canyon, a grocery store, a drugstore, a shoe repair shop, a beauty shop, and a service station. At the retail businesses, which had union contracts with District 50, the "Shortcreekers" gradually replaced former employees with members of their uniquely insular faith. When in 1961 concerned UMWA members urged a boycott, then-president Harry Mangus rightly concluded that to do so would be technically illegal and could invite a lawsuit for damages.⁶

Union politics, however, further complicated such setbacks. In 1962 former District 22 president Harry Mangus confided in John L. Lewis to frame nonunion mining's advances within the context of "membership turmoil of an extreme nature." While district leaders defended their own positions by hotly debating a proposed combination of presidential and secretary-treasurer's duties, the rarity of their visits to local union meetings blinded them to an incipient revolt: "The men speak with disrespect about the morals of the District officers, and rumors are abundant about some of the International Officers. In many local meetings the International is being condemned severely and no apparent defense has been or was made by anyone."[7] Leading members' grievances, recent Welfare and Retirement Fund eligibility cuts invalidated members' medical cards where employers fell behind in royalty payments. While inflationary healthcare costs and the coal industry's postwar decline would have stressed the Fund under any administration, Lewis and Boyle's intention to preserve union operators' profitability let eligibility cuts take precedence over higher royalty demands.[8] Locally, the Fund's medical director controversially eliminated coverage for the county hospital in Price, which forced members to travel 30 miles farther to Dragerton. For some, this now meant driving "110 miles one-way with no motel or hotel accommodations available for the patient's families."[9]

Along with many organizers, Mangus felt that the Fund "is one of the main things that is keeping the members in the U.M.W. of A." But as International leaders deflected criticisms, employers took careful note: "A steady campaign is being conducted to brain wash their employees . . . claiming that the miner is not receiving his just dues . . . and for the amount that the Company pays into the Royalty Fund they can create better coverage than what the Fund can." Absent an able leadership, he predicted nonunion operators stood "a good chance of success. . . . If [miners] cannot obtain any benefits by being a member of the U.M.W. of A . . . they will not hesitate to go non-union."[10]

Taken together, Stevenson's and Mangus's observations challenge our preconceptions to reconsider the complexity of forces confronting labor unions decades before their precipitous decline during and after the 1980s. On the eve of coal's resurgence, organizing defeats allowed a once-peripheral nonunion sector to establish a hitherto unknown legitimacy and resilience that expanded rapidly over the ensuing years. While some nonunion miners articulated anti-UMWA sentiments on the basis of past experience, these played only a supporting role in operators' struggles at this time. Although union negotiators periodically made tactical mistakes, a systemic crisis within the UMWA model appears incipient by these years. Above all, standard contracts' higher costs were unacceptable to small producers. In their view, the UMWA had become less of a crusader for workplace justice than a proxy of protection for their less efficient competitors. Reciprocally, unionists viewed their adversaries not as virtuous entrepreneurs bringing jobs to economically struggling regions, but as upstarts threatening to replace well compensated, secure jobs with precarious work and substandard conditions.

In an exception to coal markets' contraction during the 1950s, the Tennessee Valley Authority constructed new coal-fired power plants throughout East Tennessee, eastern Kentucky, and southeastern Ohio. This agency awarded contracts on the basis of price alone, which encouraged the proliferation of small, nonunion operations. Here, industrial safety increasingly suffered from federal laws that exempted small mines from many safety requirements. Subsequently, this purchasing policy intensified regional labor strife and accelerated a nascent health and safety crisis. As small-mine owners fought the UMWA to defend some of the only well-paying jobs left in southern Appalachia, union members similarly resisted the downward pressure on industry conditions. At times, "organizing" supplemented mimeographed leaflets and idealistic appeals with pick handles and dynamite.[11]

Undoubtedly, these struggles had a cancerous effect upon the morality of union officers most heavily involved in it. In the union's District 19 in eastern Kentucky and Tennessee, Lewis's assistant Tony Boyle directed many of these campaigns. Historian Curtis Seltzer ably summarizes the tenor of violence on both sides:

> Clay and Leslie counties in eastern Kentucky bore the brunt of UMWA efforts in that state. The UMWA filed suit on September 11, 1951, for $2 million in damages against 612 defendants—including coal operators, judges, and sheriffs—for interfering with the union's right to organize and assemble peacefully. Tom Rainey, the UMWA international board member who was leading the organizing drive there, had his car dynamited in January 1952. Rainy claimed it was the third car to be blown up and the seventeenth dynamiting or machine-gunning in the area since the organizing drive began. Charles Vermillion, a UMWA organizer, was murdered in his parked car outside Hyden, Kentucky, in August 1953. He and three other UMWA members had been ambushed and wounded in January of that year. On June 24, 1952, three more union organizers were ambushed, prompting Lewis to ask Kentucky governor Lawrence W. Wetherby to use his authority to stop the "reign of terror."
>
> At the same time, a federal grand jury returned indictments against thirty-six UMWA members, charging conspiracy in their organizing

drive. The grand jury indicted the union members . . . for conspiring to "deny certain citizens the right to refrain from joining a union." In Virginia, Charles Minton, a former UMWA field worker, filed a $350,000 damage suit against the UMWA in February 1952, charging that the union had fired and blacklisted him because "he refused to . . . murder two owners of the Gladeville Coal Co." . . . The terms of the out-of-court settlement were never made public. . . . The legal papers on the case had disappeared from the Wise County, Virginia, courthouse when reporters, investigating Boyle, looked for them in the early 1970s.[12]

Ultimately, even such extreme tactics failed to stem nonunion mining's gradual proliferation: "There were simply too many targets in too many places. Too many miners needed jobs—and jobs that paid anything. The Eisenhower administration was neither helpful nor particularly hostile. Lawsuits stopped Lewis cold."[13]

Defending their common interests, the UMWA and unionized coal companies supplemented increasingly fruitless organizing with collusion against potential competitors. With this conflict most severe in the

FIGURE 4.3. UP&L's Castle Gate coal-fired power plant near Helper, Utah, delivered "coal-by-wire" that gave miners hope for industrial stability during the 1950s. Photo courtesy of the Western Mining and Railroad Museum.

southeast, echoes of these tensions reached western coalfields, where until the late 1960s markets remained weaker. In Utah, the UMWA quickly tried to block nonunion entrants once their hostility became known. In October 1967, Stevenson's communication to UP&L—"that we would not tolerate 'scab coal' being burned under their boilers"—led the company to drop consideration of Plateau as a supplier. A letter-writing campaign that month pressured Governor Rampton to suspend state highway funds for a road only useful to Swisher Coal. In 1968, similar pressure led the school board to hold up coal deliveries from Swisher "pending receipt of an analysis" of its quality.[14] These strategies, however, only slowed the pace of change.

While traditional class antagonisms still gave nonunion miners plenty of reasons to consider the UMWA, its own shortcomings increasingly led some to view reform inseparably from organizing's future. In the breech, however, antiunionists supplemented purges of union supporters with a rhetorical defense of their workers' right to stay union free. While union officials, antiunionists, and rank-and-file miners competed to define coal's future, those who later followed in their footsteps did so within a transformed cultural context: Organizing failure left emotional legacies not easily countered by economistic appeals. As setbacks mounted, operators gradually shifted tactics from the "stick" of aggressive union busting to the "carrots" of paternalistic union avoidance.[15]

In September 1961, membership outrage over Fund cutbacks contributed to Mangus's narrow defeat in a three-way race for District 22's presidency. His successor, Kaiser miner Frank Stevenson, had been active in local and district politics since the 1950s and was sharply critical of previous organizers' sparse accomplishments. Stevenson was also a member of the LDS church, which may have been a factor in his election, as Mangus had recently locked horns with the church over its employment of UMWA members at its nonunion "welfare" mine in Emery County.[16] Like many upstarts before and after, Stevenson's new role allowed him to better appreciate his predecessors' difficulties.

Stevenson's closest collaborator at this time, Frank J. Sacco, also came from Kaiser where he had served for twelve years as the local's president. Born in Grand Junction, Colorado, Sacco came from an Italian Catholic family and first mined coal in 1935 as a thirteen-year-old alongside his father. While he idolized Lewis and for many years supported and defended Tony Boyle, his credentials as a rank-and-file advocate included a successful fight against electoral fraud in the 1949 District 22 election, a reputation for intolerance of financial irregularities, and his voluntary resignation as district vice president in a 1957 cost-saving measure.¹⁷ In his capacity as an appointed International representative, he led organizing drives throughout Districts 22, 27 (Montana and northern Wyoming), and 15 (Colorado and New Mexico) from 1965 to 1972. Freed from the need to campaign for reelection, Sacco demonstrated professionalization's benefits as he worked with less distraction than previous district officers. However, as a principled man, Sacco's discovery of his superiors' more controversial practices eventually prompted an irreconcilable break.

As he assumed his duties, Sacco initially focused on two properties near Wellington—Knight Ideal Coal Company at Dugout Canyon and Premium Coal Company at Soldier Canyon—that produced nonunion coal "within the very heart of our organized mines".¹⁸ Shortly afterward, Knight Ideal's owners sold out to Kennecott Copper, who closed the mine and retained it as an investment.¹⁹ While most Knight Ideal miners had long resisted UMWA appeals, several now provided hostile cores of antiunion opinion where new mines opened. In January 1967, Sacco found that six out of ten miners employed by Plateau's new mine at Wattis had previously worked at Knight Ideal. That April, Plateau's general manager, Wayne Baker, adopted Knight Ideal's model of a "private," or "company," union, and formed the Castle Valley Workers' Association (CVWA) to exclude the UMWA. Former Knight Ideal miner Danny Price served as tipple supervisor, as well as CVWA president.²⁰ When Ura Swisher opened his operation along Gordon Creek in August 1967, he employed three former Knight Ideal miners, as well as the company union strategy. As Sacco and Stevenson approached his employees, Swisher claimed they already had a union that they preferred to the UMWA.²¹

For several of these men, it was not ideological opposition to solidaristic principles, but negative personal experiences with cutbacks to the Welfare and Retirement Fund that inspired the greatest hostility. At Swisher, Stevenson identified one former Knight Ideal miner, Alonzo Thayn, as the "ringleader" of employee antiunionism. Thayn had once been a United Mine Worker and told Sacco that in the mid-1960s he broke with the union "over a medical bill which the Fund refused to pay." Another miner here rebuffed Sacco for the same reason: "In the year 1958 he was employed by the [unionized] Columbine Coal Company, and was hospitalized. This company was given a post-dated agreement by Harry Mangus, then president of District 22, for this reason [he] had to pay the hospital bill, even though he had a valid 85 H.S. [medical card], for this he is very provoked."²²

Perceptions of Fund effectiveness subsequently became a major point of contention during organizing drives in Utah. When Swisher employees met to discuss joining the UMWA in July 1969, a third antiunion miner denounced its medical program specifically. At Plateau, Wayne Baker circulated a December 1968 *Wall Street Journal* article that highlighted the West Virginia Disabled Miners' and Widows' protests of benefit cutbacks. In response, Fund managers in Washington, DC, attacked the activists' credibility, while local union supporter Charlotte Herzon praised the Fund's effectiveness in a letter to Plateau miners' wives. Yet throughout this year, the balance of credibility remained on the union's side. In a 1969 letter to Frank M. Stevenson, skeptical miner Danny Price admitted, "We don't doubt [the Fund] is good" and raised instead the practical concern that "you avoid ever saying how you plan to get it for us. . . . Doesn't our employer have to agree to pay into the fund before we can have it? . . . How long do you estimate we would have to stay on strike to get the company to agree to pay the extra cost?" In a signed affidavit, Stevenson remembered one bargaining session that July where Plateau's negotiator interjected, "We are not foolish enough to say our plan is as good as the UMWA's" and described the limited plan of their smaller operation as a necessary reality of the free market, where "some people drive Cadillacs and some Volkswagens." The full extent of the Fund's shortcomings was not publicly revealed until late 1972, as the growing Miners for Democracy movement attracted whistleblowers with inside information, and a court order gave the group authority to edit half of the *United Mine Workers Journal*. Even after a frank discussion of the Fund's problems began, however, its medical program stayed competitive with most nonunion plans until June 1977.²³

At Premium's Soldier Canyon mine, owned by the Marinoni family, organizers' reports provide another window into nonunion miners' evolving outlooks in these years. In 1963, then-IEB member Arthur

Biggs noted several "in the lower age bracket" who were "not too concerned with the protection and security of our plan for age reasons, etc." The few employees not related to the owners feared that by organizing, they "would either be laid off, or the mine would be closed and then reopened with only the Marinoni brothers working." On the other hand, all reportedly felt "satisfied with their employment," "treated better now than they were when they worked in the union mines," and enjoyed being paid two dollars more per day than union wages. Biggs also recalled their wives' preferences for higher wages, the difficulty of "trying to compete with home television programs," and "complaints against the operation of the Welfare Fund affecting the limitation of doctors and poor services they received."[24]

While this portrait anticipates the UMWA's later challenges, Premium's miners periodically considered unionizing. In January 1969, employees' desire for a pension led a majority to join the UMWA and petition for an NLRB election. After the Marinoni family arranged one through a private insurance company, the miners withdrew their sup-

FIGURE 4.4. An idle Soldier Creek Mine, 2015. Once one of few nonunion properties in Carbon County, during the 1970s its owners, nonunion miners, and UMWA organizers struggled mightily to decide their industry's future. Photograph by author.

port and the union cancelled the election.[25] Two years later, another attempt ended when the UMWA lost an NLRB representation election by nine votes against four. Such sporadic interest had typified small coal-mine organizing throughout the postwar years, and probably did not come as a shock to cautiously optimistic union officers. Given victory's uncertain likelihood, however, these miners' ability to wield the threat of union organizing to win concrete gains outside of the contractual union framework is remarkable.

In 1966, Sacco's first organizing campaigns targeted the SUFCO mine near Salina Canyon and Sun Valley's Dog Valley mine on the opposite side of the Emery–Sevier County line. When he checked into Salina's Shasheen's Motel to begin these projects in late August, SUFCO employed eight miners and Sun Valley only three. At that time SUFCO operated as a local partnership between brothers Vernal and Neal Mortensen, their relative John Mortensen, and local investor Guy Huntsman. In 1965, the mine produced only 61,437 tons of coal (or 0.013 percent of state output) with seven employees, each of whom worked five or six days a week during the winter and only one-and-a-half days per week in the summer.[26] In 1966, Sun Valley owner Paul Anderson sold this mine to his son Boyd, employee James Dickert, and venture partner Robert Eddy. It produced even less, and like SUFCO marketed to consumers in Utah and Nevada.[27] While their small sizes made organizing difficult, UMWA director of organization John T. Kmetz supported both initiatives. His fear that each might "affect the markets of commercial operators which have long been under UMWA contract" proved well founded, as Coastal States' 1974 purchase of SUFCO helped expand the property into its current status as Utah's largest single producer.[28]

Matching the union's strategic perspective, organization appealed to both companies' employees. At SUFCO, Howard Christensen had been in contact with Sacco since the mine began its slack season in May, at which time all eight employees expressed an interest in joining the union. To avoid a retaliatory layoff, they had agreed to postpone organizing until the fall. Having arrived in Salina, Sacco viewed Sun Valley more speculatively. While in September he found support among the three miners it employed, he waited two months to file for an NLRB election in the hopes that further hiring would strengthen their power. Ultimately, Sun Valley employed only four miners that winter, all of whom signed union cards.²⁹

Christensen's outreach to Sacco is interesting in light of his position as president of the company-controlled "Independent Union of Southern Utah Fuel Company." This body's leadership included another UMWA supporter, vice president Gale Laier, as well as a company foreman, secretary Don T. Huntsman. In addition to its role as a buffer, this "union" financed the company's healthcare program through an eight-cent royalty on mined coal. However, Christensen and Laier disapproved of management's cost-saving decision to exclude five employees from membership in it and saw the UMWA contract as superior. Management's control over the "Independent Union" is further supported by all employees' claims—including those of Christensen and Laier—never to have seen a written copy of their contract. During a mandatory company meeting on September 23, employees queried about the cause of their dissatisfaction submitted "a long list of complaints."³⁰

Within the first week of his arrival, Sacco secured union cards from eight of SUFCO's twelve employees. Factors that limited support from the remainder included fear of foreclosure on personal debts, familial relationship to owners, and a personal preference for nonunion operation. On October 6, Stevenson filed for an NLRB representation election. Subsequently, Sacco felt "everything is going our way" and communicated "high hopes of winning down here." Days before the election, eleven employees and their wives attended a "highly successful" rally at Salina's city hall.³¹ Preserved within the UMWA archives at Penn State is a draft leaflet Sacco authored for distribution during the campaign's final days. Its confidence in health and retirement benefits' stability is indicative of the respect most unorganized miners had for UMWA contracts at this time:

> The outstanding benefit of UMWA members is received by the fact that they are beneficiaries of the United Mine Workers of America Welfare and Retirement Fund. The total figures are impressive—more than two billion dollars spent for pensions, medical care, funeral and other benefits. Individually, it means simply that you and your families are fully covered for hospital care, including medications and physicians' bills. It also means that if you want to you can retire at the age of 55 with a $100-a-month pension with the freedom to work outside the coal industry, if you are able to find employment, still retaining your miner's

pension. However, on the other side of the coin, your employer cannot force you to retire at any age under our contract if you are physically able to work and want to continue to do so....

The Welfare Fund is not the only benefit in our contract.... You also will be able to elect a Mine Safety Committee that could shut down the mine, or any part of it, if a truly dangerous condition exists.

After listing dollar amounts for wages, paid lunches, weekend pay, eight paid holidays, fourteen days' paid vacation, job security, house coal at cost, a grievance procedure, paid show-up time, and miscellaneous benefits, it optimistically concluded: "If you become members of our Union, you will receive protection under what is possibly the greatest labor contract in the United States today. You cannot fail to give your families the economic benefits that will become yours and theirs when you work under the banner of the United Mine Workers of America."[32]

On November 17, the tally of sixteen ballots revealed a close UMWA win with eight votes in favor, three votes opposed, and five ballots challenged. Emboldened, Stevenson contacted Sun Valley Coal on November 30 to invite a card check of the union's majority as a prelude to collective bargaining. After Sun Valley rejected the overture, it took until January 17 for Stevenson and the NLRB to determine the mine's small size required a certification election to proceed through the Utah Labor Relations Board. On March 3, 1967, this board oversaw an inconclusive election with two votes for the union, zero against, and six challenged ballots. Eleven days later, it certified the UMWA as bargaining agent.[33]

On February 12, 1967, Sacco met again at Salina's City Hall with ten supportive SUFCO unionists and charter members of Local 1485. Four days earlier, the NLRB's investigation had determined a final vote of ten to six in favor of the UMWA. While the assembled appreciated the tally, five months of pressure since the drive began had taken a toll on morale and enthusiasm. Fourteen days after the initial election, Stevenson filed an NLRB charge against SUFCO for "acts of coercion, intimidation, and threats of closing the mine." On February 7, truck driver Gale Laier filed paperwork that charged his late January termination was retaliatory for union support and his refusal to act on a bribe. That same week, a clerical employee pressured three union supporters into signing an anti-UMWA petition. Collective bargaining had not yet even begun. Regrouping at the Salina meeting, Sacco optimistically recalled the union's history to remind the men: "You have no fear of losing your jobs. This union will protect you.... You now belong to an effective organization." Anticipating delaying tactics, Sacco called for unity, yet he also frankly acknowledged that "God will only know when they will sign our contracts."[34]

Following the union win at SUFCO, Sun Valley similarly began to profile and intimidate its employees. On November 18, miner Dar Heaps recalled Boyd Anderson's threats to shut down the mine if employees voted for the union. Anderson combined direct economic pressure with the promise of future rewards: "We were discussing the matter of bidding on more coal orders and he told me, that he wouldn't dare bid on any coal orders until he contacted all of the employees to see how they would vote. Both Dickert and Anderson told me that if the men voted the union out, they would pay the employees 40 cents-a-ton royalty." Wayne Christensen related that supervisor Tom Heaps (misleadingly) warned him of high UMWA dues and membership application fees, and described an inflated level of dissatisfaction among union miners at the nearby Browning Mine. Terrence Jorgensen and Terry Crain recalled a November 26 threat that "if we joined the U.M.W. of A., we would get fired." On December 2, Sun Valley fired union supporter Wayne Christensen and replaced him with owner Boyd Anderson. Although the union filed an unfair labor practice charge, NLRB Region 27 director Clyde F. Waers felt "the board would not assert jurisdiction under its existing standards" and refused to issue a complaint.[35]

Over the following two years of inconclusive bargaining, harassment escalated while the unity of both workforces disintegrated. SUFCO retained attorney Stephen J. Beeley, a professional negotiator from the antiunion Utah Industrial Council. Sun Valley similarly employed lawyer Don V. Tibbs of Manti. Both companies' unwillingness to propose more than "a yellow dog contract," along with their attorneys' expertise at delay, conceded little to Stevenson during on-again, off-again negotiations. Against the NBCWA proposed by Stevenson and supported by Local 1485, SUFCO most strongly objected to seniority language that established the right to rehire idled miners, a safety committee with the authority to withdraw employees from areas of immediate danger, and the Welfare and Retirement Fund.[36] Sun Valley similarly found the NBCWA "so unrealistic, in the size of our operation, that we cannot at this time consider entering into such an agreement." Sun Valley did have serious financial liabilities, as revealed by subsequent litigation, which included a $62,500 debt to the Small Business Administration that had accompanied the mine's 1966 sale. The dry nature of the mine's coal also necessitated hauling in 600 gallons of water a day, while a dirt band in the middle of the seam slowed mining and raised its cost. Though Sun Valley refused to let the union examine its financial statement, Tibbs wasted over a month of Stevenson's time looking into the possibility of obtaining it.[37]

In his own letters to each managerial team, Stevenson protested that "the employees . . . and the Union are anxious to reach an agreement and bring this matter to a conclusion." His suggestions to "continue negotiations immediately" to avoid "a considerable delay in the contract negotiations which is to say the least, intolerable" convey the image of a man outmatched or unaware of his opponents' strategy.[38] The more protracted the bargaining became, the more management gained through employee demoralization. While union records of the Sun Valley drive drop off after December 8, 1967, they indicate that one unionist left the bargaining unit by accepting a position as foreman, and only one of the four who helped to bring the union in was still employed by March 1969. Sometime during or after 1968, the union "had to abandon their efforts because of a lack of interest on the part of the employees."[39]

As the fall of 1967 began, SUFCO replaced union activist Charles Black with Wayne Bennett, a son-in-law of the company's president. With little economic power during the slow summer months, the best pressure Stevenson could bring was an NLRB charge against SUFCO for having "refused to bargain in good faith." While this restarted negotiations, it also prolonged irresolution.[40] Finally, on November 8, 1967, Stevenson authorized the first and only strike for contract recognition to occur during any Utah organizing drive in this period. On the first day, Local 1485 erected a picket line on the road to SUFCO's mine where coal trucks passed. At 5 AM the second day, supportive union members arrived as reenforcements. As strikers conversed with the stopped station wagon of a foreman and three antiunion employees two hours later, four highway patrolmen intervened to break the picket and allow the car through. As the first coal trucks arrived, "one patrolman got on the fender of a lead truck, one got on the fender of the truck following, and instructed the truck drivers that they could go through the picket line." While a hasty message to Governor Rampton brought the UMWA an apology from state patrolmen and a reduction in force, they remained to escort trucks throughout the day.⁴¹

On November 13, Stevenson brokered a verbal agreement with a federal mediator to end the strike. While its details are unclear, the strikers' return to work without a contract proved extremely demoralizing. In retrospect, Stevenson's decision to end the strike in exchange for promises, rather than a signed contract, repeated a historic pattern that ensured the death of this effort just as it had at American Fuel in 1946 and Coal Creek in 1950. In written statements, strikers Marvell Anderson, Verge Kennedy, and Art Robinson recalled that when they returned to work, stockholder Marvin Mason confronted them with a humiliating barrage of insults and threats. Anderson remembered Mason's taunt: "You showed your god dam colors. . . . You are lower than a snake for standing on the picket line yesterday and then coming to work today." After Kennedy arrived at the bathhouse, he recalled Mason looked right at him and said, "There is one guy amongst you not worthy of being a scab; not enough man in him to make him a good scab. . . . You came sneaking back without a contract." Robinson recalled a less ambiguous greeting: "You son-of-a-bitch, you came crawling back. If it wasn't for us you would starve, and you didn't get the contract signed either." Striker Howard Christensen remembered antiunion miner Max Curtis's welcome: "You look like that other scum up there, the lowest grade of humanity," as well as SUFCO's president: "Guy Huntman picked up a handful of dirt and threw it in the air and said: 'You sure are a chicken-shit bastard.'"⁴²

While Stevenson's compromise won the pleasure of additional negotiations with Stephen Beeley, a thinning correspondence record suggests their last meeting may have occurred in November 1968. Three months later, eleven SUFCO employees sent a two-sentence petition to Frank Stevenson: "We the undersigned employees of Southern Utah Fuel Company want to handle our own affairs. We no longer want you to represent us." While seven names had been against the union from the beginning, as Stevenson forwarded the message to new International director of organization Michael Widman, he drew no connection to the post-strike experiences of signatories Art Robinson and Marvell

Anderson. By now Local 1485 had disintegrated, and the remaining two members had not paid dues since November.⁴³

Throughout these campaigns, long periods of inaction while the UMWA waited for national or state labor board decisions proved highly demoralizing to newly unionized miners, who endured years of surveillance and managerial harassment without the protections of a union contract. In addition to labor law, the Fund provided another albatross that provoked managerial hostility while tying the basic protections of union representation to a substantial profitability reduction. Yet the one factor the union controlled—its decision to call and then end the SUFCO strike after only five days—seems to have been most damaging. Thus, Stevenson's continued prioritization of marginally helpful federal mediation over an approach centered on rank-and-file activity may be included among the reasons for the defeat.

Successful as an entrepreneur in several industries and politically active in neoconservative circles, Plateau Mining Company founder and general manager Wayne Baker emerged as a prophet of antiunionism during these years. While living in Roy, Utah, during the mid-1950s, his journey to coal mine operator began almost accidentally. Hearing of a recently closed mine's liquidation prices for its equipment, he purchased a truck with a small loan and began reselling machinery, scrap metal, and other materials from closed coal mines and the railroads that formerly served them. After Lion Coal Company closed its Wattis mine in 1964, Baker's Mountain States Machinery Company purchased the property and equipment, but had difficulty finding a buyer. Undeterred, with local investors he graded a new road to a higher, untapped coal seam where he opened a new mine on an experimental basis. After nearly ten years of adversarial relations with the UMWA, he now committed to managing the mine as a nonunion operation.⁴⁴

In his 2008 autobiography, Baker's hostility to the UMWA appears undimmed by time. When he earlier reclaimed equipment from Spring Canyon, "they threatened to shoot our workers with rifles . . . [and] the sheriff . . . wouldn't do anything about it. . . . [W]e had to join [construction] District 50 of UMWA in order to salvage the mines without trouble." During collective bargaining sessions in 1969, he described Frank Stevenson as "a drunkard" and a "union thug," determined to "force me into the union or put me out of business." He also denounced the ethics of union supporters who "salted"—or applied for work to support an organizing drive—at his mine. Of them he remembered that "several of the men who had supported the union quit" immediately after their one-vote victory in an NLRB election.⁴⁵ Raised by a conservative LDS family on a Wyoming ranch during the Great Depression, Baker's determined ideological antiunionism proved extremely formidable to the UMWA, and played a major role in establishing nonunion mining's foothold and legitimacy in Utah.

While his memoir remains an invaluable primary source, UMWA organizing records paint a far more active picture of his agency as a union resister. While at former Knight Ideal miners' suggestion he established a company-controlled union, seventeen of his employees signed UMWA membership cards from June 1966 to April 1967.⁴⁶ Of these, nine were laid off when the mine shut down for one month while Baker formally organized Plateau Mining Company, one quit due to an injury, and three quit for other reasons. On April 3, the UMWA charged Baker with five employees' illegal termination "because of their membership in or activity on behalf of a labor organization." NLRB Region 27 director Clyde F. Waers refused to issue a complaint, however, finding "no evidence" that the layoffs were "in any way related" to union membership. Pointing to three of the employees' later rehiring, and the "separate and distinct" nature of the new company's "records, bank accounts, and book keeping," Waers found "no evidence of any employer interference, restraint, or coercion" in violation of the National Labor Relations Act.⁴⁷ Over the next several years, NLRB investigators' findings frequently differed from the UMWA's perspective, and affirm many labor historians' critique of this body's politicized and linear drift away from its origins as an aggressive defender of workers' rights. Authoring an appeal to one unfavorable ruling in 1969, District 22's attorney A. Wally Sandack likened the board director's conclusions to "an Alice-in-Wonderland fantasy."⁴⁸

Amid NLRB inaction, employer intimidation increased. UMWA supporter Chris Padilla felt so pressured by Superintendent Floyd Tucker's promotion of the CVWA and threats to fire union supporters that he asked District 22 "not to contact him at his home again because he was afraid that someone would see [an organizer] and report it to the company."⁴⁹ At a meeting on company premises on April 20, 1967, Baker secured employees' signed consent for CVWA representation. Padilla recalled the meeting's intimidating atmosphere: "How else could we vote when Baker was in the area with [supervisor] Danny Price looking on[?] We had no choice [but] to accept. We would all lose our jobs if we opposed Price or Baker." Miner Claud Bell agreed: "I either signed, or else." Having missed the meeting, Russell Curtis complied with Baker's request to visit his home in Carbonville, where he signed the statement without reading it.⁵⁰

In 1968, production increased with additional investment from Sundance Oil Company of Denver and the purchase of a new continuous mining machine. While UMWA supporters applied to Plateau to help the organizing drive, the father of undecided employee Elvin Bygre noted widespread pro-union sentiments, as "the men are all rattled up and dissatisfied with the conditions there. Old Baker is slavedriving the men all the time." Out of thirty employees, twenty-one signed union cards by December 13. Management responded predictably. One supervisor ended social communication with his long-time friend Gary Pilling, and transferred him to a less desirable job after he "started to push our union and [tried] to enforce safety."⁵¹ In mid-January, Baker held two employee meetings on company property where he promised to raise wages, share profits, and invest a company welfare fund in the stock market to benefit employees as Plateau grew. In mid-February, he raised wages to thirty-four dollars a day. While these efforts to sway employee opinion seem to have had some effect, the UMWA still retained a majority of employee support. After a March 6 NLRB election resulted in a seventeen-to-eleven win for the union (with six challenged ballots), the International chartered UMWA Local 1612. To represent Plateau in negotiations, Baker hired Salt Lake antiunion attorney S. Lyle Johnson.⁵²

One day after the first negotiating meeting in May, "Mr. Baker had a party at the mine site and told the employees present that he would go to hell first before he would sign our agreement." While he stalled at the bargaining table, like the management of the Sun Valley mine he stopped bidding on new coal orders. Slowing down his operations, that summer he was able to lay off several union supporters. By July 31 Plateau's workforce had shrunk from thirty-five to between eleven and fourteen. Less provocative than a company-wide "lockout," this strategy facilitated a purge under the guise of reduced business. As he anticipated a strike for contract recognition, Baker corresponded individually with employees to identify their views. To those he felt were unreliable, he supplied additional antiunion arguments. As Local 1612 president Elvin Byrge reported one such ultimatum: "YOU HAVE THREE CHOICES: Stay the way we are and meet with the union any time they want to meet or accept the new insurance that Plateau offers or GO FIND ANOTHER JOB! I WON'T PAY 40 CENTS PER TON!" Soon after, Baker fired Byrge, and by December 2, 1969, Plateau employed only "about 5 bosses and 6 classified workers."[53]

Baker's aggressive purge of Plateau's workforce contrasts with his opponent's comparatively timid response. Stevenson first attempted to resolve the May layoffs through negotiations; which it took him until August 28 to recognize as futile. Subsequently, he filed an NLRB unfair labor practice charge. On December 23, 1969, new Region 27 director Francis Sperandeo refused to issue a complaint, defined the union's delay in protesting the May firings as "acquiescence," and found a second round of firings in October having been "properly" conducted. In April 1970, NLRB officers in Washington, DC, denied District 22's appeal.[54] Outmaneuvered, on June 1 Plateau's seven employees filed an NLRB decertification petition. The next month Stevenson conceded his defeat: "The UMWA claim no interest in representing the employees of Plateau Mining Company."[55]

Like Wayne Baker, Ura Swisher opened a Carbon County mine in these years after an earlier coal career that involved passionate clashes against the UMWA. During the 1950s, Swisher operated a mine in Meigs County, Ohio, that violently resisted organization. District 6 president Thomas A. Williams recalled the tenor of this conflict: "One of our organizers, the late Joseph Kostecka, was brutally beaten by thugs during this drive and spent a considerable amount of time in the hospital as a result; his assailants were never found." International director of organization John T. Kmetz also noted Swisher's management of a mine that had recognized the union in District 19, Tennessee, where "because of failure to pay Welfare Fund Royalties . . . legal proceedings were instituted." In June 1967, Swisher leased land near the former Consumers townsite from Colombine Mine owner and NBCWA signatory Dr. F. V. Colombo. In August, Swisher rejected Sacco and Stevenson's overture to discuss a UMWA contract: "Swisher refused to do so and informed us that he was not going to force the United Mine Workers on his employees and that if we didn't stop harassing him, he wouldn't even talk to us in the future."[56] Anticipating an organizing drive, Swisher advertised for nonunion miners from familiar territory in Ohio. He also hired a few former Knight Ideal employees. As his mine began development work in mid-1967, he paid four dollars per hour—a rate higher than the union scale. He also signed a highly favorable contract unread by the nominal leaders of a company-controlled union: the "Gordon Creek Workers Association."[57]

By September 29, 1967, Sacco had collected union cards from three of the mine's six employees. In December, Stevenson informed Swisher of majority support and proposed collective bargaining. Swisher rebuffed this approach and pointed to the presence of a union contract already in existence. Over the next year, Swisher Coal grew slowly and hired carefully. By November 1968, only five of twelve employees had signed UMWA cards. By March this support appears to have shrunk, as Stevenson described the ten men employed: "Five . . . came in with Swisher from Ohio and three are Carbon County's most well-known scabs from the Knight Ideal Coal Company. . . . Two of the employees we feel can be depended upon and will support the United Mine Workers of America."[58]

Finding themselves at the center of a growing conflict between union and nonunion sectors, Swisher Coal's employees moved cautiously to advance their interests through the most convenient frameworks at their disposal. In May 1969, ten out of twelve miners creatively used the auspices of a Gordon Creek Workers Association meeting to gather on company property during working time to discuss their grievances against persistent substandard conditions. After some discussion, they concluded that they "wanted a $4.00 per day raise; 5 cent raise on royalty per ton; job seniority; and for the employer to pay all of vacation. . . . They discussed going on strike if necessary." Having communicated these concerns to their employer, Swisher responded with a request for time to consider. A month later, company union trustee and anti-UMWA miner Alonzo Thayn "called a meeting and asked how long we should give Swisher to give us what he wanted. Everybody was present but Cox and Curtis [and] they voted unanimously that we had to have the demands immediately." As Thayn's subsequent reluctance to pass on their concerns became evident, seven employees contacted the UMWA during the last week in June. On July 1, Stevenson felt confident enough to petition for an NLRB election.[59]

Swisher responded, like Baker, with offers to "grant wage increases, paid vacations, and other benefits . . . to discourage employees from joining District 22." At the same time, Thayn and supervisor Kent Pilling pressured employees to sign a petition that expressed support for the GCWA as bargaining agent. Two miners recalled their cryptic encouragement to sign because "it would help protect our jobs," and saw the petition as a trick to identify union supporters.[60] In response, the UMWA filed two unfair labor practice charges on July 18. The NLRB dismissed both of them two months later, after director Sperandeo decided the Gordon Creek Workers Association was a legitimate labor organization and that a recent settlement between it and Swisher Coal "remedies everything."[61]

After the UMWA appealed in October, Director of Appeals officer Irving M. Herman issued a mixed verdict on April 24, 1970. Ordered to investigate the charge, Sperandeo set a hearing in Price for January 12, 1971. After a second hearing on April 27, Stevenson shared his optimism that "we are in a good position of getting a favorable decision" at a third hearing set for June 1. While he rightly predicted that "Swisher will be ordered to bargain with our Union," organizer Jess M. Vicini's September 1972 update to the long-quiet Swisher Coal file summarized the erosion of miners' support: "UMWA withdrew from a second election order by the NLRB because the district felt we would lose the election. There is no interest being shown at this time."[62]

Events at Plateau and Swisher coal repeated—with variations—the same organizing trajectories established at SUFCO and Sun Valley. While majorities of miners took risks in hopes of winning a real union's protection, District 22's president and chief negotiator Frank Stevenson appears outmatched and outmaneuvered by opponents who fought with the tenacity of what they saw as a life or death struggle for their businesses' survival. Given Stevenson's past experiences with the NLRB, his willingness to wait two years for a favorable ruling at Swisher Coal contrasts dramatically with the intimidation working miners faced daily. While successful at Wyoming's Kirby mine in

FIGURE 4.5. Picket of Plateau's opening, May 27, 1969. Union officers' and pensioners' prominence suggests working miners' limited roles during organizing drives. *From left*, Frank Roybal Sr., Bill Ward, Frank J. Sacco, Frank M. Stevenson, Melvin Taylor, James Madrigal, Louis Dalpiaz, John Juliano, and Sam Colosino. Used with permission from the Eberly Family Special Collections Library, Pennsylvania State University Libraries.

1962, Stevenson never imitated former IEB member Malio Pecorelli's resolve to lead newly unionized miners through a steadfast contract strike as long as eighteen-days (or more). Perhaps, like other UMWA leaders, he was unprepared for shifts in NLRB and Labor Department attitudes. As historian Charles Perry (1984) concluded, while the approaches that worked in the past appeared increasingly inadequate, the union nationally failed "to alter adequately its basically defensive strategy, developed to deal with nonunion competition in a declining industry."[63]

In contrast, the management teams of all four of these mines exercised decisive and unchallenged control over workplace operations. While in the aftermath of these drives Sun Valley went out of business, SUFCO, Swisher, and Plateau soon attracted new and deep-pocketed investors that allowed them to purchase the latest equipment and steadily expand. As the UMWA increasingly faced actual—rather than potential—competition, its failures in these years would have significant long-term effects.

While Pecorelli successfully applied an earlier era's militancy to organizing dilemmas in the 1960s, he was also a different man, raised in a different time, who operated under a different International administration. Stevenson, by contrast, learned the arts of union officialdom during a period of close collaboration with unionized employers amid relative state tolerance. And as Stevenson's experience with Kaiser miners' brief loss of autonomy had demonstrated, union mines' overriding need for stability required limited rank-and-file activity. International president Tony Boyle, who followed Utah organizing closely at this time, also probably exerted greater control over organizers' strategy than his aging predecessor, Thomas Kennedy, had during his 1960–1963 tenure.

Unfortunately for union supporters, Boyle not only approached mass mobilization skeptically, he silenced any discussions of setbacks. When Plateau held its opening celebration on May 27, 1967, Stevenson, Sacco, and other officers joined former Lion Coal Company employees to picket the road leading to the mine. This picket was largely an attempt to influence radio personality and actor Art Linkletter, a Plateau investor and also a union member. While Baker's brother drove Linkletter through the picket without pause, Stevenson later mailed in photographs of the action for publication in the *United Mine Workers Journal*. To print this story might have mobilized additional pressure, or at least stimulated a needed discussion about the challenges organizers faced and the possibility of revising their strategy. Yet while Kmetz agreed the photographs would help the organizing drive, Boyle tolerated little criticism of his administration's competency and personally prevented their publication.[64]

By June 1969, Frank Stevenson and the International's organizing department recognized the probable necessity of a contract strike at Plateau yet remained officially discouraged from going ahead to organize such an action. On September 19, Stevenson again described Baker's intransigence directly to Boyle, who sent additional negotiators but again declined to authorize a strike.[65] Relaying this conservatism, International Director of Organization Michael Widman's September 30 recommendation to "wait a little longer" to see if an unfair labor practice charge might affect Baker's disposition appears to have been hopelessly naive. On October 8, Stevenson astutely identified a final chance

[Handwritten margin note: UMWA leaders brushed on criticism of their tactics + inactivity]

to use his supporters' strongest weapon, and recommended "that we strike the mine at an early date.... [W]e will take immediate action upon hearing from you." As he waited for a response, the next day Plateau's miners detected preparations for an impending round of layoffs, which subsequently curtailed the union's capacity to interrupt production. Stevenson again requested strike authorization on October 15, yet Boyle's orientation remained ever-legalistic. He instead instructed Widman to refer the case to the International's top lawyer to investigate additional legal options. This Widman obeyed, communicated a denial of strike authorization, and encouraged Stevenson to file a new unfair labor practice charge. While talk of the necessity for a strike continued through December, little potential to win one remained.[66]

Such a conservative and top-down negotiating style constrained organizing efforts at Swisher Coal as well. During initial communications with Dr. Colombo, Stevenson and Sacco brought up a clause in the NBCWA that required owners to ensure any subleased coal lands were mined by union labor.[67] However, after a September 1967 meeting, "Stevenson charge[d] the district was making headway with Colombo when Widman, in the presence of him and Sacco, had assured Dr. Colombo he had nothing to worry about; that we would not file legal action which resulted in Colombo's refusing to negotiate with the district." While Widman's cordiality to a NBCWA signatory is in line with the conduct of social equals discussing mutually beneficial business, it took a potentially decisive tool off the table and forced the district into a protracted and resource-demanding campaign.[68]

As with the Plateau picket, organizers' efforts to publicize the Swisher drive were similarly silenced by the highest levels of the UMWA presidency. On October 10, 1968, Swisher supervisor Art VanWagenen fired UMWA supporter Bud Pilling after he refused to cross a picket line erected by union miners during the first national contract strike in almost twenty years. Recognizing his sacrifice, District 22 filed an NLRB grievance on Pilling's behalf and helped him find a new job at the (union) Carbon Fuel mine. Weighing the time such a case might take to fight against his family's immediate economic needs, a month later Pilling withdrew his charge and abandoned his request for reinstatement to accept a $96 settlement—the equivalent of three days' pay. As with the Plateau picket, Sac-

FIGURE 4.6. Swisher miner Budd Pillings and his wife. Fired for refusing to cross union miners' picket of his nonunion property during a national contract strike, UMWA advocacy secured a settlement check for his unfair labor practice charge. Used with permission from the Eberly Family Special Collections Library, Pennsylvania State University Libraries.

co mailed in a photograph of Mrs. Pilling holding the check for possible *Journal* publication. Mr. and Mrs. Pilling's sentiment that "they appreciated everything done in their behalf," might have boosted morale and provided proof of the union's ability to help its victimized supporters. However, Boyle's rejection of the idea revealed little sympathy for the time and energy required to win an NLRB complaint: "Mr. Pilling apparently decided he would rather have $96 than to pursue his charge against Swisher. I certainly don't consider this any victory for the UMWA and if Mr. Sacco sent the picture for publicity purposes, I am adamantly opposed to giving the matter any publicity whatsoever." While Pilling's settlement was modest, the UMWA subsequently suffered greatly for its inability to protect union supporters whose mines it picketed during national contract strikes.[69]

Only under unique circumstances at Castle Valley Mining and American Coal did Boyle's elite negotiating approach succeed. Here, organizing drives initially encountered sharp resistance from Shirl McArthur, Huntington's former mayor, energetic booster, and "extremely anti-union" owner of both companies.[70] For decades, McArthur managed the LDS Church's cooperative, nonunion mine above Orangeville in Emery County. While some UMWA support existed here throughout the 1960s, miners expressed only lukewarm desire to unionize and balked at the prospect of a contract strike. In 1972, UP&L purchased this property to fuel the new power plants it then had under construction. That year it expanded the mine's operations from 19 employees producing a hundred thousand tons of coal a year to 150 who expected to produce a million. Eager for stability and unwilling to take on the UMWA, the major utility signed a contract that April.[71]

McArthur also managed Castle Valley Mining, a subsidiary hired by Peabody Coal to conduct development work on two historic small mines in Huntington Canyon: Deer Creek and Wilberg. While fourteen of the company's twenty-five miners signed union cards by January 1967, organizers stopped approaching additional employees at this time "because we were instructed by president W. A. Boyle to leave this mine alone since he was working the matter out with Peabody Coal Company Officials." Faithful to those he represented, Stevenson protested that, along with safety concerns, "the employees have complained to this office that they want a union now because the company is forcing them to work nine hours a day while being paid for eight hours with no lunch period." Though "certain" he could win a representation election, Stevenson deferred, and urged patience to union supporters. Perhaps as a cunningly evasive strategy, McArthur initially promised to sign a UMWA contract when the mine was in full operation, yet insisted on remaining nonunion during the "prospect" period. He maintained this strategy for the next three years. In April 1970 Stevenson noted, "This company is up to their usual tricks of intimidating employees by using threats of mine closures, reduction of force, discharges, etc.," and (perhaps learning from earlier defeats) suggested "that we take immediate action." After a June NLRB election ended in a seventeen to seven defeat, District 22 filed an unfair labor practices charge. In response, McArthur also retained S. Lyle Johnson's now reputable legal services.[72]

While apparently ready to deploy a familiar strategy of antiunion resistance, on March 3, 1971, McArthur reversed course and signed the standard national contract.[73] While it may have delayed success for four years, Boyle's strategy of "bargaining to organize" worked. Two months earlier, Stevenson and McArthur had reached an "oral understanding" with Peabody's senior vice president of operations. While details are unclear, the millions of dollars Peabody had saved through sweetheart contracts secretly negotiated elsewhere may have given them plenty of reason to consider the union as an acceptable business partner. A year later, Castle Valley Mining and American Coal Company merged and

FIGURES 4.7 AND 4.8. Huntington *(above)* was a small, agricultural community with significant outmigration and an unclear future before 1970. UP&L's Huntington power plant *(below)* provided new relevance for Emery County's coal as high-voltage power lines and a two-mile conveyor belt connected the town and once-marginal Deer Creek mine to regional consumers. Photo Credit: Special Collections, J. Willard Marriott Library, University of Utah.

dedicated their output to UP&L's new Huntington and Hunter power plants. In a transformation analogous to Geneva and Kaiser Steel's earlier impacts, this victory at Utah's newest and largest captive mines created new centers of union power within once-sleepy agricultural communities in western Emery County.[74]

If operators' victory in five out of seven coal mine organizing drives from 1966 to 1971 set the stage for nonunion mining's local emergence, similar setbacks nationally nudged collective bargaining into an increasingly defensive position. In secret and behind members' backs, Tony Boyle responded to increased nonunion competition and union operators' concerns over productivity and cost disparities by negotiating reduced-royalty agreements, usually allowing twenty-cent-per-ton payments into the Welfare and Retirement Fund rather than the forty cents per ton that miners believed their companies were paying. While his Machiavellian approach helped struggling mines stay open and allowed other benefits of union contracts to be observed, it failed to fund the union's health care and pension commitments and eventually outraged most union members. While on two occasions in District 22 Stevenson forwarded operator proposals for "sweetheart" royalty rates to the International along with ambiguous requests for "guidance," this study has not uncovered any evidence of him actually signing off on such a contract in Utah. During their last bargaining session in 1969, Baker remembers that Stevenson flatly rejected such an offer.[75]

Regionally, a connection becomes increasingly clear between organizing setbacks and sweetheart proliferation. While Tony Boyle makes an attractive villain, his eventual offer of a reduced-royalty contract to Colorado's Bear Coal Company may be understood as a tactical retreat following his organization's failure to unionize its Utah competitor at Premium Coal. And given strip-mine operators' intense hostility to Fund royalty payments that essentially subsidized less productive underground miners, had Boyle not offered discounted royalty payments to several Colorado properties or to Peabody's Black Mesa operation near Kayenta, Arizona, it's unclear whether any UMWA contracts would have been signed there at all. As Boyle's successors discovered, forcing such operations to pay the full royalty ignited potentially insurmountable wrath.

While the International's strict control of information suppressed awareness of mounting problems for most members, organizers witnessed these failures firsthand, and faced the moral pressure of squaring their own material comforts with their duty to the miners whom they interacted with daily under difficult and collaborative circumstances. Through these years of setbacks, Frank Sacco developed an increasingly vocal critique of his superiors, and in 1972 broke with the Boyle administration for good. At Plateau, he concluded that Baker's original evasion of the District 50 contract and establishment of a company union had only been possible through Stevenson and District 50 representative Wilbur McCready's inattentiveness, as these men had earlier agreed to protect the jurisdiction "even if it meant a pickett [sic] line." At Swisher, Sacco identified that the UMWA had a legal right to sue Colombo for violating the lease provision of its contract, which he communicated to Boyle who declined to press the issue. And perhaps distracting Stevenson from all of these drives, Sacco noted an increasing number of spurious trips to Salt Lake City that coincided with unauthorized telephone charges billed to District 22. With the state's capital only a two-and-a-half-hour drive from Price, Stevenson billed the union for overnight hotel stays when only brief business engagements or a trip to the airport was required. As Sacco tabulated thirty-six visits in 1966, sixty-one in 1967, and thirty-seven by October 1968, he suspected Stevenson was pursing an illicit affair at union expense. Most concerning to Sacco, on multiple occasions Stevenson vaguely excused himself from organizing meetings with supporters at nonunion mines. Sarcastically, Sacco suggested in late 1968 that "it would be much cheaper to move the District office to Salt Lake City," and warned "it would be a grave mistake" to appoint Stevenson to the district's vacant IEB seat.[76]

As Sacco reported this behavior to an indifferent Boyle, he noted a growing coldness from Stevenson himself. In a November 27, 1970, meeting at the Price district office, Sacco and fellow District 22 International representative Frank J. Roybal confronted Stevenson for circulating rumors that they "couldn't be trusted," "were causing dissension," and "would be transferred out of District 22." They charged Stevenson directly with concealing financial reports and correspondence, and instructing the district's secretary to keep the safe locked any time Sacco was in the office. Failing to come to any agreement, at this meeting's conclusion the opponents pledged to continue working together despite their differences for the sake of the union.[77]

By March 1971, however, Sacco encountered a new set of appalling circumstances that he could no longer ignore. Sent to organize Decker Coal Company's strip mine near Sheridan, Wyoming, Sacco arrived in the extreme northeast corner of that state which at the time fell under the administrative jurisdiction of Montana-based District 27. As Sacco sought support from union members at Big Horn Coal Company's Local 2055—an adjacent strip operation—rather than a cadre of articulate supporters he encountered a workforce seething with anger over a recently signed sweetheart agreement. In violation of the standard NBCWA contract, Big Horn mechanics now had to purchase their own tools; older members were denied graduated vacation pay; new jobs were not posted for fair bidding; lunch breaks for some employees were as short as twenty minutes; work weeks varied greatly in length and were not evenly distributed; no panel of laid-off miners existed; shift preference was not observed; and to the Welfare and Retirement Fund the company paid only twenty-cents-per-ton royalties.[78]

After Sacco confronted R. J. "Dick" Boyle (Tony Boyle's brother and president of District 27), the latter acknowledged the substandard conditions and rationalized International acquiescence before them because "they're a small company." A more realistic explanation may be that Big Horn Coal had tenaciously opposed the UMWA ever since it was organized in 1945, and negotiations may have reached a point where the Boyles felt significant concessions were necessary to prevent the property from going nonunion altogether. Now, however, this strategy appeared difficult to reverse. If Big Horn's men could not demonstrate superior working conditions and a strong contract to their counterparts at Decker, what chance did an organizer have? And if nonunion properties proliferated, how could the union resist further concessions in the future?

Sacco took another year to break with Boyle and expose these findings. In that time, he discovered numerous additional sweethearts, some of which were signed in his presence and almost all of which were with highly productive strip mines now opening across the West. Most outrageous was the secretly negotiated 1968 "Sub-bituminous and Lignite Agreement," which allowed twenty-four western mines operated by sixteen coal companies in Alaska, Arizona, Colorado, Wyoming, North Dakota, and Montana to pay twenty cents per ton rather than the normal forty cents per ton. Despite the arrangement's deliberately misleading name, many of these producers mined high quality bituminous coal.[79]

After he confronted the International president's brother, Sacco was transferred from Wyoming to District 15 and assigned to organize Mid-Continent Coal and Coke Company's miners in Glenwood Springs, Colorado. Here, however, his presence appeared fruitless, as the company created a shell "union"—the Redstone Workers Association—which signed a three-and-a-half-year contract in December 1971. This prevented the UMWA from appealing for an NLRB election until 1975 and ensured Sacco's closest contacts became demoralized over organizing's apparently slow and fruitless pace. By summer 1972, Sacco concluded that there was nothing further he could do, and that the only reason he had been sent there was to isolate him from friends and supporters. Adding further insult, Sacco's superior, District 15 president Sylvester Lorenzo, denied his requests to return to Dragerton, Utah, where his wife struggled in his absence with a number of medical issues. In June, Sacco contacted a local lawyer for help. He also reached out to Miners for Democracy—a band of union dissidents centered in the eastern United States coalfields who were rapidly gaining traction in that year's repeat of the 1969 International election. On July 26, he resigned as an International representative, returned to his old job driving trucks at Kaiser Steel, and devoted his free time to coordinating the reform movement across the West.[80]

While employer activism and restrictive labor law takes much credit for organizers' defeats during the Tony Boyle era, union strategy also shares a part of this blame and in retrospect appears to have been woefully inadequate. While the NLRB's lethargy slowly sapped workers' strength, at key moments union negotiators relied on its machinery long after the futility of doing so became apparent. Yet for all their faults, factors greater than individuals fueled nonunion coal's contested rise. Reviving markets attracted wily entrepreneurs as well as vast sources of investment capital. Even if alternative tactics had been employed, it is unclear whether any would have guaranteed success. The sweetheart contract, perhaps, reflected not so much the malice of its signatories as the balance of their power. While organizational setbacks failed to equalize price and cost disparities between union and nonunion coal, union operators weren't stable enough to weather an all-out fight against the UMWA. Nor were existing union members any more eager for an industry-wide showdown, as they were policed by high unemployment as much as prospective members were by restrictive labor law and indifferent NLRB staffers.

While no party could move decisively forward, the sweetheart contract emerged as the union sector's collective sigh. Through a web of demagoguery, censorship, and intimidation, Tony Boyle outwardly projected the image of a capable professional and anointed heir to John L. Lewis. Behind the smoke and mirrors that masked corruption and polished his image, working miners' worsening conditions, nonunion mining's steady rise, and benefit programs' slipping solvency condemned his presidency to an inevitable implosion.

As coal production recovered over the ensuing decade, union miners across the nation's coalfields fought to overcome the legacy of recent organizing failures. Increasingly, nonunion mines not only undercut UMWA markets, but the booming workforces organizers approached contained a significant minority of miners describable as "unorganized" only through the word's most literal meaning in the past tense. Such men who had tried to make collective bargaining work and learned hard lessons from defeat did not easily forget what had often been transformative and traumatic life experiences. Winning these ex-members back, and countering their influence within expanded workforces, would require a tremendous commitment of resources and talent. While a series of escalating national contract strikes further strained relations between union and nonunion miners, an unprecedented membership revolt gave the UMWA an opportunity to revise its strategy. If, at its best, Miners for Democracy demonstrates rank-and-file democracy's potential to revive an ailing labor union, its failures also expose the limitations of such a dream.

CHAPTER 5

Carbon County, USA

Utah's coal reserves have been estimated at 27.8 billion tons, with 13.9 billion easily recoverable. If Utahans mined six million tons a year, the state's coal would last over 2,300 years.

—Governor Calvin L. Rampton, 1975

IN 1969, UMWA DISSIDENTS and liberal supporters coalesced around the presidential candidacy of District 5 IEB member Joseph A. "Jock" Yablonski. In a December 9 election characterized by widespread fraud, he won a significant 46,736 votes compared to W. A. "Tony" Boyle's 80,751. As Yablonski, his wife, and their twenty-five-year-old daughter Charlotte spent the Christmas holidays at home taking a much-needed rest from preparations to contest the election, three strangers from Ohio appeared in Clarksville, Pennsylvania, and began nervously and systematically studying the outspoken former candidate's home. Well fortified with alcohol on the night of December 31, the trio sliced Yablonski's phone line, took a screen door off its frame, and removed their shoes before tip-toeing upstairs with a .38 caliber pistol and a .30 caliber M-1 rifle. Awakened by a pair of shots, Mrs. Yablonski woke up screaming while her husband fumbled in the dark, too late, for a nearby shotgun. Moments later, the killers exited the same way they had come, undisturbed by a family dog they had earlier befriended.[1]

"What Are You Doing Here In The Upper Areas?"

FIGURE 5.1: Political cartoons, reprinted in MFD's newsletter *The Miners' Voice*, satirized an increasingly distant UMWA hierarchy. A 1969 Herblock cartoon, © The Herb Block Foundation.

Amateurishly, Paul Gilly, Claude Vealey, and Aubran Martin left a slew of fingerprints throughout the house and were quickly apprehended. Gilly's wife, Lucy, and Vealey began talking first. They told a federal district attorney about the $5,200 they had been paid for the assassinations, and who had acquired it for them. More than any tonnage statistics, organizing setbacks, lifestyle largess, or gaffe comments before the media, the Yablonski murders demonstrated the naked criminality of the Boyle regime, the depths to which it was prepared to go to maintain power, and, for millions of readers who followed the story as it made national headlines, the unrecognizable distance bureaucratization had taken labor unions from their roots in the heroic past.

As police investigators linked the murders back to the UMWA's highest levels, Yablonski's friends and supporters organized the MFD movement the following April to carry on the work the fallen reformer had begun.[2] After they convinced the Labor Department to supervise a rerun of the election in 1972, MFD's rank-and-file slate of Arnold Miller for president, Mike Trbovich for vice president, and Harry Patrick for secretary-treasurer won by 70,373 votes to 56,334.[3] As the first slate of working miners elected to these offices in over half a century, their victory represented the most serious and successful attempt to democratize a major American labor union during the 1970s–or any time since. Shortly afterward, a federal court found Tony Boyle, District 19 secretary-treasurer Albert Pass, and field representative William Prater guilty of orchestrating the Yablonski murders. They spent the rest of their lives in prison.

Although in 1969 no organized Yablonski campaign existed in Utah, far from being solid "Boyle County," coal miners here shared many of the concerns of eastern miners and participated actively in the reform process. Yet while reformers gained ground nationally, an uncommonly restrictive nominating procedure in District 22's constitution facilitated the persistence of district officers hostile to reform until 1977. These leaders' performance during key events, their opposition to Miller's agenda as administrators and IEB members, and the inability of rank-and-file activists or Miller himself to solve the crises of an increasingly divided union sharply curtailed the options available to any subsequent union official. After reformers won District 22's election on March 12, 1977, the issues they faced were in many ways more daunting than those which confronted Miller four and a half years earlier. Through their experience, MFD illustrates both the potential and the limits of democratization alone to revitalize an American labor movement.

Indicative of mounting dissatisfaction, Utah miners' growing concerns about their union's functioning is perhaps best preserved in their direct appeals to International presidents. As in the East, those who fell through the cracks of benefit and safety programs had the strongest reasons for writing. Twice in 1971, Mrs. John Henderson of Dragerton wrote on behalf of her disabled fifty-six-year-old son, Gladwyn, who had still not received a pension two years after submitting paperwork that documented a thirty-three-year career in mining. Her father had been a UMWA member since 1902, and his brother had helped bring the union into Utah. In response, Boyle's assistant, Gerald Griffiths, promised to forward the inquiry to Fund managers, yet he checked Mrs. Henderson's optimism with a formulaic sentence repeated to thousands of denied claimants: "[As you know] benefit eligibility must be determined by the Fund under its governing rules and regulations since the Fund has always been a separate entity from the union." With no recognition of irony, he also noted the fifty-year service pin recently awarded to her husband and communicated Boyle's "warm compliments" and "every good wish" for "an honor he so richly deserves after being a member of this union for so many years."[4]

Other veteran miners, and often friends and family members writing on their behalf, similarly protested Fund managers' apparent indifference to years of work and dedicated union membership. Seventy-year-old retiree and Columbia Local 6089 charter member J. Lorin Winn protested his exclusion from a pension, and provided references for twenty-six years of work in union mines.[5] Julian M. Paiz penned a "letter of inquiry and of gross injustice in the denial of the pension, small as it may be, to Mr. Martin Smolich . . . [who] had his back smashed in the mine at Peerless, Utah, and had to wear steel braces all the time for three years before he could take them off at all."[6] Clorinda Cordova demanded of Boyle: "My father has always been a union man and very faithful for all the 35 years he worked in the coal mines and I would be very interested to know how anyone can justify denying him his benefits."[7]

In 1971, Don Logston lamented the gaps in Fund coverage: "Although I have twenty-five years in the mine I am not old enough to receive the miners pension, therefor [sic] after one year my benefits under the Welfare Fund were terminated. . . . I will never again be able to work . . . and I cannot buy any medical insurance, I've tried but no insurance will sell." While Logston supported Boyle's congressional testimony in favor

FIGURES 5.2 AND 5.3: In May 1969, International president Tony Boyle characteristically addresses a District 17 convention underneath a giant hanging portrait of himself. And again, from another angle *(below)*. Used with permission from the Eberly Family Special Collections Library, Pennsylvania State University Libraries.

of expanding Medicaid, he included a potentially threatening proposal: "I wish to ask you if you thought that a petition signed by every coal miner in District 22 would help your stand I and several other disabled coal miners could get this petition signed and we could send it to you." As the principle defendant in disabled miners' and widows' soon-to-be successful *Blankenship v. Boyle* lawsuit, and having recently had his evasion to retirees' protests confronted by a wildcat strike of forty thousand miners led by the same, Boyle balked at Logston's suggestion of grassroots mobilization to instead recommend that "you contact your neighbors, friends and relatives and request them to write letters to Utah's congressmen . . . and ask them to support our bills."[8]

Nonunion coal's proliferation concerned many members as well. As discussed in the previous chapter, despite organizers' best attempts to maintain UMWA control over a majority of the nation's tonnage, little frank discussion of the obstacles these organizers faced ever made it to the general membership's attention. Thus, apparently unaware of the progress of ongoing campaigns, in 1968 Castle Gate Local 5916 recording secretary R. H. Tweddell decried that "apparently very little effort is being put forth" to organize Plateau and Swisher Coal and wrote the International directly for an update. In addition, he said, "We have inquired about progress toward organizing the mine in Salina Canyon but cannot seem to get any definite information concerning this property." Geneva Steel widow Mary G. Lopez raised two other concerns when she asked Boyle if remarrying would alter her benefits payments, and if a survivor's benefit for Black Lung existed. Though he had died in a mining accident, she related, "If my husband was here to speak for himself his cough wouldn't have let him do it."[9]

While for years the International had responded to such questions individually, growing discontent with benefit cutbacks forced District 22 president Frank M. Stevenson to field criticism in increasingly public forums. As Plateau mine owner Wayne Baker circulated a 1968 *Wall Street Journal* article that described gaps in Fund coverage among his pro-UMWA employees, Fund managers hurriedly responded that "there is meticulous machinery for examining applications for benefits, and [an] elaborate appeal[s] mechanism exist[s]. . . . This is really big business, and it requires a special kind of experience, knowledge, and dedication to serve as trustee and administrator." As for the Disabled Miners and Widows of West Virginia, "there are only a handful of members in reality, in spite of the noise they have been able to generate. They are led by some 'cute' lawyers very savvy about public relations if not the law."[10]

In campaign materials for the 1969 and 1972 elections, Boyle's supporters evaded such concerns with an ominous baiting of "outsiders." Thus, the District 22 Committee to Elect Tony Boyle and Slate framed its struggle as one to "protect the UMWA from distruction [sic] by outsiders" who "are strong forces out to destroy your Union." While "TONY BOYLE is reputed to be the shrewdest and smartest contract negotiator in the nation," the Miller Team "will have lawyers do this for them." In another advertisement the committee denounced "Arnold Miller and his lawyer advisors." Additionally, this body used red-baiting and race-baiting, as in late November when it "informed" its audience that at the district office, MFD's two observers read "material from Moa [sic] Tse Tung, The Black Panthers and H. Rap Brown."[11]

Not so easily dismissed, however, are Boyle's rank-and-file supporters' letters. These suggest the legitimate fears many had of gambling an imperfect present on the outcome of a less certain future, as well as the super-human image of his own abilities Boyle had long projected. As "A Greatful [sic] Coal Miner's Wife of Darrell Norton" argued in a letter to the *Sun Advocate*,

> All I can say is thank God for Tony Boyle and the dedicated officers of the United Mine Workers of America. No honest coal miner can say truthfully that they have been hurt by the union, but if Tony Boyle gets defeated in this election anything can happen and God pity us all.
>
> There isn't anyone I know that wouldn't like to have the medical Insurance the United Mine workers have in times of illness, and now thanks to the efforts of the Union Officers a coal miner who has contracted the terrible disease Black Lung from working underground breathing in foul air can be compensated.
>
> We know what we have now. Many people all over the nation are enjoying the fruits of our efforts, but no one knows or could possibly promise any better than we have now, so don't turn your backs on the officers that have your interest at heart or maybe you may find that you are biting the hand that is feeding you, and, then it will be too late.[12]

While the *Helper Journal* denied any space to critics as it covered the Boyle campaign, from 1969 to 1972 the more balanced *Sun Advocate* printed eleven articles that raised serious questions about the union's internal functioning. Topics covered in these articles included increasingly restrictive Fund qualifications, the manipulative orchestration of the 1969 election, the illegal use of the *United Mine Workers Journal* to campaign that year, Boyle's connection to the Yablonski murders, and his embezzlement of union funds.[13]

By 1970, speakers at the union's most public events—annual Labor Day celebrations in Price and Helper—denounced the "threats against the solidarity of the union." The following year, "Mr. Stevenson called for unity among the United Mine Workers in standing behind [Boyle] and the other international officers," while another speaker warned, "The United Mine Workers of America is being attacked in the courts of our nation's capital." Amid MFD's 1972 progress, Boyle assigned District 14 president Henry Allai to address the celebration. According to the *Sun Advocate*, Mr. Allai denounced Boyle's opponents with little nuance: "'Vote for your friends—Defeat your enemies.' This was the theme of the Labor Day message."[14] However, by then Boyle no longer controlled members' information administratively. In July a federal court ordered the union to allow an MFD editor to arrange half the content of *United Mine Workers' Journal*. Henceforth, the message of reformers entered the living room of every union miner in the country. According to Frank Sacco, its revelations "hit miners and their families like a thunderbolt from heaven." By September, the campaign's headquarters had received about seventy-five letters of inquiry from miners in western states.[15]

Frank Sacco's political trajectory parallels that of most MFD leaders, who had publicly supported Boyle for years only to become increasingly disillusioned by the late 1960s. When in 1964 maverick "Cadillac" Steve Kochis reached out to District 22's largest local in an ephemeral bid to challenge Boyle, Sacco's response embodied historian Curtis Seltzer's observation of a "political culture [that] has always fostered organizational loyalty."[16] To Sacco, Kochis's modest platform—"it is time we elected a new president and put the union back in the hands of our membership"—was "an insult to our president." Rather, he argued, "President Boyle was brought up and schooled by the greatest labor leader the world has ever known, John L. Lewis.... The Leadership of Boyle... is our guarantee that our membership will continue to have its rights and privlidges [*sic*].... [O]utstanding men cannot be replaced."[17] At one Kaiser local meeting in these years, he argued against an opponent who dared to modestly suggest that "it was a healthy situation to have others running against our International Officers." In 1969, Sacco, Stevenson, and International representative Frank Roybal Sr. conspired suspiciously with Boyle to wrangle control over the Horse Canyon miners' ballot box from Local 8003 vice president Edwin Alberts, who had unreliably expressed a "bitter attitude" toward Boyle. While Sacco increasingly criticized President Stevenson's performance, in 1970 he assured Boyle that his concerns remained publicly muted "because of the long standing relationship that you and I have had and of my true loyalty to you and this union."[18]

In a 1967 speech to SUFCO miners, Sacco shared a more nuanced view, admitting that "almost everything that could happen to a human being or a human institution has happened to this union.... [W]e may have some problems down here. I have some evidence of this; but I want you to understand that we can't solve these problems [by] merely being cynical about them or merely by talking about them amongst yourselves."[19] While he shared the podium and quietly listened to the 1971 Labor Day message, by 1972 he remained silent no longer. In the last week of July, Sacco penned a letter of resignation not only to District 22 and President Boyle but to the *Sun Advocate* as well. In a rare move for any union officer, he explained his return to driving trucks at Kaiser Steel, which

> I am confident will provide me with peace of mind, tranquility and solace.... I have been unable to enjoy of late as a representative of the United Mine Workers of America... in view of the sweetheart contracts negotiated in District 27 in derogation of working miners' interests... and other incidences of harassments and reprisals, I find that I can no longer have any interest and in good conscience, can no longer perform my duties.[20]

By resigning his position, Sacco leant the movement a much-needed boost of authority. Now as a rank-and-file member, he became "the chief local MFD organizer in Utah."[21] Sacco began working closely with John

Kuzio, a young Pennsylvania miner MFD sent to District 22 as its representative and observer in Price. By early August, the two had established contacts with about "half a dozen" allies.

One of the first to support MFD, Horse Canyon miner Carl Norton of Wellington had a wider social network than most. Employed there since 1945, Norton was also an elder in the LDS Church, a former commander of the American Legion, a three-term Wellington city councilman, and tied by marriage to Carbon County's large Greek community. Norton had supported Yablonski in 1969, and with Kuzio now began building the movement's profile through evening visits with acquaintances he knew to have similar concerns. At Hiawatha, Bill Jones of Ferron had grown up in Emery County and also began mining during World War II. In September he estimated that 70 percent of the men at his mine "will go to Miller with a little prodding," and began distributing MFD campaign materials at work. And like many coal miners' wives and daughters, Mrs. Frank Feichko of Price was appalled at retired and disabled miners' arbitrary treatment. After a two-hour discussion with Kuzio in August, she pledged that "she would hit all the stumps and soap boxes—if she talks to one man or a hundred men (miners) she is going to do it."[22]

Five days after Sacco resigned, District 22 began holding nomination meetings. By late August, three locals nominated Miller and eighteen nominated Boyle.[23] To expose Utah miners to the national movement, MFD activists organized a rally at the College of Eastern Utah for Saturday evening, September 9. Here, Yablonski's son and attorney Joseph "Chip" Yablonski and MFD candidate Harry Patrick spoke during their tour of western districts. Patrick advocated for contract ratification by rank-and-file vote, district autonomy, health and safety enforcement, a pension increase, reduction of officers' salaries, and increased western organizing. He also contrasted disabled miners' and widows' eligibility cuts with the revelation that "every man who is an international or district officer will retire on at least four times the rate as the rank and file miner." Of the assassination of his father, mother, and sister, Yablonski dryly added, "It's pretty clear right now who financed it, and if you want to put a murderer back in office it's your privilege."[24]

The meeting attracted a crowd of eighty, mostly working miners. This may have discouraged some organizers, who Price native and historian

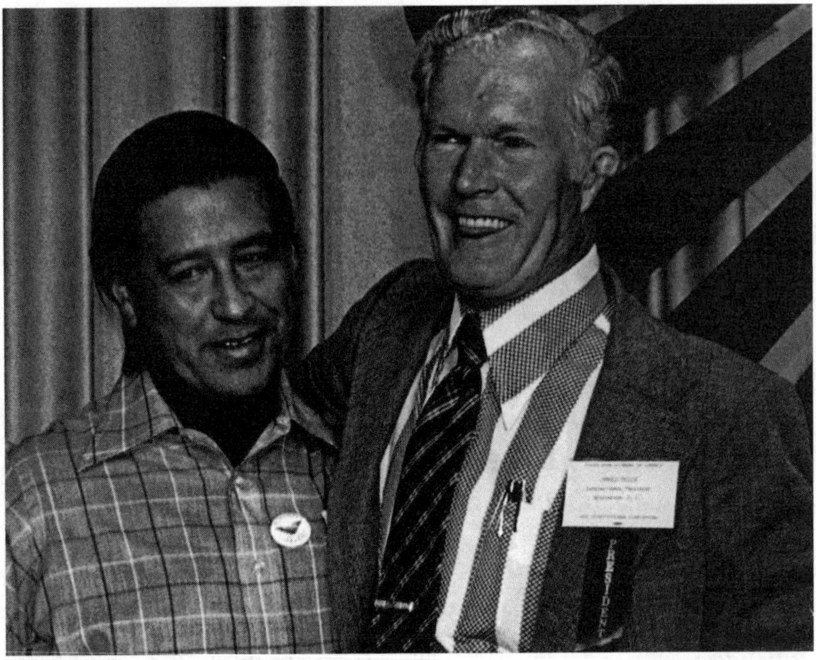

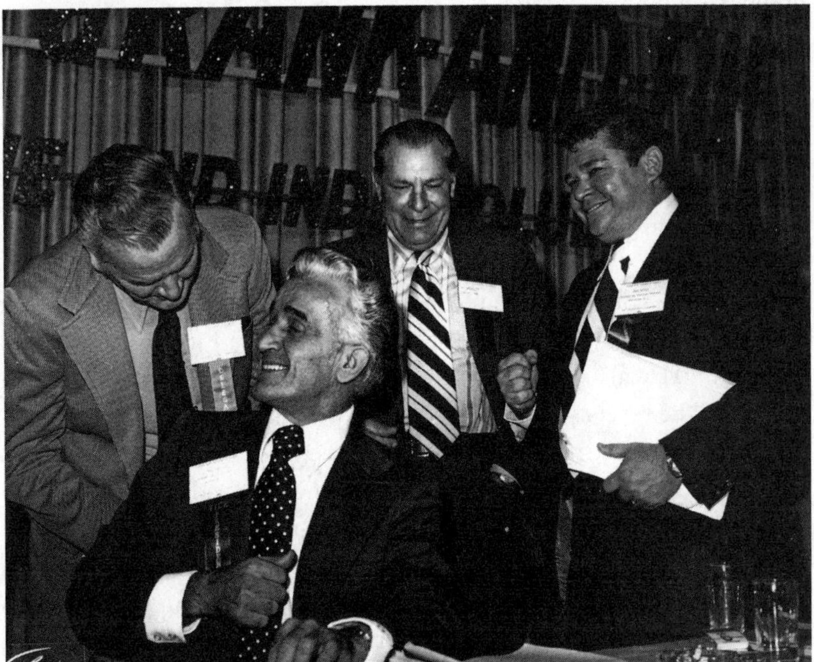

FIGURE 5.4. *Opposite*, at the 1973 UMWA national convention, Miners for Democracy's victorious presidential candidate Arnold Miller introduces guest speaker Caesar Chavez *(above)*, and shares a laugh with fellow reform officers Mike Trbovich (vice president, seated) and Harry Patrick (secretary-treasurer, *far right*). The convention rewrote the union's constitution into the most democratic of any major American labor union and demonstrated an unprecedented spirit of optimism and inclusiveness. Used with permission from the Eberly Family Special Collections Library, Pennsylvania State University Libraries.

Richard Jensen noted had "expected a capacity crowd of 1,000 people."[25] However, the rally appears to have energized several attendees, whose letters to the editor initiated an unprecedented debate in the pages of the *Sun Advocate*. From September 7 until the paper closed the debate on November 23—"pending the raising of any new issues"—eight supportive letters appeared. As in the East, disabled miners, miners' wives, and miners' widows spoke out first. The opening letter, by An Enraged Coal Miner's Wife reveals through its anonymity the strength of historic pressure against internal union dissent. Its writer denounced the fund's arbitrary eligibility criteria and poor investment record, as well as Boyle's weakness on safety, and challenged the innuendo against "outsiders" and lawyers by asserting her ties to the coal industry and revealing that Boyle had hired lawyers from a firm that represented coal operators. A Disgruntled Pensioner also refused to sign his name to a favorable report of the MFD rally "because I know that Frank Stevenson will have my pension cut off." A UMWA member for the Miller Slate added a denouncement of Boyle's effective subversion of nominal district autonomy:

> In District 22 Tony Boyle has quietly eliminated three elective offices and has controlled the election of District 22 president by making pay rollers out of the opposition—as a result—Dist 22 has one Boyle man holding four elective positions on two pay rolls with a salary of $23,000 per year plus more than $1,000 per month expenses. The record shows and proves that Boyle has quietly destroyed autonomy in Dist. 22 which Boyle claims exists—Boyle is a real phony and should be removed as President of the International Union.[26]

Don Logston, however, wrote twice under his own name. While he had earlier appealed to Boyle personally for redress, he now denounced sweetheart contracts, Fund mismanagement, and the mounting evidence of internal criminality to a community audience.[27]

On October 28, Boyle himself spoke on a campaign stop before an audience of three hundred at Carbon High School. Here he denounced the "propaganda" of "outsiders," and warned that Miller's team was "going to take over the union, waste your assets, and destroy your union welfare fund." In its final preelection advertisements "The Pro-Union Team" repeated its superior executive experience.[28]

On December 1 and 2, members of Utah's fourteen locals cast ballots in silent rooms as Labor Department and MFD observers looked on. Nationally, Miners for Democracy's slate won with 70,373 to Boyle's 56,334 votes. In District 22, 1,251 voted for Boyle and 909 for Miller, with the latter winning majorities in eight of twenty-seven locals. Taking 42 percent of the District 22 vote (43 percent in Utah), Miller's showing demonstrates a substantial rise in support from the early days of the campaign, and a major increase from Yablonski's weak, if dubiously accurate, showing of 5 percent in 1969.[29]

Compared to Utah, MFD supporters appear to have had weaker prospects in neighboring western states. In the Pacific Northwest, few links appear to have been made with Canadian miners in British Columbia or Alberta. Nearby, Washington State's coal industry had almost totally collapsed, and while some miners complained of trouble getting Black Lung benefits and arbitrary exclusions from pensions, two supporters reported that "Sam Nichols, District 10 President, has shown at local meetings [that] his sheer presence intimidates potential MFD supporters from Speaking Out." By September, no formal reform movement had yet coalesced, and in 1972 MFD's observers were a pair of sympathetic health care workers (and union members) from Seattle.[30]

At the center of District 27, Montana's union miners were similarly weak. Most locals consisted almost entirely of pensioners, while newer strip mines in southeast Montana remained largely unorganized. Though a handful of veteran members contacted MFD, few publicly supported the movement. West Virginia journalist Tim Cogan served as district observer, where he noted an atmosphere of intimidation in nomination meetings. At one local, "No Miners for Democracy candidate is nominated. The Boyle slate wins without a vote. Outside of the local president and [district president R. J. "Dick"] Boyle, no local member has made a sound. The meeting sets a new District 27 speed record: 12 minutes." At another:

> The actual voting moves in super-slow motion, as it wears on and on, it becomes clear that these men do not understand the voting procedure, do not understand that Boyle has already won by acclamation. Some of these men worked for sixty years in the mines. Once rugged men, the backbone of the most militant union in the land, they are now docile, confused, afraid. Living so long under autocratic rule, they have not the habits of exercising their democratic rights. Even when safeguarded by a neutral Department of Labor.[31]

At least three locals, however, nominated the Miller slate. As Cogan noted, individual miners who stood up to break the ice made a significant difference: "Every time a miner has had the courage to stand and place that slate in nomination, every time there has been a head-to-head battle between Tony Boyle and Arnold Miller, every time Arnold Miller has won."[32]

Elsewhere in District 22, supporters were far more geographically isolated from one another. In Arizona, a handful of retirees living in Phoenix and some sympathetic liberal organizations contacted MFD, but few links appear to have been initially made with working miners at Black Mesa's strip mines. In October, however, Kuzio began working with John Mix Sr., who campaigned in Kayenta. Wyoming miners' participation was similarly limited, though men at Amax Coal's strip mine in Gillette were interested enough to hold a special meeting to read an MFD outreach letter on August 3, 1972. MFD's own ambiguous attitude toward strip mining, however, might have given these men additional pause. Privately, many of its leaders agreed with *Miners Voice* editor Don Stillman, who in an exchange with Dine Researchers—a Navajo group opposed to strip mining—shared that "we would like to see all strip mining abolished and are working to that end."[33] Publicly, however, Miller noted that "Western miners face the same problems Eastern miners do," and appealed for "Equality of union brothers." Despite this effort, tensions between strip and underground miners probably weakened the movement's appeal.[34]

Colorado gave MFD the second-most western support and carried District 15 for Miller in 1972. Yet unlike Utah coal mining's concentration, the

Rocky Mountains fragmented coal communities across four corners of a geographic uplift. The oldest southern coalfields lay almost four hundred miles from recent growth in northwest Colorado near Craig. The Somerset region, in the central-western slope, and Nucla, in the far southwest, remained over a hundred miles apart as well. While the union's traditional base was hit hard by industry restructuring, Colorado Fuel and Iron's four-hundred-man Allen Mine at Weston supported MFD, nominated its slate, and warmly welcomed Harry Patrick and Chip Yablonski when they spoke in Trinidad. In northwest Colorado the campaign developed its largest number of contacts, where it won one nomination election and barely lost a few others. Only in the Paonia-Somerset region and New Mexico did support appear largely absent.[35] In New Mexico, Kaiser's underground miners near Raton largely supported Boyle while strip miners in the western part of the state remained mostly nonunion.

Upon taking office, the situation facing Miller's Administration has been compared to that of the French after Napoleon, the Spanish after Franco, and, more recently, the fledgling democracies that sprang out of the Arab Spring. Miller may have underestimated the struggle ahead when, with most MFD activists' support, he dismantled the organization after regional elections in most districts the following summer. As District 5's newly elected reform president Louis Antal optimistically summarized, "The need for MFD has ceased to exist and we now must devote our time to rejuvenating the union that we all want to serve and improve."[36] While most activists desired to quickly heal the rift within their union, several scholarly observers have identified MFD's formal disillusion as a mistake that deprived reformers of an important organizational vehicle.[37]

At the International level, the 1972 election brought about the swiftest changes. As he took office, Miller cut his own salary from Boyle's princely $50,000 per year with a $25 per diem (totaling approximately $359,000 in 2018 dollars) to $25,000 per year with no per diem. Former officers' family members who worked in highly paid positions of questionable value were fired, and Miller similarly reduced the salaries of other officers, legal counsel, and the International staff. Signaling the end of an era, the Washington, DC, headquarters' Cadillacs were auctioned off. Under Don Stillman's editorship, the *Journal* transformed from a fawning propaganda organ with minimal member input to an award-winning publication. During the December 1973 International convention in Pittsburgh, members rewrote the UMWA constitution into the most democratic of any major American labor union. At least one ambitious policy plank died a rapid death, however, as talk of moving the International headquarters from Washington "back to the coalfields" ceased soon after the new administration discovered the value of maintaining its presence in the nation's capital city.[38]

Contractually, the new administration's greatest chance to revise the terms under which miners worked came during the November 1974 UMWA-BCOA negotiations. After union members struck for twenty-four days, for the first time in their history they exercised an unprecedented right to read the proposed contract's terms before voting to approve or reject it. Notably, this contract added a week of paid sick leave, a sickness and accident benefit plan, a pension increase, an increase in the number of paid days off from twenty to thirty, a cost-of-living escalator, and improved job bidding. With additional helpers mandated on equipment, increased safety training, and recognition of miners' right to withdraw from hazardous areas, at the time of its passage it was viewed as the best in the union's history. However, it also contained some notable limitations. The contract contained no right-to-strike provision, which many hoped would reduce the threat of lawsuits. An additional grievance step failed to empower miners, and only further increased negotiators' case backlog. Perhaps most importantly, the Welfare and Retirement Fund now separated into four distinct Health and Retirement Funds, with different benefits for miners who retired in different years.[39]

While coal's recovery put the industry in a greater position to pay expanded benefits, and rapid growth gave miners more confidence to strike, the union probably lost its best opportunity to win two of MFD's principle goals at this time. In 1969, Yablonski had promised to demand "a substantial increase to the 40 cent per ton royalty" that had been unchanged since 1952. He also hoped to alter grievance procedures "in order to create stability in the industry . . . restore confidence of the membership in the union and eliminate the unjustified discharges of large number of miners and the prolonged work stoppages which result therefrom." While in 1974 Miller hoped a militant strike could force coal companies to pay a higher royalty, members voted to return to work before BCOA negotiators budged. And instead of returning stability to the coalfields, his grievance procedure led many to view wildcat strikes as more effective to immediately resolving disagreements. While a shortage of experienced miners left companies reluctant to fire every militant, International leaders paid heavy fines while hurriedly ordering miners back to work. As such strikes proliferated, they proved so damaging to union finances—and Miller's rapport with the rank-and-file—that some critics concluded coal companies were even provoking them on purpose.[40]

In the West, two specific conditions tempered many miners' enthusiasm for the early Miller administration. First, Miller personally opposed strip mining from an environmental standpoint.[41] Second, his first regional initiative attempted to merge four districts covering eight western states into an enlarged "District 22" with offices in Denver. While this would have saved the cost of keeping multiple offices open for the benefit of only 6,755 working and retired members, these savings might have been offset by the higher costs of district officers' travel. Probably even more important, as Local 9958 president and Miller supporter Harold L. Alger predicted, "The miner, for whose benefit the Union is supposed to exist, will work at the will of the company for months—even years, while his case follows the contractual settlement of disputes procedure all over the country." To a four-man commission sent to poll their views, Utah miners similarly related "the disorganization[,] delays[,] and excessive expense of a distant office" during the years all district officers worked out of Rock Springs, Wyoming.[42]

During the summer of 1973, Millers' delegates Rich Bank and Bernie Anderson held a series of regional meetings to present the merger proposal and record members' concerns. Unfortunately, they were unable to report on the mood of northwest Colorado's strip miners where coal production was expanding the fastest: "Because of a security problem on August 24th, the remaining schedule was altered. . . . [M]eetings set for Aug 25 in Hayden and Aug 26 in Steamboat Springs were cancelled." At Lafayette, near Boulder along the Front Range's Denver Basin coalfields, members shared "considerable concern about the need to organize new, non-UMW miners opening up in the West. The Operating Engineers . . . were seen as a principal threat to the UMW." Members here also asked whether wage scales at strip mines could be raised to meet the slightly higher pay nonunion properties were then offering.[43]

As the healthiest center of underground coal mining left in Colorado, the Somerset region along the North Fork of the Gunnison River was of particular importance to the UMWA. In late October 1972, Arnold Miller had noted it was the only major coal region in the district where no MFD campaign had yet been organized. When Bank and Anderson arrived there that August, they were particularly eager to improve relations. Unfortunately, their meeting in Paonia got off to a rocky start. When, contrary to their expectations, miners discovered that Miller himself had not arrived with the commission, Bear Coal's local union president Don Morrow, who chaired the meeting, "gave . . . no support at all and left it up to the floor to decide if the meeting should continue. A majority of those present indicated that they wanted to hear from us, though a significant minority preferred to walk out." Of those who stayed, many expressed dissatisfaction with District 15's IEB member Arthur Biggs, who remained in power as a Boyle appointee and now worked with the Miller Administration out of either rekindled altruism or personal opportunism. Paonia miners felt that "the [disinterested] service they have received from Biggs," long inaccessible from his Denver office, was "an example of the service they can expect from the new merged district." They lamented few visits, slow grievance processing, and organizing's unclear and mysterious pace. While Miller leaned on Biggs for stability during the administrative transition, Bank and Anderson concluded "the 200 men at the Paonia meeting were good, tough UMW men who have legitimate grievances and concerns. . . . Unless the present deep-seated grievances among western miners are relieved, organizing efforts in the West will be doomed to failure. . . . [W]ithout the full support and cooperation of the local miners, it is unlikely that the UMW will be able to mount a sustained organizing drive in the west." While Miller shifted after hearing miners' concerns, and dropped the merger proposal after members rejected it in a September 1, 1973, referendum, each damaged his image and provided ammunition to his opponents.[44]

Upon taking office in December 1972, Miller fired the twenty IEB members—including Frank M. Stevenson—whom Boyle had unconstitutionally appointed. Reflecting a cost-saving response to mine closures as well as the decline of membership democracy, Stevenson was one of seven leaders in the union's twenty-five districts who simultaneously held the positions of IEB member, district president, and district secretary-treasurer.[45] To keep the union functioning until new elections could be held, Miller appointed Frank Sacco as International representative and acting secretary-treasurer, and Wellington coal washer plant Local 1206 officer Louie Kosec as acting IEB member. Keeping the presidential seat he won in the 1965 election, Stevenson challenged these appointments in federal district court.[46] His relationship with Sacco continued to deteriorate, and in March 1973 Stevenson refused to let him examine the union's books until he heard from his attorney. In response, Sacco refused to issue Stevenson a paycheck. In June, a court decision allowed Stevenson to hold the positions of president and secretary-treasurer simultaneously.[47]

On December 11, 1973, Utah miners had their first chance in eleven years to elect representatives to all three District 22 positions. While he had avoided joining Sacco in early public support for the movement, former International representative and Horse Canyon Local 8003 president Frank Roybal Sr. opposed Stevenson for the IEB seat while Kaiser Local 9958 president Harold Alger challenged Stevenson's ally, H. A. Browning, for district president. While Roybal's three nominations represented 38 percent of District 22's membership, neither his nor Alger's names appeared on the actual election ballot, as rules established in 1953 still required any candidate to secure a minimum of five nominations. In the intervening years of coal mining's contraction, District 22 declined from twenty-six to sixteen locals, and the five-nomination requirement matched the most restrictive of any UMWA district. Unintentionally, the western merger initiative delayed a district constitutional convention until August 1974, at which time delegates liberalized the nomination process. Meanwhile, in 1973 only one candidate's name appeared for two of three executive offices, which forced miners to elect the "uncontested" Stevenson and Brownfield, as well as Andrew J. Smith for secretary-treasurer and William J. Crissman for subdistrict board member. While Miller's principled support for district autonomy led him to abstain from intervention in the 1973 elections, the limited resources available to reform candidates led to their success in only eight districts. In seven others, members elected IEB members at least somewhat hostile to Miller.[48]

Contesting his exclusion, Roybal immediately protested the election's restrictive orchestration as well as Stevenson's use of incumbency's advantages. As district board members admitted to a conflict of interest, Roybal appealed to the International.[49] In early April 1974, Miller brought the case to an IEB hearing. While the board sided against Roybal, his visit to Washington, DC, allowed him to strengthen his political relationship with Miller, and to bring back to his membership "a true message ... a lot different from the picture that had been painted to our people by our District Officers."[50]

Simultaneously, Roybal employed another tool available to union dissidents, the Labor-Management Reporting and Disclosure Act of 1959. Better known by the names of its congressional sponsors, section (e) of Title IV of the Landrum-Griffin Act forbids unions from denying candidates a "reasonable opportunity" to be nominated in internal elections. Designed to combat union corruption, this law provides legal tools for internal challengers but no enforcement mechanism outside of federal courts. Unfortunately, Roybal's attempt to use the act is a textbook case in labor law's lethargic and frustrating pace.[51]

In early 1974, Roybal brought his case to the Department of Labor. Although on May 13 the department's acting chief, Branch of Elections and Trusteeships, John N. Niswander issued a supportive opinion, pretrial hearings did not begin until July 15 and oral arguments were not heard until November 7.[52] On January 21, 1975, the department brought *Dunlop v. District 22 United Mine Workers of America* to court, and on April 1, federal district judge Aldon J. Anderson instructed both parties to file additional memoranda. It was not until July 22 that Anderson agreed with Roybal and instructed the secretary of labor to organize a new election "as soon as practicable."[53] Still in office, Stevenson appealed this decision to the Tenth Circuit Court in Denver which upheld the lower ruling. Finally, from January 14 through 16, 1976, members were allowed to choose between both candidates, and elected Roybal with 1,056 votes against Stevenson's 984. Clinging to power, Stevenson challenged *this* election, which prevented Roybal from taking office until Anderson dismissed his suit six months later. Finally, on July 16, 1976, Roybal took office. Eight months later, a separately filed case secured a new election for the remaining four district positions.[54]

Though western coal was responsible for only 5 percent of national tonnage in 1969, Miller's administration recognized its growing importance and made its organization a priority. MFD's 1972 platform identified nonunion western coal as a major concern and sympathized with those hesitant to join the UMWA "because these coal miners see the same greed and corruption in our Union that we see." This document posited that under Boyle, the union share of tonnage fell because "so-called 'organizers' in our union are fat and lazy and afraid to sit down with these non-union miners and convince them of the benefits of being union" and envisioned that "modern organizing techniques by men who mine coal, not by porkchoppers who haven't been in the pits for 30 or 40 years, will be employed." This assessment probably gave organizers of that period too little credit, and furthermore underestimated the difficulty of their tasks. Not only did Miller rely on several individuals left over from the Boyle era, but his administration ran into identical problems when newly organized operators refused to sign contracts.[55]

As coal's recovery appeared increasingly solid by the early 1970s, many viewed organizing optimistically for the first time in years. In the first Utah drive conducted under reform leadership, in April 1973 Miller-appointed organizers Frank Sacco and Arthur Biggs reported a revived interest among Premium Coal's miners. While those who supported this effort shared much of the optimism captured in Barbara Kopple's film *Harlan County, USA* (1976), unlike the successful strike that began at Kentucky's Brookside Mine that same year, events at Premium were more typical of most organizing trajectories, and left a bitter legacy that cut short many members' hopes for just how easy an organizing revival would be.[56]

With twelve employees producing 141,850 tons a year, Sacco and Biggs's reports noted a continued lack of adequate pension coverage as a significant persisting grievance, with a forty-seven-dollar daily wage slightly less than union averages. At a May 10 NLRB election, miners voted twelve-to-zero to elect the UMWA as their bargaining agent. As the International chartered Local 1909, what appeared to be a victory evaporated on June 7 when the Marinoni family announced they would be closing the mine the next day. While Premium had lost sales in 1972, it never released a financial statement to the union or attempted to bargain—though it did take the precaution of hiring the same antiunion lawyer who had served Wayne Baker and Shirl McArthur just a few years prior.[57]

An equal problem to the UMWA contract may have been a lack of sufficient capital to invest in needed mine improvements, as well as the

TABLE 5.1. UNION ORGANIZATION IN THE BITUMINOUS COAL INDUSTRY
(percent of total employment)

		EAST		WEST		UNITED STATES	
		Underground	Surface	Underground	Surface	Underground	Surface
UNION	United Mine Workers of America	88.0	42.8	73.3	35.5	87.4	41.5
	Operating Engineers				16.9		3.3
	International Brotherhood of Electrical Workers				11.5		2.2
	Southern Labor Union	1.3	1.0			1.3	0.7
	Progressive Mine Workers	0.4	1.0		11.3	0.4	2.8
	International Construction Workers Union				0.3		0.1
	Utility Workers of America				1.2		0.9
	Other			7.5	3.8	0.5	0.2
NON-UNION		10.1	55.2	19.1	19.5	10.4	48.3
TOTAL		100.0	100.0	100.0	100.0	100.0	100.0

SOURCE: Mine Enforcement and Safety Administration (MESA) Survey: Union Organization in the Bituminous Coal Industry, November 1977.

increased costs of meeting the 1969 Federal Coal Mine Safety Act's new regulations. Like MFD, this act was a product of the Black Lung movement and prevented many tragedies over subsequent years by requiring additional hiring and safety-related investments. However, this necessarily reduced productivity at all mines, which stressed marginally profitable operations and gave nonunion owners additional incentives to avoid UMWA contracts' added costs. In Utah, North American Coal cited the act as a major factor in its 1972 decision to shut down Castle Gate and Kenilworth, which laid off 240 men. Thus, the Marinonis' hastily posted closure notice read in part that "the increased cost of doing business, attributable in substantial measure to Government regulations and restrictions, cannot be offset by income sufficient to place the company in a profit position."[58]

Internally, an organizing department memorandum estimated that in recent years the mine had realized a profit of approximately sixty-three cents per ton of coal mined, a margin that gives credence to the Marinoni brothers' claim that "the company could not afford the UMWA Welfare and Retirement Fund tonnage royalty payments." As the final summary of organizing activities concluded, perhaps the greatest tragedy of this drive is that neither the union nor the miners ever had a chance to critically evaluate the profit structure for themselves: "It should be stressed again, however, that the company's profit figures may be drastically understated; we don't know, without knowing what the partners were paying themselves." Though the UMWA provided health insurance for six months and a twenty-five-dollar weekly cash benefit to all twelve unemployed miners, Miller acknowledged his organizers' concern that the situation had "really given the union a black eye reputation among nonunion miners in [the] District 22, Price, Utah region."[59]

Demonstratively, Premium miners' eventual support for the UMWA indicates the union's historic stature as well as the favorable opinion much of "the unorganized" still held of its national contract. Though employers preferred avoiding the union through paternalism, most miners saw single-employer benefit plans as inferior. Furthermore, by 1973 comparatively few nonunion miners in the West had experienced the consequences of a failed organizing drive. This allowed the Premium campaign to proceed with an optimistic faith in new leaders' abilities that was harder to come by in later years. Not only did the UMWA have the most to offer at this time, but subsequent overtures to nonunion miners would be interpreted through the setbacks of the early Miller era.

FIGURE 5.5. During the 1970s, organizers across the West struggled to bring union traditions into an era fraught with new obstacles. Despite occasional victories, mounting frustration and significant setbacks became increasingly common. Used with permission from the Eberly Family Special Collections Library, Pennsylvania State University Libraries.

Elsewhere in District 22, a June 1973 contract signed with Rosebud Sales Corporation's 1.6 million-tons-per-year strip mine in Hanna, Wyoming, proved more lasting, and can also be attributed to Sacco and Biggs's talents.[60] Regionally, surface miners at Great National Corporation's Sundance Mine near Gallup, New Mexico; Pittsburgh and Midway's mines at McKinley, New Mexico, and Steamboat Springs, Colorado; North American Coal's Indianhead mine in Zap, North Dakota; and Peabody's second strip mine at Black Mesa, Arizona, joined the UMWA and secured contracts. These successes were eagerly reported in the *Journal*, along with members' editorials and appeals for support.

These victories, however, were overshadowed by western mining's faster expansion, particularly in strip mining. One of the biggest setbacks occurred at Utah International's Navajo strip mine near Farmington, New Mexico. Providing energy for the nearby Four Corners coal-fired power plant, in 1971 it was the largest single producer in the country. After earnestly starting an organizing campaign early in 1973, Miller called the drive off in mid-July. After following many heavy equipment operators from construction into strip-mine employment (and eager to expand its jurisdiction), the International Union of Operating Engineers beat the UMWA to establish itself as sole bargaining representative for the mine's employees. Rather than backing his supporters' efforts to decertify the Operating Engineers and call a new NLRB election, a conciliatory Miller entered high-level talks with his rival, and on July 20 contacted former New Mexican deep miner and recently hired organizer Anthony Mascarenas:

> We both agree that labor has enough to do without fighting each other. We are attempting to hammer out a jurisdictional agreement to our satisfaction, and we feel any continued effort to decertify the IUOE at Navajo would only jeopardize future relations and negotiations.... Although we all obviously wish that our organizing drive at Navajo was a more victorious occasion, I am confident that we have taken some of the first important cuts into the non-UMWA coal production.[61]

While Miller concluded this letter optimistically, a month later staffers Rick Bank and Bernie Aronson concluded their tour of the West with a far more sobering assessment:

> The western districts presently account for 25 million tons of non-UMWA coal and 18 million tons of UMW coal every year. Total western tonnage is expected to rise to a minimum of 300 million tons in the next 17 years. All indications are that the West represents the new developing coalfields in this country. Unless the present deep-seated grievances among western miners are relieved, organizing efforts in the west will be doomed to failure. The present dissatisfaction and disunity among western UMW miners will damage whatever positive image of the UMW we seek to project to non-UMW miners. In addition, without the full support and cooperation of the local miners, it is

FIGURE 5.6. *Opposite*, coal's western boom in one graph. From 1970 to 1977, coal production on federally owned land increased at an average yearly rate of 29.9 percent. Mines in Colorado, Montana, New Mexico, Utah, and Wyoming accounted for 98.5 percent of this total growth. Also indicated here is strip mining's rapid expansion on Navajo lands in northern Arizona. From the President's Commission on Coal, *Coal Data Book*, 1980.

COAL PRODUCTION ON FEDERALLY ADMINISTERED LANDS, 1947-1977

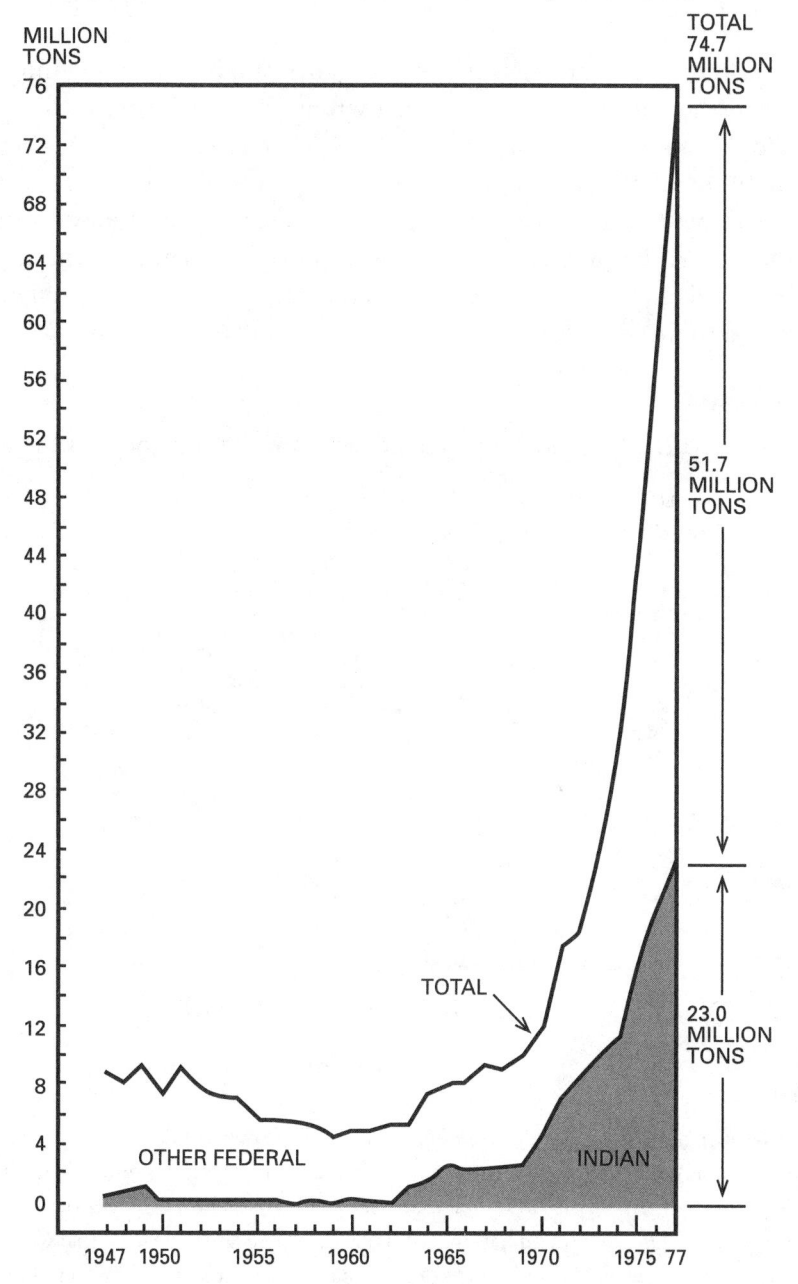

MILLION TONS

TOTAL 74.7 MILLION TONS

51.7 MILLION TONS

23.0 MILLION TONS

TOTAL

OTHER FEDERAL

INDIAN

1947 1950 1955 1960 1965 1970 1975 77

Source: U.S. Geological Survey: Federal and Indian Lands Oil and Gas Production, Royal Income, and Related Statistics

unlikely that the UMW will be able to mount a sustained organizing drive in the West.[62]

Aware of the formerly marginal region's rapidly increasing importance, the following summer Miller wrote a personal letter to all District 22 members that urged unity in support of western organizing.[63] In 1975, International organizing director Tom Pysell reiterated the seriousness of these stakes for *Journal* readers: "As coal moves west, the UMWA has to move with it or we're finished as a union. The companies plan tremendous high production strip mines in the West and if that tonnage isn't produced under UMWA contract our bargaining leverage is down the tube."[64] That January, a strike at fifteen western strip mines won a new pattern contract—the Western Surface Agreement—which the *Journal* predicted would be "a big boost to the ex-

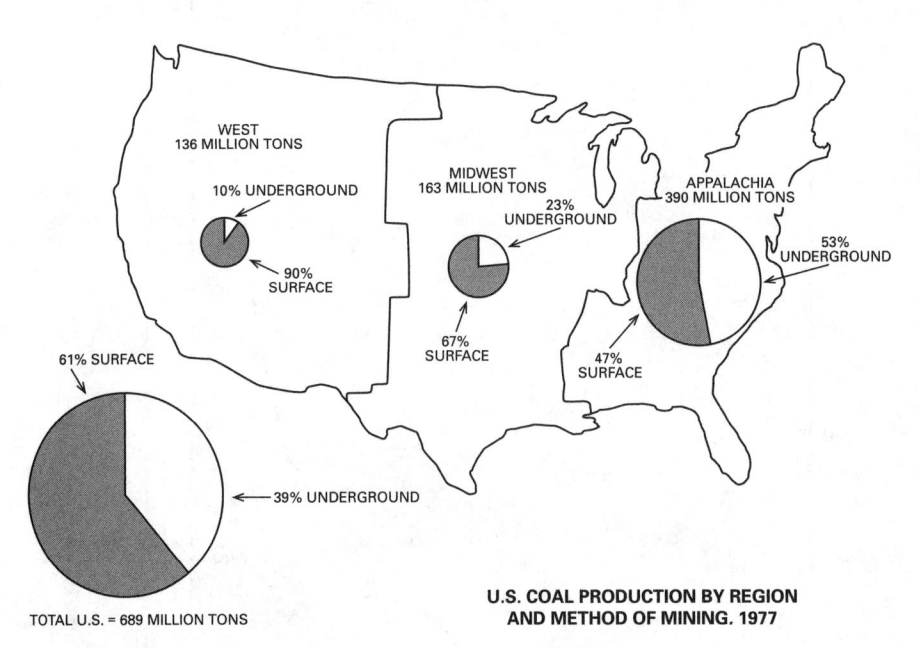

WEST
136 MILLION TONS
10% UNDERGROUND
90% SURFACE

MIDWEST
163 MILLION TONS
23% UNDERGROUND
67% SURFACE

APPALACHIA
390 MILLION TONS
53% UNDERGROUND
47% SURFACE

61% SURFACE
39% UNDERGROUND

TOTAL U.S. = 689 MILLION TONS

U.S. COAL PRODUCTION BY REGION AND METHOD OF MINING. 1977

FIGURES 5.7 AND 5.8. *Above and opposite*, while increased demand led to more coal employment nationally, eastern underground mines' higher production costs left them vulnerable to market fluctuations. As railroad and power-line construction increasingly integrated national coal markets, it became apparent that western strip-mined coal was best poised to dominate the industry's future. From the President's Commission on Coal, *Coal Data Book*, 1980.

SELECTED COAL PRICES

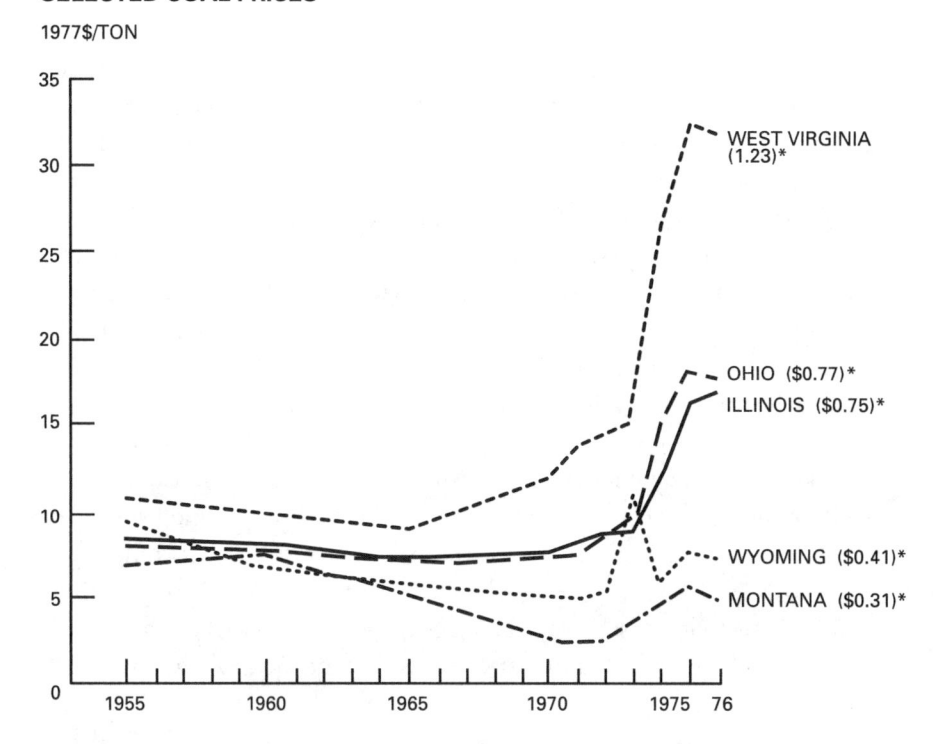

1977$/TON

* 1976 Btu-adjusted price (1977$/million Btu) assuming State average Btu contents:

West Virginia	13,000 Btu/pound
Illinois	11,200 Btu/pound
Ohio	11,300 Btu/pound
Wyoming	9,000 Btu/pound
Montana	8,300 Btu/pound

panded organizing drive ordered last year by President Miller." Veteran union officers' leadership in these drives suggests long-serving technocrats' potential to work effectively with reform leaders as members of the same team.[65]

By that spring, only Amax Coal Company's Belle Ayr Mine near Gillette, Wyoming, refused to sign. On March 24, it restarted production with a workforce of new miners and a majority of former strikers. This strike, and intermittent contractual negotiations, continued until the summer of 1976. In retrospect, this struggle's location within the booming Powder River Basin may have provided the decade's greatest test for the UMWA. Like Utah, where union operators regarded Wayne Baker's defiant campaign against the union with interest, the eyes of every strip mine in the West now turned to Gillette.⁶⁶

In 1975, Amax was the third-largest coal company in the United States. While it had multiple mines in the East and Midwest under UMWA contract, Amax's decision to invest in Wyoming exemplified two trends: the shift in coal production toward highly profitable western strip mines, and operators' desire to mine this coal free from the entanglements of UMWA contracts. Amax's plans were challenged by their workforce, however, which joined the UMWA in November 1971 to form Local 1854. On March 27, 1972, Amax signed a contract.⁶⁷ Yet in 1975, it refused to sign the pattern Western Surface Agreement for three main reasons: It objected to the tonnage-royalty financing of the Health and Retirement Funds, the common termination date of the Western Surface Agreement, and strikers' reemployment rights.⁶⁸ While avoiding these provisions would no doubt increase Amax's profitability, perceptions of union weakness and the end of sweetheart contracts may have inspired the company to employ a level of resistance it had not considered in 1972. Having retained his IEB seat, Stevenson played a critical role at Amax where he quickly recognized the strike's significance. On September 30, 1975, he wrote candidly to Miller:

> I believe it is of major importance to the membership involved in work stoppage at Amax . . . and the entire membership of our great union in all UMW districts that you involve yourself in the negotiations in attempting settlement at an early date since this matter is of grave international importance and our union may be hanging in the balance. . . . [I]n as much as you are the international president, your leadership is necessary in securing the contract.⁶⁹

This letter's tone speaks favorably to Stevenson's foresight and intelligence, and is notable for its exception to the hostility that otherwise characterized the two men's relations.

In Gillette and at union offices in Utah, concerned miners identified and proposed several alternate strategies to break the bargaining stalemate. On November 19, 1975, two Amax miners drove over ten hours to attend a meeting of District 22's Coal Miners Political Action Committee in Price. According to District 22 president H. A. Brownfield, these miners "were asking for a District-wide, unauthorized work stoppage in support of their contract strike." With the International buried in lawsuits from summer wildcats at eastern mines, Brownfield recognized the proposal's impracticality and denounced it the next day in a letter to the district's membership.[70]

By January 1976, Kaiser miners had contributed $12,950 in donations to the Amax strikers. Writing to Miller that month, Harold Alger asked the question of every unionist faced with a lengthy and seemingly deadlocked strike: "What can be done, other than continue to contribute money till we go broke, to assure Amax, other watching operators, and the country that we are determined not to lose this mine and not to abandon these men?" Considering three options much closer to legality, he suggested: "a memorial period or periods national in scope and determined in character; a mass march into Wyoming from all surrounding districts; [or] every miner in the country taking a week graduated vacation at the same time." Anticipating Miller's concerns, he argued for accepting massive financial risks, and implored, "Does this give you concern for 'the fund'? If Amax wins this one then all, including the retired, will suffer far more! There must be something we can do! Should you be worried about breaking the contract, remember that the operators have allready [sic] gone this route. . . . [T]hey are out to break the Union!" In response, Miller revealed the limitations of MFD's earlier faith in the ease with which "modern organizing techniques" could be implemented. Though he applauded Kaiser's support, he also warned, "As you are probably aware, the labor laws of this country do not favor unions and some of the actions which you have suggested could entail some severe legal consequences for the UMWA." Instead, he urged Alger to place his faith in the negotiating skills of Mike Trbovich, then head of the UMWA's Western Bargaining Council.[71]

Internally, organizing setbacks fueled growing factionalism among International officers, which Miller noted in his response: "Unfortunately, there are those who feel differently and have attempted to destroy our western organizing program."[72] In June 1975, the IEB demanded Miller replace the organizing department's acting director for the western region whose personal irresponsibility and mismanagement had become clear. While Miller recognized his own appointee's poor performance, he insisted on the need to keep him in office until a suitable replacement could be found. Five months later,

Miller suspended District 6 IEB member Karl Kafton for breaking an assignment to remain in Gillette to boost strikers' morale. Two years later, the Stansbury mine in Wyoming refused to sign a second contract and precipitated another lengthy strike. After seven months, director of contract administration Steve Galati found the strike's principle organizer and longtime union official Merrill Thornock guilty of "sheer negligence" for failing to hold meetings or take a consensus of the employees' opinions for two months: "As a consequence, the employees were now refusing to follow any directions." In April 1976, the IEB's anti-Miller faction delivered its own blow with a budget that dramatically cut western organizing, and that summer Miller and Trbovich broke publicly over the latter's refusal to head a western organizing commission. By then, Amax strikers charged Miller for using their strike as "a political pissing post, and a 'Siberia' to send insubordinate Board members to."[73]

Aside from a few benefit events and a personal visit to Gillette, Miller developed little strategy other than to send IEB members and International organizers to meet with strikers, who spent a year and a half picketing their mine while it continued to operate. Though visiting board members' reports reveal much about the mood of these men, their arrival appears to have done little to rouse their spirits while the sporadic nature of external support contributed to "a continuing series of build ups and let downs" detrimental to morale. In early 1976 Miller and Trbovich recognized further visits by an IEB commission to Belle Ayr as futile, and on February 3 Trbovich recommended that the commission be dissolved. The strike ended shortly after June 1976, at which time there were only two full-time pickets left.[74]

During what may have been three of the most challenging years for any International president since the 1940s, Miller became increasingly overwhelmed. At one January 1976 meeting, Local 1854 members instructed their financial secretary to write him with a strike update and a plea for decisive action: "We think we can still win, but only with the all-out effort of the International. . . . In short lets [sic] either get in to this Amax strike with all we've got, immediately, or lets [sic] get out of it." Though it demanded an urgent response, the letter appears to have gone unread. Stapled to its first page in the UMWA archives is a handwritten note: "Rich, This letter was found buried on AM's desk."

It is quite old. Should we respond?" and in a different ink a response: "Leave it lie at this point, Rich."[75]

Communications at this time suggest the possibility of alternate trajectories. Harold Alger had correctly noted that the NBCWA gave the union the authority to call "memorial periods" for essentially strategic reasons—which the UMWA used for five days in 1974 to demonstrate resolve and shrink operators' prestrike stockpiles.[76] Miners could take graduated vacation days, and no law forbade hosting a mass march into Wyoming. Any of these tactics could have helped make the Amax strike a national issue. Furthermore, a tradition also exists within the UMWA of accepting tremendous fines in order to win a nationally important strike. To win the Welfare and Retirement Fund in November 1946, John L. Lewis led a national strike despite the threat of a $3.5 million fine (about $41 million in 2018 dollars) by federal courts. In April 1947, operator resistance to the Fund again led the union to endure a $1.4 million fine and a Taft-Hartley injunction.[77] During the high-profile, nationally significant 1989 strike at Pittston Coal Company's mines in Virginia, West Virginia, and Kentucky, the union accepted $64 million in fines to defend the Fund from an existential threat. Even if the union had made an all-out effort, been unsuccessful, and conceded defeat, it would have left a more positive legacy than it did by indecisively dragging the strike out for another six months.

In Utah, District 22's members and officers recognized western strip mines' superior tonnage and supported the priority Miller assigned to their organization. But they also expressed concern about the growth of nonunion underground mining in their state.[78] By 1971, Plateau had expanded to produce 700,000 tons a year and employ seventy men. That year, Wayne Baker sold the property to United Nuclear Corporation, which subsequently constructed a new $750,000 preparation plant connected by conveyor belt to the mine itself. By 1979, Plateau employed 225 men in three shifts.[79] Swisher Coal increased its annual production to 250,000 tons by 1975, in which year General Exploration Company of Dallas purchased the company and opened a second mine in upper Huntington Canyon. After winning a major contract, Swisher constructed a new processing plant in Wellington. By 1978, it produced 530,000 tons and employed 160 miners.[80] Soldier Creek reopened in 1976 under its new owner, California Portland Cement, and by 1978 employed 115 and produced 550,000 tons a year.⁸¹ All three companies subsequently expanded further. Though "a very irritating thorn in the side of every Union man in the District," retired unionists who still used coal stoves and heaters observed these properties' growth with a particular grudge. With metallurgical coal poor for home use and most companies unwilling to sell house coal to nonemployees, Plateau and Swisher's willingness to sell to anyone forced these individuals to suffer the indignity of purchasing "'scab' coal in order to keep from freezing."⁸²

While earlier organizing drives had left a troubling legacy, increasing district factionalism also complicated subsequent efforts. When in 1975 Alger alerted the International to the rise in nonunion tonnage in Carbon County, he wrote Miller directly rather than proceeding through district officers. In fact, Alger explained that he had "been instructed by my local union not to advocate organizing by district officials, or IEB members," and instead preferred to receive men accountable to the International's organizing department. The parallel between this inquiry and R. H. Tweddell's 1968 letter (as described earlier in this chapter) is striking. Not only has organizing's pace and problems remained similarly opaque and unknown to most members, but a persisting lack of trust between local and district officers remains. In both instances, direct appeals from rank-and-file members to International presidents failed to receive adequately detailed responses, and the vertical nature of these communications mirrored hieratical organizing models that relied heavily on professional staff while possibly underutilizing the support, input, and advice of local union members. Apparently unaware of Alger's appeal, a month later Alger's coworker at Kaiser and fellow officer of Local 9958, recording secretary William Preston, penned a worried message asking Miller "why organizer's [sic] were [sent] to this area from outside District 22, for the purpose of making a survey in the Salina, Emery & Carbon area."⁸³

Alger's appeals also convey unfamiliarity with the record of 1966–1972 through an optimism radically at odds with those drives' timetables. In June 1975, he asked for organizers "in order that good house coal might become available to us by this winter."⁸⁴ Miller forwarded these requests to the organizing department, which that summer sent two organizers to contact nonunion miners. The following February, John Kuzio also arrived on an organizing mission to Utah. After Kuzio described his progress to a meeting of Deer Creek miners, Local 1769 President Harold Hansen wrote to Miller that "the membership felt like Mr. Kuzio needed more help in our area. We are requesting more help for organizing in District 22."[85] Evidentially, Miller took this request seriously, and his organizing department sent additional organizers to Utah during the mid- to late 1970s.

While the IEB's 1976 budget cuts limited these organizers' resources, nonunion miners also appeared increasingly cool to their overtures. At Plateau and Swisher Coal, several who had experienced the organizing failures of 1966 to 1969 were likely to have still been working and could be expected to have acted conservatively whether they agreed with their employers or not. The legacy of defeat appears clearer at the Dog Valley mine, which reopened under new management in 1975. Here, organizers got as far as filing for an NLRB election before withdrawing a petition "because of lack of interest." After Soldier Creek reopened in 1976, organizers secured and lost an NLRB election. Even though the four organizers assigned to that drive filed unfair labor practice charges, the effort failed to bring the mine under contract.[86] While nonunion operators pointed to the higher wages, steady work, efficient operation, and lack of conflict that (at its best) nonunion mining provided, UMWA miners' worsening strike record in the East—as reported in the *Journal* as well as the *Sun Advocate*—also negatively impacted the UMWA's image.[87]

The rapidity of coal's boom carried a final, intrinsic problem for organizers. Near Factory Butte west of Hanksville, Atlas Resources' new Dirty Devil strip mine promised to become a major producer in the late 1970s. By April 1978, organizers obtained membership cards from fifteen of eighteen employees. Atlas initiated a familiar process of delay, however, when it fired five prounion miners. This forced the union to try to settle their reinstatement case before it called for an NLRB election. Possibly eager to avoid unionization but more probably overburdened by financial mismanagement and the high cost of trucking coal to the nearest railroad at Green River, Atlas filed for bankruptcy in 1979. While in retrospect it appears that this drive drained precious resources to little effect, at the time District 22 had every reason to believe this property would soon become a major producer.[88]

In contrast to the rapid pace of western coal mining's expansion, District 22's administrative evolution also appears to have been woefully handicapped by an overreliance upon the regulatory machinery of a slow-moving and at best halfheartedly supportive state. In the two and a half years it took the Labor Department and the courts to consider Frank Roybal's case, dramatic changes occurred in District 22. From 1973 to 1976, significant organizing setbacks tilted western strip mining's epicenter—the Powder River Basin along the Wyoming-Montana border—decisively toward a nonunion direction. In Utah, members who observed these developments gravitated toward one of two responses. Among many who had supported Miller, increased dissatisfaction inspired a second revolt in April 1976 that echoed MFD's trajectory and tone but not its organizational coherence. Others, disillusioned with Miller and his opponents, approached the 1977 district and International elections with lackluster interest. As coal operators threw down the gauntlet at the start of that year's national contract strike, picket-line tensions exploded into the greatest outpouring of miners' anger since 1950.[89]

In 1976, dissatisfaction with persisting "Boyle-loyalists" on the IEB and within District 22 inspired a second miners' revolt. Disillusioned with these officers' handling of his first grievance in thirty-one years, one miner confided in Miller that "local 8003 can't do anything to help us. The company knows after a grievance goes to District 22 they will win it, [so] why talk with local 8003"? Furthermore "the men that run District 22 are all Boyle men and they aren't doing anything to help you. But I guess you know all of that." In the summer of 1975, Alger denounced the IEB's attack on wildcat strikers in a letter printed in the *Journal*: "Those we have elected to represent us in the IEB are now joining our persecutors . . . to punish and chastise us for using the only sure weapon we have. . . . Our greatest enemies are those we have taken from the rank and file (whatever happened to them?) and placed in a plush chair they now think they own, to take the money from those they look upon as servants."[90]

That December, Local 9958 created a committee to study the voting record of IEB members in detail. In April, it responded to the budget cuts with letters of protest to every IEB member. These letters specifically cited the need for additional organizing, funding for the UMWA's legislative body—the Coal Miners' Political Action Committee—and denounced the board's practice of keeping its minutes secret.[91] District

FIGURE 5.9. In 1977, Utah, Wyoming, and Arizona miners elected a reform slate of Utah men and MFD veterans to District 22 office. *From left*, president Bill Jones, secretary-treasurer Louis Pestotnik, subdistrict board member Harold Alger, and IEB member Frank Roybal Sr. Courtesy, *Sun Advocate*.

president Brownfield seems to have sided with the IEB, and circulated the statement by its spokesman to all local unions.[92] Following Roybal's instatement as IEB member on July 30, 1976, Local 9958 activists campaigned against the remaining officers. Citing poor handling of grievances, a 600 percent increase in district expenditures "out of all proportion to services rendered," vague expenditure itemization, and obstruction against Roybal, members passed a resolution without dissent that Brownfield, Smith, and Crissman be recalled from their positions. A petition to this effect quickly gathered 534 miners' signatures, was circulated with an introductory letter to all district locals, and was forwarded to Arnold Miller.[93]

Though it proceeded more quietly than the Roybal campaign, the Department of Labor filed a second suit that allowed reformers to confront district officers in a special election held on March 12, 1977. On June 29, the reform slate of president Bill Jones, secretary-treasurer Louis Pestotnik, subdistrict board member Harold Alger, and IEB member Frank J. Roybal Sr. took office.[94] Unfortunately, national events almost immediately undermined this administration's chances to improve on district organizing. On July 1, 1977, the Health and Retirement Funds' trustees enacted unprecedented deductibles for what had been free coverage: $250 annually for hospital bills and $500 ($2,045 in 2018 dollars) for nonhospital care. Reasons for the cuts were multiple and included royalties lost through wildcat strikes, inflationary health care costs, and the harsh winter of 1976–1977, which had disrupted the production of some union mines. Beyond the shock of the announcement itself, its timing two weeks after the June 14 International election appeared highly suspicious. Miller, who had campaigned for reelection in Utah that April, left his base unprepared for this announcement. Like Tony Boyle and his IEB opponents, Miller's attempts to stabilize the fund's revenues by discouraging wildcat strikes failed to provide his membership with any realistic alternatives. Subsequently he received much of the memberships' anger for these cuts, which led to a widening gulf between him and his base.[95]

In Utah, miners' feelings of betrayal were immediate and overwhelming. Local 9958 recording secretary William Preston protested to Miller, "Where there was once trust, can now only be distrust. Where once our membership was free from worry . . . there is now only a feeling of despair. Where once we had something better to offer nonunion coal miners, to join our ranks we now have nothing." Preston went on to articulate one of two widespread responses to the cuts: "The coal operators think they have found a way to bring our membership under thumb. But this will not be so, because we will fight them as we have in the past. And we will not ratify the next contract until it assures us that this will not happen again."[96] Most union miners shared Preston's anger, struck for 110 days that winter, and rejected two contracts before they approved a third by a thin majority. While the strike prevented even greater concessions, its length and divisiveness proved disastrous for relations with nonunion miners, and it ended with the dismantling of the multiemployer healthcare fund.[97] In September 1977, four miners at American Coal projected another alternative: to leave the UMWA and form a separate union. While the majority of their local rejected the attempt, that they were angry enough to organize the meeting, confident enough to send International officers a hotly worded letter inviting them to attend and defend their record, and resonant enough with so many other miners' anxieties that they were able to draw a crowd of 450 participants, speaks volumes to the changes running through coal country.[98]

Through these years, MFD's Utah experience illustrates a nationally significant story in a disproportionately relevant context. Containing

FIGURE 5.10. In 1977, some 450 union miners packed Emery High School's gym to consider breaking away from national bargaining. Overwhelmingly pro-UMWA, the crowd cheered for unity and disregarded the proposal. Courtesy, *Sun Advocate*.

District 22's headquarters as well as the bulk of its membership, Utah miners played key roles as union officers, ambitious reformers, and dedicated organizers in a region of decisive significance. While local MFD leader Frank Sacco performed his preferred work as an organizer comparatively well, convincing miners to join the UMWA proved much easier than convincing employers to sign off on standardized contracts. And while the labor department offered tools to Sacco's allies, this body's inertia ensured that by the time reformers had a chance to implement changes, national setbacks almost immediately curtailed their potential.

Ultimately, it remains inconclusive what difference reformers' victory in the 1973 District 22 elections could have made. Stevenson and Brownfield might have processed some grievances unsatisfactorily, and they might also have lacked the negotiating skills needed to win contracts by the mid-1970s. But experience suggests that coal operators could have delayed grievances and stymied collective bargaining as effectively under a reform administration as they did under one partially composed of former Boyle supporters. While Harold Alger and Local 1854 members' suggestions to break the Amax deadlock deserved the serious consideration of a wider audience, they also pushed the boundaries of what is possible under American labor law. Perhaps, from the 1970s onward, alternative strategies to traditional collective bargaining may have contained the most useful options for unorganized workers and union members to consider. Yet those who racked their brains to identify them did so in a losing race against time. As Miller grew increasingly alienated from the rank-and-file, International functioning disintegrated into accusations, red-baiting, and proliferating staff resignations. For a winning strategy to have persevered in the 1970s, frank discussions of organizing's limitations would have had to have been conducted long before.

Perhaps, if a stronger leader had been able to rise to the UMWA's presidency, and had he not been undermined by a hostile IEB, he might have experimented tactically with greater success. Yet it remains unclear whether personal talents alone would have sufficed to overcome the systemic crisis the union sector found itself in by the mid-1970s. A negotiator would have to have been skilled indeed to convince the industry to sign off on a grievance procedure efficient enough to forestall the epidemic of eastern wildcats that so depleted the union's treasury, or, alternately, for extremely efficient strip mines to continue so heavily disproportionate payments to a benefit fund principally enjoyed by the underground competitors it was putting out of business.[99]

A bigger "what if" may be whether any victorious options remained open to the UMWA by the mid-1970s at all. As evident at Amax, Miller failed to break the same contractual deadlock that had bedeviled multiple predecessors, and which by January 1976 Local 1854 financial secretary Victor Henry lamented as "the old familiar U.M.W.A. rut."[100] While union negotiators refused to budge on their most central demands, they also failed to mobilize the pressure necessary to force companies to sign. While miners, organizers, staff experts, and elected officers enjoyed a freer debate about tactics, none proposed altering the demand for forty-cent-per-ton payments into the Welfare and Retirement Fund. Perhaps, to the awareness of American unions as the prisoners of a restrictive legal regime, it may be added that some—like the UMWA—also became fatally wedded to their most popular programs.

With Miller as unsuccessful in raising BCOA members' royalty payments in 1974 as Boyle had been in 1971, organizing remained the only way to boost the ailing Fund's revenues. Yet as organizers targeted the most productive nonunion properties, miners became increasingly receptive to employer arguments that claimed the union had ulterior motives. As early as February 1974, organizing department officers noted that strip miners at Gillette's Belle Ayr mine and the McKinley mine near Gallup, New Mexico, had independently voiced the same complaints "regarding the royalty payment being sent to help the Eastern Miners." At McKinley, they suggested "that the voting strength of each member be decided by the amount of tonnage produced at the mines and not by the size of the Local Union. Members complained that Pres. Miller was against strip miners. We could not change their minds, so we suggest that each member be sent a letter from Pres. Miler clarifying his stand."[101]

While Miller quickly ended his support for proposals to limit strip mining, the elimination of sweetheart contracts left a royalty structure so rigid it inspired fierce resistance from Canada to New Mexico. While organizers appealed to miners—often successfully—on the basis of solidarity, ethics, or safety, the Fund provided the financial rock upon which negotiating broke. And as nonunion operators flush with new investment quickly pointed out, unlike the historic image of substandard nonunion mines, with the latest mechanization they could now afford safety improvements and competitive benefits with more than enough left over for higher wages.[102] As likely, the seemingly impossible situation Arnold Miller faced would have driven many a braver and more competent person to the ill health, distraction, and defections that characterized his later administration. With organizing offensives essentially at a stalemate, it now remained up to working members to defend their union's gains from those who sensed its growing weakness.

CHAPTER 6

Hell or High Water

> There is no tomorrow in a coal mine. It's either safe now, or men aren't going to mine coal.
>
> —Arnold Miller, 1972

ON THE EVENING OF DECEMBER 19, 1984, twenty-two working miners and five onlooking managers in the fifth right longwall section of the Wilberg coal mine near Orangeville, Utah, prepared to set a world record for tonnage produced in a twenty-four-hour shift. Like their sister mines Deer Creek and Des-Bee-Dove, Wilberg's output was dedicated to UP&L's Hunter and Huntington power plants. Since 1979, the three coal mines had been managed by Emery Mining Corporation (EMC), an ambitious offshoot of local coal-trucking firm Savage Brothers. Not only were Wilberg's longwalls the most mechanically efficient machines yet invented to mine coal underground, they had been ordered, installed, and operated by several former Kaiser Steel miners who were elite veterans of the first crews ever to use the technology in the United States. Despite two years of heavy layoffs, a decade and a half of topsy-turvy union politics, and lingering mixed feelings over a recently concluded month-long strike, everyone present had a reason to be excited. All were extremely competent, well-compensated, locally respected professionals working at the cutting edge of their profession. Universally, face workers on longwalls were

FIGURE 6.1. In December 1984, the Wilberg Mine Fire killed twenty-seven miners attempting to set a world production record. In addition to a faulty air compressor, other factors that contributed to Utah's worst coal mine disaster in sixty years included inadequate safety enforcement, increasingly competitive markets, and declining rank-and-file power. Courtesy, *Sun Advocate*.

the best of the best in any mine. By the end of their shift, most anticipated being recognized as the best coal miners in the world.

Shortly after nine pm, an Ingersoll-Rand air compressor with a bypassed temperature safety switch probably overheated and started a fire near the section's air-intake passageway. As the fire spread to supporting coal pillars, the ventilation system blew carbon monoxide and smoke directly into the face where miners worked. Complicating an escape, rock falls had blocked two alternate exits for weeks. Four miners attempted to use them, with three stopped by a blockage in the return air, or tailgate, passageway. A fourth crawled through a rubble-filled bleeder passage that connected to the sixth right section, where he collapsed a few hundred yards later. Following experienced miners who donned air-purifying self-rescuers and ran into billowing smoke with zero visibility, only one miner from fifth right, Kenneth Blake, successfully escaped. With rescue workers unable to contain the fire, Emery mining sealed Wilberg's portals for a year to suffocate the flames. Utah's worst mining disaster since 1924 affected all connected to the industry—and for many to this day is remembered as "the year without a Christmas."[1]

Although a full treatment of the Wilberg disaster is beyond the scope of this work, it serves as a useful bookend through its demonstration of militant unionism's decline throughout Utah's coal country. On June 18, 1980, Wilberg miners had initiated a wildcat strike over the unsafe installation of seventeen-ton longwall supports, which Emery Mining attempted in violation of regulations that mandated minimum clearances for underground transportation and a certified electrician's supervision.[2] This strike was one of at least six wildcats that had occurred there from 1980 to 1982, some of which resulted from far less threatening conditions such as objection to management participation in a crude yet physically harmless practical joke.[3]

Despite this history, miners made no similar effort to stop the 1984 push for a world production record amid far more dangerous conditions. Six days before the accident, Wilberg Local 2176's safety committee concluded a two-day inspection which found sixty-eight unsafe conditions, half of which related to fire hazards. One day before the fire, federal Mine Safety and Health Administration inspectors concluded a six-week inspection that cited Emery Mining for twenty-seven viola-

FIGURE 6.2. In 1982, wildcat strikers at Wilberg used ski masks to hide identities. Courtesy, *Sun Advocate*.

tions—nine of which contributed directly to the disaster—yet allowed the mine to stay open.[4] Only a year before, a nonfatal fire that began December 29, 1983, at Emery Mining's nearby Des-Bee-Dove mine disrupted production through March and demonstrated the urgency of reevaluating fire precautions.[5] Despite that uncanny precedent and the revelation of recent warnings, by December 1984, neither union nor federal inspectors had a mechanism to immediately stop production. And this time, the working men and women of Local 2176 no longer felt able to employ their own.

By the 1980s, such challenges to management prerogatives as the member-initiated wildcat strike had become increasingly unusable. Winning a key demand to end labor instability, in the 1978 NBCWA operators won a clarified right to discharge and discipline miners who advocated or participated in a wildcat.[6] Emery mining invoked this clause when it suspended seven of the miners who initiated the June 18, 1980, strike. Further empowering management, layoffs that began at eastern mines in 1978 and at western mines four years later ended the labor shortage that gave coal miners (and the militants among them) a decade of job security unmatched in basic industry.

Repeating the pattern of the 1950s, now even dedicated union supporters accepted work at nonunion mines when they provided the only alternative to unemployment. At union mines, workforce solidarity weakened as operators found it cheaper to offer existing workers overtime than to call back their union brothers from lists, or "panels," of laid-off miners. As one eastern miner described at a 1985 conference in Price, "You got your neighbor next door starving and you're sitting there doing double shifts. . . . I always wondered why they worked us Saturdays—it's more money—and then somebody explained to me—it doesn't cost 'em any more working us, it costs 'em less. They're not paying any more for your benefits when you're working that Saturday or that Sunday."[7]

During one of the era's last wildcats in February 1982, picketing Wilberg miners demonstrated the tactic's fading utility when they wore ski masks to avoid being identified. These strikers did not embrace coverage

FIGURE 6.3. While an earlier owner went bankrupt in 1972, by 1979 Price River Coal mined profitably at Castle Gate with expanded loading facilities where a town once stood. Photo courtesy of the Western Mining and Railroad Museum.

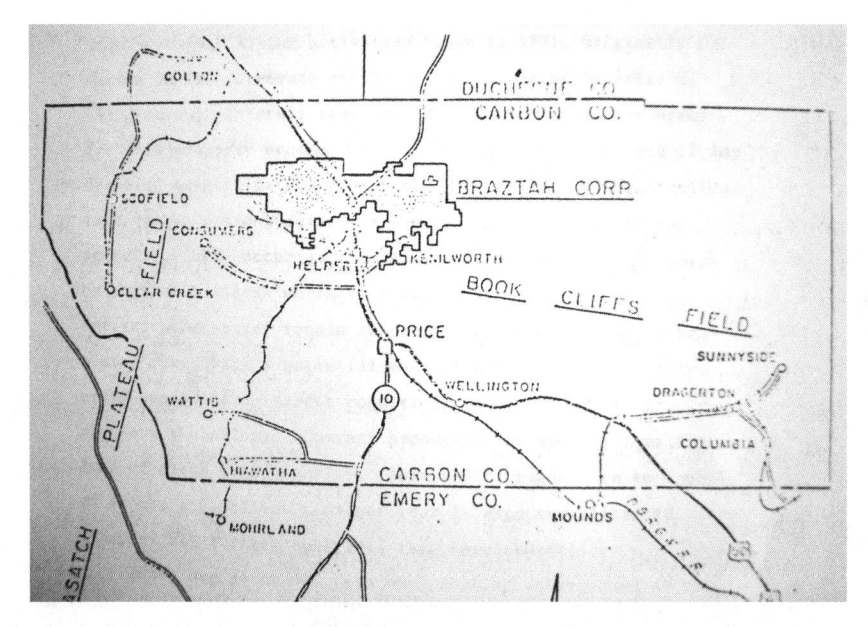

FIGURE 6.4. By 1974, Braztah Corporation had accumulated massive holdings where multiple local companies had once produced. Restructuring significantly altered national coal strikes' effectiveness. Photo courtesy of the Western Mining and Railroad Museum.

by a historically supportive local press, and some even threatened *Sun Advocate* and *Emery County Progress* journalists as they photographed their picket. In spite of these precautions, one former Deer Creek supervisor remembers that these men—"the magnificent seven"—were eventually identified and fired.[8] As such stoppages became impractical, militants at area mines adopted increasingly desperate forms of resistance that included vandalism, sabotage, and the phoning in of bomb threats. Despite the immediate satisfaction of temporary results, these strategies failed to achieve any long-term result other than eroding public sympathy.[9]

As the UMWA's control over coal production decreased, increasingly lengthy and divisive national contract strikes alienated nonunion miners and sapped union members' morale. Unlike the strikes of the 1940s, coal mines were no longer predominately owned by individual companies entirely dependent on one or a few mines' output for their entire corporate survival. Not only was ownership consolidated, it had been increasingly absorbed by energy conglomerates with assets in several industries—and with fewer vulnerable nodes of production. Perhaps at Castle Gate's former townsite these changes had become the most visible. In 1973, the Los Angeles–based McCulloch Oil Corporation's Braztah subsidiary purchased the property as part of a massive investment into several Carbon County coal properties. After relocating its residents and their houses to a subdivision west of Helper, Braztah leveled the town to expand coal-loading facilities. In 1979, a New York–based energy conglomerate and the nation's largest coal consumer, American Electric Power Company, took over. With more capital than its earlier Utah owners could mobilize, Castle Gate's miners now conveyed coal continuously from longwall systems to a new unit-train loading facility. Up Hardscrabble and Spring Canyons west of Helper, Braztah also purchased and retained control of what had been the Carbon Fuel and Spring Canyon mines. In 1975, Valley Camp Coal—a subsidiary of Quaker State Oil—similarly acquired Clear Creek's mines and began building a new loading facility near Scofield. At Hiawatha, Pennsylvania's Sharon Steel Company purchased U.S. Fuel's property in 1980. While outside capital allowed these mines to survive and grow, striking miners could now only interrupt a fraction of their parent companies' overall revenue.[10]

During national contract strikes in 1971 and 1977, picketing at nonunion operations only briefly stopped production and probably reduced UMWA strength over the long term. Such tactics proved far more successful in Appalachian coalfields, where car caravans of picketing union miners shut down several nonunion producers, particularly in the early months of the latter strike.[11] In Utah in 1971, crowds of union miners that varied in size from 25 to 250 formed picket lines along the roads to Plateau and Swisher Coal. Apparently, these actions were member-initiated and were never officially organized by union officers. At Plateau, 15 to 20 out of 60 employees refused to cross picket lines while the mine kept producing. At Swisher Coal, mining ceased early in the strike while the company trucked stockpiled coal to its customers, yet after three weeks the property reopened with a full crew. After the picketed companies filed lawsuits against the UMWA, district officers convinced their members to abandon the practice.[12]

While Utah UMWA members attempted no picketing during the month-long national contract strike in 1974, several hundred tried the

FIGURE 6.5. Union miners picket road to nonunion Plateau mine during national contract strike, October 1971. Courtesy, *Sun Advocate*.

tactic again during the passionate 1977–1978 strike. As tensions escalated, only Emery County's nonunion Trail Mountain mine closed temporarily in deference to pickets. At Soldier Creek, antiunion miners carried concealed guns in the buses that shuttled shift changes. Miner Elven Stokes sympathized with the UMWA and reported this to them and the Carbon County Sheriff's Department. As he refused to cross picket lines soon after, he was fired in an almost identical repeat of Bud Pilling's situation in 1968. He, too, appealed to the NLRB, which ruled in favor of Soldier Creek, who had terminated him just two days prior to the end of a sixty-day probationary period. In retrospect, asking miners to refuse to cross picket lines without the prior knowledge of solid majority support was ultimately counterproductive. By failing to develop a strategy that allowed union sympathizers to maintain their positions (and their audiences) at these mines, picketing inadvertently contributed to the removal of those most likely to play an activist role during subsequent organizing.[13]

As the union lost ground, strikes became longer and more divisive. Faced with operators' demands for concessions, union presidents' weaknesses, nonunion miners "hitch–hik[ing] on our strength," and backlogged grievances, several miners' frustrations escalated into violence during strikes in 1971, 1977, and 1981.[14] At Plateau in the first year, some who crossed the picket line had their car windows broken. At the mine itself, private security guards hired by Plateau set fire to a company car, though it is unclear whether they did so in solidarity with the picketers or in an unsuccessful attempt to discredit them. One picketer was charged, however, with throwing a rock that broke the window of a bus hired to transport Plateau employees to the mine. Meanwhile, Plateau owner Wayne Baker recalled receiving threatening phone calls, and placed one of his own to District 22 president Frank M. Stevenson.[15] After eighteen days, Plateau and Swisher Coal filed civil suits and unfair labor practice charges against the UMWA that prompted district leaders to abandon picketing.[16]

Events in 1977 escalated much faster. Twenty-four hours into the peaceful strike, Carbon County's long-serving sheriff Albert Passic escorted chartered buses of nonunion miners through picket lines.[17] While many union miners had grown up with, liked, and voted for the popular Democratic-leaning sheriff, their reaction was explosive. The following night, December 7, "county roads were littered with tacks, rocks, and broken glass." A bridge on the road to Plateau was anonymously burned and prevented forty miners from returning to their homes. The next day

FIGURES 6.6 AND 6.7. Union miners block road to Swisher Coal's mine with rocks and a burned-out car *(above)* and light a bonfire of railroad ties on the road to Soldier Creek *(below)*, December 1977. The same night, strike supporters burned the bridge to Plateau's mine. Courtesy, *Sun Advocate*.

they were shuttled home and the afternoon shift brought in via helicopter. On Friday, December 9, strikers ignited a bonfire of railroad ties in the middle of the road to Soldier Creek and similarly obstructed the road to Swisher Coal with rocks and a burned-out car. As nonunion operators bused employees through picket lines the following week, one Plateau miner was hospitalized after a rock broke through a window and struck him in the face. Two other buses had their tires slashed. After federal

FIGURE 6.8. Utah Highway Patrol monitors road to Plateau mine as chartered buses transport workforce, December 1977. Courtesy, *Sun Advocate*.

judge Don V. Tibbs ordered 180 picketers to appear at a December 13 hearing, an anonymous caller phoned in a bomb threat to the Carbon County courthouse. Three days later, Tibbs issued an injunction that limited picketing to five persons standing fifteen feet apart at each mine. Providing further assistance, Governor Scott M. Matheson mobilized seventy-five highway patrolmen to create a combined presence of a hundred law enforcement officers to monitor pickets. Unable to stop production with such numbers and fearful of additional legal costs, union leaders halted picketing for most of the remainder of the strike.[18]

During the seventy-seven-day national contract strike in 1981, UMWA leaders decided against picketing nonunion mines at all. As individuals, a small number of militants symbolically opposed nonunion production when they burned a bridge leading to the Soldier Creek mine and called in a bomb threat to the Trail Mountain mine. Amid these elevated passions, four nonunion subcontractors working on the Hunter Plant became the targets of some militant unionists' frustration. First, they received threatening letters telling them to quit their job. On April 9, pipe bombs loaded with BBs exploded within minutes of each other outside two of the contractors' homes. Four days later, one of the targeted contractors, thirty-nine-year-old mechanical engineer William Robert Stilson, was driving his car down 100 North in downtown Price. After a red Ford pickup flashed its lights, Stilson stopped as a man he didn't recognize approached him. After saying, "Hi, scab," the man shot Stilson in the shoulder with a .22 caliber pistol. Stilson survived, but the assailant eluded capture. At least one of the contractors, along with his wife and family, moved out of the area shortly thereafter. These actions brought no sympathy to union electrical workers or coal miners, but inspired popular condemnation and the posting of a $10,000 reward.[19]

Local militancy's decline, as well as a growing east-west rift, appeared increasingly visible as Utah miners voted two to one to accept a concessionary contract their eastern brethren rejected by the same margin. Emery Mining recognized an opportunity and approached District 22 officials directly to negotiate a separate contract—a move that historian Charles Perry (1984) recognized as an opening salvo in the BCOA dissolution. Horse Canyon's miners similarly supported national collective bargaining's fragmentation when they picketed U.S. Steel for refusing to join other Utah operators to negotiate a separate agreement from the BCOA-UMWA pattern that would allow them to return to work early.[20] Speaking for many miners eager to go back to work, the *Sun Advocate*'s editors argued,

> Eastern and western coal markets differ. Buyers of eastern coal are eastern utility companies and European countries. Western coal mines serve western power plants and Asia. The very nature of the product differs regionally; western coal burns cleaner (and more economically) than eastern coal. Labor and management should constructively respond to these differences by creating separate bargaining arms for the east and west. Western workers should negotiate with western managers and the same situation should apply to the east. There is no reason for westerners to endure a strike they do not really want.[21]

District 22 officers Harold Alger and Louis Pestotnik Jr. argued against this trend, and in a joint letter to the editor the following week, opposed the "un-schooled and juvenile innuendo" of an east-west divergence they likened to company "propaganda" designed "to divide and conquer." While Emery Mining's owner lamented his highly efficient mines' disproportionate contributions to the pension fund, Alger and

Pestotnik denounced this "dog-in-the-manger concept" with an affirmation of the union's historical solidarity:

> The United Mine Workers have never quibbled over just what area of the country gave the most for the benefit of all. Neither have we counted dollars and cents against human suffering, or the fact that some locals are in a position to do more than others, or conditions in one mine that may enable the employees of that mine to contribute more or less than another.... [T]he United Mine Workers must stick together. We have no choice, and those who hitch-hike on our strength must walk beside us, or fall the harder!"[22]

While in many ways representative of the best union traditions, by 1981 the current of miner opinion began to shift away from such an encompassing notion of solidarity. That year an opinion poll of 256 Emery mining employees found a majority supported returning to work early under a separate contract. The BCOA rapidly declined in importance after this year as well, and went from representing 130 coal-producing companies in 1981 to only 32 in 1984.[23]

As the 1981 national contract neared its September 30, 1984, expiration date, the UMWA's recently elected International president Richard Trumka knew an urgency existed to break the pattern of lengthy national strikes that had characterized collective bargaining in coal over the preceding decade. With a worsening employment situation (almost 50,000 out of 155,000 nonretired UMWA members were currently laid off) and the UMWA controlling a declining share of national tonnage, neither the membership nor union operators could stomach another three months of lost production. Trumka's solution, welcomed by most members, changed national negotiations with two major revisions. First, with as many companies as possible, the union signed interim agreements that allowed members to continue working under the terms of expired contracts while negotiations for new ones proceeded. After they were signed, any changes in benefit payments or wages would be applied, retroactively, to the date of the prior contract's expiration. And for holdout companies who refused to sign interim agreements, "selective strikes" could apply additional pressure. With a smaller number of miners idled, the UMWA could better support them with weekly benefit payments from a strike fund sustained by working members.

On the eve of the 1981 contract's expiration, all of Utah coal producers had signed interim agreements except for Emery Mining, which with 635 employees working at Wilberg, Deer Creek, and Des-Bee-Dove was the state's largest coal employer. It was also, according to ton-per-man statistics from the Mine Safety and Health Administration, *the* most efficient underground coal company operating in the United States. Emery Mining's chief objection in 1984—which lingered as a perennial source of disagreement until Deer Creek's 2015 closure—centered on tonnage-royalty payments to retired miners under the 1950 pension fund. While the UMWA identified five Emery Mining employees whose earlier careers would soon allow them to retire under the terms of the 1950 fund, the company's managers framed its funding structure as unfairly discriminatory. With UP&L's ratepayers vocally dissatisfied over high electricity prices, Emery Mining estimated in could save $15 million over the next five years if its payments to the shared fund were cut.[24] As general manager Bill Zeller put it a week after the selective strike against his company began,

> Because EMC does recognize that it has a responsibility as part of the coal industry to help fund the "1950 plan," Emery has already paid over $40 million into the fund. Additionally, Emery has agreed to pay its legal share of the 1950 trust's "unfunded liability," which could amount to as much as $20 million. EMC's total contribution into the 1950 trust would then be as much as $60 million. Isn't that more than a fair share, considering that none of Emery's employees are covered by the 1950 funds?
>
> Emery mining is penalized for being the most efficient and productive large underground coal mine in the nation.... In a nutshell, Emery Mining has to pay nearly twice as much per man into the 1950 and 1974 trusts because Emery workers are nearly twice as productive and efficient as the national average. Forcing EMC to contribute according to tons produced rather than man-hours worked is penalized efficiency, and that is wrong! The result is that the less efficient coal companies in the east are subsidized by Emery Mining and rewarded for their inefficiency.[25]

As the National Bituminous Coal Wage Agreement's once-universal terms diverged into company-specific contracts, Zeller now asked,

> Why is it that most other UMWA coal producers here in the west are not required to contribute to the 1950 fund? Make no mistake about

it, the 1950 trust benefits primarily the eastern coal companies. That's why during the first half of 1984 western UMWA coal companies produced over 12,500,000 tons but paid contribution into the 1950 trust on less than 25 percent of this tonnage. Emery Mining must compete with these western coal producers, and yet they are able to play by one set of rules, while Emery Mining is forced to play by another. If EMC and its employees are to have long term job security, we must keep the cost of our coal competitive.

The interests of our own employees and the communities in which we live must come before the interests of the eastern coal companies. Emery mining must remain competitive with other western coal companies if we are to provide for our employees and others.[26]

Opposing the company's stance, a crowd of approximately twenty retired miners and wives of retired miners picketed its offices as the strike began. Supporting their concerns in a letter to the editor, strike supporter and miner's wife Alene E. Hansen cited the large number of 1950 pension fund beneficiaries living throughout District 22. Despite the vagaries of its funding structure, she described it as an essential and irreplaceable program worth defending:

> Mr. Bob Henrie gives us the impression that all the money that Emery Mining Corporation pays into the 1950 fund goes back East and the miners here never benefit from that fund. Where does Mr. Bob Henrie and Emery Mining think the money comes from that supports our miners and widows of District 22? It comes from the 1950 pension fund and benefits trust fund whose headquarters are located in the east.... If the UMWA doesn't take care of their own, who will? Welfare? The state of Utah? Or no one? Where does the money come from to support the coal miners where the companies they worked for have shut down, such as Latuda, Rains, Kenilworth, and Spring Canyon? It comes from the 64 cents a ton royalty that all union mines pay.[27]

Having retired rather than run for reelection as a district officer in 1981, Harold Alger remained a respected and well-recognized force of moral authority. In a pair of letters he applauded the strike, questioned whether UP&L would actually pass cost savings on to ratepayers, and defended the logic of continuing to share benefits nationally:

FIGURE 6.9. A union supporter pickets Emery Mining's Huntington office during a comparatively calm selective strike in October 1984. Courtesy, *Sun Advocate*.

> As miners switch from mine to mine or state to state because of economics or job opportunities, we want them protected. Both working and retired. Since the miner is such an important contributor to the national energy, we think he should be entitled to national (geographically

TO MINERS WHO HAVE PICKETED PLATEAU

One of the greatest benefits we enjoy in our wonderful land of America is the right and opportunity to be and act as independent free men. The basic freedoms for workers, men and women to work for whomever they choose, or become employers themselves and go to work each day at their jobs by their own choice free from threats or force by some outside group are among the rights enabling this to be the most desirable nation in the whole world in which to live.

We feel that these are the basic principles we stand for in not submitting to the threats and acts of violence by members of the United Mine Workers of America who are trying to scare or force us to stop working. We have no argument with you fellow miners some of you are neighbors and community or church associates. We think we know many of you well enough to believe that you cannot help but be ashamed of your actions during moments away from the mob when you pause to think of what you are doing in permitting yourself to be part of a "gang" attempting to take from us rights that you believe in and would fight to keep for yourselves.

Proudly we are a part of the vast majority of loyal American workers who have had the courage of their convictions and remained independent men and women, refusing to bow to the pressures of union organizers who would have them turn their affairs over to the unions and pay the union leaders money with which to conduct their class warfare, often opposing the very economic and free agency principles upon which a sound economy, industrial progress, and happy self-respecting lives are based. We are proud to be counted among the seventy-five percent of all American workers and eighty percent of all Utah workers who have chosen to keep their independence from unionism and stay free from the control of union leaders.

Yes, we are proud to declare that like our early national founders, we refuse to be pushed around and forced into some herd or be stuffed into a mold too small for our individuality. We still like to be free, independent men, who stand up for our beliefs rather than crawl into the tranqualized; we want to enjoy the rewards of our own efforts rather than feeling that what we do get comes from belonging to a gang that acquired it through some warfare.

At Plateau, without having to pay money to some union officials, skilled workers receive a daily wage of $38.00 and our health care, paid vacations and holidays, retirement pay and other benefits are equal to or better than what you receive under the United Mine Workers of America contract. They are especially better in that the insurance and pension benefits cannot be changed or cancelled at the whim of some union leader.

We do not feel that you and we as individual coal miners should be fighting each other. We feel you have the right to turn your affairs over to union officers, if that is the way you want to exist, and we feel we have the equal right to remain independent free men. The country and mining industry are big enough for both kinds and we should both be free to choose which course we want to follow.

Plateau Mining Employees

The Foregoing Letter Published And Paid For By The Following Plateau Employees:

Ken Miller	Keith Barker	Richard Guymon
Ben Blackburn	Doug Sitterud	Bill Durham
John Melo	Jim Atwood	Kay Dunn
Leon Safley	Ken Brown	Paul Knuckles
Lynn Anderson	Mel Cohen	Jay Woodruff
Jerry Price	Wilford Nielson	Tom Wood
Clemont Bentley	Roy Nielson	Mel Atwood
		David Winder

FIGURE 6.10. Plateau Mine's response to pickets, October 1971, signed by employees. Note the co-option of miners' traditional language, new understandings of freedom, shifting perceptions of union leaders, and unapologetic pride. Courtesy, *Sun Advocate*.

The public forum

VIEW FROM THE OTHER SIDE

Editor:

The ad by the Plateau Mining Employees could give someone a cock-eyed view of the situation; I would like to set the record straight.

The warfare to which the ad refers, and that we Union men fought, was against low pay, poor and unsafe working conditions, lack of laws and rules to protect miners from unscrupulous employers. My father, for instance, had been fired for attending an organizing meeting, for not buying from the Company store and even for refusing to contribute to a Christmas fund for a superintendent.

The high pay, health care, paid vacation, retirement pay, etc., which you enjoy, you only get because the U.M.W. of A. has made such things standard in the industry. Your employer is aware that should he pay you less than we get you would join us to get it. To put it bluntly, you people are riding a horse you neither saddled nor bridled and you don't even have guts enough to lead your own bronc along behind!

The great majority of the coal mine operators are far, far ahead of what they were in what you call the "class warfare" days. Most of them are aware that the employer and employee are after the same things; safety, security, profit. For the most part we-work together now, rather than fight.

The "Gang" to which we belong, however, is made still necessary by suckers such as yourselves who would if necessary, give away everything we have gained. If it were not for the U.M.W. of A. believe me, you would be facing the necessity.

Watch just how long those of you who honored the picket line last! Should you make it a matter of chosing sides, I choose the U.M.W. of A.!

Personally, I don't even want your kind in the Union any way; since the majority of you tend to be dippy-birds and head bobbers in front of the boss and cry babies with your fellow workers.

A "gang" member for 26 years and good for many more.

Harold L. Alger
Sunnyside, Utah

FIGURE 6.11. During the 1971 strike, Kaiser local 9958 president Harold Alger responds to Plateau mine's antiunion letter. Note the defensive tone, Alger's use of historical memory, and prounion minorities' precarious position. Courtesy, *Sun Advocate*.

speaking) protection. We have long since learned that, in the long run, local (company) protection is just not dependable.

Productivity varies with conditions. Payments to the fund by the amount of coal produced is the only fair way it can be done. Should conditions at any mine (including those of ECM) cause a drop in production, there would be a corresponding drop in the amount to the fund. EMC would penalize those mines with chronic problems with roof, rib, gas, or other conditions attributable to nature.[28]

After a month, the strike ended with a compromise. For half of the contract period, payments into the 1950 pension plan would now be based on man-hours worked. For the other half, it remained based on tons produced. While neither party got exactly what they wanted, both came closer to understanding previous formulas as dated and in need of revision. Speaking after the strike for working miners, however, Emery Mining employee Gregg Powell ambivalently wondered, "Was it really the '50s plan we were striking for? Or did Emery just need to deplete their stockpiles? We were out for a month, but we all lost."[29]

Historically, strikes have always provided platforms for society's quietest and most taken-for-granted members to express long-dormant concerns within unusually broad public forums. Like UMWA members, during the era's national coal strikes an emerging minority of antiunion voices became increasingly outspoken as well. In October 1971, twenty-two Plateau employees purchased and signed an advertisement that condemned "the threats and acts of violence by members of the United Mine Workers of America" and affirmed pride in remaining "independent men and women, refusing to bow to the pressures of union organizers." Though the document closely mirrors then-owner Wayne Baker's writing style and political ideology, it is possible that these miners wrote it themselves. Equally interesting is the fact that three of the signatories had signed union cards during the UMWA organizing drive at the mine in December 1968.[30] By 1971, their loyalties—however idealistic or pragmatic—had clearly shifted. Similarly unprecedented, amid outrage over the Fund's July 1977 copayment announcement, one antiunion observer countered "Harold Alger's mindless mouthings about non-union miners" to reclaim the language of "scabs" whom, she suggested, "are performing valuable functions to help stop the spread of infection caused by unions and their outrageous demands which, if unchecked, could lead to the death of the economy."[31]

As the 1977 strike began, community members penned six sharply critical letters to the *Sun Advocate* opposing the UMWA's conduct.[32] While none of these writers self-identified as working miners, union miners' family members wrote twice. The letters expressed outrage at the Fund's managers' decisions to suspend benefit payments for the duration of the strike and envisioned a bleak future for the union should it fail to win back the lost coverage. After the 1978 contract codified a $200 deductible for physician and medication costs ($100 for retirees) and dissolved working miners' multiemployer healthcare fund into privatized, company-specific plans, the outrage of one veteran miner's daughter shifted against the union itself: "Now, however, I believe the union has grown to the point that it cares only for the survival of itself and its leaders, and not for the individual miner that gave his lungs and life to pay for its so called existence."[33] For those more sympathetic to the union and its strike, idled miners' privations provided a discouraging example. By March, union miners had lost up to $6,000 in wages, and many depended upon food relief and unusually frequent servings of venison to feed their families.[34]

By the latter part of the 1970s, another blow to unity came when congressional revisions to the Clean Air Act further divided Appalachian and western miners' regional interests. With American steel increasingly threatened by international competition, most observers understood that coal's long-term future lay in centralized electricity generation. Eager for predictable fuel supplies, as new power plants came online they signed coal contracts that often lasted twenty or twenty-five years. Such a contract could make the difference between a mine staying open or closing down and a community thriving or losing its entire economic base. Subsequently, mining communities and their congressional representatives fought passionately over the act's wording, interpretation, and revisions.

Detailing specific emission maximums for particulate matter, sulfur dioxide, and nitrogen oxides, the original 1970 Clean Air Act made using lower-sulfur western coal a cheaper option than installing advanced flue-gas desulfurization systems, or scrubbers, to remove the greater amounts of sulfur common to eastern coal. Beyond regional electric demand's steady growth, western coal benefited tremendously from the original act and made significant inroads to midwestern and eastern markets in the early to mid-1970s. Facilitating a major market transformation, in 1972 the Burlington Northern railroad began work on the Gillette-Orin line, which at 127 miles was the longest new piece of mainline railroad to be built in the United States in forty years. For the first time it connected Wyoming and Montana's Powder River Basin to national rail networks passing through Nebraska, with grave implications for eastern miners. In Utah, unprecedented interest in Carbon and Emery Counties' generally hotter-burning, lower sulfur underground-mined coal raised commercial mines' output statewide.

As boosters welcomed ever-higher production figures, residential growth, and prosperity's long-awaited regional-return; they reacted with horror to revised standards passed in 1977. Seen in the west as a political subsidy to eastern miners, they required all new power plants to install scrubbers with the "best available control technology." As Utah Coal Operators Association president Roger Markle summarized at the 1977 Fuel Symposium at the College of Eastern Utah, "Western coal is compliance coal. Eastern utilities can burn low sulfur Western coal without expensive add on equipment and still meet the EPA standards. It doesn't make sense for the government to require scrubbers on all power plants and then require 80 percent of the sulfur to be removed.... It's especially stupid to require Western power-plants to have the scrubbers when they meet the standards without." While union negotiators might be able to debate the terms and compensation under which western coal was mined, federal legislators now made decisions affecting whether western miners would have future jobs at all. Sharing many western miners' growing frustrations, Markle dryly predicted, "If the East will leave us alone, we will be okay."³⁵

In a final pair of organizing drives undertaken at the height of coal's long western boom, two defeats in Utah suggested an ominous new trend. The first setback came in 1979 at Soldier Creek, and probably stunned the union in the one-sidedness of miners' voting. In 1974, the Marinoni family had sold their idled property to California Portland Cement, which reopened the mine in 1976 after a year of rehabilitation. Despite the deep divisions that picketing had caused during the 1978 strike, UMWA organizers gained enough support to feel comfortable petitioning the NLRB for a union representation election. Two days before the vote, ten UMWA locals in Carbon and Emery Counties ran an advertisement in the Price, Utah, *Sun Advocate* to extend an early welcome to the Soldier Creek miners. Beyond their concern with conditions at Soldier Creek itself, union miners understood that their organization's survival depended on its ability to organize new mines as coal production increasingly shifted west. To highlight the benefits of union membership, they emphasized that nonunion miners would gain credit toward a UMWA pension, medical coverage for their families, protection against unfair dismissals and discrimination, seniority-based job bidding on new positions, retirement benefits, and mandatory safety training. The following Wednesday, the *Sun Advocate* surprised many with a report on the election's outcome: Soldier Creek's eighty-four miners voted seventy-six to eight to remain nonunion.[36]

In his assessment of the vote, District 22 president Bill Jones cited no specific incidents of illegal campaigning by management. While his observation that some workers feared "being fired or penalized if it was discovered who voted for the unionization" suggests an intimidating environment, it also indicates little faith in majority support. Perhaps more importantly, Jones acknowledged shifting perceptions of union membership's value. While unions historically promised better pay and benefits, after a 110-day strike the previous year he noted, "the threat of losing working time while negotiating a contract," was a legitimate bread-and-butter concern.[37]

Traditionally, historians sympathetic to the UMWA who have pondered its challenges in this period have preferred to generalize about "large new surface mines . . . in the booming mining regions of the west," operated by "huge, antiunion multinational corporations" as the union's principle nemesis. Even labor lawyer and historian Thomas Geoghegan, an MFD veteran and UMWA staffer during the early and mid-1970s who is strongly sympathetic to the pressures nonunion workers face, simplified geography in his own account: "The coal industry was moving West, and in the West it was hard to organize the new strip mines, or surface mines. Not because of the 'culture' out West (Utah, in labor history, is at least as radical as Virginia), but because the mines out there were surface mines, not the deep underground mines where solidarity was automatic and the Union was a matter of life and death."[38]

Located in the Book Cliffs at the base of an eight-thousand-foot high plateau, in 1979 Soldier Creek's miners worked underground with three continuous mining machines to extract coal via the room-and-pillar method. In these inherently dangerous conditions, they depended on high levels of teamwork, coordination, and trust as equally as union miners who worked in nearly identical environments just a few miles away. And compared to other conglomerates then investing in Utah coal, a relatively small company owned the mine and used its output exclusively to fuel three cement plants in California and Arizona. Challenging generalizations of the UMWA's principle opponents in this era, Soldier Creek miners' historically significant vote demonstrates antiunionism's ascendency as an ideological power within western underground coal mining's traditionally prounion regions. The 1979 campaign's timeline also marks a shift from the general pattern of prior campaigns, where majority support for the union came first, and defeat at the hands of wily employers came second. Compared to the uncertainty of what joining a union had come to mean, the mine's vice president and general manager Don Ross likely spoke for much of his workforce when he concluded that "the employees felt as shown by the vote that wages and benefits were adequate to meet their needs."[39]

Developed at the peak of coal's western boom in 1981, industry giant Coastal States spent $125 million to open the Skyline mine as Carbon County's newest and largest producer. With rosy predictions of future demand, it anticipated that within a few years it would produce five million tons a year and hire as many as nine hundred employees. Though located near Clear Creek and Scofield, these historic mining camps with long-dwindling populations had vastly insufficient infrastructure to support such a workforce. Instead, the mine's planners built new roads over mountain passes to draw commuters from the larger towns of Fairview and Huntington in addition to established routes that connected it with the Helper-Price area. The UMWA understood that an organizing campaign here would have major ramifications for its regional future and engaged its employees throughout the mine's development period. However, this effort similarly failed to win over a majority. The UMWA still offered fairness, defined benefits, representation, a degree of control over the work process, and the affirmation of industrial solidarity, but Skyline's owners offered slightly higher wages, comparable benefits, and a more believable promise of steady work.⁴⁰

Since the heady and optimistic days of 1973, much had changed in America's coalfields. Not only had failed organizing drives left a bitter legacy, but the NLRB's increasingly proemployer orientation, the Miller administration's inability to substantially advance organizing, and the rise of internal factionalism contributed to a snowball effect: The less tonnage the UMWA controlled, the longer, more costly, and more alienating its national strikes became. Observing this trend, industrial customers who valued stability as well as price shifted purchasing to the nonunion sector. As the UMWA's power declined, undecided miners fearful of layoffs had even less incentive to join. Within this transformed context, nonunion operators' strategies of paying high wages and providing competitive benefits replaced earlier repressive methods to successfully stymie organizing throughout the industry.⁴¹

If widespread layoffs, organizing setbacks, and nonunion coal's elevation to a majority of national tonnage closed the historical window where new leadership had the best chance to revitalize organized labor, from the 1980s onward labor struggles in many traditionally unionized industries have become increasingly defensive and protracted. Yet the historical hindsight that allows us to assess the beginning of organized labor's long decline was not apparent to its participants in these years. For many who had fought the hardest to establish a well-paid career in mining, civil rights activism overlapped with union membership to broaden its meaning even as long-term opportunities for reform diminished. While historians have rightly noted that such groups made inroads into the labor movement during the very years it lurched into a steady, national decline, the era's high-water marks of working-class feminism and civil-rights unionism retain a profound relevance into the era of #metoo and #blacklivesmatter.⁴² By examining how identity shapes union membership, scholars looking more closely at the long 1970s may not only better understand deunionization, they might also recover those traditions most essential to labor's future.

PART III

SMC: 1949 (p 206)
Socio: 1967 (p 207)

CHAPTER 7

El Movimiento

He taught us kids, and he learned from United Mine Workers, that if you don't stand for your rights as a human being, that you weren't going to be anything unless you did, and you weren't going to respect yourself.

—Rose Sandoval, 1972

AT ITS 1890 FOUNDING CONVENTION, the UMWA passed a resolution remarkable among American labor unions: "No local union or assembly is justified in discriminating against any person in securing or retaining work, because of their African descent."[1] Subsequently, interracial unionism's meaning has varied widely, as members through the decades have struggled to balance their anxieties and beliefs with the necessity of organizing workers of diverse backgrounds. Finding the International presidency of W. A. "Tony" Boyle unresponsive during the 1960s, many racial and ethnic minorities participated actively in the MFD movement and supported several western organizing drives. Racial differences, however, never entirely vanished beneath class unity. While miners of European heritage had dominated leadership positions throughout most of District 22, minority unionists still faced an uphill struggle to make their own needs heard by those who campaigned under the slogan of reform. By decade's end, many sought redress for racial discrimination through independent organizations and legal channels as well as traditional labor unions.[2]

While in some respects regional civil rights and Chicano movements enriched and rejuvenated labor organizations, unions' subsequent decline raises alarming questions for more than just prospective minority members. Through their departure coalfield communities have lost anchoring democratic vehicles, which—despite their limitations—had over the course of the twentieth century provided millions of working-class Americans cooperative and interracial frameworks for solving problems previously interpreted through racially exclusive ideologies. While New Dealers disagreed over industrial democracy's ideal extent, all understood that reciprocal relationships had long existed between economic inequality and political racism. Legalizing unions in 1933 was not a political reward to a powerful labor lobby, a core value of the (still deeply segregationist) Democratic Party, or even

FIGURE 7.1. In 1954 a *Tribune* photographer visiting Price noted Utah miners' uniquely high level of residential and occupational integration. Two decades later, many union miners' children became powerful advocates for civil rights and workplace justice. Used with permission, Utah State Historical Society.

just a creative policy plank to win voters. It gave millions of workers a stabilizing stake in their jobs, their coworkers, and the state at a time when democracies retreated globally before demagoguery, authoritarianism, and war. By giving millions of previously marginalized citizens a say in the most important decisions that affected their lives, the New Deal did more than confront poverty. It transformed democracy from an abstract and ritualistic principle into a practical part of millions of Americans' lives. By making democracy real, the New Deal made it worth defending.

Prior to 1942, ethnically European and Japanese Americans formed the majority of Utah's coal miners, with African Americans and ethnic Mexicans present in smaller numbers. Unsurprisingly, many union members retained prejudices common throughout American society at the time. Tellingly, from 1938 to 1950—years of the union's greatest influence and during which its founding organizer, Frank Bonacci, served the county as Democratic state legislator—the Price *Sun Advocate* promoted at least eight minstrel shows. Many miners enjoyed these performances, and at least two appeared at the densely populated, unionized coal camps of Rains and Castle Gate in 1939. In 1971 and 1972, the Green River Mutual Improvement Association and the Huntington Cub Scouts performed the last minstrel shows ever promoted by local newspapers.[3] Interviewed for oral history projects in the 1970s and 1980s, several retired miners and former union officers spoke freely in language then dated as offensive by national standards, suggesting a limited commitment to interracial unionism.[4]

Prior to 1927, Sunnyside may have housed the highest concentration of black residents in Carbon County, where as many as 200 worked a hot and heavy job loading and unloading the 800 slow-burning outdoor ovens that reduced coal to coke. At a production peak in 1920, as many as 64 may have lived in Mohrland just over the Emery County line. At the north end of Helper, several black families lived in a segregated area known as "Color Town," and to the west in Spring Canyon, "ten or fifteen," lived at Rains.[5] Coal's decline in the years preceding 1930 appears to have had a major demographic impact, as that year's census reported only 39 and 31 black residents in Carbon and Emery Counties, respectively. Fon Lemaster, who grew up in Hiawatha during the 1930s, recalled that shopping visits made by one black miner and his wife were such unusual events that "every kid would come along and

FIGURE 7.2. A longwall operator at Plateau mines more coal in the mid-1980s than a workforce of hundreds did in 1933. A mechanical sheer removes coal from the face, which falls onto an underlying conveyor belt for automated transport out of the mine. Hydraulic supports maintain roof integrity. The entire system is mobile and follows the cut deep until the entire panel is extracted. Photo courtesy of the Western Mining and Railroad Museum.

follow 'em. . . . We'd follow them to the store, and we'd wait for them to come and then we'd follow them till they took back for Mohrland."⁶

Amid declining coal markets, increased job competition, anti-immigrant sentiment, and a conservative political climate, the Ku Klux Klan organized "klaverns" and cross burnings in Carbon County during the early 1920s. In 1925, Castle Gate miners, managers, and supervisors organized Utah's last officially recorded lynching after black miner Bob Marshall allegedly shot night watchman J. Milton Burns, who may have been a Klan member. Unlike other murders committed in those years, the specific circumstances of this one ignited a reservoir of hate that revealed the darker side of a county uniquely proud of its melting-pot identity. After a hiding Marshall was turned in three days later by his roommate, police deputies released their prisoner to an angry crowd. As word spread, prominent citizens as well as women and children piled into approximately a hundred vehicles that converged near Wellington, where Marshall was tortured to death by slow hanging for over ten minutes until his neck was broken. While a photographer documented the event and many citizens subsequently traded postcards of a dying Marshall, none of 125 grand jury witnesses identified the ringleaders, all of whom were released after going through the motions of a criminal investigation.[7] Summarizing the extent of segregation in Carbon County ten years later, black miner and Helper resident Robert Brown remembered that

> over in Price, we couldn't go to the theaters. Couldn't go into the restaurants. Because that was mostly a white, Mormon [town]. . . . [North] of Price, we could go anywhere we wanted to go. We could go into restaurants, hotels, the theaters, or wherever we wanted to go. 'Cause, actually, we went to dances and stuff there in Helper. But we couldn't go over in Price. 'Cause Price was off limits to Blacks. . . . Helper is right in the heart of the coal mining industry. And there were a lot of blacks that lived down in Helper that worked in the mines.[8]

While the 1940 census found 18,459 Carbonites distinguishable into 18,199 "white," 37 "negro," and 223 "other races," World War II's boom in steel production substantially altered Carbon County's racial makeup.[9] Facing a tight labor market, Kaiser and Geneva Steel aggressively recruited from neighboring states to staff metallurgical coal mines in eastern Carbon County. Relocating largely from Colorado and New Mexico, ethnic Mexicans represented perhaps one half of the 2,000 new residents who moved to the East Carbon–Sunnyside area by 1944.[10] Retirees' obituaries suggest the extent of these migrations, and list birthplaces that include Canjilon, Coyote, Dulce, El Rancho, Los Martinez, Questa, and Tokay in New Mexico; Marshall and the San Luis Valley in Colorado; and Penjamo and Zacatecas, Mexico.[11]

As postwar coal output dropped, captive mines experienced comparatively fewer layoffs than those producing for the general market. Thus, the 1970 census found 1,621 vaguely classified "Hispanics" in Carbon County, most concentrated in the same community. Two years later, Kaiser manager Joe Palacios and mechanic Richard Cordova estimated their workforce's Mexican composition at 40 percent and 60 percent, respectively. As coal employment boomed over the ensuing decade, over

800 additional Hispanics moved into Carbon County by 1980.¹² As mine employment rose, ethnic Mexicans' personal networks and cultural infrastructure attracted a disproportionate number of minority miners. While the Hispanic population figure rose from 1,621 in 1970 to 2,423 in 1980, the same demographic in Emery County had grown by only five persons to a 1980 total of 119.¹³

Interviewed by oral historians in the 1970s, many of those who grew up in Carbon County during and after World War II recalled unpleasant personal encounters with discrimination. In 1972, University of Utah's American West Center interviewed nine Mexican Americans who grew up in Carbon County, eight of whom described negative encounters with local prejudice. Mrs. Rosa Sandoval recalled many ethnic Italians' hostility, who "seem to think that they are better than Mexicans. They're lighter complexioned and this and that." Describing her children's ambivalent relationship to their heritage, she mentioned, "My children aren't learning Spanish in our home because they feel ashamed. And I can't force them to learn if they don't want to. They don't want to be different. But they know their grandparents' background and they are really proud of being a Mexican."¹⁴ Reflecting on her childhood in East Carbon during the 1940s, Clorinda Cordova recalled policemen who arbitrarily arrested Mexicans and being forbidden from speaking Spanish at school. Her husband, Richard Cordova, also remembered the ban on Spanish, as well as the prejudiced owner of one lounge: "He had a blackjack and actually beat people out of his beer joint. He had a regular billy club. A Mexican walked in there and he was after him with the billy club."¹⁵ Alice Ramos felt most whites believed that "because you were a Mexican you didn't have any rights at all, they treated you the way they treated the kids, and you couldn't say anything." In 2017, Roma Valdez remembered sitting down with her husband at the last free table in a Carbon County restaurant during the 1950s. With their orders in and water glasses on the table, they were asked to leave when a white couple appeared.¹⁶

In 1949, ethnic Mexicans in Helper laid the foundations for future civil rights activism when they established the *Sociedad Mexicana de Cuauhtemoc*, known commonly as the Mexican lodge. Shaped uniquely by its time, this organization had much in common with societies and spaces prior generations of immigrants had established, such as

Castle Gate Italians' *Stella D'America*, the Greek Orthodox Church in Price, Martin Millarich's Slovenian Hall in Spring Glen, Finnish Miners' Hall in Clear Creek, or the Greek coffeehouses found in many company towns. The lodge promoted cultural pride through activities such as dances, maintained a treasury, and offered practical and financial assistance for community members in need. Later it hosted a weekly radio show on KOAL, and inspired local veterans to create a chapter of the GI Forum. The lodge continued to operate into the early 2000s, at which time its members disbanded and donated its remaining funds to a charity.[17]

Over the years, ethnic Mexicans gradually played a larger role in professional organizations. By the mid-1950s, Kaiser Steel hired its first Mexican American managers. The five Palacios brothers of regional celebrity are among the many beneficiaries of this policy. Their parents, Maria Palacios Rojas and Gumercindo Palacios, had moved from Santa Eulalia, Chihuahua, Mexico, to mine coal at Sego, Utah, in 1923. John, Manuel, Robert, Pete, and Joe all mined coal at Kaiser, and all five became mine foremen or superintendents at regional mines. In 1961, John Palacios oversaw the installation and operation of the first longwall mining system in the United States at Kaiser. This technology's extreme efficiency has allowed Utah's underground mines to stay competitive to this day, and Palacios's pioneering experience made him a sought-after mining consultant internationally.[18] Within the UMWA, by the 1960s James Madrigal served as president of Spring Canyon Local 6210. His brother, Paul, also became active in union politics into the 1980s.

Inspired by the growing national civil rights movement, in December 1967 a coalition of longtime advocates, proud World War II and Korea veterans, and younger activists came together in Salt Lake City to form Utah's largest organization identified with the Chicano movement, the SOCIO. Through the 1970s and early 1980s, this organization maintained a high profile as it combined local activism with state political initiatives through its Salt Lake office. Nationally, Utah's Chicano movement is unique for its early positive relationship with the state, which at the time was headed by liberal Democratic governor Calvin L. Rampton. Although many white Utahans' retained significant anti-Mexican prejudice, the latter's smaller proportionate numbers may have allowed progressive leaders to greet their movement more warmly than their counterparts in neighboring states. Comparatively, granting equal rights to Mexican Americans had greater economic stakes (and probably triggered qualitatively deeper racial anxieties), in California, Arizona, Texas, or Colorado. While those states' governments regarded Chicano organizations with more alarm, Rampton began an immediate collaborative relationship and invited SOCIO's members to serve on an advisory council on Hispanic affairs. Invited in 1975 to contribute to the *Sun Advocate*'s Statehood Day commemoration of the seventy-ninth anniversary of Utah's admission to the union, Rampton wrote admiringly about diversity's historical benefits in Carbon County:

> The coal mining industry . . . has provided the incentive for many diverse ethnic groups to emigrate to our state. Through the common bond of mining, they have intermingled and cooperated, and learned to appreciate the strengths of one another. Through this process, Utah's cultural heritage has been enriched, as we have had the benefit of being exposed to the lifestyles that are different from that of the majority of our population. This has served as a democratizing influence as well, as it is a proven principle of the American experience that diversity in a society is essential to a functioning democracy.
>
> Such an influence is also beneficial to the ethnic groups themselves, as members have opportunities to participate in community and state leadership, assume responsible positions in the business community and thereby effect change for the betterment of the people they represent.[19]

Demonstrative of moderation's success in Utah, SOCIO activists won a major early victory in January 1968, when the state legislature passed a bill to establish a fund to assist minority students with access to higher education. In 1971, the state permanently institutionalized its dialogue with Chicano concerns when it created a minority ombudsman position. By the early 1980s, SOCIO had branches in fourteen Utah counties. In addition to cultural events, educational advocacy, voter registration and lobbying, it worked with the Department of Corrections to reduce recidivism by 40 percent among Hispanics, trained the first Hispanic parole officers ever hired, supported migrant workers' practical and legal needs, provided crisis relief and job training, and lobbied for expanded minority employment in construction and education.[20]

FIGURES 7.3 AND 7.4. Chicano Conference on Equal Opportunity in Salt Lake City, October 1971. Through local branches and state politics, the SOCIO expanded educational and professional opportunities while promoting cultural pride. Photo Credit: Special Collections, J. Willard Marriott Library, University of Utah.

In Carbon County, activists organized a Price SOCIO chapter on August 18, 1968.[21] By 1972, its members had established a Chicano studies program at the College of Eastern Utah (CEU), which in 1978 commissioned a large mural to commemorate Chicano history. Harassed and fired by white colleagues at Wellington's public elementary school, teacher Rose Sandoval won a lawsuit that awarded her back pay as well as a commitment from Utah's Teacher Aid Program to hire ethnic Mexicans for 25 percent of new teaching assistantships.[22] In 1973, Governor Rampton appointed leading East Carbon activist Clorinda Cordova to the Policy Advisory Council on Spanish Speaking Affairs, where among her accomplishments were increased bilingual education funding and support for minority businessmen. Also in 1980, SOCIO pressured the city of East Carbon into compensating victims of police brutality, firing one abusive policeman, and requiring sensitivity training for its other officers. Throughout the decade members raised Chicano culture's profile with numerous letters to the Price *Sun Advocate* and assisted many in the resolution of day-to-day conflicts. As a young man in the early 1980s, Jim Valdez served for a time as the chapter's vice president where, among other duties, he negotiated with construction and power plant employers in then-booming Emery County on behalf of workers affected by discriminatory treatment and layoffs.[23]

Within a society broadly characterized by discrimination, union coal mines offered ethnic Mexicans unique opportunities for higher wages, occupational advancement, and protection from prejudiced employers. Describing his experience in other industries, Richard Cordova contrasted his career as a Kaiser mechanic with his mid-1950s experience in Utah's then-booming uranium mines:

> Before I came to work in Kaiser I went to Monticello looking for work, and this guy who owned this uranium mine, he was from Texas, and I asked around town for some employment and they sent me over to this pool hall and that's where this guy was. And he says "Are you Mexican?" and I says "Yes" and he says, "Well, I'll put you to work tomorrow, I'll pay you fifty cents a day and you'll work your ass off," and I said, "No sir, mister, thank you" and I hit him one. I walked out and that's as far as I went looking for work.[24]

Joe Palacios added, "Well, in coal mining . . . there has always been the higher wage you wouldn't be able to find anywhere else in common labor. Say for instance, if you worked in Salt Lake for $2 an hour, you would have to hold two jobs in order to get what you're getting here, in comparison to $6 or $7 an hour."[25]

During regional organizing drives in the 1970s, many ethnically Mexican and Navajo miners emphasized discrimination as a factor that led them to support the UMWA. During a 1975 contract strike at the Sundance Mine near Gallup, New Mexico, Lester Livingston recalled, "They pay you on the basis of what color your skin is—not what kind of job you do. The Navajos get the lowest, then the Mexicans and Spanish and the Anglos.... Discrimination on the wages is the biggest problem—that's the big thing." Fellow miner Gilbert Olguin agreed: "If you had a name like Olguin or Gonzales, you'd probably get a little more than if you had an Indian name.... [I]f your name was Smith or Jones you'd get a little more. If there was any firing to do, they'd pick on the Indians or on the Olguins or Gonzales." A year later, Robert Dimas described the strikers' determination: "It took us 18 long hard months to win our battle.... The company tried everything from starving us out to bribing us, but no way, we were fed up by this coal operator and we survived it."[26]

At Kaiser and Horse Canyon, many Chicano miners appear to have supported union reform and produced some of the movement's active leaders. Although by a thin margin Tony Boyle carried District 22 in the 1972 elections, the 44 percent of Horse Canyon's 297 voters and 37 percent of Kaiser's 543 voters who supported Miller represented the greatest numerical concentrations of MFD support in the state. During the national contract strike in October 1974, members of Kaiser Local 9958 unanimously passed a resolution in support of Miller's presidency and bargaining team.[27] Following MFD's victory in December 1972, Miller's administration organized elections in each district to recompose the union's IEB. In Utah, Horse Canyon Local 8003 member and former International representative Frank Roybal Sr. challenged incumbent and Boyle-loyalist Frank M. Stevenson for this position. At Kaiser and Horse Canyon, he gained two of his three nominations with two-thirds' majorities. Disqualified that year on a technicality, Roybal sued to secure a reelection in 1976 at which time he won the position.[28]

Richard Cordova maintained stronger links to the Chicano movement and similarly moved into union politics. Idled during the 1971 national contract strike, he attended the State Chicano Unity Conference in Salt Lake City and became a SOCIO activist, where his wife, Clorinda, served as chapter president. Interviewed in June 1972, he emphasized his union support, but criticized leadership for having marginalized minority participation. Asked about Kaiser, he lamented, "The only Mexican American they have on the local level is the door-keeper." As for attendance at union meetings, he replied, "[There was participation] until the Mexican found out that he wasn't going to get nowhere. Now there's hardly any attendance, because what is the use of being a member when all you are doing there is being a rubber stamp for these other officials?"[29] In 1979, the State Chicano Unity Conference in Salt Lake City honored the Cordovas with the Labor and Chicana of the Year awards. The labor award specifically recognized Richard Cordova's service as UMWA Labor Day activities chairman, as well as his management of the emergency food program during the 110-day national coal strike of 1977–1978. His later activities included service as Mine and Safety committeeman, executive of SOCIO, and chairman of Miners' Aid during the 1981 contract strike. In district elections that year, he ran for and won the IEB position.[30]

Nationally, while UMWA reformers were themselves of multiracial and multiethnic backgrounds, in campaigning before predominately white union members with a range of racial tolerances they struggled to balance electoral considerations with minority unionists' concerns. At MFD's 1972 conference in Wheeling, West Virginia, strategists appealing to pragmatism advocated what has been called a "No Blacks, No Hunkies" approach to candidates' selection. Interestingly, sons Chip and Ken of the martyred Polish-American Jock Yablonski were among the strongest advocates of this strategy and supported selecting Arnold Miller for his plainspoken style and all-American appearance. As historian Paul Nyden has noted, Miller's experience might have been inferior to other potential candidates, such as black miners Robert Payne and Levi Daniel, Hungarian Lou Antal, and Mexican American John Mendez.[31] Black miner and MFD activist William Finley challenged the necessity of the policy in his successful 1973 campaign for District 5's IEB position, despite his refusal to follow the Yablonskis' advice to withhold his picture from campaign literature. While Arnold Miller succeeded in his bid for union president, his lack of administrative experience repeatedly undermined his effectiveness. Resentment at being sidelined into the vice president slot may have also contributed to Trbovich's subsequent break with Miller. This had significant repercussions for western organizing, with Trbovich outright refusing a 1976 directive to head an organizing commission in the region.[32]

As a newly elected Miller struggled to manage a union staffed by multiple opponents at district and local levels, his search for allies occasionally placed him at odds with some minority members' concerns. By October 1973, Navajo miners at Kayenta, Arizona, developed significant criticisms of their Anglo local president, Loren Williams. While they noted racial discrimination in promotion and working hours, unsafe working conditions, and selective safety enforcement, their lawyer, Eric Swenson, summarized

> numerous complaints . . . concerning Williams, and concerning the performance of the UMW. . . . Many clients have been working for Peabody for 3 or more years, but have had no opportunity to elect their own union head. They feel it is unjust to have imposed on them a non-elected union head, an anglo, who dominates a nearly all-Navajo union local. Many have complained of Mr. Williams' refusal to act on complaints of unsafe working conditions. . . . They feel Mr. Williams encourages an insulting and demeaning attitude by the anglo employees, and lends active approval and support to Peabody's racially discriminatory practices. Our clients feel that Mr. Williams represents the company, and not the workers. . . . Mr. Williams seems to be a rather bad hangover from the Boyle era.[33]

Williams caused additional tension by refusing to live among his fellow miners at the same trailer park and intervening to get his son hired at a skilled position ahead of Navajos with more seniority. While Miller promptly asked his Navajo ally Tom Shirley to investigate, he also defensively noted that "since my administration began, I have never received one complaint about the leadership of Loren Williams. In fact, he has been singled out many times as being an outstanding local union president." Miller may have seen Williams as an effective partner, if not an ally, as in 1972 Williams had confided in Frank Sacco to discredit Boyle, oppose Stevenson, and expose Peabody's sweetheart contract. While he may have been helpful in internal politics, tensions between Williams and Navajo miners continued, with the local president still in office by May 1975. That month, 250 Kayenta and Black Mesa miners—90 percent of whom were Navajo—initiated a wildcat strike to resolve fifty-one backlogged grievances. To end the strike, Peabody sued the union for $12,000 in damages.[34]

From 1974 to 1976, two grievances arose at Kaiser that pitted the best traditions of UMWA antidiscrimination against incumbent district officials' perceived indifference. At the mine's bathhouses, Kaiser posted positions for third shift lampmen—a maintenance and custodial position—as "steady graveyard." In 1971 and 1976, Ray Bustos and Arnando Tollis took the positions, but protested with the schedule's interference with their family lives and overlapping with union meetings. Reviewing the matter with Local 9958 president Harold Alger, they discovered that both jobs had been posted in violation of the union contract, which since 1942 maintained rotating shifts at all mine positions. Subsequently, Bustos and Tollis filed grievances in 1974 and 1976, respectively.[35]

Ray Bustos appealed his case for two years before he received a final unsatisfactory judgment that International president Arnold Miller declined to challenge. Throughout the process, he documented instances of district president H. A. "Dell" Brownfield holding meetings to discuss the grievance without allowing him the opportunity to be present. At a March 6, 1975, hearing, he suggested the other lampmen refused to rotate because the day shifts frequently allowed them to make four rather than two hours of overtime. In his view, rather than sympathetic advocacy, IEB member Frank M. Stevenson maintained that "it didn't have nothing to do with the case" and "acted like a prosecutor and [Bustos] was on the witness stand on trial." Despite two supportive arbitration precedents and Kaiser's own deference to the union, Brownfield and Stevenson refused to push the contract angle, maintaining instead that the other lampmen's prior practices be respected.[36]

Bustos felt the district's handling of his case "was nothing but discrimination" and "playing favoritism." Tollis and Alger suspected Stevenson's reluctance to pursue the grievance stemmed from his brother's employment as one of the day-shift lampmen who refused to rotate. In March 1975, Bustos appealed to Arnold Miller directly for support, mailing him a notarized petition with four hundred (out of five hundred possible) Kaiser supporters' signatures. Advocating for Bustos, Alger wrote four times to the International's Contract Department and twice to Arnold Miller, complaining that the district officials "never at any time made a serious attempt to *win* the case for the Union" and that "all their efforts were haphazard and amateurish and even sloppy."[37]

Beyond the immediate outcome of this one situation that affected comparatively few individuals, Harold Alger feared that such favoritism could have broader consequences for UMWA's future in the West, where "the contract we are so busy selling these new union men is being given away to our companies even more rapidly." He pointed to the grievance's drawn-out and unsatisfactory handling as contributing to depleted morale, which affected "those who even question the feasibility of paying any dues, let alone twelve bucks, to have our causes lost; we can lose them for nothing outside the union!"[38] This particular grievance case is further significant in its demonstration of executive-level factionalism affecting local members directly. In 1975, Frank M. Stevenson led the UMWA's organizing drive at the Belle Ayr strip mine in Wyoming's Powder River Basin. At the time, the union understood this effort would have major ramifications for its regional future, and beneath Miller's evasion of appeals to confront Stevenson may have been a desire to preserve a functional relationship. Furthermore, it must be understood that throughout his presidency appeals for local interventions increasingly overtaxed Miller's capacities to respond. Bustos's petition, which lay unread in Miller's files for three months until an administrative assistant stumbled across it, was not the first important letter to fall through the cracks of an inexperienced executive's disorganization.[39]

In District 22, members alienated by Brownfield's and Stevenson's conduct supported a reform slate in the March 1977 District 22 election. Antipathy for Miller's handling of the lampmen case may have further eroded his support at Kaiser, which in International elections that year gave him 44 votes as opposed to 189 for Harry Patrick and 79 for Roy Patterson.[40] An original leader of MFD, Patrick's attempt to carry reform beyond Miller's limitations failed that year, and split a three-way race to reelect Miller with barely 30 percent of the vote in the International election. Also visible at Kaiser, many miners' abstention from voting indicates a level of disillusionment with the democratic process.[41]

Throughout western districts, overlapping Chicano and UMWA traditions inspired activists in many coal-mining communities. At the

International's optimistic 1973 convention, organizers invited United Farmworkers president Cesar Chavez to speak. The assembled delegates personally donated more than $3,000 to his organization and passed a motion to contribute an additional $10,000. Explaining unionism's advantages to unorganized miners, Joe "Moose" Martinez, Leroy Baca, and Louis Sandoval served as regional organizers in the late 1970s and early 1980s. Frank Roybal Sr.'s son, Frank Roybal Jr., served as Local 8003's militant president until Geneva fired him for leading a 1975 walkout in defense of union safety inspectors. At Labor Day celebrations in Carbon County, Chicano families blended identity and union politics by attending in traditional Mexican dress.[42]

In 1984, SOCIO's float won first place in Carbon County's annual Labor Day parade, and by the quantitative accounting of its membership statistics it appeared to be a healthy organization. With a reported total of 313 members in Carbon County, it claimed 106 in Price, 77 in Helper, and 116 in East Carbon.[43] In 1986, however, SOCIO abruptly disbanded statewide. Chicano historian Jorge Iber suggests a long-term structural instability unsustainably wed an unpaid activist base to a professional staff almost entirely dependent on outside funds. Increasingly, paid personnel performed the tasks volunteers formerly had, which may have reduced grassroots perceptions of the need for involvement. For working-class Chicanos, multiple and otherwise physically demanding jobs limited the free time most had available for activist work and led to burnout among some over the long run. For others, SOCIO may have become a victim of its own success. As many who benefited from its programs increasingly assimilated into middle-class lifestyles, personal distractions and professional responsibilities competed with volunteer participation.[44]

For Chicana women, inadequate daycare facilities exerted a uniquely difficult pressure. While some, like restaurant owner Clorinda Cordova, had the income and scheduling power to juggle married life, work, and political careers, many others struggled against the combined limits of familial expectations and lower-paying employment. As an early-1980s SOCIO proposal for a minority women employment program summarized,

> American Society has always confined minority women to a different and, by most standards, inferior status. . . . We have found that the frus-

> trations of providing day care for dependent children, in an area where day care facilities are inadequate, may prohibit some clients from entering or retaining some kinds of jobs. Child care is the most serious problem experienced by single parents.... Single parents need high enough income to support their families and to pay for day care for younger children. Therefore, women who are single parents are in special need of training that emphasizes preparation for higher-paying jobs which offer career prospects. For female clients, only non-traditional careers reliably offer enough income to support families and present an alternative to public assistance. For the minority female this problem becomes more acute, in as much as the opportunity for these higher paying jobs has really never existed.... In Utah, women earn only 51 cents for every dollar earned by men.... Low-paying, dead end traditional jobs for women are hardly an attractive alternative to public assistance.[45]

As the author of the report of Scott Matheson's 1984 Governors' Task Force on Integrating Women into the workforce similarly concluded,

> Occupational segregation, poor compensation, and limited career opportunities are primarily rooted in longstanding cultural male-female stereotyping which, despite the facts, continue to assign men to the work-place and women to the home.... The barriers best considered in this forum are equal pay for equal work, inadequate or non-existent child care, lack of access to transportation, inflexible work schedules and hours, and inadequate health insurance.

Among its policy recommendations, the report identified two fundamentally urgent unmet needs: (1) "The state should provide, through legislation, a mechanism for health care coverage for all civilian employees." (2) "Allocate state funds to assist in the development and implementation of company-sponsored child care alternatives."[46] Radical sounding today for a study commissioned by a Republican governor, these findings testify to the advances civil rights and women's movements had made throughout society by the early 1980s. Unfortunately, while identifying the problem was comparatively easy, little political will to follow through on such recommendations existed in Utah (or nationally) at the time.

Throughout its history, SOCIO also struggled with a dual identity as a membership organization and professional nonprofit. Like unions, many civil rights–era organizations struggled to retain their base through the late 1970s as they developed deeper relationships with state agencies, heavier reliance on legal competency, and existential dependence on diminishing funding sources. As Utah activist Orlando Rivera warned in 1972:

> If SOCIO ever does get to the point that its greatest interest is in self-perpetuation [or] raising money for its own existence then I think SOCIO will have lost its purpose.... SOCIO's purpose isn't for its own sake as many institutions that now exist have found themselves becoming but rather SOCIO should continue to be a vehicle through which those ... in our society that suffered from lack of representation, lack of adequate employment, lack of education [and] lack of involvement in the total community ... can become a full-fledged member of the society of which [one] exists.[47]

In 1976, SOCIO's Salt Lake City–based director, Robert Nieves, worked for over a year without pay to make up for his organization's budgetary shortfall. At this time SOCIO began its prisoner recidivism program, which netted $300,000 from the Department of Corrections over three years. Increasingly, the organization chased funding for similarly specific projects, and by early 1980 received funding from such powerful institutions as the United Way and Kennecott Copper Corporation. While this afforded financial stability, it shifted the group's operations. As Nieves remembered, "Sometimes you've got something against this part of the system, but they're giving you funds. How can you then go ahead and jump all over the guy? He's giving you the funds.... [Y]ou can't bite the hand that feeds you.... You can't jump all over [a politician] when you know you're receiving money from him." In exchange for 501(c)3 tax-exempt status, SOCIO's organizational scope narrowed to exclude political participation "in politics except for board of registration and political orientation." Yet, as funding sources decreased by the mid-1980s, SOCIO could neither afford a large staff nor retain its members' involvement.[48]

In later years, the terrain upon which union and Chicano activists met did not vanish so much as shift, like the UMWA, to new social bases and battlegrounds in Emery County. Materially, far-eastern Carbon County, where the richest cross-pollination of civil rights and union tra-

FIGURE 7.5. Co-op miners march near Huntington to protest substandard conditions, poor pay, and discriminatory treatment during an organizing drive from 2003–2005. Courtesy, *The Militant*/Terri Moss.

ditions occurred, experienced major blows to its economic foundation. In 1982, Horse Canyon closed, and Kaiser's Sunnyside operations experienced the first of several closures in 1987. In recent years, the nearest coal mines have been the nonunion West Ridge and Lila Canyon properties, and East Carbon–Sunnyside's economic survival largely depends upon a 1989 decision to host a landfill catering to distant urban centers, employing a small minority of the workforce mining once had.

In Emery County, mining jobs remained more stable, and a comparatively smaller Mexican American population slowly increased. As one employer experimented with hiring undocumented Mexican miners in a bid to keep costs low and the UMWA out, these men experienced unique discriminations based on their national origin, language, and appearance. Complicating their struggle for acceptance, social and geographic distance between assimilated Mexican Americans and recent immigrants, as well as the Chicano movement's decline by the late

1980s, forced many of these men and women to build latter-day advocacy movements more slowly.[49] To date, the last major effort to organize a workforce of aggrieved coal miners under the UMWA in Utah had its roots in the cooperative civil rights and union activist worlds of the late 1970s. In the early 2000s, this struggle reinforced the potential synergy of the two movements, yet through its defeat pessimistically reemphasized traditional collective bargaining's fading effectiveness. Here, at Emery County's nonunion Co-op mine, a smaller workforce largely composed of ethnically Mexican miners similarly experimented with legal options and union frameworks in a protracted struggle to address uncommonly substandard conditions.

While by 1979 most nonunion properties matched or exceeded union wages and encouraged miners' increasingly professionalized image, labor relations at Co-op embodied some of the worst stereotypes of nonunion operation. A comparatively smaller operation, it employed only 45 miners who produced 200,000 tons annually at the height of the energy boom. Located at Huntington Canyon's Trail Canyon fork, its owners essentially established a company town, which had 100 residents by 1980 and actually petitioned Emery County to incorporate that year. Co-op grew in significance until 2003, when it produced over 1 million tons at a second mine near Bear Canyon.[50]

While the fundamentalist LDS Kingston family and business empire worked the mine with its own members in earlier years, by the 1970s it began recruiting undocumented Mexican immigrants, who they felt could be compelled to work for substandard wages and benefits. By 1979, many of them had grown increasingly dissatisfied with conditions. While they had been promised "wages equal to and better than miners in other mines . . . workman's compensation . . . and comfortable and habitable housing," that year many received $4.50 an hour for labor normally compensated at between $9 and $11 an hour. One miner's wife, Patsy Zavala, complained that when they first moved there, their trailer didn't have a bathroom for four months. And despite chilly fall nights at high altitude, they also had had no heat for the previous six months. Others noted inferior safety conditions and blamed the company for Huberto Leon's death in 1978 and Roberto Lopez's serious injury in 1979.[51]

Though a legal resident, Zavala's husband spoke poor English and the couple felt reluctant to relocate given the probable difficulty of finding a new job. Seeking assistance, they reached out to the UMWA through Deer Creek miner Jorge Velasquez, who put them in touch with organizer Louis Sandoval. Sandoval may not have felt it possible to organize a traditional union campaign at this time. Rather, he put the eighteen miners most interested in change in touch with attorney Anthony Ayala who filed a suit for $1.3 million in compensatory damages. While Ayala filed paperwork to protect the miners from deportation pending their cases' outcome, by November only eleven undocumented miners remained at the mine. The rest had left, fearful of mining officials' retribution. While defending itself in court, Co-op's owners organized a company-controlled "union" this year to keep miners from petitioning for a certification election.[52]

While the company continued to operate with lower wages and undocumented labor for the next two decades, in 2003 miners—including several who had worked here since the 1970s—undertook a major campaign to organize under the UMWA. With pay averaging between $5.25 and $7 per hour, and without health insurance or pension benefits, conditions here appalled International officials who felt them more reminiscent of "the early days of coal mining when workers were treated more like property than human beings" than anything still expected in the twenty-first century. After El Salvadorian immigrant Bill Estrada was fired for union support in September, the union filed unfair labor practice charges while seventy-three miners struck. The drive became a major UMWA priority, with seven Co-op miners welcomed as guest speakers at that year's special convention in Las Vegas, and multiple articles on the strike running in the UMWA *Journal*.[53]

One week before an NLRB representation election in December 2004, management "discovered" thirty strikers' lack of legal authorization to work in the United States and fired them in an effort to tilt the vote. This failed to halt the effort's momentum, and after a year of striking, in 2005 victory finally appeared likely when the NLRB ordered the company to bargain with the union. Soon after, the company provided a final and devastating blow when it closed the mine entirely. While the Kingstons experimented with transferring their coal-mining operations to the long-idled property at Hiawatha, coal markets' significant plunge after 2007 halted these plans. As Utah's coal production has decreased sharply since that year, there has been no comparable organizing effort since.[54]

At its best, the UMWA's continued willingness to organize all miners despite their immigration status evokes its earliest struggles in all regions of the United States. During lengthy Utah strikes in 1903–1904 and 1922, many Utahans of northern European and LDS backgrounds had attacked Italian and Greek strikers as much for their national origin and cultural traits as for their economic demands. With a progressive new president of the AFL-CIO, racial and gender minorities' increased representation in union offices, and experimental new formations such as the Service Employees International Union's "Change to Win" federation, the Co-op strike symbolized the hope many labor supporters had for unionism's revival during the 2000s. While the campaign suggested what many hoped a revived labor movement could look like, its negative conclusion underlined traditional collective bargaining's persistently tenuous utility.

If identity provides a nuanced look into some miners' greatest challenges, it opens additional windows into the hidden world of rank-and-file union activism during the 1980s. Minority activists formed independent networks under their own control, critically evaluated the best tools to confront discrimination, and reached out to embattled strikers who waged the decade's strongest challenges to deunionization. Just as importantly, they developed creative alternatives to traditional labor union hierarchies and practices. Nowhere was this culture more visible than during the 1985 Seventh National Conference of Women Miners in Price, which over 250 participants from fourteen states attended and where International UMWA secretary-treasurer John J. Bonovic and District 22 president Mike Dalpaiz appeared as speakers. Born into a coal-mining family in Sunnyside, John Medina—now employed as antidiscrimination director for the Utah Industrial Commission—led one workshop at the conference, and Richard Cordova led another.[55]

The Price conference attracted not only UMWA officials or legal advocacy organizations but Terry Florin, coordinator of a national network of women firefighters, and strikers Margret Skidmore and Norma Hottermio, whose participation in the Phelps-Dodge strike defended the United Steelworkers' future in Arizona copper. Elsewhere, the Lady Miners of Utah connected with Hormel strikers at Austin, Minnesota; Decker Coal strikers in Wyoming; oil refinery workers in Salt Lake; Molybdenum miners in Colorado; and coal-mining women across the country.⁵⁶ As artifacts of these gains, by 1985 women appeared alongside men in UMWA advertisements, coal industry pictorials, and broadened solidarity's language to include new phrases like "brothers and sisters." Like racial minorities, their fight for acceptance and representation broadens our understanding of miners' long struggle for democracy throughout the twentieth century.⁵⁷

CHAPTER 8

A Quiet Revolution

My last year in the mine I was a classified miner helper. It's a mystery to me how I maintained my position after seeing the things I have seen. I did a lot of fighting for the rights I'm supposed to already have.

—Carolyn A. Booker, 1979

WITHIN THE POPULAR ICONOGRAPHY OF COAL, negative stereotypes of uncaring corporations, indifferent polluters, and worker victimization abound. Most commonly, these are visually represented by stark, black-and-white photographs of coal-smeared, usually white, usually male faces. However, the stories of power plants and the mines that serve them are as social and diverse as the worlds of any observer. Gendering coal's history transcends the most persistent stereotypes, speed limits, security fences, and preconceptions to reveal the profound social changes associated with coal's long twentieth-century rise and fall. In the monuments erected throughout the country to honor the victims of mine disasters, women's names have grimly staked their growing share of claims to the risks and benefits of coal employment. Perhaps, it is to the detriment of future generations that we do not commemorate life as frequently or as publicly as we commemorate death. Nannette Wheeler's name can be seen among others on the Wilberg Mine Memorial. But balancing the memory of Nannette's sacrifice should be the memory of the unusual and illuminating circumstances of Sherri Walters and Jim Williams' lofty marriage.

FIGURE 8.1. A ladies' auxiliary is ready to defend the union. Photo courtesy of the Western Mining and Railroad Museum.

On July 1, 1982, accompanied by six witnesses and Castle Dale's justice of the peace, the couple exchanged wedding vows on the roof of the thirteenth floor of No. 1 unit, Hunter Power Plant, 256 feet above the ground. While original plans called for the ceremony to take place atop one of the plant's much higher smoke stacks, these had been scaled back for safety and logistical reasons. Still, from the vantage of the power plant's roof, the wedding's participants must have enjoyed one of the best views available of the booming industrial and natural landscapes that together had brought them here. The couple first met while working at the plant, where Jim was planning-scheduling department supervisor and Sherri was a training department secretary. Born in Kanab, Sherri moved to Castle Dale with her first husband whom she later divorced. In her early thirties and needing a job, she found a well-paying position in the energy industry rapidly expanding throughout Utah's coal country. Economically independent at the time of her marriage, she exercised greater discretion in the choice of a second husband than most prior generations of Emery County women could have probably imagined. This time, she remained more happily married for the rest of her life.[1]

A decade before, such a celebration would have been unthinkable. Emery County couples almost universally married young and rarely included self-supporting wives. Divorce was equally uncommon. Indications of local gender expectations may be gained from the passionate dress-code debates that raged throughout Carbon and Emery County classrooms and households during the contentious autumn of 1972. As the *Emery County Progress* noted, "While the parents may have agreed to Levis for the girls, the students turned thumbs down. The boys don't want to see the fair sex in blue jeans . . . and the girls themselves prefer denims of dress quality, weight and color, pink, for instance."[2] That spring, a joint committee of Emery High students and parents defended traditional expectations when they adopted the following list of unacceptable dress for girls:

> Ten-ounce boy-cut denims with or without rivets; tank tops; halter or harness tops; any clothing which is deliberately tattered or torn; T-shirts or sweat shirts; see-through clothing of any kind; shoes which damage floors; low cut necklines that become immodest; blouses and slacks that expose bare midriffs; any clothing with undesirable or repugnant letters, slogans or pictures.[3]

During the 1970s, residents of Carbon and Emery Counties experienced the many cultural changes that transformed American life nationally. In dancehalls, high schools, a community college, and municipal parks built by cowboys and coal miners, birth control, folk music, disco, political activism, and recreational drugs introduced thousands to alternative lifestyles and ideas. Even support for the Vietnam War fractured within the strongly patriotic region. For the previous five years, *Sun Advocate* editor Robert Finney ran numerous pieces disparaging antiwar protestors. After helping close friends in Helper bury their son in June 1971, he penned a biting editorial against the seemingly interminable conflict.[4]

By challenging gender roles and limited professional opportunities, men and women in Carbon and Emery Counties reflected a national desire for change. As a sign of the times, Planned Parenthood opened an office in Carbon County in the fall of 1971. The next year high school students, parents, and administrators argued passionately on both sides of a fight for women's rights to wear pants and men's rights to grow hair. Within the workforce, women entered a number of nontraditional occupations. In 1974, Bonnie Hansen and Mitilda Hatch became the first women construction flaggers. In 1976, Joan Murray became the first woman electrical worker when she began a UP&L apprenticeship. In 1980, Frances M. Palacios became the first woman from East Carbon to become a lawyer. In sports, Ralean Hatt broke the gender barrier in little league baseball, and Arline Shade because the first woman victor of a demolition derby. While not every change had the prominence of Sherri and Jim Williams' wedding, through a kaleidoscope of mostly unheralded personal struggles, the sexual revolution came to eastern Utah through local gumption and a boom in fossil fuels.[5]

Of all the traditionally male occupations women entered in the 1970s, perhaps none was more rigidly gendered than underground coal mining. Miners' identities, health care, pensions, recreational and consumptive patterns, restrooms, and bathhouses were male breadwinners' unmistakable constructions. As women began mining coal in 1973, many men feared more than increased job competition. As one female miner remembered, "The men's hero identity was kind of destroyed.... People thought if women could go underground, mining couldn't be as hard and ugly as they thought."[6] Subsequently, men's sexual harassment, hazing, and resentment of women miners weakened many workforces' historic solidarity. Despite this treatment, many women miners fought for professional and peer acceptance as working miners and, most often, as union members. What followed was one of the most dynamic mergers of civil rights and union activism during the era: the Coal Employment Project and Coal Mining Women's Support Team.

This was not the first time women struggled for acceptance within the UMWA. In the mid-1930s, several Utah locals organized miners' wives into ladies' auxiliary units. Such formations were products of an era when labor's power was far from certain, and unions depended upon male workers' wives and community support to meet picketing and logistical strike challenges. Perhaps most famously, such organizations played crucial roles during the massive (if ultimately unsuccessful) strike that swept Southern textiles in 1934, and the United Auto Workers' more successful factory occupations in Flint, Michigan, in early 1937. During their initial organizing efforts in early 1933, the radical National Miners Union introduced auxiliaries' effectiveness to coal

THE ROCK SPRINGS Daily ROCKET

WESTERN WYOMING'S HOME NEWSPAPER

ROCK SPRINGS, WYOMING, SATURDAY, JULY 28, 1951 — PRICE 5c

Union Office Picketed — A touch of irony was added to the strife-torn District 22 United Mine Workers office Friday afternoon as office workers proclaimed the bastion of labor as being "unfair to organized labor." District officers, however, contended that they had been informed that they were nt to recognize any picket line and were to carry on their business as usual. Shown picketing the office are, left, Mrs. Malcolm Condie, wife of the International Board member from the district, who only recently resigned his post because of internal strife in the district, and Mary Butkovich, right, who was dismissed Thursday evening.—(Daily Rocket Photo by Jim Wegner)

District 22 UMW Office Picketed; Officials Ignore Picket Line

By JIM WEGNER

FIGURE 8.2. *Opposite*, in 1951, two union secretaries from District 22's Rock Springs office protested discriminatory layoffs that ignored seniority. *At left*, former IEB member Malcolm Condie's wife supports Mary Butkovich *(right)*. Used with permission from the Eberly Family Special Collections Library, Pennsylvania State University Libraries.

miners in New Mexico and Utah. Having replicated the model, as the UMWA gained security in its position it appears to have disbanded most ladies' auxiliary units by the 1940s. It did, however, continue the Labor Day tradition of electing a ceremonial "Coal Queen." Beyond the local celebration, this tradition used coal miners' seventeen- to twenty-six-year-old wives and daughters' physical attractiveness to promote coal consumption and local investment through beauty contest coverage in industry and regional magazines.

During World War II, a shortage of male miners led some employers to recruit women as tipple workers, despite state laws that forbade their presence "in or around any mine." Most male miners, however, were opposed. In 1944 the IEB instructed Wyoming miners to forbid any additional women from joining the union, and asked District 22 president Alfred Carey "to endeavor, at the earliest possible time, to eliminate the employment of women around any mine." At Local 2328, this created an unstable situation, where a recording secretary noted, "We have some women that do belong [to the union] and some that don't belong. And we are having trouble every meeting night, asking us why don't we stop the girls from working or make them pay dues."[7]

While the UMWA did not organize secretarial workers at coal companies, in 1951 District 22's Rock Springs secretaries were members of at-large District 50 Local 7525. Following the tumultuous 1949 district election, incoming officers provoked a revolt among these women. Newly elected secretary-treasurer Arthur Biggs suspected they had leaked internal information to his rivals during their contested ouster. In July 1951, he fired Ann Jelaco, who had worked as former district president Houston Martin's personal secretary, and her sister Mary Butkovich, who had also worked in the office as a secretary for three years. Biggs added insult to injury, however, when he asked Butkovich to stay aboard long enough to teach her work to a new employee. She immediately protested Biggs's disregard for her seniority, and that day the two women picketed the office. While two district auditors who were working inside left the building in respect of their action, Biggs and board member Leon Wisniewski remained inside and continued to work. Joined by supporters that included former district officers' wives, Butkovich and Jelaco carried signs that provocatively claimed, "District 22–UMWA Unfair to Organized Labor," and received front-page coverage in the *Rock Springs Daily Rocket*. In an editorial to the *Sun Advocate*, Jelaco situated her treatment within miners' historical struggles:

> [Mary and I] would like to know how any individual reading this would feel if he or she is told, "I will have to lay you off because you are someone's sister and in a Union office are being replaced by another girl, who you are asked to teach your work to." No employer or coal company in this country, where there is a Democracy, has ever done this to anyone. It is evident then that we did not have to be told to fight for our rights by the use of a picket line and appeals to the International office. Our father, having been a union man much longer than this "So-Called Union Officer" has raised us to be union people with the Union principle.[8]

Butkovich denied the charge of leaking information, protested via personal letters to John L. Lewis, and appealed her case for back pay to the IEB. On October 23, this body awarded the two women a minor settlement but denied their claim for reinstatement on the grounds that district officers had the right to select secretaries. In a last letter to Lewis, Butkovich indulged in none of the flatteries common to miners' letters at this time. Instead, she framed her struggle within the context of members' declining strength within the organization:

> I had every means of winning my case had I been given true justice by the IEB, and I feel if cases like mine are to be ignored by the International that the union principles fought and died for by miners in the past years has only been a worthless cause as there is no longer brotherhood among the coal miners—it is every individual for themselves trying to get on top even if they have to step over innocent and defenseless persons. This is exactly what the present District officers are doing and getting away [with] because of the high position and large salaries permit them to do so, but when the majority of the coal miners who have only been sitting back find out the true facts of injustices done by these officers the past incidents won't just be forgotten.[9]

While Butkovich and Jelaco's grievances preceded women miners' struggles by over twenty years, their case suggests the complexity of the UMWA's century-long relationship with women. Through direct employment as well as unpaid work feeding male miners, washing their clothes, and maintaining their households, coal mining has always required women's labor. While coal employment and union traditions could empower women and lead them to broader civic roles, male miner's biases ensured their presence—and participation—remained contested.

During the 1970s, a trajectory of the UMWA's acceptance of women miners may be traced through its organ, the *United Mine Workers Journal*. In 1972, a back-page cartoon satirized the very idea as laughable. Thirteen months later, a more frank discussion took place in an interview with three male employees of Virginia's Clinchfield Coal Company, where several women had just applied. All three expressed hostility toward the concept. But when two women actually began working underground in Letcher County, Kentucky, a *Journal* article portrayed them favorably, pointing out their fathers' roles in the mine's earlier organization. In June 1974, the first letter to the editor by a woman miner appeared, and in March 1976 a fifteen-page feature on women in the UMWA contained a full page of photographs, four letters from women miners, and an interview with Gloria Johnson, treasurer of the Coalition of Labor Union Women. At its October 1976 convention, the union sat its first two female delegates. While it was easier for editors to adapt to changing political realities than it was for rank-and-file miners to change long-held attitudes, discursive change suggests the inroads women made.[10]

Obstacles women coal miners faced included exclusion from higher-paying and technical positions, discrimination on job biddings, exclusion from union meetings, sexual harassment, lack of bathroom and changing facilities, superstitions about women being bad luck underground, and social pressure to quit mining. Biological difference presented further barriers. As little work clothing existed in women's sizes, men's proportions shaped safety equipment and led to ill-fitting shoes and hardhats for women. Underground restrooms rarely existed, and some women became dehydrated and prone to bladder infections through efforts to minimize the vulnerability and awkwardness of biological breaks. And after coming home from a shift, most women miners' families still expected them to assume the primary responsibility for housekeeping and childcare.[11]

While male miners frequently questioned women's physical capacity for heavy lifting, their success discouraging women from entering higher-paid and higher-status positions operating mechanical equipment at the face led to their disproportionate concentration in entry level positions where the most upper body strength is required. While they shoveled conveyor belts, built concrete walls to guide ventilation, bolted roofs, or covered pillars of coal with rock dust, women faced disproportionate and nearly constant scrutiny. Where company policies may have required a miner to seek assistance with a strenuous task, women frequently feared that to do so would raise doubts about their competency. As a result, those who persevered in mining often shunned assistance and subjected themselves to greater strain.[12]

In a 1980 study of sexual harassment, CEP found "17% [of respondents] have been physically attacked while working as miners, while ten percent say they have been searched for smoking materials in a sexually suggestive manner. . . . Fifty-three percent of the respondents reported that they have been propositioned by their bosses on at least one occasion . . . [and] seventy-six percent of the women reported that they had been propositioned by a co-worker." Above ground, married miners' wives could be among women miners' harshest critics. As Helper native Rebecca Montoya observed, "Women miners often faced judgments from other women in the community that questioned their morality, their ability to be proper mothers, and even the safety of their husbands with what was perceived as less capable miners." Living in Fairview in 1979, Irene Sanderson Nielson commuted to work at Valley Camp's Belina mine and remembered, "The church (LDS) did not have any social events for widows or singles at that time and many of the women were afraid of me working too closely with their husbands."[13]

Despite such obstacles, mining offered women unparalleled financial opportunities. In 1973, researchers at Brigham Young University calculated that miners' average annual wages of $11,904 ($69,734 in 2018 dollars) averaged 68 percent higher than those in the service sector where most women worked. Furthermore, local women in service work may have found traditional employment increasingly scarce as the energy boom developed. According to a 1979 report of the US Civil Rights Commission, the spouses of arriving male workers raised the educational level and work experience expected for traditional women's jobs in several energy boomtowns. However, farsighted employers challenged by high turnover and insufficient applicants may have viewed women miners as a way to obtain needed workers without increasing the strain upon community infrastructure. In this context, the further the boom developed, the more the opportunity—and the pressure—for women to participate in it became.[14]

Hired in small numbers after 1973, women initially fought for acceptance as individuals. Utah's first female miner, Shirley Haycock, started as a belt shoveler at Kaiser in 1974. After gaining experience, she bid on a job driving a "buggy" that shuttled coal underground. As the only woman employee for over a year, Haycock understood her pioneering role. Reflecting on her career, she recalled always "trying to keep everything above board, so if other women wanted to go underground they didn't have a bad reputation to fight." For her this meant maintaining a relatively low profile, not flirting at work, not telling dirty jokes, and keeping her car seat covered with an old blanket during the thirty-mile drives home to shower. On her first day at Kaiser, male miners initially refused to work alongside her before backing down once she entered the mine.[15]

Defending their jobs, women miners frequently inverted conservative criticisms to emphasize mining's compatibility with traditional gender roles. While applying to the Deer Creek mine was her own decision, Rose Oviatt emphasized the consent she had obtained from her fiancé to do so. Likewise, Hiawatha miner Agnes Pierce noted the support of her husband and three children for her decision to work underground. Mentioning "a son in the Air Force, a son in the marines, and a married daughter" as proof of her maternal competency, Carol Mecham described mining as an opportunity that enabled her to support two younger children at home. Employed as an underground safety inspector at Hiawatha, former waitress Deloris Reed framed her identity in similar terms as "a divorcee and mother of a 12-year-old son and an 11-year-old daughter, [who] wants to provide her family with a better life." Joy Huitt pointed to the increased time she had with her husband and her ability to contribute to six children's college savings to demonstrate how coal mining improved her performance as a mother and wife beyond her prior occupation as a nurse. Starting her work underground at age forty-four, Huitt noted, "The younger girls that come to work in the mines have a little trouble with the men, but I don't because I'm old enough to be a lot of their mother.... I'm thought of as 'mom' and with that comes respect.... I'm a good Christian woman and I'm not out for anyone's husband."[16]

Those who allowed journalists to photograph them at work and conduct interviews, however, were extremely cognizant of their stories' effect. Beyond the scrutiny of public spotlights, many who played key roles in challenging exclusionary practices have not had their names or stories included in written records. Locally, a story is told of one female miner at Kaiser who, where a separate bathhouse did not exist, refused to drive home covered in coal dust and decided to shower at the mine alongside her male coworkers. While the discomfort her act created helped motivate company officials to provide separate facilities, her action was unconnected to any organization and unreported in the local press. In workplaces throughout coal country, many such transformative moments remain recorded only in memories.[17]

Relationships between women miners and the UMWA were not initially warm. While Deer Creek miners Carol Mecham and Ruth Oviatt recalled being excited to attend their first union meeting, reporter Joe Rolando concluded that Hiawatha safety engineer Deloris Reed "doesn't have any problem working in a predominately male occupation because she works for the company and not the UMWA." Referring to male miners in her interview, Reed agreed that "as long as you don't work directly with them you're alright." Employed at Hiawatha a year later, Agnes Pierce lamented her male coworkers beliefs that "a woman's place is at home taking care of the children and doing the cooking. Some say it and some don't." As one of only four women in Price River Coal's workforce of 160 in 1978, Joy Huitt concluded, "The bias against women miners was everywhere then.... [W]omen were not encouraged by local [union] officers to go to the local meetings. They let us know they wanted us to pay our union dues and shut up."[18]

If women's initially sparse hiring demonstrates the "tokenist" approach of reluctant companies, a series of legal victories won by the CEP opened doors for many more. The organization began after an accidental discovery in April 1977, when two public interest groups—the East Tennessee Research Corporation and Save Our Cumberland Mountains—based in Jacksboro, Tennessee, attempted to visit an underground coal mine to better understand the industry so influential to their communities. While the mine's owner was initially very cooperative, when he found out that one of the staffers to go on the tour was a woman, he cited male miners' probable objections and refused to allow her to enter the mine. As CEP founder Betty Jean Hall later summarized:

> Members of the ETRC staff, who were very disturbed by this situation, began to brainstorm about what could be done. After some research, they discovered Executive Order 11246 (as amended) which has forbidden sex discrimination in employment by federal contractors since 1968. Since most coal companies, particularly in the Tennessee area, have federal contracts with the Tennessee Valley Authority (TVA), a legal handle on the problem became apparent. Coal companies were violating presidential order by not hiring women to work in the mines![19]

After receiving a start-up grant from the Ms. Foundation in August, these founders organized their efforts under the name of the Coal Employment Project:

> The first three months were spent documenting the problem and traveling around the coal fields of Tennessee and Kentucky to visit women and men miners, to determine the extent of interest in mining jobs by Appalachian women, and, in general, "to test the atmosphere of the coal fields." Two questions still lingered: (1) how many women were there in the mountains who really wanted the job? And (2) were most women, who had been brought up in a "traditional way," physically capable of handling coal mining jobs. The doubts raised in those questions quickly melted when, in practically every coal mining community visited, several women were identified who were seriously interested in coal mining jobs. Further, it became clear, that while mining is hard work, most women can do the job as well as the average man.[20]

While coal's story after 1978 is usually written as one of increasing layoffs and diminishing expectations, CEP activists were guided by the now largely forgotten optimism of western energy boomtowns during the Carter years and the second energy crisis. As they understood it,

> the time was right for launching an attack on the discriminatory practices of the coal industry because it was one of the nation's biggest growth industries. With president Carter's goal of doubling coal production by 1985, the federal government was projecting 45,000 new coal mining jobs annually until 1985. CEP would not even have to deal with the issue of "taking men's jobs away."[21]

In December 1978, the fledgling coalition of lawyers, unionists, and rank-and-file women miners won a landmark decision when the country's second-largest coal producer, Consolidated Coal Company, paid $360,000 in back wages to a group of 78 women it had discriminated against in Tennessee, Virginia, and West Virginia. The company also agreed to hire women in 25 percent of entry-level positions until they made up 32.8 percent of the workforce.[22] In the West, the US Department of Labor set a similar precedent when in 1979 it ordered Decker Coal Company of Decker, Montana, and Big Horn Coal Company of Sheridan, Wyoming, to pay $200,000 in lost wages to 186 female plaintiffs. Although both companies had signed equal opportunity agreements with the federal government, Decker's mine had only hired one woman since 1972, and Bighorn admitted hiring no female employees as it expanded its workforce from 46 to 231 over a four-year period. In their settlements, both companies agreed to henceforth staff 10 percent of entry-level blue-collar jobs with women. Nationally, women miners grew from 4.2 percent of new hires in 1978 to 11.4 percent in 1979, and stayed around 8 percent through 1984. By December 31 of that year, 3,825 women had started underground coal-mining careers.[23]

One of CEP's most successful and long-lasting efforts was facilitating working women miners' formation of statewide support networks. By 1984, these had been organized in seven states and served multiple roles. In addition to maintaining a connection to legal advice, they assisted women miners and prospective women miners in sharing news about job openings, lessons for successfully integrating into a workforce, job-specific knowledge male miners may have been less likely to share, and coping strategies for overcoming biological difference. Perhaps most importantly, these organizations played an intangible, psychological role providing women miners a sympathetic ear for their problems and a confidence-boosting reserve of moral support. CEP staff facilitated regional and national communication among women miners by helping support groups get organized, publishing a newsletter that shared their stories, and organizing and financing annual national conferences. The first national conference, held in West Virginia, brought together 50 women miners, including some from as far away as Wyoming and New Mexico. The sixth conference, held in 1984, drew over 200 women delegates.[24]

As the number of Utah women miners increased, so did their capacity for collective action. By 1979, the few employed at Price River Coal coordinated to make sure at least one of them attended every union meeting. By 1981, some 190 women mined coal in Utah. On January 31 of that year, a crowd of 90 persons gathered at the La Salle Café in Helper to discuss the formation of a women miners' support network. Along with women miners, prospective women miners, and some of their husbands, friends, and relatives, national CEP director Betty Jean Hall and assistant director Joyce Dukes attended. Those present at the meeting formed the Lady Miners of Utah (LMU) and agreed to meet thereafter once a month. Ann Byerley, Faye Lee, Elnora Clark, Carolyn Booker, Joy Huitt, and Judy Franco composed the group's initial board.[25]

While CEP's national staff identified freely with feminist politics and regularly interacted with the movement's leading personalities and organizations, women coal miners did not always share the same understanding of their role. As staffer Connie White noted during a pilot training program for women, "We'll have everything from very politically-aware feminist women to gun-toting Tennessee mountaineer women. And there will be everything in between, including several women who have very traditional lifestyles and values, except for their job aspirations." Similarly, Utah miner Ann Byerley explained her group's practical motivations in one interview: "We want to solve problems, we are not women libbers. . . . We want to work with the men. We want to work to support women, the families, and the community."[26] While both expanded women's opportunities, many women miners strategically deemphasized sexual difference in order to be accepted in the workplace. This approach has been observed among underground women coal miners elsewhere and remains commonly employed by strip miners in Wyoming, where today women make up 20–25 percent of the workforce. Scholars have recognized such "unacknowledged feminism" to be present in other traditionally male industries at this time. At the CEP's first national conference in 1979, a motion to establish a women's caucus within the UMWA had actually been defeated because of how divisive delegates feared it would be.[27]

Already, women faced a number of charges from suspicious union members. For decades the accusation of "dual unionism" had been levied against almost anyone advocating participation in labor-related projects outside of the UMWA, and by the early 1980s many still appeared uncomfortable with the idea of collaborative organizational work alongside nonunion miners. Kaiser miner Irene Pritchett remembered her initial request to district officers for paid time off while away on CEP business—a courtesy extended to men for UMWA activities: "As I feared, someone asked if CEP was Union. Since we do have some ladies in our Utah group who are not union miners, my request was denied. They did suggest we convince these nonunion ladies to purchase a union card, then the U.M.W.A. would support our CEP actions here."[28]

By contrast, some nonunion companies seem to have recognized women's presence as an opportunity to demonstrate progressive credentials. Thus, while Wyoming's Amax Coal Company fiercely battled the UMWA, they were among the first to welcome women to strip mining. In 1978, the company's vice president of human resources, Thomas F. Connors, wrote to *Coal Mining Women's Support Team News* editor Millie Walters "to congratulate you on your efforts to expand opportunities for women in the coal industry," and noted that "with the organizational abilities and dedication you have shown to date, I am sure you will succeed. Be assured that AMAX Coal shares, and in most cases exceeds, your goals." Connors ordered a subscription to the newsletter and purchased twenty-four "Women Can Dig it Too!" T-shirts.[29]

At SUFCO, former manager Glen Zumwalt recalled, "We had quite a few women who worked for us. . . . I don't know if we were the first in Utah but we had women underground at SUFCO in 1977. We weren't looking for the stereotype. We weren't looking for the guy that had 10 years in the coal mine and knew how to do everything. We were looking for people with values. You can learn to do all kinds of jobs."[30] In 1979, Amax gave activist miner Laurie Castleberry an extra day of leave without pay to attend the National Conference of Women Coal Miners in West Virginia, and initiated a program "where area foremen go to training sessions that help them to recognize the potential value of women as workers, and help them change behaviors that stop women from becoming as knowledgeable and productive as they might be." Plateau similarly supported LMU activist Gene Byrge and paid her plane fare to attend a national CEP conference in 1981.[31]

This experience, however, appears to have been uneven, and contrasts with many nonunion mines' preference not to hire women at all. From her work, Joy Huitt generalized:

> I've met nonunion women, and it seems like they work under great fear. They're not really free to communicate. They have to be so careful about what they do so that they're not implicated for trying to organize a union. The companies often rotate the women on different shifts to keep them separated. They have no job protection. They can't relax. There is a lot of turnover. You make money, but you don't have any rights. If we had a problem with sexual harassment, we'd go to someone in our local, or to the district or international union. There are channels, and eventually, someone is going to hear you. If you try that in a nonunion mine, you don't have a job the next day.[32]

While the national CEP office welcomed some nonunion companies' support, they employed strategic identities as a labor and civil rights organization. Thus, after receiving one company's request for an upcoming national conference's schedule, staffer Joyce Dukes responded with a version of the agenda that had all union-specific workshops omitted. While she admitted to feeling a bit "like a chicken," she undoubtedly was correct to recognize that "coal companies don't seem too keen on supporting projects that are union-oriented."[33]

As time went on, relationships between women miners and the UMWA notably improved. By the mid-1980s support team members and UMWA organizers frequently shared information and contacts. UMWA locals increasingly gave women time off, paid vacation days, and funding to attend CEP events. In its publications, advertisements, and campaign art, the UMWA increasingly printed images of women miners as well as International resolutions of support for their organizations and needs. Speaking in 1985 at women miners' seventh national conference in Price,

FIGURE 8.3. National conferences of women coal miners gave rank-and-file activists rare opportunities to meet one another, share experiences, and find mutual support. The Lady Miners of Utah's custom T-shirts stand out in 1982 and suggest the unique organizational coherence this state chapter had. Courtesy of Archives of Appalachia, East Tennessee State University, Coal Employment Project Records.

International secretary-treasurer John Banovic recognized that "we have to organize. We have to revitalize the labor movement, and as the fastest growing segment of the labor force, women are playing a crucial role. You are emerging as leaders in our unions because you are qualified, you are motivated, and because of all workers, you have the most to gain."[34] As the UMWA's new International president, Richard Trumka officially endorsed women miners' national conferences in 1983 and after. Reaffirming this support five years later as the Tenth National Conference of Women Miners organized, he invoked history to support women miners' ongoing efforts:

> The United Mine Workers of America has always upheld the belief that "an injury to one is an injury to all" and this statement applies to problems that UMWA women have experienced in the coal industry, such as job discrimination and workplace harassment. To give less than our full attention to the concerns of women miners would be a disservice

FIGURE 8.4. CEP's 1985 national conference in Price brought together many interested in a more inclusive labor movement and represents hidden chapters of working-class feminism pioneered by coal miners and their supporters during the 1980s. Courtesy of Archives of Appalachia, East Tennessee State University, Coal Employment Project Records.

to our entire membership, and a betrayal of the best traditions of our Union.... I make this endorsement not only as a demonstration of solidarity with our Union sisters, but in recognition that this conference addresses issues facing all UMWA members, such as mine health and safety and family leave.[35]

Like most of CEP's leadership, Joy Huitt came from a proud family of union coal miners. Born in Powhatan, Alabama, she moved to Utah after her father got a job at Horse Canyon during World War II. He had been a longtime union activist and fought for the UMWA during earlier Southern campaigns. Ann Byerley grew up in an LDS coal mining family and learned from her father what conditions were like in the days of handloading coal. Before mining, she was a divorced mother of two holding two full-time, low-wage jobs. Gene Byrge grew up in Helper where her father mined coal until he was laid off in the 1960s. Her earlier

FIGURE 8.5. In 1986, Rita Miller and Joy Huitt became the first women elected to district UMWA office. Courtesy of Archives of Appalachia, East Tennessee State University, Coal Employment Project Records.

career involved office work, bartending, and work as a bank teller. Like Byerley, she left her first husband after he became abusive. Similarly, Wanda Lankford, Elnora Clark, and Rita Miller left their first husbands after their deficiencies became known. All entered coal mining in their forties and had a variety of prior work experience.[36]

Faye Lee stands out as one of the younger active members of the Lady Miners. Born to Italian parents in Standardville, she was thirty-three years old in 1981 and drove a shiny new pickup truck with a front license plate that read "Liberated Woman." She also left her first husband—a truck driver and a miner—after he developed "a roving eye" and a drinking problem. She came to mining after working numerous waitress and bartending jobs, for financial reasons as well as miners' healthcare benefits which greatly helped her diabetic child. At Deer Creek, she experienced a taste of what underground mining might have become had women continued their advance to parity numbers. Here, Lee worked on an all-woman team on straight day shifts where she performed a variety of maintenance duties, masonry work, and motor equipment operation. In 2014, she recalled an initial battle for acceptance:

We ate in a lunchroom with some of the guys. At first it was really hard; they were nasty-mouthed, very nasty-mouthed. One day one of the men was really giving me a rotten time and I stood there and ate and listened and listened. I got up and grabbed some rock dust and started throwing it on the side of the kitchen, then I threw it at him. He said, "You have no business under here." I said, "I'll gladly quit if you will take care of my children. I have four children. If you will pay for my children, I'll quit today. I'm here because of them. I'm not here to impress you. I'm not here to date any of you. I'm not here for any reason other than to take care of four children that need a mom, a house, food, and medical. If you'll take care of them, I'll quit." After that day we . . . became friends. To this day I'll never forget him because to this day we were best of friends. He hated women underground, but I explained and we became really good friends.

As time passed,

I'd go under there and I felt secure. My boss was fantastic, my crew even better. I had the best crew anyone could ever, ever have. The crew that I had made you feel so good. . . . I'd lost a son at the time, and my crew kept me strong. . . . They made you feel like you were always protected. . . . You know, women weren't supposed to be able to do it, and my ex-husband said, "You can't do it. You're not woman enough." Being able to prove to a lot of people that I could do anything that I set my mind to do. Just to go in there and say, "I can do it." And I really did love the mine. I don't know, there's something about being underground. The family that you make under there, that's pretty special.[37]

Into the late 1980s the Lady Miners met monthly and shared community, coping strategies, self-education, and connections to legal support. For working and prospective women miners, they gave advice and helped with a number of unfamiliar procedures, from getting hired to filling out Mine Safety and Health Administration, Equal Employment Opportunity Commission, and union grievance paperwork. Through traditional gender roles, they also raised their community profile. During mine rescue team competitions, International Days festivals, and Labor Day celebrations, they prepared and served hundreds of lunches to support participants and raise funds. During the October 1984 selective strike at Emery mining, the Lady Miners brought coffee and donuts to those on the picket line. Amid relief efforts for the Wilberg mine fire, the Lady Miners coordinated logistics, provided food, and transported missing miners' family members from the Salt Lake airport to Price. They were also assigned some of the more difficult tasks, such as calling missing miners' families to let them know that recovery efforts were being postponed when the mine was sealed to extinguish the fire. The following June, the group reached a high point of its influence when they hosted CEP's national conference at the College of Eastern Utah in Price. Approximately 250 women miners attended.[38]

The Lady Miners also continued to develop their relationship with broader movements for social justice. At the 1981 Labor Day parade, the Lady Miners' float won third place. Decorated in green and white for support of the Equal Rights Amendment, its front featured the CEP emblem—a crossed pick and shovel within the Venus symbol—followed by crib blocks and a large pile of donated coal. During a 1982 Christmas party at the Cowboy Club in Wellington, the Lady Miners held "a short business meeting . . . on the ERA coalition and rallies to keep the movement alive." Several LMU activists joined the Coalition of Labor Union Women, and attended its events including a 1984 conference in Salt Lake City.[39]

Within the UMWA, women's influence continued to expand. In November 1978, the IEB unanimously passed a resolution in support of "our sisters who are working to widen options for women in coal mining." At the International convention in 1983, delegates unanimously supported a resolution to include parental leave demands in upcoming BCOA negotiations. Subsequently, a joint union-BCOA committee began to study the issue, and later parental leave was written into union contracts. Women miners also fought for the Family and Medical Leave Act of 1993.[40] Nationally, many women miners identified with union reform, and endeavored to carry the movement started by MFD forward even as the opportunities to do so narrowed. In 1983 and 1984, the LMU organized public showings of *Harlan County, USA* (1976) in Price, Helper, and East Carbon. Very much a product of the MFD movement, the film describes its origins and electoral struggles as well as the 1973–1974 Brookside strike. Assisting CEP with strategy and legal help, former MFD leader Joseph "Chip" Yablonski served on the organization's national board.

FIGURES 8.6 AND 8.7. Fay Lee *(top)* celebrates the Hiawatha mine women's team's tug-o-war victory at the 1984 Labor Day celebration. While historically marginalized groups breathed life into union reform, organized labor's subsequent trajectory has limited the impact—and the memory—of their accomplishments. While Chicano miners Paul Madrigal and Richard Cordova *(bottom)* blended civil rights and union activism, food relief efforts during the 1977–1978 national contract strike demonstrated national collective bargaining's increasing length and bitterness. Courtesy, *Sun Advocate*.

By the 1984 Labor Day celebration in Price, the changing status of women miners was clearly visible. While the organizers continued a fifty-one-year-old tradition of ceremonially appointing a Labor Day queen to rule over the event, the Hiawatha mine women's team provided alternative role models when they won an annual tug-of-war competition.[41] Two years later, Joy Huitt ran for and won District 22's secretary-treasurer position to become the first woman ever elected to district office. Rita Miller also ran that year and was elected as the district's first woman auditor. Nationally, these years saw women miners reach a high-water mark of influence within the UMWA.[42]

Compared to neighboring states, the LMU formed one of the most organizationally cohesive and long-lived support groups. Reflecting the feminist movement's egalitarian ethos, CEP's national office did not require support teams to adopt any uniform organizational structure, and in 1981 its newsletter noted a recent survey's conclusion: "There seems to be no overall pattern or steps to organizing. The two western groups [are] examples: Wyoming has a loose, no-membership structure and consists of a network of people who can be called when a woman experiences a difficult situation or needs help and advice. Utah, on the other hand, is tightly controlled into a membership organization with dues, fund-raising plans, and community participation."[43] In 1979 and 1981, Wyoming women miners in Gillette and Kemmerer formed support-group branches. In Arizona, one Navajo woman miner got in touch with CEP in 1981. As in Utah, a well-publicized organizing meeting brought 103 women together in Kayenta where a CEP staff person, Peabody officials, Local 1924's union president, and a Job Service representative explained the opportunities available to women. Although attendees decided to form a support group, it does not appear to have functioned for long. By August 1983, CEP's mailing list noted only 10 names for the state. While a few revived the effort in 1985, by 1987 no Arizona group existed.[44]

Despite a worsening employment situation, in 1983 CEP established a western office in Denver in the hopes that the region's disproportionate growth would continue despite an eastern coal mining decline. That fall about twenty-five women miners near Paonia, Colorado, organized to form the first support group in that state. After one of the largest nonunion mines, Colorado Westmoreland, hired a strongly prejudiced manager, the group succeeded in getting the company to stop harassing one pregnant miner and eventually won her a transfer to light duty and received assurances that she would be rehired after having her child. Mary Welsh also won her job back after she was fired for suspected union organizing. Spiraling unemployment, however, soon limited this growing interest. As western CEP director E. Michelle Smith noted, "Everyone agrees a support group would be a good idea and is needed, but acknowledge[s] that people right now are afraid for their jobs and not ready to do anything to disturb the status quo." A heavy blow came in 1985, when Westmoreland's Orchard Valley mine closed down, laying off 230 miners including 22 of its 23 women miners. As the second major closure in the North Fork valley, it left the Colorado support team with only three working members.[45]

In 1981 Utah producers projected plans to hire an *additional* 9,529 miners by 1990, but a year later the western energy boom collapsed. In 1982, employers laid off 36 percent of Utah's coal miners, and nationally 60,000 lost their jobs by 1984, including 40 percent of women miners.[46] While plans to expand female recruitment depended upon continued growth, women miners' decision not to confront a gendered seniority system led to their disproportionate rate of dismissal. Increasingly, women miners experienced heightened community and financial pressure to stay at home while men continued working.[47]

At CEP's 1985 national conference in Price, workshop participants had their understandings of layoffs' pressure preserved on videotape during filmed sessions. As one saw it, "A lot of women that we work underground with, they're passed over for promotion pretty much all of the time, and the company gives more bullshit stories than you can shake a stick at but some of them are scared to make waves because they're intimidated." A strip miner agreed, "If management doesn't want a woman to run a bulldozer, or run a dragline, a scraper, a haul truck, or any of it, she's not gonna get there no matter how much seniority she's got. . . . If you're a woman: look out!" A third underground miner similarly summarized:

> See, what they want you to do, they want you to come there, and just be shoveling. They don't want you to learn nothing. They figure that this shoveling, it's a lady's job. . . . They want to move them somewhere so they won't be anywhere around production, so they can't even be at the [face]. . . . [T]he women just can't do it. That's just how they feel. And you

just have to show them that you can do it. . . . You know, a lot of women are hesitant to make waves, we've got women where all they want to do is ride a buggy and they tell you, "I don't want to do nothing I don't want to make no waves I just want to get my check and go home."[48]

Nationally, unemployment played havoc with the CEP's legal strategy. In June 1978, Betty Jean Hall had summarized, "Coal is also one of the nation's biggest 'growth industries.' Government studies project a yearly average of up to 45,000 new coal mining jobs until 1985 . . . up to 186,000 new job slots. This presents an excellent opportunity for women and minorities to claim a large percentage of coal mining jobs, without displacing present workers or precluding traditional applicants." During a 1981 interview on a Salt Lake City radio station, she reiterated the point: "I think we've said at CEP that if we could ever get to the stage where we had fifteen or twenty percent women in every mine, we could go out of business and feel really good about it because the problem would take care of itself. But that's where we've gotta get to." At the time, women appeared on track to attain this goal, making up 11.4 percent of all new hires in 1979. In 1983 they did even better, making up 57.1 percent of new hires in Utah. Direct numbers, however, underscore the standstill this advance had come to. In 1983 Utah coal mines hired only seven new employees.[49]

Upon taking office, Joy Huitt recalled encountering growing hostility from her fellow union officers, whom she believes deliberately sabotaged her effectiveness.[50] If these recollections are valid, they may indicate a resurgence of sexist attitudes, as well as the tentative nature of women's gains. Huitt's campaign also ran into the same formidable geographic barriers that for decades had discouraged rank-and-file members from running for district office. With 4,800 voting miners in three states, Huitt put a lot of miles on her car to gain twelve locals' nominations and win by 296 votes. Being laid-off actually helped, as she would have otherwise experienced greater difficulty finding the time to campaign. Having a large supportive family, strong community roots, and an active grassroots organization behind her also made a difference.[51]

After the election, Huitt continued her earlier activism, served as national CEP board member, part-time western regional organizer, and outreach liaison to women in nontraditional industries. While she shared the

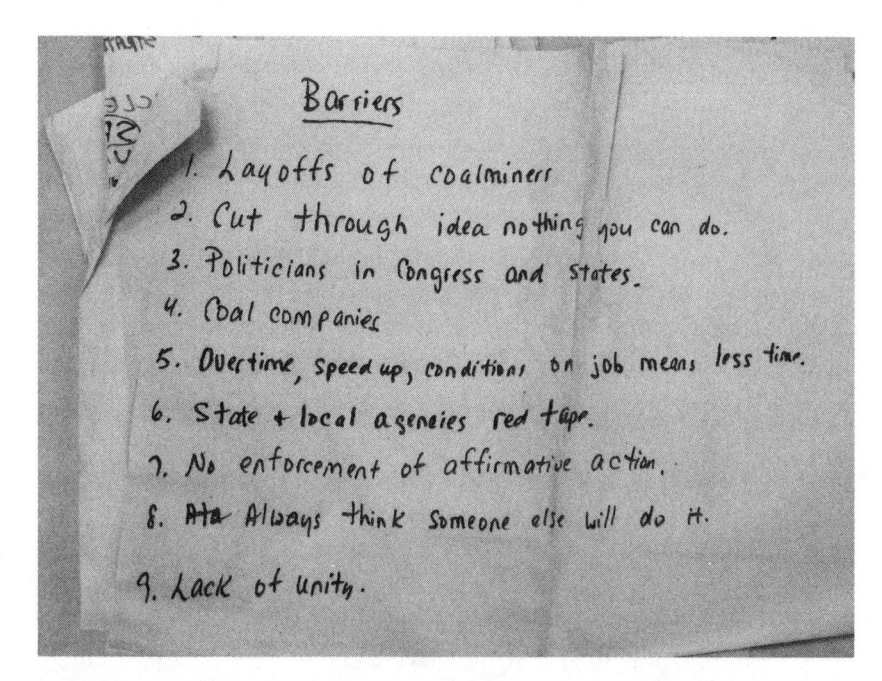

> Barriers
> 1. Layoffs of coalminers
> 2. Cut through idea nothing you can do.
> 3. Politicians in Congress and States.
> 4. Coal companies
> 5. Overtime, speed up, conditions on job means less time.
> 6. State + local agencies red tape.
> 7. No enforcement of affirmative action.
> 8. ~~Ata~~ Always think someone else will do it.
> 9. Lack of unity.

FIGURE 8.8. CEP's workshops preserve records of rank-and-file activists' growing frustrations by the mid-1980s. Courtesy of Archives of Appalachia, East Tennessee State University, Coal Employment Project Records.

CEP model with Salt Lake City oil refinery workers, Colorado molybdenum miners, and Arizona copper miners, her own organization pondered its growing sense of mission drift. In 1986, CEP hired consultant Barbara Rusmore to visit its Utah chapter, hold an organizing workshop, and evaluate its prospects. While she felt the meeting went generally well, and applauded the participants' energy and personal bonds, Rusmore sensed an "ongoing weakness" in "a persistent and insidious problem with internal communication." Rita Miller may have developed a substitutionist leadership style, "to just do things and not think ahead and involve others," while organizational contact work depended disproportionately on Charlene Adamson. Noting a discrepancy between the group's purposes and projects, Rusmore warned that

> community projects and getting to the national convention overshadowed any educational or outreach work. When this was brought to their attention, it was largely explained by the fact that times have changed

and few of them are currently working in the mines so they feel a bit out of touch. No one addressed how, in this recessionary time, could Lady Miners help women miners keep their jobs or get on the few jobs that open up.... They did budget in money to travel to other areas to help set up new support groups as well as money for a brochure and various kinds of informational programs. So the material is there, I just didn't get a feeling for how an outreach campaign would really happen, except around parental leave.... A group that has been pretty static for several years may have the tendency to get entrenched and not grow. That may be happening here.... The potential exists to try to do too many things that don't have a great enough financial and/or organizational return. Frustration and burnout are lurking around the corner.[52]

Already, CEP had adapted its mission to follow many members' drift into different industries. At a 1984 meeting in Utah, consultant Mike Clark updated the Lady Miners with the national organization's future directions project: "While we all agreed that it was very important for CEP to continue having its primary focus on coal mining women, we also felt that CEP should look at the possibilities of exploring sex discrimination in (1) utilities; (2) gas and oil; and (3) trucking." Many Lady Miners followed such trajectories themselves, and by 1987 most of the group's members worked outside coal mining. Rita Alderson and her son managed a bottled gas company, before she moved on to drive trucks at a Nevada strip mine. Rose Hurtado opened a restaurant in downtown Price. Gene Byrge finished a B.S. in sociology, experimented with creative writing, learned to fly airplanes, and applied to jobs as a community organizer. Glenda Cloward became a construction worker. Rita Miller became a UMWA district officer at the same time she studied truck driving.[53]

CEP's legal strategy also had additional shortcomings. In some western regions, CEP staffers noted strong cultural biases against any activism designed to exploit the threat of legal action. As sociologist Kristen Young shared in 1983, "In Colorado the attitude of male blue collar workers toward litigation was very negative, and ... the workers seem to feel that nothing was so terrible that it required resorting to the courts. Women have been run out of the mines for filing suits and, as in the east, black-listed." While this prejudice compounded the emotional pressure on women who waited years to fight through appeals, layoffs gave employers additional tools to indirectly retaliate. After filing a discrimination case through the Equal Employment Opportunity Commission, one Colorado woman accepted an early settlement after her employer fired her husband in retaliation.[54]

When one Clear Creek miner complained of sexual harassment that included male miners' peepholes drilled into women's changing areas, CEP staffer Nancy Burnett provided referrals to regional lawyers along with contact information for eastern women who had fought similar cases. Before filing her own lawsuit, Burnett recommended, "After talking with some of the women miners . . . who have gone through this type of case, you could decide whether it is the best route for you. As I explained, some women who have gone through such 'peephole' cases (and many are currently still going through litigation after more than two years), would not do it again. Some other women would. . . . [T]alk to some of these women to get an idea of both points of view."[55]

At Hiawatha, Aggie Pierce may have fought women miners' most bitter legal campaign in Utah. In 1985 she was one of six women miners with a total workforce of 250. Through union channels, Utah's Labor Relations Board, and the Equal Employment Opportunity Commission, she filed complaints against her employer for verbal sexual harassment, which she noted included such phrases as "you don't belong here," "this is a man's job," and "you are taking a man's job away from him." After her son died in an accident at the same mine in 1982, she filed a suit against the company for neglect. Over the next three years, she noted, "Since that time the harassment has been speeded up beyond endurance. . . . The bosses have talked very crude, belligerent, and filthy to me. It's gotten to the point that the rest of the people I work with have picked up on this and know that it is accepted so they go along with it and join in." Amid escalating stress, Pierce's doctor began treating her for high blood pressure.[56]

In many ways, Pierce's determination embodied the historical contingency of Utah miners' blends of union and civil rights activism. Demonstrating the progress male miners as well as the UMWA had made, Bob Tiny, president of Hiawatha's Local 6363, supported Pierce's suit and accompanied her to hearings in Salt Lake. Broadening the meaning of solidarity to include support for union sisters, Frank Roybal Jr., now at Hiawatha, joined five additional witnesses who testified on her behalf. In spite of such support and her own determination, competitive pressures and slack markets led Hiawatha to lay off 150 miners, or half its workforce, in 1985. Pierce remained but was laid off in 1988, shortly before the mine closed down for good.[57]

For CEP, layoffs further increased tensions over direction and control between its staff—based in Oak Ridge, Tennessee—and its decentralized coalfield membership. In 1987, a serious rift developed between one board member and the group's founder and chief legal counsel, Betty Jean Hall. Beyond the personalities involved, many working members desired to gain full control over the national organization, and in early 1988 Hall resigned in deference to their pressure. Those who remained, however, probably lost more than her legal competency or effectiveness at grant writing. Most likely, more potentially deep-pocketed donors felt a greater kinship with a legal advocacy organization broadly allied with mainstream feminism than they did with a network of working coal miners heavily involved in union politics. Into the early 1990s, CEP struggled to match its earlier stature. In 1999 it disbanded.[58]

Like the UMWA's connections to the Chicano movement and Navajo miners, women coal miners represented a politically active population eager for rank-and-file empowerment. Yet, unlike the public sector, service, transportation, or teaching industries, coal employment's decline frayed one of the era's most promising manifestations of working-class feminism. Subsequently, American underground coal mining became largely resegregated by sex, with only about nine women working underground in Utah during 2016. Women's long history in British coal mines prior to 1842, underground women miners' international experience, and women's success at surface mines in Australia and Wyoming cast doubt upon essentialist arguments that disparage female biology. Had oil prices remained high after 1982, women's predicted influx into underground employment may have continued "undermining gender," opened the last skilled positions to women, and remade underground coal mining into a far less isolating and arduous place for women to work.

CHAPTER 9

Unbridled

> Leadership is hard to find, and you can't get the youth involved. . . . Almost everybody . . . now, most of them are burned out. They started back in the sixties. And they're still the same people there. Very few people are coming in young that get involved. I don't know. They're too involved with this new generation of fast music and—and . . .
>
> —Robert Nieves, Chicano activist, 1985

FROM 1950 TO 1970, over three hundred thousand American coal miners lost their jobs due to mechanization and declining markets. Employers who stayed in business needed few new workers, and when they did a pool of unemployed, skilled miners was readily available. By 1970 that reserve was disappearing, and as production revived operators hired younger workers to fill over one hundred thousand newly created mining jobs.[1] Particularly in the West, many of these new workers did not come from mining families, were unattached to the UMWA, and had not experienced the deference to authority older miners had accepted in the years of precarious employment. While coal miners' median age dropped from forty-six in the late 1960s to thirty-one in 1977, the aggregate statistic obscures the generationally bifurcated nature of the workforce.[2] In the midst of a divisive internal struggle and bargaining setbacks, UMWA organizers increasingly faced the difficult task of "selling" their union across a generational divide.

While veteran miners in their forties and fifties led Miners for Democracy, a younger generation's entrance to coal mining proved far more destabilizing for union power. While pension and health benefits had dominated older miners' concerns and led many to support MFD, those at the start of their careers had a greater interest in immediate cash wages and minimal strike interruptions. Though some younger miners embraced militancy, joined New Left labor organizations, and attempted to construct a base of radical power, their influence during the 1980s was marginal and declined rapidly with layoffs. More commonly, younger miners new to the area as well as to the industry reflected national cultural moods better than coal mining families' traditional unity. For many, nonunion mining's efficiency and competitive prospects mattered more than union contracts' mechanisms for fairness and control.

The UMWA keenly recognized young miners' growing numbers, as well as their tendency to ask, "What have you done for me lately?"[3] As early as 1967, the union's research department identified their significance, "both from the standpoint of making good members of the UMWA and training them to assume responsible positions in the organization."[4] In 1969, researcher Joseph Brennan described his view of an emerging generation gap:

> During [the 1950s and '60s] sons did not follow fathers into the mining industry. Thus, continuity—which is the keystone of tradition—has been broken. We are faced, therefore, with attempting to maintain a tradition among younger miners who for the most part have no real contact with it. . . . Our union is an old established organization. . . . We must offer young men an opportunity to participate in and help determine the destiny of the UMWA. . . . We can no longer proceed as we have in the past, because this new era has brought with it a group of young, smart, aggressive and restless men who have the potential to build our union or tear it apart.[5]

Presenting at a Washington, DC, conference on coal miner safety in 1970, former CIO organizer and UMWA supporter Mike Ross added:

> Miners under 30 often appear hostile to both company and union,

FIGURE 9.1. *Opposite*, from the President's Commission on Coal, *Coal Data Book*, 1980.

AGE DISTRIBUTION OF ACTIVE UMW MINERS, 1967-1975**
(percent of total)

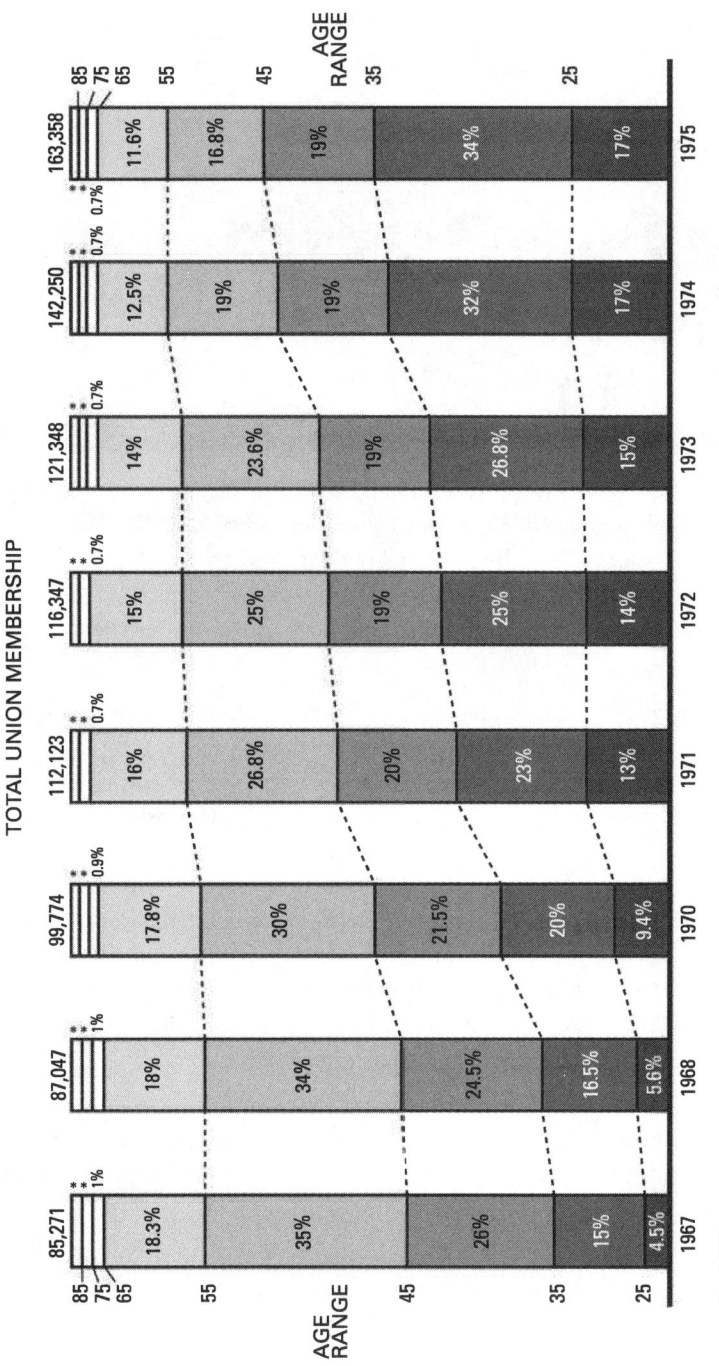

TOTAL UNION MEMBERSHIP

Age Range	1967	1968	1970	1971	1972	1973	1974	1975
Total	85,271	87,047	99,774	112,123	116,347	121,348	142,250	163,358
85	*	*						
75						**	**	**
65	1%	1%	0.9%	0.7%	0.7%	0.7%	0.7%	0.7%
55	18.3%	18%	17.8%	16%	15%	14%	12.5%	11.6%
45	35%	34%	30%	26.8%	25%	23.6%	19%	16.8%
35	26%	24.5%	21.5%	20%	19%	19%	19%	19%
25	15%	16.5%	20%	23%	25%	26.8%	32%	34%
<25	4.5%	5.6%	9.4%	13%	14%	15%	17%	17%

* <0.5%
** 1969 data not available

Source: United Mine Workers Health and Retirement Funds

FIGURE 9.2. At a district level, union leadership demography is evident in this photograph of the 1970 Labor Day committee in Price, Utah. Note standing, *far left*, Paul Madrigal; standing, *center*, Frank M. Stevenson; and seated, *second from left, middle row*, Louis Pestotnik Jr. Used with permission from the Eberly Family Special Collections Library, Pennsylvania State University Libraries.

cynical and disillusioned. Essentially an undisciplined, action-seeking person, now often from a cross-cultural background compared to the older man, far more influenced by TV and national norms, the young worker is unlikely to accept the older miner's relationship to the union uncritically.

Increasingly, they come from outside the coal towns and are high school graduates.... They are bright; some are wild, try to work without much sleep and the beginning of drug usage has been noted.... It is not yet clear what kind of role the young miner will play.... They are now faced with fresh problems and current issues on which past experience sheds only little light.[6]

As union reformers organized, many looked to younger miners optimistically. Comparing Joseph Yablonski's unsuccessful 1969 presidential bid with Arnold Miller's meteoric triumph in 1972, UMWA scholars Marsha Nye (1973), Richard Jay Jensen (1974), Paul J. Nyden (1974), and Maier Fox (1990) all cite the rise in youth employment as a decisive counterweight to longtime incumbent Tony Boyle's support among pensioners.[7] Considering Boyle's advantages of incumbency and well-manicured image as an effective technocrat, heir to John L. Lewis, and living connection to the union's glory days, for a working miner, local union president, and occupational safety activist like Miller to rise from obscurity to the top position in one of the largest labor organizations in the country was by any measure incredible. While Yablonski's years of service as one of few International Executive Board members still elected by his district had enabled him to develop networks of sympathizers and allies, executive experience, political sophistication, and a national profile, Miners for Democracy and its unknown slate of candidates had to build all of these (and more) from scratch. Though the cultural and political shocks spanning 1969 to 1972 may have increased public skepticism of many elites' pretensions to competency, a strong case can be made that demographic shifts within the coal mining workforce played a major role tilting the odds decisively against the presiding status quo. Contrasting job creation with retirements, Nyden estimated approximately 37,214 new workers were mining coal in 1972, a significant number when comparing Yablonski's 46,073 votes to Miller's 70,373.[8]

Although many younger miners may have supported reformers in the early 1970s, it is important to note that an older generation led the insurgency itself.[9] The first rumblings of dissent arose in the early 1960s in response to benefit cuts for pensioners and widows. In 1966 and 1968, unauthorized strikes protested Boyle's handling of national contract negotiations. Disabled miners and widows began to independently organize in 1967, and Yablonski and Miller joined the opposition as the Black Lung associations formed in 1969. In Utah, all leading MFD activists had begun mining coal by the late 1940s.[10]

Prior to the 1973 energy crisis, it was difficult to anticipate the rapidity with which industrial growth would outpace the tedious and factional process of union reform. In common with nearly 200 energy boomtowns throughout the Intermountain West, accelerated growth strained Carbon and Emery Counties' social fabric.[11] From 1970 to 1980, their populations rose by 41 percent and 122 percent respectively. Utah coal employment surged from a nadir of 1,155 miners in 1968 to 4,296 in 1982. Despite the inherent dangers of underground work, many found coal mining to be extremely rewarding. In 1977, Emery County had the highest wage and per capita income in the state along with an unemployment rate (4 percent) almost half the national average. Two years later, Carbon County placed second behind Salt Lake County in the per capita income category. Reflecting the influx, 65 percent of Carbon High School students in 1980 had parents from outside the county.[12]

While the infrastructural and social disruptions of boomtown growth are better documented, sociologists have published a number of studies with direct relevance for union organizing. John Gilmore (1976) described "integrating the newcomers into the community without driving out the old-timers" to be "a key problem" in energy boomtowns. Thomas Greider and Richard Krannich's (1985) comparative study found "an apparent decline in reliance on neighbors as sources of social support." William R. Freudenburg (1986) found "a lower density of acquaintanceship," leading to "a degree of anonymity that greatly decreased the effectiveness of deviance control." Michael Smith, Richard Krannich, and Lori Hunter (2001) noted "a decline in trust," confirming earlier observations of "a collapse of established informal social structures" during years of rapid growth.[13]

In her 1980 poem "Coal Brains," miner Laurie Castleberry satirized the rising individualism she saw unfolding in Gillette:

> The poor fool's brain has turned to coal,
> A black chunk in an otherwise empty bowl.
> At first glance it's solid, which may seem fine,
> But a closer look shows fragments breaking 'way with time.
>
> There was a real mind there one fine day,
> 'Till big bucks washed true thought away.
> Thoughts turned to snowmobiles, trucks and a boat,
> Work was the castle with a deep money moat.
>
> A company number left the fool unnamed,
> 'I make twelve bucks an hour,' 5544 proclaimed!
> You've lost sight of your life, you've lost touch with your home,
> You gave up the real things for things you could own.
>
> Now the company owns you, your body and soul,
> 'Cause the poor fool's brain has turned to coal.[14]

Interviews with those who relocated to Utah to mine coal at this time suggests that many carried with them outlooks and goals that differed from most born in mining communities. Like Wayne Baker, Robert Trapanier's career in Carbon County demonstrates the sociological changes that accompanied coal's revival. Born in Rhode Island, he used enrollment at Utah State University as a way to see the West while he pursued degrees in business and accounting. After assessing the average accountants' pay and the additional degrees needed for top promotions, he left college to pursue high-paying jobs in phosphate, coal, and the last of Park City's silver mines during the early 1970s. After that mine closed, Trapanier relocated to Helper and worked at Braztah's Spring Canyon No. 5 mine in 1978. While he had supported the United Steelworkers in Park City, he developed a number of criticisms of the UMWA:

> One thing that I was taught is a strong work ethic, and one thing I didn't really like with the union mine, it's like all the guys they were anti-company. There was always this friction. . . . For instance if you were a company foreman, you weren't allowed to do any work, and if you did any work, anybody in the union could turn you in to the company and get a shift's pay. Even if a foreman lifted up an electric cable—heavy cable—to help drag it, [he] was not allowed to do that. Every section was assigned an electrician, and a mechanic, and you had certain jobs. And if you weren't busy in that particular job you didn't have to do anything. You know I saw mechanics and electricians sit on their butt for eight hours you know, a mechanic waiting for somebody to break down, and the same with electrician. And they weren't allowed to help, they did the one thing and that was it.
>
> In a nonunion mine, the foreman is kind of just like the lead man. He is the foreman but he also does some work, you know, if somebody is sick he might do their job for the shift. And I didn't think that was bad. You know, if the company is not prosperous you're not going to have a job. That's the way I looked at it. And I think the pendulum can go too far one way or the other.[15]

Like many who shifted between opportunities at different mines, Trapanier began working at Beaver Creek, where a new owner managed the mine Ura Swisher opened years earlier:

> I was a little leery because I'd heard all these stories in union mines about how they're slave drivers and they fire you on a whim and you had no protection and so on and so forth, but I didn't find that to be the

case at all.... I found in a lot of ways you were not hampered by archaic union rules, you know, it's like the company gave a choice one day, 24th of July was a paid holiday, and they left it up to men, would you rather have the 24th of July or the Friday of deer hunt? And it was overwhelming to the men it was the Friday of deer hunt people wanted off. But in a union mine that would have been hard to do, you know, because there are just a lot of rules in place.

We got raises and the benefits were better than a union mine. So I think there wasn't any desire on the part of the men to join a union. Exactly the opposite really.[16]

While he enjoyed mining, Trapanier approached the profession not as a life-long career but as a high-paying means to save the money needed to become a small businessman himself. By the mid-1980s he had purchased three hotels in Carbon County, whose rooms he rented to miners and railroad workers. In 1980 and 1981, Trapanier made political waves by running as a rare Republican for state representative and for Helper's City Council. Unsuccessful in either election, and with his properties going from fully occupied to entirely vacant as mass layoffs began, Trapanier left a declining coal industry to pursue a successful career as the owner of a Lehi restaurant. Through his educational background, financial goals, and political dispositions, Trapanier embodied the changes then sweeping Carbon County, and provided an archetype for a new type of miner.

While the UMWA fought for new and undecided constituents, like other unions it increasingly did so within a transformed material and cultural landscape. After their introduction in 1948, continuous mining machines produced unprecedented amounts of coal with far smaller work forces. After 1961, longwall systems accelerated this trend. The American coal miner now worked in smaller crews, and often directly alongside his supervisors. Rather than riding a "mantrip" of empty coal cars with a hundred of his fellow miners, by the late 1980s coal miners were more likely to drive through the mine with a handful of passengers in a converted jeep or truck. If solidarity is organically produced in the workplace, this re-creation of nonunion miners' "workscape" must have had significant implications for their willingness to join a union.

In housing, miners' social environments became increasingly separated from their professional relationships. Of Carbon County's original company towns, by 1971 only Castle Gate, Clear Creek, East Carbon, Hiawatha, and Sunnyside still supported operating mines. Wattis and Consumers had been entirely dismantled, and in their place new companies Plateau and Swisher Coal operated after years of inactivity. In 1975, McCulloch Oil Corporation relocated the entire town of Castle Gate to a subdivision west of Helper to expand coal-loading facilities. Clear Creek and Hiawatha persisted, though each experienced substantial outmigration. In the 1970s, Hiawatha's owner, U.S. Fuel, remained one of few mining companies in America that still sponsored such institutions as an amusement hall, community roller staking, a Thanksgiving banquet, a town Christmas tree, an annual daddy-daughter dinner, and a ladies' Wednesday night bowling league, all within walking distance of their employees' homes.[17]

Even within such towns, persisting community traditions faced new competition for miners' attention. When in October 1973 many Hiawatha residents attended a bike rally organized by a community organization, others "packed their camper for a few days to visit at Scofield Lake," "took a weekend vacation and traveled to Salt Lake to visit their son," "traveled to Huntington Canyon for a hike and picnic," or "took . . . a camping trip in the Uinta Mountains and visited Flaming Gorge." While all union miners enjoyed vacations over the same dates, they increasingly approached recreation as individual or family activities. Unthinkable for their parents a generation prior, coal miners in the 1970s could even afford travel to such exotic destinations as Hawaii and Las Vegas.[18]

Those whose lifetimes straddled the company-town era were in a unique position to note the social impacts of residential decentralization. In 1982, Louise Fossat recalled a poignant moment soon after her move to Helper:

> After we left Peerless the sunshine came out, there was this one morning, it was after the winter and I was expecting a new baby and I walked out on the porch, you know, what a glorious morning it was and there wasn't a soul to say hello to. That had never happened to me before. It wasn't that I didn't have neighbors or anything but you know, before you could always go out and somebody was shaking their rug or they were yelling at the neighbors. I never felt so alone as I did that morning that I stepped out there and here is this wonderful and beautiful sunshine and there wasn't a soul to share it with.[19]

A son of Greek immigrants, John Mahleres later perceptively noted the technological changes that remade American culture nationally, and appeared particularly dramatic in Carbon County:

> We didn't have five people in the family, and have five cars outside, five automobiles, five boats and five trailers and everything else. There was one car, and it was the family car, and you could plead and beg and everything else . . . once in a while you might be able to use it. . . . People didn't have any means of transportation, there weren't too many cars, there wasn't any television, all we had was a radio and everything else, so that's why they were close, close knitted . . . because, "Hey, let's have a party then. Or lets go down to church and have a dance or let's do this," . . . and that's what brought everything the closeness. . . .
>
> [Now], when a family starts growing up, Joe wants a car, Bill wants a car, Sadie wants a car, you got four cars. Well, "We can go," "We can go to Provo," "We can go to Salt Lake," "We can go," "We don't want to party, we don't want to do this. We got TV!" We're engrossed with this, we like this. So eventually it all breaks off and falls away. . . . [Before] there was no place to go, you couldn't go anywhere. . . . They had a community picnic up in Scofield or community picnic down in Price or big dance down [at] church or big dance at the Silver Moon where everybody congregated, not just the Greeks or anybody the whole community was communicating you knew one another and nobody cared whether you were Greek or Italian or Dago . . . or nothing.[20]

Like transportation, miners' recreation also became increasingly individualistic. In Spring Canyon west of Helper, coal camp residents once hiked over a ridge to fish along Beaver Creek. By 1975, those who commuted to work at Braztah's No. 5 Spring Canyon mine could now tow private powerboats to fish in any of over twenty regional reservoirs. Throughout the decade power sports including motocross, four-wheeling, OHV-driving, and water-skiing grew rapidly in popularity. While team sports also grew with the counties' population, coworkers and neighbors now composed fewer homogenous teams. As longtime Hiawatha resident Ezra Buttery observed, "We used to have one of the best ball teams in the county. King Coal took everything around here and they used to have their own little league team. . . . Now they send the kids down to Wellington to play ball."[21]

COAL MINE FATAL AND NON-FATAL INJURIES 1950-1978

NON-FATAL INJURIES PER YEAR

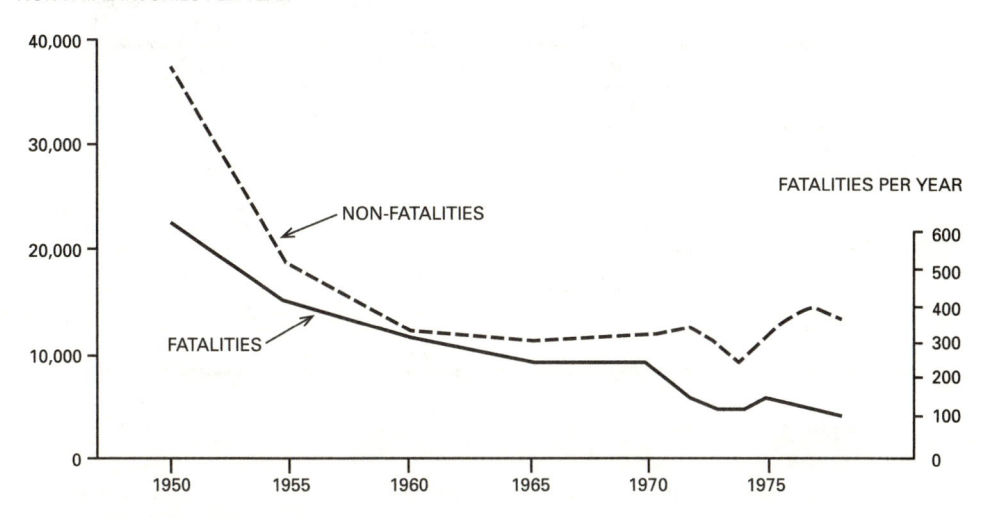

Source: Mine Safety and Health Administration

FIGURE 9.3. While the 1969 Coal Mine Safety Act had an immediate effect reducing mass–fatality incidents, coal mining's rapid expansion, and its reliance on an increasingly young and inexperienced workforce, led to a rise in debilitating injuries few miners were prepared to tolerate. From the President's Commission on Coal, *Coal Data Book*, 1980.

While miners had once gathered at company-built amusement halls to watch films, hear music, and attend dances, these activities now took place at urban centers or in private homes in increasing isolation from coworkers. In 1976 local papers first listed TV schedules, and by 1982 miners could rent a VCR and VHS cassettes, and watch films alone or with families. Instead of eating and conversing in neighborhood restaurants owned by former miners, they now enjoyed fast food at McDonalds (1979), Kentucky Fried Chicken (1980), Arbys (1981), and Wendys (1984) in newly constructed buildings adjacent to Price's Highway 6/50 onramps. Reacting to lost commercial activity, Price and Helper businessmen organized downtown redevelopment committees with mixed success.[22]

Perceptively, union strategists increasingly recognized that young miners' loyalties to a collective workplace organization could not be

TABLE 9.1. BCOA WILDCAT STRIKE LOSSES, 1964–1978

YEAR	MAN-DAYS LOST	YEAR	MAN-DAYS LOST
1964	129,800	1972	515,600
1965	160,700	1973	529,200
1966	485,800	1974	1,023,800
1967	109,500	1975	1,417,400
1968	630,700	1976	1,950,300
1969	626,500	1977	2,283,400
1970	593,100	1978*	229,500
1971	565,000	1979*	261,800**

* Preliminary
** First 9 months.
Source: Bituminous Coal Operators Association.

TABLE 9.1. Nationally, wildcat strikes' frequency spiked first in the late 1960s during protest movements led by disabled miners and widows and West Virginia miners' near-unanimous support for the Black Lung strike in early 1969. As employment boomed, accident rates increased, and a younger workforce chafed at lengthy grievance processes, wildcats crescendoed in 1977. After an exhaustive, 111-day national contract strike that winter, their use—and effectiveness—declined dramatically. From the President's Commission on Coal, *Coal Data Book*, 1980.

taken for granted. In his exhaustive 1974 dissertation on reform efforts within the UMWA, Paul Nyden noted that "the vast majority of young miners rarely even attend local union meetings" and predicted, "If [they] do not take an active role in UMW affairs, the UMW will be in deep trouble within the next few years." Writing in 1975 to the *United Mine Workers Journal*, John Bradford of District 20's Local 1288 lamented, "The young have a tendency to stay away from the union hall more than the older" and suggested incorporating a by-law to fine members for nonattendance. In the same issue, Larry Cani of District 5's Local 4426 described the importance of "the new men between ages 18 and 35" being able to "see grievances being settled in their behalf by our capable mine committee" to understand the value of active participation.[23]

Unfortunately for young miners and the UMWA, seeing a grievance settled on their behalf within a timely manner became increasingly unlikely after 1974. Changes to the NBCWA that year added an extra step to the grievance procedure which substantially backlogged new cases. Those who resorted to wildcat strikes in attempts to bypass the process increasingly divided the interests of working miners from the union's older membership.[24] While waiting for weeks to resolve a grievance could be fatal to a working miner, for older miners, pensioners, and widows each ton of coal unmined by an idled signatory represented a direct financial loss to the increasingly troubled Health and Retirement Funds.

Furthermore, the Supreme Court's *Boys Markets* decision (1970) clarified US labor law to declare any strike initiated over an "arbitrable" grievance during the life of a union contract to be illegal and subject to punitive injunction. Coal operators understood their strategic advantage, and could provoke a strike and fine its participants whether they had violated the contract or not. In the summer of 1975 and 1976, local grievances at eastern mines twice generalized into regional "anti-injunction" strikes that defied judges for several weeks, and involved 80,000 and 90,000 of the union's 125,000 members respectively.[25] Consequently, the UMWA's financial health suffered, and wildcats alone

FIGURE 9.4. As employers gained more tools and unions paid more fines, direct action to control a workplace became increasingly untenable. Fired in 1975 for defending his embattled local president, Horse Canyon miner Larry Krantwashl's one-man picket fails to stop production. Courtesy, *Sun Advocate*.

cost the Funds $81.2 million in lost royalties during the life of the 1974 contract. In response, older union members, UMWA officials, and political commentators increasingly criticized both the wildcat tactic and the young men who led them.[26]

In eastern mines, some projects of the American New Left appear to have served less helpfully as supplements for the UMWA's leadership crisis and more as additional fuel poured onto a growing fire. Maoist organizations provided much of the impetus behind the Miners'-Right-to-Strike Committee, which romantically equated the image of defiant strikes with the health of labor organizations. In Utah, the Socialist Workers Party (SWP) provided the most ambitious and ideological effort to provide militants a networking vehicle. As the largest non-Stalinist socialist group to emerge from the New Left, the SWP had approximately three thousand members in 1977. Having followed the decade's upsurge in many unions, in 1978 it encouraged its members to pursue careers in unionized centers of American industry, where they hoped to reinvigorate a radical, working-class left.[27]

In 1976, the SWP organized its first Utah branch in Salt Lake City. In 1982, at least five members established another in Price after they began working at the Wilberg and Deer Creek mines. In July, twenty-five people attended its office's grand opening in the Oliveto building at 23 South Carbon Avenue in downtown Price. These socialists' ability to gain a hearing suggests the liberalization of 1970s American culture, and contrasts strongly with the UMWA's historically rigid anticommunism. Over the next several years they organized political discussions, held forums on regional strikes, ran for local political office, and had campaign and event notices respectfully announced in the *Sun Advocate*.[28] Their overall strategy, however, seems in retrospect to have been as doomed by timing as by political marginalization or a demanding internal organizational culture. As longtime SWP activist Berry Sheppard noted in his memoir:

> We mistook the struggles that had occurred in the late 1970s, above all the great 1978 strike of the coal miners, and the development of Steelworkers Fight Back, as signaling the beginning of similar, broader battles. In fact, these were exceptions to the general trend. What had begun to occur was a retreat of the labor movement. . . . [N]ot only did this radicalization on the economic and political fronts fail to materialize,

things began to go in the opposite direction.... We were guilty of wishful thinking, and all the [SWP] leadership ... clung to the myth of a developing political radicalization of the working class, while evidence to the contrary continued to mount.[29]

While in 1984 and 1985 activists Cecelia Moriarty and Joe Geiser ran for governor of Utah and mayor of Price in essentially propagandistic campaigns, the crest of miners' militancy had already passed. For families struggling with unemployment, radical ideology and international solidarity movements attracted limited interest.[30] Although the party never became a mass organization, and today is a declining fraction of its former size, it retained a smaller presence in several western boomtowns including Huntington, Utah, and Craig, Colorado. There, some of its members did find practical relevance—and fulfilling careers—in coal. Moriarty was an active and respected member of the Lady Miners for years and led a safety workshop at the Seventh Annual Conference of Women Miners in Price. When she left Utah to go back to school, the group threw her a farewell party and later auctioned her hard hat as a fundraiser. Geiser sunk lifelong roots into Huntington and worked at Deer Creek for thirty-one years. Geiser and other party supporters played a helpful supportive role during the Co-op strike, and the organization's paper, *The Militant*, has through its searchable online database preserved probably the best chronology of that conflict's evolution.[31]

As expressed through wildcat strikes, local militancy peaked in the period of highest labor demand, and became increasingly untenable after 1982. These strikes also suggest the centrality of company-specific conditions to employee radicalization. The twenty-one wildcats that affected Emery Mining and its parent companies support the view that the rapid rise in employment produced a particularly volatile working environment, as the Deer Creek, Wilberg, and Des-Bee-Dove mines brought together some of the newest and largest workforces in the state. As one coal operator–commissioned study concluded in 1981, at such mines a class of hastily trained supervisory personnel with "authoritarian attitudes and lack of labor relations competence" frequently directed "a 'new breed' of less-disciplined younger workers," amid few voices of experience or moderation. By comparison, local papers reported fifteen wildcat strikes at all mines in Carbon County *combined*. Regionally,

Wildcat Strikes in Utah's Coal Industry by Employer, 1968–1985*

*As reported in the Sun Advocate, Helper Journal, and Emery County Progress-Leader

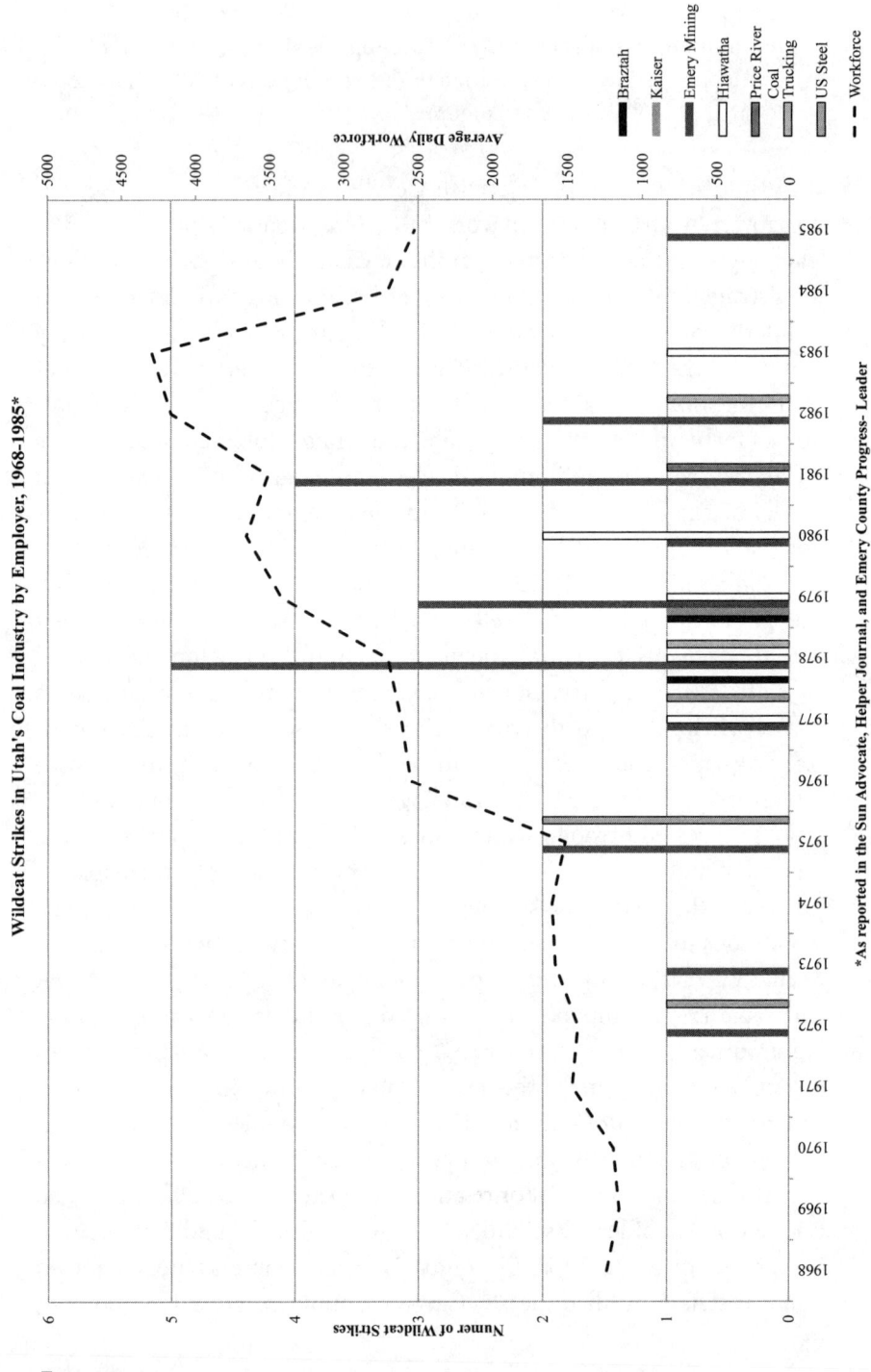

Legend: Braztah, Kaiser, Emery Mining, Hiawatha, Price River Coal, Trucking, US Steel, Workforce

FIGURE 9.5

Reported Reasons for Unauthorized Coal Strikes in Utah, 1968-1985*

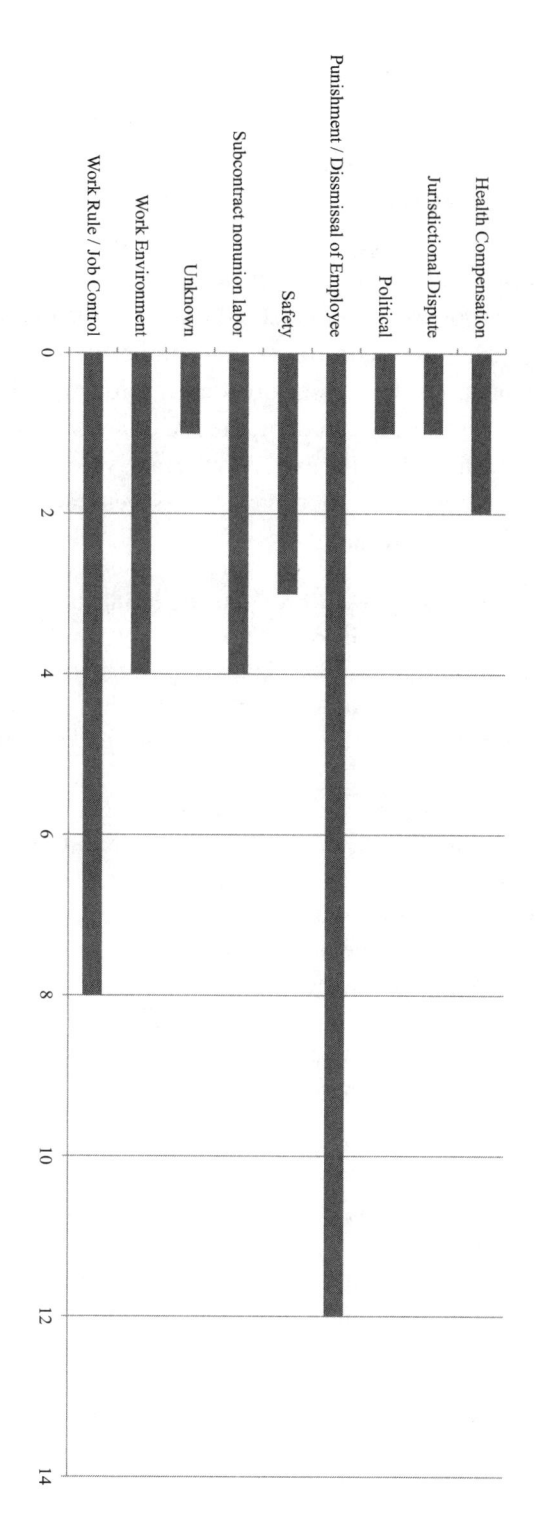

*As reported in the Sun Advocate, Helper Journal, and Emery County Progress- Lead

FIGURE 9.6

Utah miners throughout the decade appeared far less strike-prone than their eastern counterparts.[32]

Another way to understand wildcats is to break them down by category. By aggregating all reported wildcats across employers, the issues most important to Utah's miners emerge. From those unauthorized strikes reported in the local press, it appears that the issues most important were those of direct personal impact. Protection from arbitrary and unfair dismissal, control of the conditions of work, safety, and protection of union jobs from outsourcing together accounted for 86 percent of work stoppages during the life of contractual coverage. This contrasts significantly with eastern wildcats, where strikes over political and "unknown" or spurious grievances were far more frequent.[33] As Curtis Seltzer summarized,

> Wildcat strikes defined the three years following the 1974 contract, logging more than 5.6 million lost workdays, or almost 6 percent of all workdays in this period. Two kinds of wildcat strikes occurred. The most frequent erupted over local issues at a single mine. Such strikes punctuate the history of the industry despite operator and union opposition....
>
> The 1969 black-lung-strike in West Virginia had introduced a second kind of wildcat. These began at one mine, but spread because the underlying issue touched miners across the coalfields. MFD had organized at least two multistate wildcats. These kinds of wildcat strikes erupted in the mid-1970s. The issues arose from the workplace and political conditions in the coalfields, including a West Virginia gasoline-rationing plan, controversial textbooks in Kanawha County (W. Va.), shift rotation, job bidding, injunctions against wildcat strikes, black-lung legislation, and benefit cutbacks in the UMWA's Funds.[34]

From their perspective in Washington, DC, International officers and staffers who had supported wildcats during the Black Lung and MFD movements increasingly encountered their debilitating financial repercussions as their membership continued to use them. From his position in the legal department, Thomas Geoghegan recalled,

> It was as if the men, unwittingly, had stumbled upon a crude form of worker control. The companies, hysterical, were filing hundreds of lawsuits. Against us, the International Union. For a while, there was a

federal lawsuit being filed *every* day . . . no kidding, one a day. . . . Sometimes a single coal company, like Peabody Coal, would have over 150 cases pending against the International at the same time. Yet we didn't call the strikes, or approve them. They were simply happening. . . .

The scary part was that every August, in 1975 and 1976, a big, nationwide "wildcat" would start. It would start at a single mine, and then go like a forest fire from state to state. Soon it would be a national strike, burning wild and out of control. Whole districts, dry as tinderboxes, would go up in smoke. The entire Union was like a roaming mob . . . and back in Washington, we had nothing to do with it. *Nothing.* I would sit there, stunned, and every August I would wonder if this was the big, final wildcat that was predicted in the Book of Revelation. . . . [In 1976] over a hundred thousand miners were striking against the federal courts.[35]

Insulated, for a time, from the immediate financial penalties of injunctions, some miners came to view striking as a right akin to free speech. As one Utah miner denounced operators' 1977 contract proposals to fine members engaging in wildcats, "this will eliminate the only power we have to voice our opinion."[36]

On September 20, 1977, four younger members of Des-Bee-Dove Local 1859 organized a mass meeting at the Emery County High School gym to discuss seceding from the UMWA. The intertwined issues of wildcat strikes, generational tensions, and divisions between eastern and western miners appeared as clearly visible underlying tensions. Recent cuts in the Fund's medical coverage, a desire for a separate western wage agreement, aversion to the upcoming national contract strike, and a perception that American Coal Company's highly efficient mines disproportionately subsidized eastern miners' healthcare led these men's list of criticisms. While 450 miners from thirteen locals attended the event, older miners' leadership led most attendees to reject the initiative and walk out of the meeting.[37]

In a flurry of letters to the editor, District 22 officials denounced the "lads" and "boys" who had attempted "such childish immature ploys" with generational language. President Bill Jones evaded the miners' criticisms entirely and described the UMWA's historic accomplishments in depth. Subdistrict board member Harold Alger sympathized with eastern miners, blamed operators for provoking wildcats, and argued that a nationally united union remained the best vehicle to win back the lost coverage.[38] The meeting's organizers subsequently withdrew their proposal and closed ranks in support of the national contract strike that winter.[39] Yet the issues they had raised soon resurfaced, with Emery Mining citing identical concerns as they left the BCOA to negotiate for a separate contract in 1981. Frustrated as they endured a seventy-two-day national strike they had voted locally to end early, a majority of the company's employees supported the attempt.[40]

In interviews and oral histories, union supporters and opponents have frequently explained the organization's decline as generational conflict. In May 1979, retired miner Frank Massa told researchers from the Presidents' Commission on Coal that "there is no friendship between the miners like there used to be. These young miners won't talk to you and, by God, anyone who isn't on a pension doesn't even want to know your name because they think they're paying your way." In 1982 Remo Spigarelli, who had mined under preunion conditions, noted that younger miners were as a group attracted more to high wages than other benefits. John Spensko agreed these same perks allowed Swisher Coal to neutralize another organizing effort that year. Spensko also lamented young miners' higher absentee rates that disproportionately persisted at union mines. Louis Pestotnick Jr. complained that some young miners were flirting with disaster by smoking cigarettes or marijuana underground. Frank Pugliese left mining altogether to sell mining equipment after he became fed up with wildcats: "The issues of the 1970s consisted of anything. The workers would strike over anything from the roads being too slick, to anything that made them unhappy at work. Literally anything could be an issue that caused a strike."[41]

In several western states where the union enjoyed historic strength, organizers now contrasted older miners' "glue"-like support with young miners' "limited experience."[42] In contrast to Navajo and Hispanic miners' comparatively strong support for the 1974 organizing drive at Pittsburgh + Midway Coal's McKinley mine near Gallup, New Mexico, organizers also noted, "Some of the younger miners' complaints are the same as the ones we got from the Local Union 1854 Gillette, Wyoming, regarding the royalty payment being sent to help the eastern Miners." Concerned that President Miller was against strip miners, these men also suggested "the voting strength of each member be decided by the amount of tonnage produced at the mines and not by the size of the Local Union."[43]

As union power ebbed, grievance procedures bogged down, and national contract strikes became increasingly lengthy and divisive, many nonunion producers embraced the opportunity to provide a comparatively collaborative and well-compensated work environment. In the late 1960s Plateau Mining had pioneered this strategy by paying miners slightly more than union wages. In the mid-1980s the mine's newest owner, Cyprus Minerals Corporation, produced a promotional pamphlet that glowingly summarized industrial harmony's comparative benefits. To prospective commercial customers it proudly advertised that "Plateau employees exemplify a highly skilled workforce that participates in the building of the company." Although guilty of indulging in some minor historical amnesia, it proudly noted:

> The sign posted prominently at the entrance to the property, "THROUGH THESE GATES PASS THE BEST DAMNED COAL MINERS IN THE WORLD," epitomize the feelings we have about our workforce. That intangible edge that a willing and cooperative workforce gives to an organization is something that has been a part of Plateau for a number of years. Plateau's management is committed to the continuation of this philosophy for the future. Our employees have never felt the need for third party representation and have always worked with management to successfully meet the many challenges and opportunities that we have encountered through the years. . . . Productivity and a workforce of qualified employees are only part of the answer to our success. Over the years, an attitude of teamwork and cooperation between supervisory and hourly employees has enabled us to maintain a strong employee oriented environment where people count and where problems get solved.[44]

Similarly, Skyline embraced the freedom to experiment with new forms of employee decision-making and flexible compensation. Hired from SUFCO to organize the mine's initial hiring and management, Glen Zumwalt remembered:

> We had our own incentive system for our miners. We called it a bonus. Monthly they'd get paid . . . on production vs. budget [and] they also

got paid on quality. If the quality was better than what the contract required, we gave them a bonus. If it was worse, they got some taken away from them. We paid on safety. If we had a doctor-treated accident it automatically took away from their bonus. There was no added [money] for safety, it was all takeaway. There is no bonus money in accidents; we'd take away for that. They'd get paid a monthly bonus. Every day we'd chart, we had a big board and we'd chart how we did the day before so everybody knew where they were headed, what kind of bonus they would get that month.[45]

From coal mining's earliest days, operators have attempted to screen new hires for union sympathies. During the early 1970s, age provided the easiest filter, even if it sometimes let a few militants slip in. During MFD's 1972 campaign in District 15, a number of laid-off and retired miners supported the reform movement from Oak Creek, Colorado. Although two strip mines had recently opened, one miner's wife described her husband's struggle for work: "They brought in most of their men from back east and very few of the local men got jobs. In fact they hired mostly farmers and ranchers, men from surrounding towns. . . . [O]ne of the bosses made the remark that they didn't want any of the men from the [closed] Keystone mine, because they were too strong union men."[46] As a national miner shortage turned into a surplus by the later 1970s, social engineering became far easier. Not only could experienced miners be hired from far away, many from closed eastern mines now wandered western coalfields looking for work. Of Skyline's initial hiring, Zumwalt recalled:

We had the luxury of hiring 3% of our applicants; 97% didn't make it. We developed a very detailed, in-depth interview process. . . . You can get education and experience off a resume, and a lot of people use that as their main sorting technique. But you have a real tough time-getting to personal values, personal beliefs, ideas about what their job is-going to mean to them, what kind of career opportunities they want in the future, what kind of dedication they have as a person to their occupation. It didn't make any difference if it was a janitor we were hiring, or whomever, we wanted to know what made them tick and what were their values.[47]

Uniquely positioned at the top of the Wasatch Plateau, Skyline complemented its sorting of miners' personalities with new opportunities to manipulate geography: "A third of our workforce came from Spanish Fork area and Utah Valley. . . . A third . . . came from Sanpete County and northern Sevier County. . . . Actually, when we started Carbon County had the least percentage; we had more employees from Utah County and San Pete County." With a newly paved highway connecting Skyline to Fairview in San Pete County, not only could reservoirs of disproportionately conservative and traditionally agricultural workers be tapped, workforces could be separated across opposite sides of mountain ranges.[48]

As years went by, Utah's younger miners experienced two profound changes. Those who managed to keep their jobs became older miners, and encountered the conservatizing trappings of adulthood many headstrong militants in their twenties had not considered. With mortgages, car payments, recreational vehicle payments, and families, personal risks increasingly mattered as union mines encountered sharpened competition. In addition, the trauma of mass layoffs hit thousands the hardest at a time when transitioning careers was difficult. Everyone living in America's coalfields during the 1980s had a number of friends in their mid-thirties, well-trained, experienced, and heavily invested in a rewarding, high-paying industry but with little hope of ever being able to work in that industry again. And unlike the 1950s, they had far greater difficulty finding comparably well-paying industrial jobs than their forefathers had had a generation before. Regionally, similarly meteoric booms in uranium and oil shale that had welcomed coal miners' transferrable skillsets had also fizzled by the early to mid-1980s. Even outmigration to urban centers provided less of a safety valve than it once had. As thousands disappeared into neighboring states, lower-paying jobs, and entirely different industries, those lucky enough to continue mining entered an era of lowered expectations.

EPILOGUE

You fight every day, not because of what you hope to achieve, but because it's the right thing to do. You'll never be guaranteed a win, no matter how righteous your cause; fighting the good fight doesn't mean you get a happy ending. But you fight for what's right anyway, *because* it's what's right. And if you're very, very lucky, others will stand to fight alongside you. This is how great changes happen.

—Brittney Hall, Decker striker's daughter, 2006

IN MARCH 1960, coal expert V. M. Johnson summarized the dilemma then facing the unionized sector of American coal. An intelligent and perceptive observer, Johnson spoke for the largest operators whom he sensed were ill-prepared to take on an impending contest: "Just as Abraham Lincoln once said that the nation could not continue to exist half-slave and half-free, it follows that the industry cannot continue to exist 25% non-union and 75% union where other basic costs aside from wage costs are the same. It is easy to conclude that either the bulk of non-union tonnage must be unionized, or that more and more of the union operators will go non-union." Yet he was not blind to the difficulties organizers increasingly faced:

> It may be taken for granted that the nonunion tonnage will continue to grow at the expense of union tonnage.... The costs being what they are, a larger share of the market will tend to fall to them.... Aside from the quietly dying and leaving the field to non-union operators the problem of dealing with the non-union tonnage is extremely difficult, and no ob-

vious, single approach can be expected to affect a major improvement—short of a major overhaul of the UMW contract. . . . It is time that the UMW faces up to the fact that its future is in jeopardy.[1]

Concretely, Johnson suggested eliminating the paid lunch hour, as well as paid travel time to working areas within the mine. In District 8, he estimated these changes could reduce coal prices by approximately 35 cents per ton. He did not, however, recommend altering the union sector's single greatest competitive liability: the Welfare and Retirement Fund. This program had become so important to union miners and officers that to suggest an alteration was politically unthinkable, even for an operator's representative.

By this study's end in 1985, the UMWA's strategic position had declined substantially, and set the stage for Johnson's prophecy to come true. Throughout the years of booming production, industrial revival outpaced organizers' capacities to respond. Yet, as the experience of failed organizing drives shows, even if the union had multiplied its organizing budget in 1970 or 1973, it is unclear if employers' steadfast opposition to the Fund and the many tactics available to them would have prevented them from continuing to turn organizing successes into collective-bargaining failures. While the Miller administration attempted to reverse its predecessor's organizing record, it never managed to mobilize the support—or identify the strategy—necessary to reverse this trend.

By the end of the 1970s, the UMWA represented approximately 75 percent of miners in the East and less than 50 percent of miners in the West. Tonnage statistics, however, revealed greater losses: by 1980 UMWA tonnage declined to less than 50 percent of the national total, down from 90 percent in 1950 and 70 percent in 1970. Surface mines, where the union was the weakest, now produced 60 percent of national tonnage.[2] With the balance of power decisively tilted, the UMWA entered a period of decline comparable to the 1920s but lasting—to date—nearly four decades with little variance in its overall trajectory. Increasingly, nonunion operators set the standards for coal markets. As one then-contemporary observer noted, "The western tail of the industry [was now] in a position to wag the eastern dog." As union mines disproportionately closed, the UMWA's working membership dropped to its present number of approximately twenty thousand. Long insulated from commercial pressure by its direct conveyor-belt connection to the Huntington Power Plant, Deer Creek's 2015 shutdown ended eighty-two years of union power in Utah's coalfields.³

As nonunion miners encountered organizing failures personally or learned from those who had, even those who recognized union membership's advantages increasingly doubted the likelihood of winning an organizing campaign. In a world of diminishing alternatives, many eager for steady, high-paying work accepted nonunion operators' control of production in exchange for competitive pay and benefit plans. As labor historians have noted, some articulated their "right" to work at nonunion mines in a vernacular compatible with the liberal values of post-1960s American political discourse.⁴ This discursive shift, however, gained credence only in the wake of collective-bargaining and organizing failures. Throughout the 1970s, ideological antiunionists were an embattled minority within most coal-mining communities and were overshadowed by civic leaders who supported the UMWA. While America's coal industry, like its national culture, became increasingly individualistic and ideologically antiunion, it is important to note that this progression was neither natural nor consensual. It occurred only after millions of American workers experienced labor activism's limitations, and thousands of the strongest believers in collective bargaining had been fired for attempting to try it.

As the early Miller administration raced to establish a functioning organizing department, Frank Sacco's role was described in passing during the summer of 1973 as "a finger-in-the-dike" for western districts. Considering the magnitude of internal and external opponents arrayed against MFD, the nickname may be a fitting metaphor for 1970s union reform efforts in general. Unlike previous factional battles, MFD was not united by ideology or personalities, but by a deep-seated concern for the future of an ailing institution upon which all depended. As historian Michael Foley has suggested, their histories fit well into the framework of American "front porch" politics noted elsewhere in these years. In common with school busing advocates (and opponents), toxic waste cleanup campaigns, deindustrialization resistance, AIDS, and homeless activism, miners gravitated to MFD less through altruism than in response to imminent threats against their lives, livelihoods, and retirements. They organized not because they had a coherent path to victory, but because they had no other choice.⁵

Like Tony Boyle, Arnold Miller failed to find a way out of the Fund's tonnage-royalty formula. As the program's limitations became increasingly clear during his presidency, alternate proposals such as mine construction employers' fixed payments per employee hour were never seriously considered for broader adoption—and might have been a tough sell anyway to most operators. In Congress, universal single-payer health care had occasional advocates from the New Deal onward, and could have done more than anything else to nudge an ailing labor movement away from defensive protectionism and back toward workplace issues, community needs, or a reimaging of the forms and strategies needed to maintain relevance amid new challenges. It also might have opened the door to more genuinely honest experiments with collaborative production planning. However, like labor-law reform, to date the political will necessary for such a bill to be seriously considered remains perennially elusive within the halls of Congress.⁶

Probably to the detriment of the organizing department's strategic vision, the tonnage formula guided organizing toward high-tonnage targets—such as strip mines—that were the most challenging to unionize. This also fueled suspicion among some nonunion miners that the UMWA sought to "use" their productivity more than it cared about these miners' specific needs.⁷ While those who brought industrial unionism to Utah did so in response to long-accumulated grievances and pervasive, systemic injustice, when District 22 officers H. A. Brownfield and Andrew Smith reported a 1974 pair of organizing victories to the International organization, they did so in telling terms:

> Your officers are pleased to report that they with the assistance of the International Union were successful in organizing the Black Mesa area of Arizona which brought approximately 14,500,000 tons of coal annually under contract for which royalty payments are being made into your Welfare and Retirement Fund. In addition, the Gillette area of Wyoming (Amax Coal Company) was brought under contract and added an additional 6,500,000 tons of coal for which royalty payments are being made.... These two mines alone more than tripled the tonnage being produced in Utah at the present time.⁸

If the Fund soon after inspired insurmountable operator opposition, the union that controlled it also imperfectly matched strip miners' needs and identities. Just as the UMWA had earlier struggled for relevance among Emery County's small, family-owned truck and wagon mines, strip miners' needs were not identical to those of their underground brethren. While both might have had similar interests in safety, fairness, and benefits, many strip miners felt they had as much in common with construction workers and heavy-equipment operators as with underground-coal miners.⁹

By the mid-1970s, it was generally understood among observers throughout the industry that increasing revenues for a beleaguered Fund had become a major motivation for western UMWA organizing. As a perceptive *Sun Advocate* editorial noted in late 1977,

> A frog won't jump into boiling water, but if the water is heated slowly the frog will cook before he knows it. Unfortunately, it is not a frog but the United Mine Workers union simmering in slowly heated water. . . . In a little more than a year, the 1950 Pension Trust has liquidated $40 million in reserves to cover retirement checks to 81,500 beneficiaries. It is now in a pay-as-you-go situation.
>
> The 1950 and 1974 Benefit trusts have to adopt a $250 deductible policy instead of complete coverage. . . . It is this income structure that lies at the heart of the problem. It ties the present and future of union coal miners to the vagaries of a single industry. Everything depends on the constant growth of the coal industry. This growth is not certain. New energy sources threaten it. Imported steel smelted with foreign coal threatens it. And both sanctioned strikes and wildcat walkouts hurt as well.
>
> If the funds are to remain healthy during and after the "coal age," they must have tremendous reserves earning income from investments. But the three troubled funds have no reserves, and with income barely meeting expense they have no way of building them.¹⁰

As organizing's focus shifted from fundamental issues of workplace control and profit distribution to a battle over lifetime benefits for employees in a cyclical industry, nonunion miners faced an untenable choice between industrial solidarity and their employers' competitive advantage. This was not the union tradition of the mid-1930s. As late as 1949, District 22 president Houston Martin noted that "there are about fifteen or sixteen different wage scales and different contracts in this district." While coal operators and union negotiators strove to equalize rates of pay as broadly as possible, being flexible enough to consider separate contracts for individual companies extended unionism's more fundamental benefits—such as negotiated grievance processing, mine safety committees, freer speech at work, seniority, layoff panels, and general liberation from company-town serfdom—more effectively than was possible under the uniform contracts of later years.[11]

In retrospect, the UMWA's turn to national collective bargaining reflected its shift from working miners' direct representation and advocacy to industrial regulation and benefit management. National bargaining ended some of the industry's worst standards—but may have done so at the cost of turning the union contract into an increasingly unsellable product. Coal operators' withdrawal from the BCOA during the 1980s, Richard Trumka's 1984 decision to end national contract strikes in favor of "selective strikes" against holdout operators only, and the UMWA's subsequent return to negotiating contracts for individual companies were major institutional shifts that signified a recognition of pattern bargaining's impracticality. Had a European-style healthcare system existed, the UMWA would still have had to continue organizing in order to avoid being undercut by a nonunion sector. Yet the difficulty of doing so would have been reduced, as union and nonunion mines' costs and prices would have been much more comparable. With Utah's high-quality coal giving it a competitive edge against most strip-mined deposits, such an arrangement would have given the UMWA a far greater chance at maintaining its position within the state's coal mines to this day.

By the latter 1970s, postwar collective bargaining's growing problems allowed antiunion ideas to increasingly proliferate throughout coal-mining communities. Earlier in the decade, their rationalizations gained credence from the UMWA's failure to secure contracts at new mines where it had won, and then lost, majority support. While purges of union activists quashed these efforts in the short term, for those who remained such experiences demonstrated organizing's high costs and uncertain rewards. The 1977 cutbacks in Fund benefits, national contract strikes' divisiveness and violence, nonunion mines' ever-clearer competitive advantage, and the weakening of members' strength at organized mines further pushed the undecideds in an anti-UMWA direction. Although through the mid-1980s the UMWA still covered a majority of miners and coal tonnage in Utah, the events of the preceding period had decisively altered its strategic position.[12]

While the UMWA continued to exist, District 22 provided more than administrative services to members and retirees. At Wyoming's Decker strip mine in 1987 and Utah's Co-op mine in 2004, it gained the strong support of miners and led ambitious campaigns against the industry's worst conditions. Yet the tenor of these conflicts mirrored organized labor's broader trajectory. Unlike the rapid and mutually agreeable organization of the 1930s, or even the cautious optimism of the early 1970s, organizing drives from the 1980s onward have become Herculean, David-and-Goliath battles of generally dubious odds. Decker's miners struck for four years before signing a defensive contract that allowed Peter Kiewit & Sons to purge the strongest union supporters. The Co-op strike was front-page news for the *United Mine Workers Journal* for over a year, and united economic demands with an inspiring struggle for racial justice and a defense of immigrant workers' rights. Ultimately forced to reinstate fired strikers and bargain with the union, Co-op walked away from a boom in coal demand to shut down their property rather than improve conditions.[13]

This work finds itself situated within a growing body of scholarship keen to rescue the organizing battles and rank-and-file reform efforts of the 1970s era from obscurity. Yet to consider those years as one stage in American unions' century-long evolution, the options—and odds—open to reformers in those years appear to have been severely circumscribed. Among Left critics who saw themselves as heirs to MFD in the late 1970s, attacks on "the ineptitude of the Miller leadership," and the frantic perspective that "the UMWA must organize, and organize aggressively, or face the danger of annihilation," probably underestimated the growing impossibility that this task had become. Even if, through some miracle, the UMWA had managed to organize every western strip mine by decade's end, this would have stabilized Fund finances while doing little to stem the competitive pressures upon its eastern membership.[14] Whatever one thinks of Miller, or MFD's specific mistakes, more than personalities were at work in the development of union coal's long-term structural crisis.

If American workers' postwar labor union experiences have been funneled by legal restrictions and weak welfare states into unrecognizably alternative trajectories from their western European counterparts, labor historians of the 1970s have also correctly noted that rank-and-file activists sorely suffered for their lack of theoretical alternatives to traditional collective-bargaining frameworks. Like the conservatively acting "business unionists" they criticized and sought to replace, rank-and-file reformers in this era generally worked in isolation from other unions, never congealed into a single national movement, and with a few exceptions (such as the Black Lung strike in 1969) kept so focused on their own industry's employers that they rarely sought reform at the governmental level. In 1978, one faint echo of the era's unrest came in the form of the Labor Law Reform Act, which would have expedited NLRB procedures, provided financial damages for employers unlawfully refusing to bargain, and improved relief settlements for workers illegally fired for union activity. Passed in the US House of Representatives, it died in the Senate. In 1993 and 2009, repeated efforts to liberalize the union recognition process met identical fates, both times with a Democratic president and congressional majority.[15]

Peering through heated rhetoric to examine the pressures—and deficiencies—open to American unions and their antiunion opponents, each appear not so much as polar representations of moral conflicts but as uniquely complex historical products. While the shift to national contracts had the advantage of assuring miners an element of fairness, eliminating some appallingly substandard conditions, and meeting John L. Lewis's institutional needs for creating a nationally powerful organization with prominent role for himself as labor's chief coal negotiator; it also marked a turn away from visions of union power that prioritized miners' control over the work process. Replicating the UMWA model, most American unions from the CIO's 1935 founding onward depended upon bureaucratic hierarchies, limited roles for active members, and a prioritization of well-negotiated contracts over strong mechanisms for cooperative management. At best, these deficiencies allowed some nonunion employers to develop collaborative management strategies many welcomed as a relief from incessant adversarialism. At worst, the brittleness and eventual fracture of CIO models ensured the civic demobilization of the American working class, diminishing checks upon the power of society's most exploitative and unethical members, and a declining standard of living for millions.

In Utah coal, nonunion operation has inconsistently honored its founders' visions as alternatives of superior fairness. While to their credit many coal companies take great pride in safety records and continue to provide some of the best- compensated working-class jobs left in the United States, personalities familiar to any Gilded Age miner have also directed large workforces with alarmingly few checks upon their power. In 2007, coal tycoon Bob Murray blamed an "evil" mountain for the deaths of seven miners and three rescue workers during the Crandall Canyon disaster and ignored his own tolerance for unsafe practices. Days after Barack Obama's 2012 reelection, Murray angered many when he laid off 102 miners at Utah's West Ridge mine in a political stunt more concerned with rallying opposition against the Affordable Care Act than advancing any discussion about operational costs, market health, or coal mining's long-term future. The Co-op mine's exploitation of America's most vulnerable workers has earlier been described. And, in eastern mines, some rumblings of a revived Black Lung outbreak have recently been heard. Such industrial sickness does not come on acutely but is symptomatic of chronic conditions.[16]

While coal's predicament has made community survival a higher priority than workplace justice, without unions' collective vehicle many in Carbon and Emery Counties have abandoned traditional allies to embrace new and uncertain advocates. Though historically the most solidly Democratic and pro-union area of Utah, in the 2016 election Donald Trump swept coal country here and across the nation. This may have shocked some, but local observers have noted shifting signs of voter preference for years. Most commonly expressed through attitudes toward environmental regulation, this political realignment has evolved within the context of escalating layoffs and potentially catastrophic blows to regional tax bases. In the latest developments, EPA regulators have at the time of this writing pushed for the Huntington and Hunter power plants to install Selective Catalytic Reduction systems to decrease nitrous-oxide emissions to improve regional scenic air quality. This regulation would require the Huntington and Hunter plants to install an estimated "$200 million per unit worth of equipment." Huntington has two units. Hunter has three. Together, these plants employ over four hundred workers.¹⁷ As local journalist Trenton Willson has perceptively summarized,

> There are a lot of fingers being pointed towards Washington and there is a legitimate battle to be fought. Jobs are being eliminated with every indication they won't be coming back. Mining has been the staple industry here for decades and workers are finding themselves clamoring for lower paying construction, retail and tourism jobs. Mining has been cyclical over the years but has provided a comfortable living for hundreds of workers. Unfortunately, they have never been faced with such permanence until now. If we fight, we should fight for avoiding abrupt mandatory shutdowns that leave workers and their families grasping for a way to support their way of life.¹⁸

Many residents agree with passionate local commentators that the two-party political system currently represents a delineated conflict between "the men and women of America's labor movement" on one side, and "union-busting billionaires, CEOs and their political allies," working with "government officials and agencies that are determined to put an end to coal mining and coal fired power plants," influenced by "an under educated, uninformed group of people that call themselves 'environmentalists' when in fact they are simply obstructionists and preservationists" on the other. This common assessment is understandable in light of the apparent lack of any transitional planning for coal miners and their families as established power plants shift to natural gas or shut down entirely.¹⁹

While Trump's easy carry of Carbon (66.3 percent to 21.7 percent) and Emery (79.8 percent to 8.9 percent) Counties in the 2016 election demonstrates the unwillingness of many miners to face such a future without resistance, a closer look at the primaries reveals less of an endorsement for his personality and worldview. In Carbon County's Republican caucus, Trump only received 293 votes, or 29.96 percent, of the nearly 1,000 attendees' ballots. Cruz won with 60.84 percent, or 595 votes. And in the Democratic caucus, which less than half as many citizens attended, progressive candidate Bernie Sanders narrowly beat Hillary Clinton by 135 votes to 128. Forced to choose in the election between Trump and Clinton, miners voted overwhelmingly for the promise of job protections over an equally clear promise of accelerated layoffs.

Historically the dominant factor in Carbon County politics, the local Democratic Party is open to a discussion about planning for a post-coal world. What's unclear, however, is whether many locals are interested in hearing about it. While a 2017 debate between three democratic hopefuls for Utah's vacant congressional seat brought a frank discussion of alternative energies and economic diversification, only thirty local residents attended.[20]

At best, Trump's ability to revive coal mining remains to be seen and could be frustrated by his simultaneous support for coal's chief competitor: natural gas. At worst, echoes of history's darkest moments may be heard among today's authoritarian and exclusionary responses to industrial decline. There are strong community traditions against this—visible as recently as the Co-op miners' struggle for unity and justice just over a decade ago. And in local papers, progressive voices appalled at Trump's personal behavior and positions on social issues have been outspoken in criticizing his limitations. Whether he is able to perpetuate his image as the industrial heartland's crusading hero, or his base will eventually abandon him in disillusionment, remains an open question. Undoubtedly, it will depend heavily on what kind of alternatives his opponents are able to create.

Occupying a rare vantage from within the UMWA's International headquarters from 1973 to 1976, labor lawyer Thomas Geoghegan may be among the most perceptive theorists to have pondered organized labor's long post-seventies decline. While he chides many union leaders (and union historians) for their silence on membership democracy, he acknowledges that "there is a strong case to be made" against it.[21] After witnessing its effects, he gained a new appreciation for American labor law's ability to make union officials with every degree of altruism end their support for rank-and-file activity once its financial ramifications became known. Gloomily, many have taken the lesson to heart, and understand MFD today as a case in point for why "inexperienced" people should remain excluded from leadership.[22]

Yet Geoghegan, who joined MFD as a recent college graduate in 1972 and participated in the mass resignations of Miller's staff from 1975 to 1977, considers democracy inseparable from any discussion of organized labor's future. While, in the absence of political reform, rank-and-file democracy may not be sufficient to remedy the effective illegality of organizing unions, in his view it remains the only way to (1) cultivate an "'anti-statist' tradition," with an independent base of power, and (2) counter antiunion workers' critique of internal corruption and elitism. It's also probably necessary to discover whatever an alternative could be to the "collective bargaining of yore [that] now seems so twentieth century—and . . . was probably already out of date by the time the great UAW president Walter Reuther died in a plane crash in 1970."[23]

Updating his analysis in 2014, Geoghegan's *Only One Thing Can Save Us: Why America Needs a New Kind of Labor Movement* combines an eerily prescient pre-2016 assessment of the Democratic Party's looming crisis with a profound rethinking of unions' origins. In his analysis, "If the history of the New Deal teaches anything, it's that there is no way to redistribute income until we first redistribute power." Yet, if experience has again and again reiterated that traditional union organizing methods remain essentially doomed, something more than internal union reform is necessary. Before any repeat of MFD's 1972 victory could have a chance at reversing the overall picture, something closer to a repeat of 1933 might be necessary:

> Let's accept the Constitution for what it is and focus on what it does not stop us from doing: creating a crisis for the Democratic Party if it does not commit itself to labor law reform. . . . To go up against *employers* with the idea of 'bringing labor back' is futile. Labor is just too weak, far too weak. Be it a Caterpillar or a Ford, the other side can crush us. If that's the point of striking McDonalds or Macy's or Subway or Walmart, i.e., to beat the *employers* directly, I fear the worst. Yet, if the real target is the Democratic Party and not the employers, enough disruption, made up of little hit-and-run strikes, might change the world. . . . The goal is to roil the party, the way the civil rights marches getting beaten up in the South used to.[24]

While many miners helped greatly to create such a disruption through their 2016 voting, reviving an American labor movement through labor law reform could open avenues for change far less destructive to the nation's moral fabric, international standing, or commitment to its most vulnerable members. Bringing labor back, therefore, "is not just a sentimental bread-and-roses thing or even simple justice to the party's base. It is also an instrument of public policy. . . . It is a way of preserving a standard of living. That's the case we have to make: no government in its right mind would do away with organized labor as a way of stabilizing the country."[25]

Interestingly, after the 1978 strike the *Sun Advocate*'s Price editors anticipated some of Geoghegan's proposals, such as moving toward a West German–style collaborative management process of "working as partners and not as eternal antagonists." Decentralizing unions' power in favor of opening broader roles for decision making at the point of production, or embracing "minority unionism" to bypass the years of delay and winner-takes-all conflict that characterizes exclusive representation models might help as well.[26] Of course, the prospects for reimagining what industrial democracy could look may be a political project requiring more than the support of any one group for workers fighting within in a single industry. It also involves debates about how we remember the past. Although in 1933 many miners shook up the status quo by supporting radical union movements and demonstrating a willingness to strike,

> the labor movement *to some extent*—I hate to say this has been a project of the elite. In our history, sad to say, it's at least arguable that Big Government was responsible for what used to be Big Labor. I know many on the left refused to believe it: no, no, the people rose up, etc. . . . I partly agree . . . [but] while disruptions and strikes are important, they're important because that's how we get the elite in the Democratic Party to take on labor as a project.
>
> The first spurt [of union growth] also came *after* FDR had already tried a kind of European co-determination, or had at least given labor a role in setting industry-by-industry "codes." I refer here to the National Industrial Recovery Act of 1933, or the Blue Eagle Act. Yet when Roosevelt pushed this enormous expansion of labor's power, there was only a tiny labor movement in place.[27]

In one sense, the labor movement is the *alternative* to the welfare state. In another sense, it *is* the welfare state, at least as the New Dealers of long ago conceived it.[28]

If the neoliberal consensus that emerged from the New Deal's ashes is today experiencing its own fractures and defections, the question of what can replace it is driving working-class history from the margins of academic investigation to the center of national political discussion. Undoubtedly, centering this analysis on 1970s rank-and-file movements is appropriate and highly instructive. To this one might add that understanding unions' internal dynamics throughout the New Deal remains essential to explaining their postwar isolation and subsequent decline. From the independent, radical, and rank-and-file activisms of the early 1930s, to the cautionary tale of industrial unionism's bureaucratization, working-class history is ripe to field new questions about our longest-held assumptions.

Perhaps, by rediscovering ordinary people's fundamental power to transform their workplaces, their communities, and themselves, we may recover alternative trajectories and lost possibilities most relevant to our present-day values, anxieties, and concerns. Perhaps as well, we might discover shared histories that challenge our own bias and persisting preconceptions. In a democratic society, history plays a far more important role than simply introducing us to forgotten worlds beyond our grasp. Through the process of investigation, it introduces us to ourselves and to each other. History, at its heart, remains a debate about the future.

APPENDIX A

Chronology

Date	Regional	National
1869	Transcontinental Railroad completed through coal-rich southern Wyoming.	
1875	Winter Quarters developed as Utah's first commercial coal mine.	
1883	D&RGW links western Colorado to Salt Lake City along coal-rich Book Cliffs.	
1887	D&RGW subsidiary Utah Fuel Co. organized.	
1890		UMWA founded at a national conference in Ohio.
1900	Winter Quarters mine explosion kills 200 on May 1.	
1903–1904	Coal strike idles most Utah miners, ends in defeat.	
1910s	Independent coal companies proliferate in Utah south and west of Price.	
1919	No strike order given in Utah.	UMWA leads national coal strike.
1922	Strike idles most Utah mines. Although proposed wage cuts are postponed, no union recognition occurs.	As World War I's booming demand for coal ebbs, miners face mass layoffs and employer demands for wage cuts. UMWA leads a massive defensive strike.

Date	Regional	National
1920s	Overcapacity leads to increased layoffs, shorter work weeks.	Amid intense factionalism, John L. Lewis defeats his rivals to emerge as the UMWA's leader and top administrator.
1924	Castle Gate mine explosion kills 172 miners and one rescue worker.	
1928		Radical dissidents, led by the Communist Party, leave the UMWA to form the National Miners' Union.
1929		Great Depression begins in October.
1932		Franklin Delano Roosevelt elected.
1933	NMU's Utah organizing campaign ends in defeat, as UMWA members unite with sheriff's deputies to break its picket lines in August. In September, Utah coal operators sign a code of fair competition and recognize UMWA locals at their mines. Most Utah miners join the UMWA, with the exception of those employed at smaller "truck" and "wagon" mines.	
1935	Brief contract strike is peaceful, observed by nonunion mines.	National Labor Relations Act creates the National Labor Relations Board, clarifying unions' legality and employers' obligation to bargain, and providing a structure for union elections and unfair practices to be regulated by the state.

Date	Regional	National
1938	UMWA and regional CIO leaders note layoffs have brought union organizing to a standstill. Consumers, Mohrland, and Mutual mines close.	John L. Lewis and the UMWA leave the AFL to create the CIO. Intense organizing in basic industry begins. Cutbacks in New Deal programs reverse economic stabilization. Large layoffs in basic industry.
1940	National mine closes.	Coal markets begin recovering in response to World War II's demands upon American industry. John L. Lewis breaks politically with President Roosevelt over potential US military involvement.
1942	US Government's Defense Plant Corporation funds opening of Horse Canyon coal mine, construction of Geneva and Kaiser steel works at Provo, UT, and Fontana, CA.	Federal spending and private management cooperate to revamp America's economy. Most labor unions, including the UMWA, agree not to strike for duration of war.
1943		UMWA leaves the CIO. US coal miner deaths escalate in response to speed-ups, and increased hiring of inexperienced miners. John L. Lewis abandons labor peace, organizes strikes over safety and wages. Male worker shortage allows many women to assume nontraditional industrial jobs.

DATE	REGIONAL	NATIONAL
1945	Sunnyside mine explosion kills twenty-three miners.	Postwar strikes occur in many industries as industrial workers endeavor to preserve wartime gains.
1946	Contentious organizing at Big Horn Coal, a rapidly growing strip mine near Sheridan, WY.	National coal strike with mines under federal wartime control. Interior Secretary Julius Krug signs a contract with the UMWA to create the Welfare and Retirement Fund from a royalty on each ton of coal mined by a unionized producer.
1947	Utah annual coal production peaks at 7,619,378 tons. Sego mine closes.	National coal strike secures operator acceptance for Fund. Congress passes Taft-Hartley Act.
1948	Multiple organizing drives at smaller truck mines in Utah end in failure.	National coal strike. Continuous mining machine invented, dramatically increases efficiency, as well as the amount of coal dust miners breathe.
1949	Irregularities in District 22 election lead to protests, threats of violence, appeals for International review and intervention.	Last contentious national coal strike marks the end of postwar militancy. Coal industry enters long-term decline.
1950	Standardville and Royal mines close.	BCOA created. National coal contract quietly negotiated and signed behind closed doors with no strike. 9,429 bituminous coal mines and 488,000 coal miners nationally.

Date	Regional	National
1952	Sweets mine closes.	New BCOA-UMWA contract signed in September, gives $1.90 daily wage increase and increases Fund royalty by 10 cents.
1953		Fund revises pension rules to require that twenty years of service occurs during last thirty years of a miner's career. Many older retirees are cut off.
1954	Peerless mine closes.	
1955		New national contract gives a two-dollar-per-day wage increase. Coal's weakened state is indicated by Lewis not asking for any Fund royalty increase. Sweetheart contracts begin to proliferate. As unemployment rises, wildcat strikes increase over seniority, job bidding, and job security.
1956		UMWA Welfare and Retirement Fund completes construction of ten modern hospitals in formerly underserved Appalachian communities.
1958	Multiple Utah coal operators write to John L. Lewis protesting any wage or fund royalty increases and citing fears of bankruptcy. Rains mine closes.	New coal contract gives a two-dollar-per-day wage increase, improves vacation pay. AFL and CIO unite, with the UMWA still outside both federations.

Date	Regional	National
1960		John L. Lewis retires as UMWA president at age eighty.
		After running $12 and $21 million deficits in 1959 and 1960, a $17 million Fund deficit is anticipated for 1961. Managers end medical coverage for miners unemployed for more than a year, and require miner's last year of employment to have been at a UMWA-organized mine.
		7,865 coal mines and 188,000 coal miners are working.
1962		Fund cuts benefits for members working for companies who have not paid full royalties, punishing them for sweetheart deals approved by Lewis and Boyle. Extreme dissatisfaction prompts disabled miners to organize and confront Fund managers.
1963	Peerless mine closes.	Lewis's successor, Thomas Kennedy, also retires. Appointed staffer Tony Boyle assumes UMWA presidency.
		Only five UMWA districts still have officers elected by members.
		New contract negotiations happen for the first time in five years.
		President John F. Kennedy establishes a task force to study coal mine safety.

Date	Regional	National
1964	Wattis mine closes.	New coal contract gives a two-dollar-per-day wage increase, vacation pay raise; seniority clause remains vague; no raise in Fund royalties; 18,000 miners in six states briefly strike to protest contract.
1966	Latuda mine closes.	New coal contract adds a one-dollar-per-day wage increase. More than 50,000 miners strike for seventeen days in protest.
1967	Columbia mine closes. SOCIO organized in December.	
1968	Postwar coal production bottoms out as 1,155 Utah miners produce 4,316,000 tons. Community redevelopment efforts attract Koret to build major clothing factory in Price.	The Association of Disabled Miners and Widows begins meeting in Beckley, WV. Median coal miner age is 46. Disabled Miners and Widows file Blankenship vs. Boyle lawsuit against the Fund, the UMWA, the BCOA, and the union-controlled National Bank of Washington. As national union contract expires, 130,000 miners initiate a strike until negotiations end. In response, BCOA grants a three-dollar-per-day wage increase, with additional two-dollar-per-day increases in 1969 and 1970. Black Lung Disease discussed frankly at UMWA International Convention for the first time. In November, seventy-eight miners die in an explosion at a Consolidation Coal mine in WV.

Date	Regional	National
1969	Official count shows District 22 voting 1,876 to 112 for Boyle.	Black Lung Association formed by miners in Montgomery, WV.
		Black Lung strike closes nearly all coal mines in WV while state legislature debates a safety and compensation bill.
		Jock Yablonski announces candidacy in 1969 International election.
		While financially unsound, Boyle announces a major pension increase to counter Yablonski's claims of mismanagement.
		Federal Coal Mine Health and Safety Act passed, sets minimum coal dust standards, directs the Social Security Administration to provide Black Lung benefits.
		Boyle wins UMWA election using fraud and intimidation.
		Yablonski, wife, and daughter murdered on December 31.

Date	Regional	National
1970	UP&L announces plans to build Huntington power plant. Emery County experiences major demographic change, population increase, and infrastructural limitations as construction workers and new coal miners move in. Regional electric grid expanded as new high-voltage power lines connect Salt Lake City, Huntington Power Plant, and Four Corners Power Plant in New Mexico. Earth Day observed in Carbon County through community trash collection, tree plantings.	Miners for Democracy organized immediately afterward by attendees of the Yablonskis' funeral as a coalition of lawyers, volunteers, and working miners. MFD files multiple lawsuits against the UMWA for fraud and election irregularities, and publishes The Miners' Voice. Supreme Court in Boys Markets v. Retail Clerks International allows federal injunctions against wildcat strikes initiated by union members where a grievance mechanism exists. Black retired miner Robert Payne organizes the Disabled Miners and Widows of Southern West Virginia. After district UMWA officials refuse to let his group meet with Fund managers, the group initiates a strike of 25,000 that lasts for two months. Clean Air Act passes Congress. Emission requirements make low-sulfur, western coal more competitive. Strip mines produce 44 percent of all US coal. There are 144,000 coal miners nationally.

Date	Regional	National
1971		Supreme Court's Tennessee Consolidated Coal Company decision finds UMWA and large operators guilty of attempting to drive small operators out of business. Awards plaintiff $1.5 million in damages.
		Miners strike on October 1 when national contract expires. Boyle issues official strike call on October 11. Contract signed 45 days later increases top wages to $50 per day by 1973, but only secures a promise to study the possibility of raising Fund royalties.
		The Blankenship vs. Boyle decision finds "a conspiracy of . . . all parties that are jointly liable for the Fund's loss of income from the failure to invest."
1972	Union corruption and mismanagement debated openly through letters to the editor in the Sun Advocate.	MFD convention nominates electoral slate of Arnold Miller for president, Mike Trbovich for vice-president, and Harry Patrick for secretary-treasurer.
	Students' dress code at Carbon County High is contentiously debated.	In July, a federal judge gives MFD the right to edit half the content of the United Mine Workers Journal.
	District 22 votes 1,251 to 909 for Boyle.	MFD wins December UMWA election.

Date	Regional	National
1973	Frank Sacco resumes duties as a labor organizer in western states. Restrictive nomination requirements place democracy advocates at a disadvantage. Officers sympathetic to Tony Boyle retain control of District 22. Organizing victory at Premium coal ends in failure as mine shuts down.	International convention rewrites constitution into the most democratic of any major American labor union. Competitive elections in most UMWA districts. MFD disbands. Department of Labor takes over Black Lung compensation cases. OPEC oil embargo. Coal prices rise dramatically. Coal mines expand, invest in new property, miners, and equipment.
1974	Western Strip Mine Agreement signed. Amax coal, the only UMWA-unionized producer in the booming Powder River Basin, refuses to sign. Strike begins. Huntington power plant comes online. UP&L announces plans to construct Hunter Plant near Ferron. Approximately 1,600 UMWA miners idle in Utah during comparatively peaceful strike. Swisher and Plateau operate during strike with minimal interference.	Women begin mining coal underground. Electric utilities buy 60 percent of the coal produced in the US. Gasoline shortages, stations across the country begin running out. Month-long national contract strike begins November 12. Wins 37 percent wage increase over three years. Welfare and Retirement Fund split into four separate funds. Grievance procedure revised. Members vote to approve the contract for first time in UMWA history.
1975	Huntington's population reaches 2,000, more than doubling its 1970 residency.	Wildcats escalate in frequency and duration as grievance procedure proves unworkable. Beginnings of disillusionment among Miller's staff and aides.

Date	Regional	National
1976	Six additional giant coal-fired electrical generating plants are planned for central and southern Utah. Arnold Miller visits Price, speaks at a city hall rally in April. Amax strike ends in defeat. Intermountain Power Project considers building the third new coal-fired power plant in Emery County since 1970, plans adding an additional 10,000 residents to Emery and Ferron. Emery County commissioners oppose project.	A chaotic International convention reveals major divisions within the UMWA. Harry Patrick campaigns from the left against Arnold Miller in UMWA presidential election. So does IEB member and former strip-miner Roy Patterson, representing MFD defectors and traditional union officials along the union's political center and right.
1977	In June, union members sympathetic to MFD elected to District 22's four offices. In September, meeting of 450 rank-and-file UMWA members debate seceding from union. In December, 2,300 UMWA members in Carbon and Emery Counties are idled by strike. Picketing turns violent on December 9, with roads to nonunion mines blocked by fires, a burnt-down bridge, nails, and other debris. On December 16, a permanent injunction sets maximum a picket size of five individuals. Considering continued picketing futile, the tactic is abandoned.	

Date	Regional	National
1978	In March, the Construction Workers Wives for Equal Rights and Fair Treatment picket the Castle Dale Co-op to protest its owner's high prices and sexist comments. First Unit of Hunter power plant comes online.	Miners vote down the first two negotiated contracts. Some operators express frustration with national collective bargaining, and see the regional industrial interests increasingly divided. Jimmy Carter invokes Taft-Hartley Act to issue an injunction that demands miners return to work. Miners ignore it. On March 24, miners vote 58,802 to 44,457 to accept the contract. Funds primarily provide pension benefits while coal operators adopt single-employer health plans.
1979	Organizing drive at Soldier Creek mine ends in 76-to-8 vote to remain nonunion.	Arnold Miller resigns as his health deteriorates. His vice-president, Sam Church, assumes UMWA presidency. Iranian revolution kicks off a second energy crisis. Jimmy Carter supports expanded development of domestic energy sources, including coal.
1980	26 coal mines operating in Utah, 10 more planned or under development.	241,000 coal miners nationally. Strip mines produce 60 percent of all US coal.

Date	Regional	National
1981	Organizing drive at Skyline mine ends in defeat as miners vote to remain nonunion. Construction of Intermountain Power Plant begins near Delta, UT. The Lady Miners of Utah organizes. Emery Mining attempts to leave the BCOA to bargain independently. Most Utah miners support first concessionary contract. Growing east-west rift noted as some advocate for separate western regional bargaining. Coal boom peaks as 4,296 Utah miners produce 16,912,000 tons. UP&L cancels plans to build a fourth generating unit at Hunter Power Plant.	Miners vote 67,000 to 33,000 to reject a concessionary national contract. Sam Church loses credibility with much of the rank-and-file. 72-day strike wins better language around subcontracting and leasing. With annual payments to Black Lung victims approaching $1 billion per year, federal government tightens eligibility requirements on new claims.
1982	Layoffs begin. By December Carbon County has a 12.8 percent unemployment rate. Exxon abandons massive oil shale mining project near Parachute, CO.	Global energy prices drop dramatically. 30,000 to 40,000 UMWA members are unemployed. By mid-year union membership approximates 50 percent of 200,000–230,000 working coal miners. Former miner and MFD-era lawyer Richard Trumka campaigns on a slate of legal competency and rank-and-file power, defeats Sam Church to win UMWA presidency. District 22 supports Trumka 2,563 to 774.

Date	Regional	National
1983	As an unusually heavy spring snowpack melts, an April mudslide near Thistle buries Hwy. 6/50 and the D&RGW railroad tracks for months, playing havoc with coal transportation networks.	
1984	Selective strike at holdout operator Emery Mining is the only disruption in Utah. December 19, Wilberg Mine fire kills 27, shuts down mine for over a year.	First national coal contract negotiated without a nationwide strike since 1968.
1985	Coal Employment Project national conference of women miners held in Price. Rita Miller and Joy Huitt become first women officers elected to District 22.	

APPENDIX B

UMWA District 22 Locals, ca. 1983

Utah

Local Company, Type, & Location

1206	U.S. Steel Coal Preparation Plant, Wellington, UT
1261	Browning–Consol–Emery mine, south of Emery Town, UT
1681	Merged Independent Coal & Coke and Castle Gate mines at Castle Gate and Spring Canyon, UT. From mid-1970s onward specifically refers to Braztah No. 5 Mine in Spring Canyon
1769	Castle Valley–Emery Mining Deer Creek mine, Huntington Canyon, UT
1859	American Coal–Emery Mining Des-Bee-Dove mine, Orangeville, UT
1902	Western Coal Carriers, trucking, Wellington, UT
2011	Construction Workers, District 22
2123	Braztah–Price River Coal mine, Castle Gate, UT
2176	Castle Valley–Emery Mining Wilberg mine, Orangeville, UT
6363	U.S. Fuel Hiawatha mine, Hiawatha, UT
6788	Valley Camp Belina mine, Clear Creek, UT
8003	U.S. Steel, Horse Canyon mine, Horse Canyon, UT
8303	Carbon Fuel–Braztah No. 3 mine, Hardscrabble Canyon, Helper, UT
9958	Kaiser Steel mine, Sunnyside, UT

Wyoming

1307 Kemmerer, WY

1316 Diamondville, WY

2055 Sheridan, WY

2386 Kemmerer, WY

7404 Rock Springs, WY

Arizona

1620 Kayenta, AZ

1924 Kayenta, AZ

APPENDIX C

Historic UMWA Locals in Utah

Local Company, Type, & Location

5804	Lion Coal Company mine, Wattis, UT
5806	Standard Coal Company mine, Standardville, UT
5861	Independent Coal & Coke mine, Kenilworth, UT
5916	U.S. Fuel Castle Gate mine, Castle Gate, UT
6022	Peerless Coal Company, Peerless, UT
6089	U.S. Steel Columbia mine, Columbia, UT
620	Scofield, UT
6210	Spring Canyon Coal Company mine, Spring Canyon, UT
6244	U.S. Fuel Sunnyside Mine, Sunnyside, UT
6272	Blue Blaze Coal Company mine, Consumers, UT
6412	Royal Coal Company mine, Rolapp–Royal, UT
6508	Liberty Fuel Company mine, Latuda, UT
6510	U.S. Fuel Company, Mohrland–King mine, Mohrland, UT
6511	Sweets Mine, Sweets, UT
6567	National Coal Company, National, UT
6575	Mutual Coal Company mine, Mutual, UT
6597	Chesterfield Coal Company mine, Sego, UT
6984	Carbon Fuel Company mine, Rains, UT

ABBREVIATIONS USED IN THE BIBLIOGRAPHY AND NOTES

AWC-Helper: Oral Histories gathered by the American West Center, University of Utah, transcript reviewed at Western Mining and Railroad Museum, Helper, UT

CCOH-JWM: Carbon County Oral History Project, J. Willard Marriott Library, Salt Lake City, UT

CEP-C: CEP Correspondence Files, Archives of Appalachia, East Tennessee State University

CEP-CHR: CEP Chronological Files, Archives of Appalachia, East Tennessee State University

CEP-CW: CEP Conferences and Workshop Files, Archives of Appalachia, East Tennessee State University

CEP-I: CEP Information Request Files, Archives of Appalachia, East Tennessee State University

CEP-P: CEP Personnel Files, Archives of Appalachia, East Tennessee State University

CEP-S: CEP Subject Files, Archives of Appalachia, East Tennessee State University

CEP-V: Coal Employment Project Records, Video Files, Archives of Appalachia, East Tennessee State University

CGOHP-HBL: Castle Gate Oral History Project, Harold B. Lee Library, Brigham Young University, Provo, UT

CMWSTN: *Coal Mining Women's Support Team News*

DTC-Helper: Non-Transcribed Oral History Digital Tape Collection, Western Mining and Railroad Museum, Helper, UT

ECP: *Emery County Progress*, published in Price, UT

HJ: *Helper Journal*, published in Helper, UT

LOHP-HBL: Oral Histories gathered by the Charles Redd Center for Western Studies, Labor Oral History Project, Harold B. Lee Library, Provo, UT

MFD: Miners for Democracy Collection, Archives of Labor History and Urban Affairs, Walter P. Reuther Library, Wayne State University

SA: *Sun Advocate*, published in Price, UT

SLT: *Salt Lake Telegram*, published in Salt Lake City, UT

SOCIO: Spanish-Speaking Organization for Community, Integrity, and Opportunity records, J. Willard Marriott Library, Salt Lake City, UT

U-HR: United Mine Workers of America Archives, Health & Retirement Fund Records, Pennsylvania State University

UMWJ: *United Mine Workers Journal*

U-OD: Organizing Department Records, United Mine Workers of America Archives, Pennsylvania State University

U-PC: United Mine Workers of America Archives, Presidents Correspondence with Districts, Pennsylvania State University

U-PO: UMWA Presidents Office Records, United Mine Workers of America Archives, Pennsylvania State University

U-RD: UMWA Research Department Records, United Mine Workers of America Archives, Pennsylvania State University

U-ST: UMWA Secretary-Treasurer's Office Records, United Mine Workers of America Archives, Pennsylvania State University

UT-DOGM: Statewide Oral History Project, Abandoned Mines Reclamation Program, Utah Division of Oil, Gas, and Mining

WMRRM-Helper: Western Mining and Railroad Museum, Helper, Utah

BIBLIOGRAPHY

Newspapers

Emery County Progress-Leader, 1964–1985

Helper Journal, 1966–1976

Sun Advocate, 1933–1951, 1966–1985

United Mine Workers Journal, 1969–1990

Manuscript Collections

Arva Smith Newspaper Collection. Smith Residence, Price, UT.

Assorted Obituaries. Archives. Western Mining and Railroad Museum, Helper, UT.

Carbon County Coal Strike Records. University of Utah J. Willard Marriott Library, Salt Lake City, UT.

Carbon County Mining Records. Archives. Western Mining and Railroad Museum, Helper, UT.

City of Castle Gate Records. Archives. Western Mining and Railroad Museum, Helper, UT.

Coal Employment Project Records. Archives of Appalachia. East Tennessee State University, Johnson City, TN.

Ethnic Archives Oral Histories Audio Recordings. J. Willard Marriott Library, University of Utah, Salt Lake City, UT.

Ferguson Mine Books Collection. Archives. Western Mining and Railroad Museum, Helper, UT.

Frank M. Moss Records. J. Willard Marriott Library, University of Utah, Salt Lake City, UT.

Geneva Steel Records. Archives. Western Mining and Railroad Museum, Helper, UT.

Helen Papanikolas Collection. J. Willard Marriott Library, University of Utah, Salt Lake City, UT.

Hiawatha Record. Archives. Western Mining and Railroad Museum, Helper, UT.

Kaiser Steel Records. Archives. Western Mining and Railroad Museum, Helper, UT.

Labor Unions Records. Archives. Western Mining and Railroad Museum, Helper, UT.

Madge Tomsic Collection. Archives. Western Mining and Railroad Museum, Helper, UT.

Miners for Democracy Records, Walter P. Reuther Library, Wayne State University, Detroit, MI.

Miscellaneous Mining Records. Archives. Western Mining and Railroad Museum, Helper, UT.

Price River Coal Records. Archives. Western Mining and Railroad Museum, Helper, UT.

Rabail Motte History. Motte Residence, Wellington, UT.

Scofield and Winter Quarters Records. Archives. Western Mining and Railroad Museum, Helper, UT.

Small Assorted Collections. Archives. Western Mining and Railroad Museum, Helper, UT.

Spanish-Speaking Organization for Community, Integrity, and Opportunity Records. University of Utah J. Willard Marriott Library, Salt Lake City, UT.

Steve Star Collection. Archives. Western Mining and Railroad Museum, Helper, UT.

Sue Ann Martell Research. Archives. Western Mining and Railroad Museum, Helper, UT.

Sunnyside, East Carbon, and Columbia Records. Archives. Western Mining and Railroad Museum, Helper, UT.

UMWA Journals. Archives. Western Mining and Railroad Museum, Helper, UT.

Union Research Box. Archives. Western Mining and Railroad Museum, Helper, UT.

United Mine Workers of America Archives. Paterno Library, Pennsylvania State University, State College, PA.

Utah Coal Mining History Records. J. Willard Marriott Library, University of Utah, Salt Lake City, UT.

Utah Labor Archives. J. Willard Marriott Library, University of Utah, Salt Lake City, UT.

Oral Histories

Blacks in Utah. MS 453. J. Willard Marriott Library, University of Utah, Salt Lake City, UT.

Carbon County Oral History Project. Accn 1479. J. Willard Marriott Library, University of Utah, Salt Lake City, UT.

Castle Gate Oral History Project. Harold B. Lee Library, Brigham Young University, Provo, UT.

Hispanic Oral Histories. Accn 1369. J. Willard Marriott Library, University of Utah, Salt Lake City, UT.

Italian Oral History Project. J. Willard Marriott Library, University of Utah, Salt Lake City, UT.

Oral Histories. Box 1A. Western Mining and Railroad Museum, Helper, UT.

Oral Histories. Audio Collection. Western Mining and Railroad Museum, Helper, UT.

Scoville and Whittle, eds. *Yarns of Carbon and Emery Counties*. North Salt Lake: DMT Publishing, 2006.

South Slav Oral History Project. Accn 1369. J. Willard Marriott Library, University of Utah, Salt Lake City, UT.

Utah Division of Oil Gas and Mining Abandoned Mine Reclamation Program, Digital Oral History Collection. http://linux1.ogm.utah.gov/WebStuff/wwwroot/amr/miningHistory.html.

Author's Interviews

Interview with Frank Markosek and Dennis Ardohain, Price, July 2014.

Interview with Robert Trapanier, Lehi, UT, July 2014.

Interview with Duane Preston, Carbonville, UT, July 2014.

Interview with John Palacios, Price, UT, September 2014.

Interview with Jim and Ramona Valdez, Price, UT, March 2017.

Interview with Jon Passic, Myrtle Beach, FL, March 2017.

OTHER SOURCES

Ackermann, John A. "The Impact of the Coal Strike of 1977–78." *Industrial and Labor Relations Review* 32, no. 2 (January 1979): 185–88.

Albrecht, Stan L. "The Impacts Associated with Energy Developments in Carbon and Emery Counties, Utah, Part II: Socio-Cultural Impacts." Brigham Young University: Center for Business and Economic Research, 1975.

Alinsky, Saul. *John L. Lewis: An Unauthorized Biography*. New York: G. P. Putnam's Sons, 1949.

Andrews, Thomas G. *Killing for Coal: America's Deadliest Labor War*. Cambridge: Harvard University Press, 2008.

Arnold, Andrew B. *Fueling the Gilded Age: Railroads, Miners, and Disorder in Pennsylvania Coal Country*. New York: New York University Press, 2014.

Aronowitz, Stanley. *The Death and Life of American Labor: Toward a New Workers' Movement*. Brooklyn: Verso, 2014.

Baker, Wayne. *Above the Clouds: The Story of an American Entrepreneur*. Provo, UT: Press Media, 2008.

Banks, Alan. "The Report of the President's Commission on Coal: A Review Essay." *Appalachian Journal* 9, no. 4 (Summer 1982): 295–301.

Bethel, T. N. *Conspiracy in Coal*. Huntington, WV: Appalachian Movement Press, 1970.

Birecree, Adrienne M. "The Importance and Implications of Women's Participation in the 1989–90 Pittston Coal Strike." *Journal of Economic Issues* 30, no. 1 (March 1996): 187–210.

Black, Dan, Terra McKinnish, and Seth Sanders. "The Economic Impact of the Coal Boom and Bust." *Economic Journal* 115, no. 503 (April 2005): 449–76.

Boal, William M. "Unionism and Productivity in West Virginia Coal Mining." *Industrial and Labor Relations Review* 43, no. 4 (April 1990): 390–405.

Borstelmann, Thomas. *The 1970s: A New Global History*. Oxfordshire: Princeton University Press, 2012.

Boyd, Ernest W., Thomas R. Konrad, and Conrad Seipp. "In and Out of the

Mainstream: The Miners' Medical Program, 1946–1978." *Journal of Public Health Policy* 3, no. 4 (December 1982): 432–44.

Bragdon, Rebecca Ann Montoya. "Beneath a Balanced Rock: Hardscrabble Miners' Widows and Their Families' Search for Justice." PhD diss., University of North Carolina–Greensboro, 2004.

Brenner, Aaron, Robert Brenner, and Cal Winslow, eds. *Rebel Rank and File: Labor Militancy and Revolt from Below During the Long 1970s*. Brooklyn: Verso, 2010.

Brett, Jeanne M., and Stephen B. Goldberg. "Grievance Mediation in the Coal Industry: A Field Experiment." *Industrial and Labor Relations Review* 37, no. 1 (October 1983): 49–69.

——. "Wildcat Strikes in Bituminous Coal Mining." *Industrial and Labor Relations Review* 32, no. 4 (July 1979): 465–83.

Brinley, J. E., and Arthur Biggs. "Joint Report of the Officers of District 22 to the Nineteenth Consecutive Constitutional Convention of the United Mine Workers of America." Salt Lake City: United Mine Workers of America, 1957.

Bullock, David. *Coal Wars: Unions, Strikes, and Violence in Depression-Era Central Washington*. Pullman: Washington State University Press, 2014.

Cane, Paul F., Jr. "Parent Union Liability for Strikes in Breach of Contract." *California Law Review* 67, no. 4 (July 1979): 1028–48.

Cederlof, A. Philip. "The Peerless Coal Mines." *Utah Historical Quarterly* 53, no. 4 (Fall 1985): 336–56.

Christiansen, Bill, and Theodore H. Clack Jr. "A Western Perspective on Energy: A Plea for Rational Energy Planning." *Science* 194, no. 4265 (November 5, 1976): 578–84.

Clark, Paul F. *The Miners' Fight for Democracy: Arnold Miller and the Reform of the United Mine Workers*. Ithaca, NY: Cornell University Press, 1981.

Cobble, Dorothy Sue. *The Other Women's Movement: Workplace Justice and Social Rights in Modern America*. Princeton: Princeton University Press, 2004.

——, ed. *The Sex of Class: Women Transforming American Labor*. Ithaca, NY: Cornell University Press, 2007.

——, ed. *Women and Unions: Forging a Partnership*. Ithaca: ILR Press, 1993.

Cobble, Dorothy, Linda Gordon, and Astrid Henry. *Feminism Unfinished: A Short, Surprising, History of American Women's Movements.* New York: W. W. Norton, 2014.

Collins, Benjamin. "Right to Work Laws: Legislative Background and Empirical Research." *Congressional Research Service* (January 6, 2014). https://fas.org/sgp/crs/misc/R42575.pdf.

Cowie, Jefferson. *Staying Alive: The 1970s and the Last Days of the Working Class.* New York: New Press, 2010.

Curran, Daniel J. *Dead Laws for Dead Men: The Politics of Federal Coal Mine Health and Safety Legislation.* Pittsburgh: University of Pittsburgh Press, 1993.

Davis, Mike. *Prisoners of the American Dream: Politics and Economy in the History of the U.S. Working Class.* New York: Verso, 1986.

Dias, Ric Anthony. "'Together We Build': The Rise and Fall of the Kaiser Steel Corporation in the New Deal West." PhD diss., University of California–Riverside, 1995.

Dix, Keith. *What's a Coal Miner to Do?: The Mechanization of Coal Mining.* Pittsburgh Series in Social and Labor History. Pittsburgh: University of Pittsburgh Press, 1988.

Dublin, Thomas, and Walter Licht. *The Face of Decline: The Pennsylvania Anthracite Region in the Twentieth Century.* Ithaca: Cornell University Press, 2005.

Dubofsky, Melvyn, and Warren Van Tine. *John L. Lewis: A Biography.* New York: Quadrangle, 1977.

Early, Steve. *Save Our Unions: Dispatches from a Movement in Distress.* New York: Monthly Review Press, 2013.

Elmes, Gregory A., and Trevor M. Harris. "Industrial Restructuring and the United States Coal-Energy System, 1972–1990: Regulatory Change, Technological Fixes, and Corporate Control." *Annals of the Association of American Geographers* 86, no. 3 (September 1996): 507–29.

Embry, Jessie L., and Howard Christy, eds. *Community Development in the Modern West: Past and Present Nineteenth and Twentieth- Century Frontiers.* Charles Redd Monographs in Western History, no. 15. Provo: Charles Redd Center for Western Studies, 1985.

England, L. Lynn, and Stan L. Albrecht. "Boomtowns and Social Disruption." *Rural Sociology* 49, no. 2 (Summer 1984): 230–46.

Ewen, Lynda Ann. *Which Side Are You On?: The Brookside Mine Strike in Harlan County, Kentucky, 1973–1974.* Chicago: Vanguard Books, 1979.

Falk, Hans L., and William Jurgelski Jr. "Health Effects of Coal Mining and Combustion: Carcinogens and Cofactors." *Environmental Health Perspectives* 33 (December 1979): 203–26.

Farber, Henry S. "Individual Preferences and Union Wage Determination: The Case Study of the United Mine Workers." *Journal of Political Economy* 86, no. 5 (October 1978): 923–42.

Finley, Joseph E. *The Corrupt Kingdom: The Rise and Fall of the United Mine Workers.* New York: Simon and Schuster, 1972.

Fishback, Price V. *Soft Coal, Hard Choices: The Economic Welfare of Bituminous Coal Miners, 1890–1930.* New York: Oxford University Press, 1992.

Foley, Michael Stewart. *Front Porch Politics: The Forgotten Heyday of American Activism in the 1970s and 1980s.* New York: Hill and Wang, 2013.

Fox, Maier B. *United We Stand: The United Mine Workers of America, 1890–1990.* Washington, DC: United Mine Workers of America, 1990.

Freudenburg, William R. "The Density of Acquaintanceship: An Overlooked Variable in Community Research?" *American Journal of Sociology* 92, no. 1 (July 1986): 27–63.

———. "Women and Men in an Energy Boomtown: Adjustment, Alienation, and Adaptation." *Rural Sociology* 46, no. 2 (Summer 1981): 220–44.

Fry, Richard. "Fighting for Survival: Coal Miners and the Struggle Over Health and Safety in the United States, 1968–1988." PhD diss., Wayne State University, 2010.

Gardner, A. Dudley, and Verla Flores. *Forgotten Frontier: A History of Wyoming Coal Mining.* Boulder, CO: Westview Press, 1989.

Gearhart, Dona G. "'Surely a Wench Can Choose Her Own Work!': Women Coal Miners in Paonia, Colorado, 1976–1987." PhD diss., University of Nevada, 1996.

Geary, Edward A. *A History of Emery County.* Utah Centennial County History Series. Salt Lake City: Emery County Commission, 1996.

Geoghegan, Thomas. *Only One Thing Can Save Us: Why America Needs a New Kind of Labor Movement.* New York: New Press, 2014.

———. *Which Side Are You On?: Trying to Be for Labor When It's Flat on Its Back.* New York: New Press, 1991.

Gilmore, John S. "Boom Towns May Hinder Energy Resource Development." *Science* 191, no. 4227 (February 13, 1976): 535–40.

Glaberman, Martin. "Workers versus Unions in the Coal Industry." *International Journal of Politics, Culture, and Society* 2, no. 3 (Spring 1989): 373–77.

Goldfield, Michael. *The Decline of Organized Labor in the United States*. Chicago: University of Chicago Press, 1987.

González, Juan Carlos. "An Analysis of Utah's Chicano Civil Rights Movement Through S.O.C.I.O. and Its Involvement in Affirmative Action Programs, 1964–1984." Senior Thesis, University of Utah, 2013.

Grant, Don Sherman, II, and Michael Wallace. "Why Do Strikes Turn Violent?" *American Journal of Sociology* 96, no. 5 (March 1991): 1117–50.

Green, David. *The Threat of Western Coal*. Racine: GAU, 1978.

Greider, Thomas, and Richard S. Krannich. "Neighboring Patterns, Social Support, and Rapid Growth: A Comparison Analysis from Three Western Communities." *Sociological Perspectives* 28, no. 1 (January 1985): 51–70.

Griffith, Barbara S. *The Crisis of American Labor: Operation Dixie and the Defeat of the CIO*. Philadelphia: Temple University Press, 1988.

Harlan County USA. Directed by Barbara Kopple. Cabin Creek Films, 1977. DVD. The Criterion Collection, 2006.

Harvard Law Review. "Prospective Boys Markets Injunctions." *Harvard Law Review* 90, no. 4 (February 1977): 790–804.

Harvey, Curtis E. *Coal in Appalachia: An Economic Analysis*. Lexington: University Press of Kentucky, 1986.

Haverty-Stacke, Donna T., and Daniel J. Walkowitz, eds. *Rethinking U.S. Labor History: Essays on the Working-Class Experience, 1756–2009*. New York: Continuum, 2010.

Hill, Herbert. "Myth-Making as Labor History: Herbert Gutman and the United Mine Workers of America." *International Journal of Politics, Culture, and Society* 2, no. 2 (Winter 1988): 132–200.

Hinrichs, A. F. *The United Mine Workers of America and the Non-Union Coal Fields*. New York: Columbia University Press, 1923.

Horowitz, Daniel. *Jimmy Carter and the Energy Crisis of the 1970s: A Brief History with Documents*. The Bedford Series in History and Culture, edited by Natalie Zemon Davis et al. Boston: Bedford/St. Martins, 2005.

Howard, Walter T. "The National Miners Union: Communists and Miners in Pennsylvania Anthracite, 1928–1931." *Pennsylvania Magazine of History and Biography* 125, no. 1–2 (January–April 2001): 91–124.

Huitt, Joy. "For the Future." In Moore, *Women in the Mines*, 221–32.

Hume, Brit. *Death in the Mines*. New York: Grossman, 1971.

Iber, Jorge. *Hispanics in the Mormon Zion: 1912–1999*. College Station: Texas A&M University Press, 2002.

Jabanbani, F. R. *2000 Annual Review and Forecast of Utah Coal Production and Distribution*. Salt Lake City: Utah Department of Natural Resources, 2001.

Jacobs, Michael. "Coal Strike: Larger Issues at Stake." *Economic and Political Weekly* 19, no. 49 (December 8, 1984): 2073–74.

Jensen, Richard J. "Rebellion in the United Mine Workers: The Miners for Democracy, 1970–1972." PhD diss., Indiana University, 1974.

Johnson, Charles Jerome. "Coal Demand in the Electric Utility Industry, 1946–1990." PhD diss., Pennsylvania State University, 1972.

Johnson, James P. *The Politics of Soft Coal: The Bituminous Industry from World War I through the New Deal*. Urbana: University of Illinois Press, 1979.

Johnson, Tom. Review of *Women in the Mines: Stories of Life and Work*, by Marat Moore. *Labour/Le Travail* 41 (Spring 1998): 229–300.

Kelly, Robin D. G. *Hammer and Hoe: Alabama Communists During the Great Depression*. Chapel Hill: University of North Carolina Press, 1990.

Kiefer, David, and Jan Miller. "Public Budgets and Public Capital in Boom Towns." *Policy Sciences* 16, no. 4 (March 1984): 349–69.

Kimeldorf, Howard, and Judith Stepan-Norris. "Historical Studies of Labor Movements in the United States." *Annual Review of Sociology* 18 (1992): 495–517.

Kingsolver, Barbara. *Holding the Line: Women in the Great Arizona Mine Strike of 1983*. New York: ILR Press, 1989.

Krajcinovic, Ivana. *From Company Doctors to Managed Care: The United Mine Workers' Noble Experiment*. Cornell Studies in Industrial & Labor Relations, no. 31. Ithaca, NY: ILR Press, 1997.

Krantz, John. "Employment and Wages in the Coal Mining Industry." Utah Department of Workforce Services, *Workforce News* (March 2010): 1–3.

Laslett, John H. M., ed. *The United Mine Workers of America: A Model of Industrial Solidarity?* University Park: Pennsylvania State University Press, 1996.

Larson, Ken. *Carbon County Memories: Presented by the Sun Advocate.* Battle Ground, WA: Pediment Group, 2003.

Letwin, Daniel. "United Mine Workers of America: Centennial Conference." *International Labor and Working-Class History* 40 (Fall 1991): 108–10.

Lewis, John. *Till Every Battle's Won: The Brookside Strike of Harlan County.* New York: Center for Labor Action, 1974.

Lewis, Ronald L. *Black Coal Miners in America: Race, Class, and Community Conflict, 1780–1980.* Lexington: University Press of Kentucky, 1987.

Lewis-Beck, Michael S., and John R. Alford. "Can Government Regulate Safety? The Coal Mine Example." *American Political Science Review* 74, no. 3 (September 1980): 745–56.

Lichtenstein, Nelson. *State of the Union: A Century of American Labor.* Princeton: Princeton University Press, 2013.

Long, Priscilla. *Where the Sun Never Shines: A History of America's Bloody Coal Industry.* New York: Paragon House, 1989.

Lynd, Staughton, ed. *We Are All Leaders: The Alternative Unionism of the Early 1930s.* Chicago: University of Illinois Press, 1996.

MacLean, Nancy. "The Hidden History of Affirmative Action: Working Women's Struggles in the 1970s and the Gender of Class." *Feminist Studies* 25, no. 1 (Spring 1999): 42–78.

Maggard, Sally Ward. "Eastern Kentucky Women on Strike: A Study of Gender, Class, and Political Action in the 1970s." PhD diss., University of Kentucky, 1988.

McCammon, Holly J. "Legal Limits on Labor Militancy: U.S. Labor Law and the Right to Strike Since the New Deal." *Social Problems* 37, no. 2 (May 1990): 206–29.

McCartin, Joseph A. *Collision Course: Ronald Reagan, the Air Traffic Controllers, and the Strike that Changed America.* New York: Oxford University Press, 2011.

McCormick, John S., and John R. Sillito. *A History of Utah Radicalism: Startling, Socialistic, and Decidedly Revolutionary.* Logan: Utah State University Press, 2011.

Milkman, Ruth. "Two Worlds of Unionism: Women and the New Labor Movement." In Cobble, *The Sex of Class*, 63–80.

Millar, Rodney D. "The Impacts Associated with Energy Developments in Carbon and Emery Counties, Utah, Part III: Land Water, and Air Resources and Possible Conflicts of Their Use." Provo: Brigham Young University Center for Business and Economic Research, 1975.

"Miners Memorial." Miners Memorial Committee, Carbon County, Utah UTGenWeb, 2016. http://www.carbon-utgenweb.com/minersmonument.html.

———. *An Injury to All: The Decline of American Unionism*. New York: Verso, 1988.

———. *U.S. Labor in Trouble and Transition: The Failure of Reform from Above, the Promise of Revival from Below*. New York: Verso, 2007.

Moody, Kim, and Jim Woodward. *Battle Line: The Coal Strike of '78*. Detroit: Sun Press, 1978.

Moore, Marat. *Women in the Mines: Stories of Life and Work*. New York: Twayne Publishers, 1996.

Moore, William J., and Robert J. Newman. "The Effects of Right-to-Work Laws: A Review of the Literature." *Industrial and Labor Relations Review* 38, no. 4 (July 1985): 571–85.

Mulcahy, Richard P. *A Social Contract for the Coal Fields: The Rise and Fall of the United Mine Workers of America Welfare and Retirement Fund*. Knoxville: University of Tennessee Press, 1994.

Mullins, James N. "Impact of Generational Issues on Perceptions of Union Values in Select Manufacturing Industries." PhD diss., Capella University, 2012.

Muncy, Robyn. "Coal-Fired Reforms: Social Citizenship, Dissident Miners, and the Great Society." *Journal of American History* 96, no. 1 (June 2009): 72–98.

Myers, Robert J. "The Mine Workers' Welfare and Retirement Fund: Fifteen Years' Experience." *Industrial and Labor Relations Review* 20, no. 2 (January 1967): 265–74.

Naples, Michele I. "Technical and Social Determinants of Productivity Growth in Bituminous Coal Mining, 1955–1980." *Eastern Economic Journal* 24, no. 3 (Summer 1998): 325–42.

Navaroo, Peter. "Union Bargaining in the Coal Industry, 1945–1981." *Industrial and Labor Relations Review* 36, no. 2 (January 1983): 214–29.

Norris, Randall, and Jean-Philippe Cypress. *Women of Coal*. Lexington: University Press of Kentucky, 1996.

Notarianni, Philip F., ed. *Carbon County: Eastern Utah's Industrialized Island*. Salt Lake City: Utah State Historical Society, 1981.

Nussbaum, Karen. "Working Women's Insurgency Consciousness." In Cobble, *The Sex of Class*, 159–76.

Nyden, Paul J. "Coal Miners, 'Their' Union, and Capital." *Science & Society* 34, no. 2 (Summer 1970): 194–223.

———. "Miners for Democracy: Struggle in the Coal Fields." PhD diss., Columbia University, 1974.

———. "Rank-and-File Movements in the United Mine Workers of America: Early 1960s–Early 1980s." In Brenner, Brenner, and Winslow, *Rebel Rank and File*, 173–98.

Papanikolis, Helen Zeese. "Toil and Rage in a New Land: The Greek Immigrants in Utah." *Utah Historical Quarterly* 38, no. 2 (Spring 1970): 100–203.

———. "Unionism, Communism, and the Great Depression: The Carbon County Coal Strike of 1933." *Utah Historical Quarterly* 41, no. 3 (Summer 1973): 254–300.

———. "Utah's Coal Lands: A Vital Example of How America Became a Great Nation." *Utah Historical Quarterly* 43, no. 2 (Spring 1975): 104–24.

Perry, Charles R. *Collective Bargaining and the Decline of the United Mine Workers*. Major Industrial Unit Research Series, no. 60. Philadelphia: University of Pennsylvania Press, 1984.

Petersen, H. Craig, and Keith Lumsden. "The Effect of Right-to-Work Laws on Unionization in the United States." *Journal of Political Economy* 83, no. 6 (December 1975): 1237–48.

Poulsen, Jane D. "The Politics of Institutional Decline: The Fragmentation of Collective Bargaining in the U.S. Coal, Steel, and Tire Industries, 1946–1990." PhD diss., New York University, 1997.

Powell, Allan Kent, ed. *Emery County: Reflections on Its Past and Future*. Salt Lake City: Utah State Historical Society, 1979.

———. "The 'Foreign Element' and the 1903–4 Carbon County Coal Miners' Strike." *Utah Historical Quarterly* 43, no. 2 (Spring 1975): 104–24.

———. *The Next Time We Strike: Labor in Utah's Coal Fields, 1900–1933*. Logan: Utah State University Press, 1985.

———, ed. *Utah History Encyclopedia*. Salt Lake City: University of Utah Press, 1994.

President's Commission on Coal. *Coal Data Book*. Washington, DC: U.S. Government Printing Office, 1980.

Rayback, Joseph G. *A History of American Labor*. New York: Free Press, 1966.

Richards, Lawrence. *Union-Free America: Workers and Antiunion Culture*. Urbana: University of Illinois Press, 2008.

Rolston, Jessica Smith. *Mining Coal and Undermining Gender: Rhythms of Work and Family in the American West*. New Brunswick, NJ: Rutgers University Press, 2014.

Rosefeld, Jake, and Meredith Kleykamp. "Hispanics and Organized Labor in the United States: 1973 to 2007." *American Sociological Review* 74, no. 6 (December 2009): 916–37.

Saloutos, Theodore. "Cultural Persistence and Change: Greeks in the Great Plains and Rocky Mountain West, 1890–1970." *Pacific Historical Review* 49, no. 1 (February 1980): 77–103.

Savage, Carletta. "Re-gendering Coal: Female Miners and Male Supervisors." *Appalachian Journal* 27, no. 3 (Spring 2000): 232–48.

Scheffler, Richard M. "The United Mine Workers' Health Plan: An Analysis of the Cost-Sharing Program." *Medical Care* 22, no. 3 (March 1984): 247–54.

Scott, Shaunna L. *Two Sides to Everything: The Cultural Construction of Class Consciousness in Harlan County, Kentucky*. SUNY Series in Oral Public History, edited by Michael Frisch. Albany: State University of New York Press, 1995.

Seltzer, Curtis. *Fire in the Hole: Miners and Managers in the American Coal Industry*. Lexington: University Press of Kentucky, 1985.

Sheppard, Barry. *The Party: The Socialist Workers Party, 1960–1988, Volume 2: Interregnum, Decline, and Collapse, 1972–1988: A Political Memoir*. Berkeley: Minuteman Press, 2012).

Smith, Michael D., Richard S. Krannich, and Lori M. Hunter. "Growth, Decline, Stability, and Disruption: A Longitudinal Analysis of Social Well-Being in Four Western Rural Communities." *Rural Sociology* 66, no. 3 (September 2001): 425–50.

Spooner, D. J. "The Geography of Coal's Second Coming." *Geography* 66, no. 1 (January 1981): 29–41.

State Advisory Committees to the U.S. Commission on Civil Rights in the Rocky Mountain Region. *Energy Resource Development: Implications for Women and Minorities in the Intermountain West*, edited by Roger C. Wade and Jeanne Stibman. Washington, DC: U.S. Government Printing Office, 1979.

Stinner, William F., Michael B. Toney, and Stephen Kan. "Population Changes in Rural Utah." *Utah Science* 39, no. 3 (September 1978): 107–9.

Summers, Gene F., and Kristi Branch. "Economic Development and Community Social Change." *Annual Review of Sociology* 10 (1984): 141–66.

Tabor, Martha. "Women in Coal: Employment Patterns." *Off Our Backs* 10, no. 40 (April 1980): 10.

Tallichet, Suzanne E. *Daughters of the Mountain: Women Coal Miners in Central Appalachia*. University Park: Pennsylvania State University Press, 2006.

———. "Gendered Relations in the Mines and the Division of Labor Underground." *Gender and Society* 9, no. 6 (December 1995): 697–711.

———. "Moving Up Down in the Mine: Sex Segregation in Underground Coal Mining." PhD diss., Pennsylvania State University, 1991.

Taniguchi, Nancy J. *Castle Valley, America: Hard Land, Hard-Won Home*. Logan: Utah State University Press, 2004.

Taylor, Martha. "First National Women Coal Miners' Conference." *Off Our Backs* 9, no. 8 (August–September 1979): 20–21.

Thomas, Erin Ann. *Coal in Our Veins: A Personal Journey*. Logan: Utah State University Press, 2012.

Troy, Leo. "Trade Union Membership, 1897–1962." Cambridge: National Bureau of Economic Research, 1965. Accessed March 17, 2015. http://www.nber.org/chapters/c1707.pdf.

Turner, Evan. "The Impacts Associated with Energy Developments in Carbon and Emery Counties, Utah, Part I: Economic and Demographic Impacts." Provo, UT: Brigham Young University Center for Business and Economic Research, 1975.

Tyner, Wallace E., and Robert J. Kalter. *Western Coal: Promise or Problem*. Toronto: Lexington Books, 1978.

Underwood, Deborah. "The Ascendancy of Surface Mining Over Underground Mining in the United States Coal Industry: Effects on and Issues Relevant to the United Mine Workers of America." Master's thesis, Andrews University, 1987.

United States Department of Labor. Bureau of Labor Statistics. "Labor Force Statistics from the Current Population Survey." Accessed February 15, 2015. http://data.bls.gov/timeseries/LNU04000000?years_option=all_years&periods_option=specific_periods&periods=Annual+Data.

———. Bureau of Labor Statistics. "Union Membership Annual News Release." Accessed March 17, 2015. http://www.bls.gov/news.release/union2.htm.

———. Mine Safety and Health Administration. "Coal Fatalities for 1900 through 2014." Accessed May 5, 2015. http://www.msha.gov/stats/centurystats/coalstats.asp.

Utah Energy Office. *Utah Energy Developments: A Summary of Existing and Proposed Activity, 1981–1990.* Salt Lake City: John Short & Associates, 1981.

Utah Geological Survey (UGS). *Table 2.9, Coal Production and Miner Productivity in Utah, 1960–2013.* 2014. http://geology.utah.gov/emp/energydata/statistics/coal2.0/pdf/T2.9.pdf.

Vietor, Richard H. K. *Environmental Politics and the Coal Coalition.* College Station: Texas A&M University Press, 1980.

Wallace, Michael. "Dying for Coal: The Struggle for Health and Safety Conditions in American Coal Mining, 1930–82." *Social Forces* 66, no. 2 (December 1987): 336–64.

Watt, Ronald G. *A History of Carbon County.* Utah Centennial County History Series. Salt Lake City: Carbon County Commission, 1997.

Whitley, Colleen, ed. *From the Ground Up: The History of Mining in Utah.* Logan: Utah State University Press, 2006.

Wice, Marsha Nye. "Revolution in the Mines: An Analysis of the Miners' Revolt of 1969–1970." PhD diss., University of Illinois at Urbana-Champaign, 1973.

Wilkinson, Carroll Wetzel. "Critical Guide to the Literature of Women Coal Miners." *Labor Studies Journal* (Spring 1985): 25–45.

Wilkinson, Kenneth P., et al. "Local Social Disruption and Western Energy Development: A Critical Review." *Pacific Sociological Review* 25, no. 3 (July 1982): 275–96.

Winslow, Cal. "Overview: The Rebellion from Below, 1965–81." In Brenner, Brenner, and Winslow, *Rebel Rank and File,* 1–36.

Woodrum, Robert H. "Race and Industrial Transformation in the Alabama Coalfields, 1933–2001." PhD diss., Georgia State University, 2003.

Wool, Harold. "Coal Industry Resurgence Attracts Variety of New Workers." *Monthly Labor Review* 104, no. 1 (January 1981): 3–8.

Wysong, Jere A., and Sherman R. Williams. "The UMWA Health Care Program for Miners: Culprit or Victim?" *Journal of Public Health Policy* 5, no. 1 (March 1984): 83–103.

Yablonski, Joseph A. "Jock Yablonski's 1969 Campaign for the UMW Presidency: His Son Looks Back 40 Years After His Assassination." *LAWCHA: The Labor and Working-Class History Association* (Spring 2010): 16–19.

Zieger, Robert H. *John L. Lewis: Labor Leader*. Boston: Twayne Publishers, 1988.

NOTES

Prologue

1. Saul Alinsky, *John L. Lewis: An Unauthorized Biography* (New York: G. P. Putnam's Sons, 1949), 3.

2. "PacifiCorp to Close Deer Creek Mine in Huntington Canyon," *Emery County Progress* (hereafter *ECP*), December 16, 2014; Lisa Scovill, letter to the editor, *ECP*, October 22, 2013; C. J. McManus, "Deer Creek Miner Vote to Accept Contract," *ECP*, November 11, 2014; Patsy Stoddard, "Sixty Day Period for Contract Negotiations Winding Down for Deer Creek Miners and Energy West," *ECP*, October 29, 2013

Introduction

Epigraph source: William Dalrymple, leaflet, ca. 1951, box 97, folder 4, HCLA 1822, Presidents Correspondence with Districts, United Mine Workers of America Archives, Pennsylvania State University (hereafter cited as U-PC).

1. Michael Goldfield, *The Decline of Organized Labor in the United States* (Chicago: University Press of Chicago, 1987); Nelson Lichtenstein, *State of the Union: A Century of American Labor* (Princeton: Princeton University Press, 2002, 2013); Mike Davis, *Prisoners of the American Dream: Politics and Economy in the History of the U.S. Working Class* (New York: Verso, 1986).

2. Goldfield, *Decline of Organized Labor*, 205, 49.

3. Davis, *Prisoners*, 126–27.

4. Allan Kent Powell, *The Next Time We Strike: Labor in Utah's Coal Fields, 1900–1933* (Logan: Utah State University Press, 1985).

5. Kim Moody and Jim Woodward, *Battle Line: The Coal Strike of '78* (Detroit: Sun Press, 1978), 82; Paul F. Clark, *The Miners' Fight for Democracy: Arnold Miller and the Reform of the United Mine Workers* (Ithaca: Cornell University Press, 1981), 29, 103; Charles R. Perry, *Collective Bargaining and the Decline of the United Mine Workers*, Major Industrial Unit Research Series, no. 60 (Philadelphia: University of Pennsylvania Press, 1984), 51–52, 102, 126, 199, 268; Curtis Seltzer, *Fire in the Hole: Miners and Managers in the American Coal Industry* (Lexington: University Press

of Kentucky, 1985), 136; Maier B. Fox, *United We Stand: The United Mine Workers of America, 1890–1990* (Washington, DC: United Mine Workers of America, 1990), 461; Paul J. Nyden, "Rank-and-File Movements in the United Mine Workers of America: Early 1960s–Early 1980s," in *Rebel Rank and File: Labor Militancy and Revolt from Below During the Long 1970s*, ed. Aaron Brenner, Robert Brenner, and Cal Winslow (Brooklyn: Verso Press, 2010), 176, 180.

6. Fox, *United We Stand*, 507; Frank M. Stevenson to John T. Kmetz, August 7, 1967, box 13, folder 31, Organizing Department Records, United Mine Workers of America Archives, Pennsylvania State University (hereafter cited as U-OD); Wayne Baker, *Above The Clouds: The Story of an American Entrepreneur* (Provo, UT: Press Media, 2008), 137, 142–43; Dennis Ardohain and Frank Markosek, interview by author, Price, UT, July 15, 2014.

7. Advertisement, "To Miners Who Have Picketed Plateau," *Sun Advocate* (hereafter *SA*), October 21, 1971; Dave Munden, letter to the editor, *SA*, December 14, 1977; Iris H. Tatton, letter to the editor, *SA*, February 18, 1978; Name Withheld, letter to the editor, *SA*, March 8, 1978; Name Withheld, "Striker Hurts," *SA*, May 6, 1981; Name Withheld, "We Want to Work," *SA*, May 27, 1981; "Miner Firing Upheld," *SA*, July 25, 1979.

8. "Economic News Release: Union Members Summary," U.S. Department of Labor Bureau of Labor Statistics, January 28, 2016, http://www.bls.gov/news.release/union2.nr0.htm.

9. Seltzer, *Fire in the Hole*, 61–84. Note, negotiations between John L. Lewis and Secretary of the Interior Julius Krug established the UMWA Health and Welfare Fund in 1946. In 1974, revisions to the National Bituminous Coal Wage Agreement divided this fund into four separate funds, collectively known as the Health and Retirement Funds.

10. Ivana Krajcinovic, *From Company Doctors to Managed Care: The United Mine Workers' Noble Experiment*, Cornell Studies in Industrial & Labor Relations, no. 31 (Ithaca, NY: ILR Press, 1997), 45.

11. Brit Hume, *Death in the Mines* (New York: Grossman, 1971), 22–24; Seltzer, *Fire in the Hole*, 81–82; Clark, *Miners' Fight*, 17–18; Fox, *United We Stand*, 428, 443–44.

12. Andrew B. Arnold, *Fueling the Gilded Age: Railroads, Miners, and Disorder in Pennsylvania Coal Country* (New York: New York University Press, 2014), 185, 197.

13. T. N. Bethel, *Conspiracy in Coal* (Huntington, WV: Appalachian Movement Press, 1970), 3–4.

14. Ibid., 1.

15. Hume, *Death in the Mines*, 24, 66–69, 72, 75, 89–91, 99–113, 116–19; 120–52; Seltzer, *Fire in the Hole*, 85–107; Fox, *United We Stand*, 462–75; "Stopping the Disasters: What Must Be Done," *United Mine Workers Journal* (hereafter *UMWJ*), August 16, 1974.

16. Powell, *The Next Time We Strike*; Helen Zeese Papanikolis, "Toil and Rage in a New Land: The Greek Immigrants in Utah," *Utah Historical Quarterly* 38, no. 2 (Spring 1970): 100–203; Helen Zeese Papanikolis, "Unionism, Communism, and the Great Depression: The Carbon County Coal Strike of 1933," *Utah Historical Quarterly* 41, no. 3 (Summer 1973): 254–300; Helen Zeese Papanikolis, "Utah's Coal Lands: A Vital Example of How America Became a Great Nation," *Utah Historical Quarterly* 43, no. 2 (Spring 1975): 104–24.

17. Michael Stewart Foley, *Front Porch Politics: The Forgotten Heyday of American Activism in the 1970s and 1980s* (New York: Hill and Wang, 2013).

18. Daniel Horowitz, *Jimmy Carter and the Energy Crisis of the 1970s: A Brief History with Documents*, The Bedford Series in History and Culture (Boston: Bedford/St. Martins, 2005), 39; "Proposed Coal Leasing Policy Considers Regions," *SA*, August 16, 1978; "Coal Production Receives Boost," *SA*, October 18, 1978.

19. Allan Kent Powell, ed., *Utah History Encyclopedia* (Salt Lake City: University of Utah Press, 1994), 432–33; Utah Geological Survey (UGS), *Table 2.9, Coal Production and Miner Productivity in Utah, 1960–2013*, 2014, http://geology.utah.gov/emp/energydata/statistics/coal2.0/pdf/T2.9.pdf; Utah Energy Office, *Utah Energy Developments: A Summary of Existing and Proposed Activity, 1981–1990* (Salt Lake City: John Short & Associates, 1981): 44–81.

20. Clark, *Miners' Fight*, 141, 149–50.

21. "UMWA Building Set," *SA*, March 13, 1981; "UMW Installs New District 22 Officials," *SA*, April 2, 1982.

Chapter 1

1. Epigraph source: John L. Lewis, "United Mine Workers of America: The Stabilizing Force in the Coal Mining Industry of the United States," *Wyoming Labor Journal*, March 17, 1933, box 94, folder 41, U-PC. Howard Warren Browne, interview by Leslie Kelen, September 14–16, 1983, transcript, box 1, folders 14–15, Blacks in Utah, J. Willard Marriott Library, Salt Lake City, UT.

2. "Miners Memorial," Miners Memorial Committee, Carbon County, Utah UTGenWeb, 2016, http://www.carbon-utgenweb.com/minersmonument.html.

3. John Krantz, Utah Department of Workforce Services, *Workforce News* (March 2010): 3.

4. Agreement Between the United Mine Workers of America and Utah Coal Operators, UMWA-UCOA, November 8, 1933, box 94, folder 41, U-PC.

5. Powell, *The Next Time We Strike*; Papanikolas, "Unionism, Communism, and the Great Depression."

6. Powell, *The Next Time We Strike*, 38, 52, 106–13, 122–23, 168, and 175; "Strike Prevents Operations at Four Carbon County Mines: Coal Companies Turn Down Demands Made by N.M.U. Members," *SA*, August 24, 1933; "Strike Lines Broken in Four Camps: Mines Resume Activity: Leaders of National Mine Body Arrested on Charge of Riot," *SA*, August 31, 1933; National Miners Union, organizing leaflet, box 94, folder 46, U-PC.

7. Val Turri, interview by Jonson and Arriola, Helper, UT, February 8, 1972, transcript, box 3, folder 4, Carbon County Oral History Project, J. Willard Marriott Library, Salt Lake City, UT (hereafter cited as CCOH-JWM); Louis Pestotnick Jr., interview by Nancy Taniguchi, Price, May 5, 1982, transcript, box 2, folder 10, CCOH-JWM; Fay E. Thacker, interview by Mark Hutchings, March 20, 1976, transcript, Charles Redd Center for Western Studies, Labor Oral History Project, MSS OH 181, Harold B. Lee Library, Provo, UT (hereafter cited as LOHP-HBL); Willard Craig, interview by Mark Hutchings, June 12, 1976, transcript, MSS OH 221, LOHP-HBL.

8. Antonio Guadagnoli, interview by Phil Notarianni, June 13, 1972, transcript, Italian Oral History Project, box 1, folders 13–14, American West Center, University of Utah; Stanley C. Harvey, interview by Mark Hutchings, June 12, 1976, transcript, MSS OH 115, LOHP-HBL.

9. Tommy and May Hilton, interview by John Bluth, May 30, 1974, transcript, MSS OH 305, LOHP-HBL.

10. Tony Frungi, interview by Kendra Tomsci and M. Kobe, February 17, 1973, transcript, box 1, folder 17, CCOH-JWM; Tony Pestotnick, interview by Nancy Taniguchi, Price, July 3, 1982, box 2, folder 11, CCOH-JWM; Albert Vogrenic, interview by Nancy Taniguchi, Price, May 3, 1982, box 3, folder 5, CCOH-JWM.

11. Mr. and Mrs. Albert Robles, interview by Margie Archuleta, and Vincent Mayer, Dragerton, June 14, 1972, Utah Minorities Number S-26, transcript, American West Center, University of Utah, Western Mining and Railroad Museum, Helper, UT (hereafter cited as AWC-Helper); Tony Frungi, interview; UMWA Local 8003, "Resolution," July 9, 1944, box 96, folder 5, U-PC; Ronald G. Watt, *A History of Carbon County*, Utah Centennial County History Series (Salt Lake City: Carbon County Commission, 1997), 186–88; Powell, *The Next Time We Strike*, 40, 110.

12. Tommy and May Hilton, interview by John Bluth, May 30, 1974, transcript, MSS OH 305, LOHP-HBL; Manson E. Huff, interview by D. Mark Hastings, March 6, 1976, transcript, MSS OH 362, LOHP-HBL.

13. Pete Tabone, interview by John Bluth, November 7, 1974, transcript, MSS OH 82, LOHP-HBL.

14. Arthur Biggs to Senator Arthur V. Watkins, April 18, 1947, box 96, folder 28, U-PC.

15. "Cooks and Waiters Hold Benefit Dance," *SA*, May 9, 1939; "County Council of C.I.O. Decries Action Reputedly Taken by A.F.L. Affiliate; Proposes Retaliation," *SA*, July 6, 1939; "Auto Mechanics Vote Strike on Wage Demands," *SA*, April 29, 1948; "Union Organized for Oil Station Workers," *SA*, June 14, 1937; "Labor Movement Flourishes in Region Following Inception Eight Years Ago," *SA*, October 2, 1941; James Morgan to John L. Lewis, June 6, 1940, box 137, folder 8, HCLA 1823, UMWA Presidents Office Records, United Mine Workers of America Archives, Pennsylvania State University (hereafter cited as U-PO); James Morgan to John L. Lewis, November 19, 1942, box 95, folder 45, U-PC; James Morgan to Walter Smethurst, February 24, 1938, box 137, folder 8, U-PO.

16. "Students on Strike: New Bus Is Demanded," *SA*, September 14, 1939.

17. William M. Knerr to John L. Lewis, July 8, 1938, box 137, folder 8, U-PO; James Morgan to John L. Lewis, May 6, 1938, box 137, folder 8, U-PO; James Morgan to John L. Lewis, August 30, 1940, box 137, folder 8, U-PO; "Labor

Movement Flourishes in Region Following Inception Eight Years Ago," *SA*, October 2, 1941.

18. "Labor Conducts Celebration at Helper Monday," *SA*, September 9, 1937.
19. Powell, *The Next Time We Strike*, 166–67.
20. Ibid., 165–94.
21. "UMWA Agreement," *Carbon County Miner*, November 4, 1933.
22. Staughton Lynd, ed. *We Are All Leaders: The Alternative Unionism of the Early 1930s* (Chicago: University of Illinois Press, 1996).
23. *Carbon County Miner*, November 4, 1933.
24. Powell, *The Next Time We Strike*, 165–94.
25. Ibid.
26. Nicholas Fontecchio, "The New Deal for the Coal Mining Industry," box 94, folder 41, U-PC; Nicholas Fontecchio to Philip Murray, June 15, 1933, box 94, folder 45, U-PC.
27. Joe and Bessie Hinich, interview by Joe Stipanovich and Helen Papanikolas, Salt Lake City, June 19–27, 1972, transcript, box 1, folder 12, South Slav Oral History Project, J. Willard Marriott Library, University of Utah, Salt Lake City, UT; Marion Bonacci Lupo, interview by Helen Papanikolas, June 1971, transcript, box 2, folder 5, Italian Oral History Project, J. Willard Marriott Library, University of Utah, Salt Lake City, UT; Olga and Gus Halamandaris, interview by Carbon High School multicultural class, February 8, 1973, transcript, box 1A, Western Mining and Railroad Museum, Helper, UT (hereafter cited as WMRRM-Helper); Marko Yelinich, interview by Joe Stipanovich, Helper, February 14, 1973, folder 7, C-26, Ethnic Archives Oral Histories Audio Recordings, J. Willard Marriott Library, University of Utah, Salt Lake City, UT; Pete Aiello, interview by Nancy Taniguchi, November 23, 1979, transcript, box 1, folder 1, CCOH-JWM; Tommy and May Hilton, Ethnic Archives; Joe Meyers and Walt Borla, interview by Nancy Taniguchi, 1982, transcript, box 1, folder 4, CCOH-JWM; Ann and John Spensko, interview by Nancy Taniguchi, Helper, May 7, 1982, transcript, box 2, folder 15, CCOH-JWM; Anna Tolich, interview by Nancy Taniguchi, May 13, 1982, transcript, box 2, folder 18-19, CCOH-JWM; Florence and Raymond Toson, undated interview, transcript, box 1A, WMRRM-Helper.
28. Fox, *United We Stand*, 494; Matt Witt, "UMWA Wins First Major Test in

Western Organizing Drive," *UMWJ*, June 15, 1973, 9; "The Organizing Department," *UMWJ*, December 1973, 18–23.

29. Agreement Between the United Mine Workers of America and Utah Coal Operators, UMWA-UCOA, November 8, 1933, box 94, folder 41, U-PC; "Bituminous Coal Wage Agreement of 2008 Between Energy West Mining Company and the International Union United Mine Workers of America," International Union, United Mine Workers of America, 2008.

30. Agreement Between the United Mine Workers of America and Utah Coal Operators.

31. Ibid.; James Morgan to John L. Lewis, November 21, 1933, box 94, folder 41, U-PC.

32. Agreement Between the United Mine Workers of America and Utah Coal Operators.

33. John T Houghton, interviewed by Mark Hutchings, March 25, 1976, transcript, MSS OH 124, LOHP-HBL.

34. "Sweet Coal Company of Utah to John L. Lewis," February 2, 1940, box 95, folder 33, U-PC; R. A. Murray to John L. Lewis, February 3, 1940, box 95, folder 33, U-PC; Alfred Carey to John L. Lewis, February 7, 1940, box 95, folder 33, U-PC.

35. Alfred Carey to John L. Lewis, November 5, 1940, box 95, folder 37, U-PC; E. L. Cropper to John L. Lewis, November 5, 1940, box 95, folder 37, U-PC; Adolph Pyantil to John L. Lewis, November 7, 1940, box 95, folder 37, U-PC.

36. James Morgan to John L. Lewis, November 18, 1940, box 95, folder 38, U-PC; John L. Lewis to R. A. Murray, February 5, 1940, box 95, folder 33, U-PC; John L. Lewis to Alfred Carey, November 6, 1940, box 95, folder 37, U-PC.

37. Melvyn Dubofsky and Warren Van Tine, *John L. Lewis: A Biography* (New York: Quadrangle, 1977), 374.

38. Ibid., 377–79; "Miners Continue Strike as Negotiations in East Fail," *SA*, May 11, 1939.

39. Orvel Peterson to Thomas Kennedy, October 1, 1935, box 26, folder 17, UMWA Secretary-Treasurer's Office Records, United Mine Workers of America Archives, Pennsylvania State University (hereafter cited as U-ST).

40. Theo Reese to Thomas Kennedy, July 9, 1936, box 30, folder 42, U-ST.

41. A. D. Freeman to John L. Lewis, November 4, 1936, box 95, folder 1, U-PC; "National Miners Call Strike for Unpaid Finances: In Peaceful Walkout; Seek Back Wages; Company Is Awaiting Loan," *SA*, November 12, 1936.

42. G. G. Lindstrom and R. Rarish to John L. Lewis, February 21, 1938, box 37, folder 28, U-ST; Harold Olsen to Thomas Kennedy, March 25, 1938, box 37, folder 28, U-ST; "Coal Miners Work On, Wait Checks: Standard Firm Attests to Man's Loyalty," *Salt Lake Tribune*, February 1, 1939, box 95, folder 26, U-PC; Albert Roberts to John L. Lewis, February 11, 1939, box 95, folder 26, U-PC.

43. Frank Bonacci to Thomas Kennedy, October 8, 1934, box 26, folder 17, U-ST.

44. Virgil Wright and John Ross to John L. Lewis, January 19, 1936, box 95, folder 5, U-PC.

45. "Application for Exoneration," December 22, 1935, box 30, folder 42, U-ST; J. D. DeFries to UMWA, January 4, 1936, box 30, folder 42, U-ST; J. D. DeFries to Thomas Kennedy, March 25, 1936, box 30, folder 43, U-ST.

46. Dubofsky and Van Tine, *John L. Lewis*, 372–74.

47. Virgil Wright to Thomas Kennedy, October 3, 1934, box 26, folder 17, U-ST.

48. John Ross to A. D. Lewis, February 15, 1935, box 94, folder 53, U-PC; John M. Ross to A. D. Lewis, January 28, 1935, box 94, folder 53, U-PC.

49. Orvel Peterson to Edward F. McGrady, June 26, 1935, box 94, folder 53, U-PC.

50. Frank Bonacci, "Complaint," April 7, 1936, box 95, folder 7, U-PC. To "shoot coal off the solid" is to blast coal without undercutting the seam by pick or mechanical cutter. While this saves time and cost, there is a greater chance that the force of the blast may be expended outward into the air, bringing a greater risk of igniting an explosion, or into the ceiling, weakening the roof.

51. Tony Radalj to John L. Lewis, May 17, 1938, box 95, folder 22, U-PC; J. E. Brinley to John L. Lewis, April 10, 1958, box 98, folder 10, U-PC; John T. Kmetz to Frank J. Sacco, May 23, 1966, box 13, folder 21, U-OD.

52. "Report of District Officers: United Mine Workers of America District Number Twenty-Two," September 30, 1938, box 169, folder 8, U-PC.

53. James Morgan to John L. Lewis, March 24, 1938, box 137, folder 8, U-PO.

54. Ibid.

55. Dubofsky and Van Tine, *John L. Lewis*, 381–85.

56. "By-Laws of United Mine Workers of America Local Union No. 6089, Columbia, Utah," June 1934, box 94, folder 48, U-PC.

57. "Mine Workers Plan Meeting in Salt Lake," *Salt Lake Telegram* (hereafter *SLT*), April 2, 1934; "Carbon Miners Vote in Race," *SLT*, April 16, 1937; "Incumbents Win Miner Election," *SLT*, October 27, 1937; "Carbon Miners in UMW Race," *SLT*, October 9, 1939; "District 22 Names Carey as Head Man," *SA*, September 18, 1941; Frank Wilson to John O'Leary, October 7, 1945, box 96, folder 10, U-PC; "Mine Workers Ready for Runoff Election," *SLT*, December 11, 1945; "8000 Miners Hold Election in Utah, Wyoming Area," *SLT*, October 11, 1949; "Miners Holding New Election," *SLT*, May 31, 1950.

58. John L. Lewis to all IEB members and district presidents, December 23, 1944, box 96, folder 7 U-PC; "District Twenty-Two 1945 Changes of Officers," 1945, box 96, folder 13, U-PC.

59. Richard L. Thornock to Harry Mangus, October 10, 1961, box 98, folder 25, U-PC; Harry Mangus to W. A. Boyle, December 4, 1961, box 98, folder 27, U-PC.

60. Arthur Biggs to John L. Lewis, November 9, 1951, box 97, folder 10, U-PC; Harry Mangus to W. A. Boyle, December 4, 1961, box 98, folder 27, U-PC; Officers of Local 230 to John L. Lewis, March 22, 1934, box 94, folder 47, U-PC; George Cole to John L. Lewis, October 28, 1934, box 94, folder 48, U-PC.

61. Mike Eaves to Thomas Kennedy, March 8, 1962, box 98, folder 30, U-PC; W. A. Boyle to Mike Eaves, April 10, 196, box 98, folder 30, U-PC; obituary for Malio Pecorelli, *Deseret News*, December 17, 1997.

62. John L. Lewis to John Owens, January 20, 1958, box 98, folder 10, U-PC; Gerald L. Oviatt et al. to John L. Lewis, March 5, 1958, box 98, folder 10, U-PC; Andrew J. Smith to John L. Lewis, February 8, 1958, box 98, folder 10, U-PC; Ross Norton to John L. Lewis, February 14, 1958, U-PC; Willard Hughes to John L. Lewis, February 17, 1958, box 90, folder 10, U-PC; "Organizing: Teamwork Works, East and West," *UMWJ*, December 1983.

63. Resolutions Committee, Local Union 6511 to Thomas Kennedy, October 10, 1934, box 26, folder 17, U-ST; Orwell Peterson to Thomas Kennedy, October 1, 1934, box 26, folder 17, U-ST; Thomas Kennedy to Grant Charlesworth, November 13, 1934, box 26, folder 17, U-ST.

64. B. E. Christensen, N. S. Thomas, and Joe Dowd to John L. Lewis, January 21, 1938, box 137, folder 8, U-PO. Emphasis in original.

65. "UMW Head in Wyoming Supports F.R.," *Wyoming State Tribune*, October 27, 1940, box 95, folder 36, U-PC; Eugene McAuliffe to John L. Lewis, October 30, 1940, box 95, folder 37, U-PC.

66. L. Fowler, Ernest Toson, and E. R. Batchilos to John L. Lewis, July 2, 1940, box 95, folder 34, U-PC.

67. Ibid.; Resolutions Committee, Local 6788 to International Officers, November 19, 1940, box 95, folder 38, U-PC.

68. Harold Olsen to John L. Lewis, October 10, 1940, box 95, folder 36, U-PC; John L. Lewis to Harold Olsen, October 15, 1940, box 95, folder 36, U-PC.

69. Dubofsky and Van Tine, *John L. Lewis*, 390.

70. Ed L. Pinegar to John L. Lewis, December 4, 1936, box 95, folder 11, U-PC.

CHAPTER 2

Epigraph source: Officers of LU 6511, Sweet Mine, to John L. Lewis, November 9, 1949, box 97, folder 1, U-PC.

1. "Mine Blast Kills 22," *SA*, May 10, 1945; "Investigations Reveal Little to Place Blame for Mine Blast," *SA*, May 17, 1945.

2. "Mine Blast Kills 22."

3. John L. Lewis to William M. McPhie, May 23, 1945, box 96, folder 10, U-PC.

4. "Sunnyside Men Fail to Work," *SA*, May 24, 1945; "Miners Return to Work at Sunnyside and Hiawatha," *SA*, May 31, 1945.

5. "Sunnyside Disaster Report Criticizes Mine Management," *SA*, June 14, 1945.

6. Local 6244 Executive Board to John L. Lewis, December 23, 1945, box 96, folder 22, U-PC; Claude Heiner to John L. Lewis, December 21, 1945, box 96, folder 22, U-PC; John L. Lewis to Melvin Thomas, March 5, 1946, box 96, folder 10, U-PC; Local 6244, Advertisement, *SA*, January 3, 1946.

7. John L. Lewis to Mr. Cox, December 22, 1945, box 96, folder 22, U-PC; Claude Heiner to John L. Lewis, December 21, 1945, box 96, folder 22, U-PC; Harrison Combs to John L. Lewis, Jan 3, 1946, box 96, folder 14, U-PC.

8. Utah Fuel Company, Advertisement, *SA*, December 28, 1945.

9. Local 6244, Advertisement, *SA*, January 3, 1946.

10. Ibid.; Local 6244 Executive Board to John L. Lewis, December 23, 1945, box 96, folder 22, U-PC.

11. Ric Anthony Dias, "'Together We Build': The Rise and Fall of the Kaiser Steel Corporation in the New Deal West" (PhD diss., University of California–Riverside, 1995), 103; "Geneva Steel Plant Miracle of Wartime Construction," *SA*, May 24, 1945.

12. Robert H. Zieger, *John L. Lewis: Labor Leader* (Boston: Twayne Publishers, 1988), 135–36; "List of Seventy-One Carbon Service Men Killed in War," *SA*, September 13, 1945; "World War II Honor List of Dead and Missing: State of Utah," United States War Department, June 1946, Utah State Archives, https://archives.utah.gov/research/guides/wwii-army-honor-list-utah.pdf; J. E. Brinley and Arthur Biggs, "Joint Report of the Officers of District No. 22 to the Nineteenth Consecutive Constitutional Convention of the United Mine Workers of America," February 12, 1957, box 333, folder 21, U-ST.

13. "Royal Miner Dies Following Mishap Tuesday Afternoon," *SA*, February 19, 1942; "Latuda Miner Killed by Falling Roof Rock," *SA*, February 4, 1943; "Accident Is Fatal to Man in Latuda Mine," *SA*, November 11, 1943; "Falling Rock Kills Japanese Miner, 54," *SA*, December 9, 1943; "Two Hiawatha Miners Killed by Coal Fall," *SA*, January 18, 1945.

14. "Carbon Coal Output Lags," *SA*, July 22, 1943; "Labor Shortage in Carbon Is Acute," *SA*, April 15, 1943; "Mine Labor in Carbon Scarce, Says Forrester," *SA*, May 20, 1943.

15. Nancy J. Taniguchi, *Castle Valley, America: Hard Land, Hard-Won Home* (Logan: Utah State University Press, 2004), 228.

16. Zieger, *John L. Lewis*, 134–35; A. Philip Cederlof, "The *Peerless* Coal Mines," *Utah Historical Quarterly* 53, no. 4 (Fall 1985): 336–56; "Miners' Wage Figures Given by Magazine," *SA*, July 15, 1943.

17. Dubofsky and Van Tine, *John L. Lewis*, 420, 427; Zieger, *John L. Lewis*, 136–37.

18. Zieger, *John L. Lewis*, 138–40; Dubofsky and Van Tine, *John L. Lewis*, 421; "Mine Workers Ballot in Favor of Carrying Out Coal Strike," *SA*, March 29, 1945; "Failure of Orders to Arrive Here on Strike Slows Work," *SA*, April 5, 1945.

19. "Strike Still Unsettled," *SA*, August 27, 1942; "Miners Return to Work at Sunnyside and Hiawatha," *SA*, May 31, 1945; "Gordon Creek Work Stops," *SA*, May 31, 1945; "Hiawatha Mine Workers Return After Walkout," *SA*, May 24, 1945; Alfred Carey to John L. Lewis, September 27, 1944, box 96, folder 6, U-PC.

20. Dubofsky and Van Tine, *John L. Lewis*, 426–27; "Coal Strike Threat Now Near Crisis," *SA*, April 29, 1943; "District 22 UMWA Meeting Held Thursday," *SA*, February 8, 1945.

21. "Wyoming Miner Gets First Pension Check," *SA*, September 9, 1948; "Retired Coal Miners to Start Receiving Pension Checks," *SA*, August 26, 1948.

22. Dubofsky and Van Tine, *John L. Lewis*, 456–89; "Miners Continue to Back Lewis in Work Stoppage, Lewis Found Guilty," *SA*, December 5, 1946; "Miners List Grievances to Utah County Group, Relief Doubtful," *SA*, December 5, 1946; Welfare Sick Committee to International Union, December 4, 1946, box 96, folder 21, U-PC; "Operators to Blame for Mine Walkout, Says Labor Journal," *SA*, December 12, 1946; "Soft Coal 'Pension Plan' Walkout Closes Major Carbon Mines, 3600 Idle," *SA*, March 18, 1948; "Coal Strike Ends Wednesday, Miners Get Increases, Fund," *SA*, May 30, 1946; "Coal Strike Halts All Operations in Carbon," *SA*, November 21, 1946; "Lewis, Union, Contempt Upheld by High Court," *SA*, March 13, 1947; "Surplus Spuds Go to Needy Miners' Families," *SA*, February 23, 1950; "Dried Milk Added to Surplus Food Ration," *SA*, February 16, 1950; "Typographical Union Gives $1000 to Aid Carbon County Miners," *SA*, February 16, 1950.

23. Krajcinovic, *From Company Doctors to Managed Care*; Richard P. Mulcahy, *A Social Contract for the Coal Fields: The Rise and Fall of the United Mine Workers of America Welfare and Retirement Fund* (Knoxville: University of Tennessee Press, 1994).

24. "Coal Industry Leaders Express Views on What They See Ahead," *SA*, October 18, 1945; "Bright Future Seen for Coal in Utah's Economic Picture," *SA*, September 11, 1947; "Disturbing Picture of Future of Coal Industry Painted by Columnist," *SA*, June 18, 1946; "Coal Shortage Hits Provo Area Hard, BYU Installs Oil," *SA*, December 15, 1946; "Coal Haulage Is Large Single Item of D&RGW Business," *SA*, December 23, 1946; "Three New Giant Diesels Arrive for Railroad Traffic," *SA*, January 2, 1947.

25. "Disturbing Picture of Coal Industry"; "Utah's 1946 Coal Production Below 1945 Mark," *SA*, April 24, 1947; "Question for Coal Miners," *SA*, November 28, 1946; D. B. E. letter to the editor, *Salt Lake Tribune*, May 1954, box 97, folder 30, U-PC.

26. Joseph G. Rayback, *A History of American Labor* (New York: Free Press, 1966), 387–95.

27. Davis, *Prisoners*, 86.

28. Barbara S. Griffith, *The Crisis of American Labor: Operation Dixie and the Defeat of the CIO* (Philadelphia: Temple University Press, 1988).

29. "Lewis Fears Coal Surplus in 1949 as Laws of Supply and Demand Even," *SA*, January 6, 1949; "Coal Industry Leaders Express Views on What They See Ahead," *SA*, October 18, 1945; "Carbon-Emery Miners Remain Idle," *SA*, September 22, 1949.

30. "Settlement of Coal and Steel Issues Are of Vital Importance To Local Miners," *SA*, September 29, 1949; "Picket 'Violence' in Emery Labeled As 'Exaggerated,'" *SA*, September 29, 1949; "No 'Disturbing Elements' Reported from Coal Fields," *SA*, March 2, 1950; "Carbon Miners Remain Idle; Want Contract or 'No Work,'" *SA*, February 23, 1950.

31. Dubofsky and Van Tine, *John L. Lewis*, 488–90.

32. "Coal Industry Leaders Express Views on What They See Ahead," *SA*, October 18, 1945.

33. "Article Reviews Interesting History of Extraction of Coal," *SA*, December 11, 1947.

34. "Utah Fuel Coke Ovens May Close During 3-Day Week," *SA*, December 22, 1949; "Coal Industry Leaders Express Views"; Local 6511 to Arthur Watkins, April 1949, box 96, folder 46, U-PC.

Chapter 3

Epigraph source: Frank J. Sacco to Don Stillman, undated letter, ca. 1972, box 92, folder 21, MFD.

1. The following in box 97, folder 10, U-PC: Carlo Balducchi to UMWA, December 1951; Harry Mangus to J. E. Brinley, December 21, 1951.

2. William Dalrymple to John L. Lewis, July 19, 1951, box 97, folder 8, U-PC.

3. Frank J. Sacco to Charles Bergamo, December 7, 1951, box 97, folder 17, U-PC.

4. The following in box 96, folder 20, U-PC: Houston Martin to John L. Lewis, September 9, 1946; Malcolm N. McKinnon, "General Commitment to All the Employees of the American Fuel Company," August 2, 1945.

5. Arthur Biggs to John L. Lewis, December 21, 1945, box 96, folder 23, U-PC.

6. "Union Council Hits Non-Union Washings, Mines," *SA*, September 30, 1948; John L. Lewis to Joe Dowd, December 7, 1945, box 96, folder 10,

U-PC; James Stewart to John L. Lewis, October 21, 1949, box 96, folder 44, U-PC; Harry Mangus to John L. Lewis, August 21, 1950, box 96, folder 48, U-PC.

7. William Dalrymple to John Owens, July 29, 1948, box 139, folder 16, U-ST.

8. Miners of American Fuel Co. to Houston Martin, August 12, 1946, box 96, folder 20, U-PC.

9. The following in box 96, folder 20, U-PC: Houston Martin to Frank Fox, August 21, 1946; Houston Martin to John L. Lewis, September 9, 1946.

10. James Morgan to John O'Leary, February 14, 1947, box 96, folder 23, U-PC.

11. The following in box 96, folder 33, U-PC: Arthur Biggs to John L. Lewis, January 2, 1948; John L. Lewis to Officers of District 22, January 8, 1948.

12. Virgil Wright to John L. Lewis, January 13, 1948, box 96, folder 33, U-PC.

13. Malcolm Condie to John L. Lewis, January 27, 1948, box 96, folder 33, U-PC.

14. John O'Leary to Malcolm Condie, January 16, 1948, box 96, folder 30, U-PC; "Meeting Scheduled at Huntington of Non-Union Miners," *SA*, June 10, 1948; "UMW of A Officials Push Wagon Mine Organizing," *SA*, June 17, 1948; Arthur Biggs to Thomas Kennedy, July 3, 1948, box 96, folder 36, U-PC; Virgil Wright to John L. Lewis, February 10, 1949, box 96, folder 41, U-PC; "UMW of A Local to Be Chartered in Emery County," *SA*, July 15, 1948; Houston Martin to Thomas Kennedy, August 2, 1948, box 96, folder 36, U-PC.

15. Virgil Wright to John L. Lewis, February 10, 1949, box 96, folder 41, U-PC; Advertisement, ca. October 1949, box 96, folder 45, U-PC; "Emery Local 8282 Chartered by UMW of A," *SA*, August 26, 1948.

16. R. A. Murray to John L. Lewis, March 7, 1949, box 96, folder 40, U-PC.

17. R. A. Murray to John L. Lewis, April 4, 1949, box 96, folder 44, U-PC.

18. Ibid.

19. Woodruff Peacock and George L. May to Frank Fox, April 4, 1949, box 96, folder 41, U-PC; Local 8282 to John L. Lewis, November 2, 1949, box 97, folder 2, U-PC; Arthur Biggs to John Owens, December 7, 1951, box 71, folder 23, U-ST.

20. The following in box 96, folder 21, U-PC: "Memorandum from Mr. Pape," September 22, 1945; James Morgan to John J. Mates, November 27, 1946.

21. James Morgan to Senator Joseph C. O'Mahoney, November 14, 1945, box 96, folder 14, U-PC.

22. James Morgan to John O'Leary, November 21, 1945, box 96, folder 14, U-PC.

23. John Ghizzoni to John L. Lewis, November 22, 1945, box 96, folder 10, U-PC.

24. Ibid.

25. John L. Lewis to Joe Dowd, December 7, 1945, box 96, folder 21, U-PC.

26. The following in box 96, folder 14, U-PC: James Morgan to John O'Leary, January 11, 1946; James Morgan to John O'Leary, January 20, 1946.

27. The following in box 96, folder 14, U-PC: James Morgan to John L. Lewis, February 18, 1946; James Morgan to John O'Leary, February 25, 1946.

28. James Morgan to John O'Leary, January 25, 1946, box 96, folder 14, U-PC.

29. James Morgan to John O'Leary, February 25, 1946, box 96, folder 12, U-PC; ibid., March 3, 1946, box 96, folder 14, U-PC.

30. R. J. Warinner to John L. Lewis, May 2, 1946, box 96, folder 27, U-PC; Malcolm Condie to John O'Leary, September 3, 1947, box 96, folder 30, U-PC.

31. George A. Nugent to Houston Martin, April 30, 1948, box 96, folder 35, U-PC.

32. Gene Bondi to John L. Lewis, May 7, 1948, box 96, folder 35, U-PC.

33. Malcolm Condie to Thomas Kennedy, June 28, 1948, box 96, folder 35, U-PC.

34. George A. Nugent to Thomas Kennedy, February 8, 1949, box 96, folder 40, U-PC.

35. The following in box 96, folder 40, U-PC: John H. Cox to John L. Lewis, March 2, 1949; W. D. Murray to John L. Lewis, March 7, 1949; John L. Lewis to W. D. Murray, March 10, 1949.

36. William Darlymple to John Owens, March 17, 1950, box 69, folder 3, U-PC; Houston Martin to John Owens, February 1, 1949, box 63, folder 31, U-PC; Thomas Kennedy to William Dalrymple, August 4, 1948, box 59, folder 17, U-PC.

37. The following in box 96, folder 43, U-PC: William Dalrymple to Houston Martin, November 28, 1949; Alving Blackburn to Frank Fox, November 22, 1949.

38. William Dalrymple to John L. Lewis, July 19, 1951, box 97, folder 8, U-PC.

39. Carol Olson to John L. Lewis, June 14, 1950, box 96, folder 48, U-PC; William Dalrymple to Esther Cossel Jones, March 29, 1950, box 69, folder 3, U-ST; William Dalrymple to Thomas Kennedy, June 22, 1951, box 97, folder 8, U-PC; William Dalrymple to Thomas Kennedy, March 10, 1951, box 97, folder 4, U-PC; Arnold Skinner and Carl Olson to John Owens, March 20, 1952, box 74, folder 8, U-PC; Leslie G. Rice, Arnold Skinner, and Carol Olson to John L. Lewis, April 4, 1952, box 74, folder 9, U-ST; J. E. Brinley to John Owens, April 14, 1952, box 74, folder 9, U-ST.

40. William Darlymple, Organizing Leaflet, ca. 1948, box 69, folder 3, U-ST.

41. "New Coal Delivery Company Opens in Cedar City," *Iron County Record*, October 8, 1953; Obituary for W. Thuren Odendahl, *Salt Lake Tribune*, May 19, 2013.

42. J. E. Brinley to Thomas Kennedy, February 11, 1956, box 97, folder 39, U-PC; "Supreme Court Hands Down Decision in Picket Appeal," *SA*, May 9, 1957; Arthur Biggs to Thomas Kennedy, December 12, 1961, box 98, folder 28, U-PC.

43. Malio Pecorelli, "Report," February 1954, box 97, folder 27, U-PC.

44. William Dalrymple to Thomas Kennedy, March 10, 1951, box 97, folder 4, U-PC; Harry Mangus to John L. Lewis, August 21, 1950, box 96, folder 48, U-PC.

45. Malio Pecorelli to Thomas Kennedy, May 28, 1954, box 97, folder 30, U-PC.

46. Ibid.; Harry Mangus to Thomas Kennedy, September 2, 1959, box 98, folder 18, U-PC.

47. Harry Mangus to Thomas Kennedy, December 11, 1961, box 98, folder 30, U-PC.

48. The following in box 98, folder 14, U-PC: Oscar A. Glaeser to John L. Lewis, December 1, 1958; G. E. Sorensen to John L. Lewis, December 1, 1958; Walter Kennedy to John L. Lewis, December 1, 1958; Lion Coal Corporation to John L. Lewis, December 1, 1958; J. J. Holwerda to John L. Lewis, December 2, 1958; W. J. O'Connor to John L. Lewis, December 1, 1958; Western Coal Mining Company to John L. Lewis, December 1, 1958.

49. Seltzer, *Fire in the Hole*, 77–78; Dubofsky and Van Tine, *John L. Lewis*, 502.

50. The following in box 98, folder 28, U-PC: Harry Mangus to W. A. Boyle, October 10, 1961; Harry Mangus to W. A. Boyle, November 24, 1961.

51. Richard Murray to John L. Lewis, April 4, 1949, box 96, folder 44, U-PC; Mulcahy, *A Social Contract*, 117–18; "Utah Mine Strike Fights Physician," *New York Times*, February 3, 1952.

52. Joseph Kennedy to John L. Lewis, April 24, 1952, box 74, folder 9, U-ST; J. E Brinley to W. A. Boyle, April 21, 1952, box 74, folder 9, U-ST; J. E. Brinley to John L. Lewis, May 1, 1952, box 97, folder 15, U-PC; Henry Allai and John Kmetz to W. A. Boyle, August 31, 1953, U-PC.

53. John L. Lewis to J. E. Brinley, September 23, 1952, box 97, folder 17, U-PC; Frank M. Stevenson to Emmett Thomas, July 14, 1962, box 99, folder 30, U-PC; Arthur Biggs to Thomas Kennedy, October 17, 1962, box 99, folder 30, U-PC; "Lewis Telegram Directs Kenilworth Miners Back to Work," *SA*, December 29, 1949; J. E. Brinley, "Report of Unauthorized Work Stoppage of April 9, 1956," box 97, folder 39, U-PC; Oscar A. Glaeser to John L. Lewis, September 20, 1955, box 97, folder 39, U-PC.

54. J. E. Brinley and Arthur Biggs to W. A. Boyle, March 22, 1951, and April 11, 1951, box 97, folder 4, U-PC.

55. W. J. O'Connor to John L. Lewis, October 21, 1952, box 97, folder 17, U-PC.

56. "Resolutions Presented to the Eighteenth Consecutive Constitutional Convention of District 22, UMWA," February 1953, box 97, folder 17, U-PC.

57. The following in box 97, folder 23, U-PC: Pratt Lindsey to John L. Lewis, September 22, 1953; John L. Lewis to Pratt Lindsey, September 23, 1953.

58. Officers of Local 905 to John L. Lewis, March 23, 1954, box 97, folder 23, U-PC; J. E. Brinley to John L. Lewis, September 16, 1955, box 97, folder 35, U-PC.

59. The following in box 96, folder 13, U-PC: Thomas Preston et al., "Resolution," August 30, 1945; Johnny Vlakorek, Albert Robers, and J. E. Brinley to John L. Lewis, August 30, 1945.

60. R. A. Murray to John L. Lewis, September 25, 1947, box 96, folder 36, U-PC.

61. The following in box 96, folder 40, U-PC: Arthur Biggs to John L. Lewis, January 20, 1949; James Stanley, J. E. Brinley, and Pratt Lindsey, "Resolution," January 25, 1949.

62. Frank Fox to John L. Lewis, June 22, 1950, box 97, folder 1, U-PC.

63. Lloyd Noyes to John Owens, May 11, 1950, box 69, folder 2, U-ST.

64. "Minutes of the District Executive Board Meeting Held February 26 through March 1, 1951," box 97, folder 12, U-PC.

65. John Owens to Pratt Lindsey, August 14, 1952, box 97, folder 17, U-PC.

66. Henry Allai and John Kmetz to Thomas Kennedy, June 25, 1956, box 98, folder 1, U-PC.

67. Arthur Biggs to John L. Lewis, August 20, 1962, box 98, folder 33, U-PC.

68. Arthur Biggs to Thomas Kennedy, March 13, 1955, box 97, folder 39, U-PC; Paul James to W. A. Boyle, June 28, 1963, box 102, folder 44, U-ST.

69. Malio Pecorelli to Thomas Kennedy, May 28, 1954, box 97, folder 30, U-PC.

70. The following in box 96, folder 37, U-PC: Resolutions Committee, District 22 UMWA to John L. Lewis, November 17, 1948; John L. Lewis to Houston Martin, December 6, 1948.

71. Resolutions Committee, District 22 UMWA to John L. Lewis.

72. The following in box 71, folder 22, U-ST: Houston Martin to John L. Lewis, February 23, 1951; Thomas Kennedy to Burt Barham et al., March 1, 1951.

73. The following in box 71, folder 22, U-ST: Willard Craig to John L. Lewis, February 26, 1951; William Nielsen to John Owens, March 3, 1951; K. M. Rasmussen to Thomas Kennedy, February 22, 1951.

74. James Steward to John L. Lewis, February 17, 1949, box 96, folder 40, U-PC; Don Madia to Thomas Kennedy, March 20, 1949, box 96, folder 40, U-PC; Pratt Lindsey to Thomas Kennedy, October 20, 1950, box 96, folder 51, U-PC; Ross Norton to John L. Lewis, November 9, 1950, box 97, folder 3, U-PC; Tony Marietta to John L. Lewis, July 12, 1956, box 98, folder 1, U-PC; J. E. Brinley to John J. Mates, September 5, 1956, box 98, folder 3, U-PC.

75. Frank Wilson, Joe Shannon, and George Griffith to John L. Lewis, October 28, 1953, box 79, folder 29, U-ST; Henry Allai to John L. Lewis, June 29, 1954, box 97, folder 34, U-PC; "Court Grants Probation to Ex-Unionists," *Salt Lake Tribune*, November 24, 1959.

76. Multiple documents, box 96, folders 1–2, U-PC. The following in box 96, folder 45, U-PC: Arthur Biggs to John L. Lewis, September 10, 1949; Arthur Biggs and J. E. Brinley to John L. Lewis, November 3, 1949; J. E. Brinley to District 22 Executive Board, October 15, 1949.

77. Arthur Biggs to John L. Lewis, November 11, 1949, box 96, folder 45, U-PC.

78. "Form Letter from UMWA 'Vigilante Committee' Urges Removal of Fox," *SA*, December 12, 1949.

79. John L. Lewis to Thomas Kennedy, June 22, 1950, box 96, folder 48, U-PC.

80. The following in box 97, folder 12, U-PC: Houston Martin to John L. Lewis, July 24, 1951; "Minutes of the District Executive Board Held July 12 and 13, 1951"; John L. Lewis to Houston Martin, November 2, 1951.

81. "Mine Union Tackles Proposal Calling for Local Autonomy," *SLT*, September 14, 1944; Frank Hofferly to John O'Learly, July 28, 1944, box 96, folder 5, U-PC.

82. Dubofsky and Van Tine, *John L. Lewis*, 450–54; Frank Hofferly to John O'Leary, July 28, 1944, box 96, folder 5, U-PC.

83. Drew Pearson, "Merry Go Round: Union Bosses Disgust Field Worker," *SLT*, December 1946.

84. W. R. Byrge to John L. Lewis, December 17, 1946, box 96, folder 21, U-PC.

85. Frank Fox to John L. Lewis, June 22, 1950, box 97, folder 1, U-PC; Houston Martin to John L. Lewis, October 23, 1951, box 97, folder 12, U-PC; Arthur Biggs and J. E. Brinley to John L. Lewis, November 3, 1949, box 96, folder 45, U-PC.

86. R. A. Murray to John L. Lewis, March 7, 1949, box 96, folder 40, U-PC; Joe Dowd to John L. Lewis, November 2, 1949, box 97, folder 1, U-PC; Malio Pecorelli, "Report," March 1954, box 97, folder 27, U-PC.

87. R. A. Murray to John L. Lewis, May 26, 1948, box 96, folder 35, U-PC; James Steward to John L. Lewis, August 8, 1949, box 96, folder 41, U-PC; Grover C. Nichols to John L. Lewis, September 7, 1960, box 97, folder 7, U-ST; Harry Mangus to John L. Lewis, March 9, 1954, box 97, folder 29, U-PC.

88. Joseph A. Yablonski, "Statement," August 11, 1969, box 23, folder 33, Miners for Democracy Collection, Archives of Labor History and Urban Affairs, Walter P. Reuther Library, Wayne State University (hereafter MFD).

89. Arthur Biggs to John L. Lewis, July 15, 1951, box 97, folder 12, U-PC.

90. Arthur Biggs to Kenneth Davis, November 16, 1950, box 69, folder 3, U-ST.

91. Arthur Biggs to Tony Boyle, August 14, 1961, box 98, folder 27, U-PC.

92. Arthur Biggs to John L. Lewis, August 20, 1962, box 98, folder 33, U-PC.

93. The following in box 97, folder 34, U-PC: Frank J. Sacco to Thomas Kennedy, March 8, 1954; Henry Allai and John Kmetz to John L. Lewis, June 11, 1954; John L. Lewis to Henry Allai, June 15, 1954.

94. The following in box 97, folder 41, U-PC: Joseph Yablonski and Peter Phillippi

to John L. Lewis, February 24, 1956; Frank M. Stevenson to John Owens, October 26, 1955.

CHAPTER 4

Epigraph source: Harry Mangus to John L. Lewis, March 9, 1954, box 97, folder 29, U-PC.

1. Powell, *The Next Time We Strike*, 189; Frank M. Stevenson, "District 22 UMWA: 1969 Production Report," box 5, folder 7, U-OD; "Labor Day Celebration Committeemen," *SA*, August 25, 1966; "Helper Labor Day Celebration Huge Success," *SA*, September 8, 1966.
2. Baker, *Above the Clouds*, 132; Frank M. Stevenson, "District 22, UMWA Monthly Report on Organization," September 1968, box 8, folder 16, U-OD; William A. Bear to Arthur Biggs, December 6, 1968, box 12, folder 8, U-OD.
3. Frank M. Stevenson and Paul James, "Joint Report of the Officers of District 22 to the Twentieth Consecutive Constitutional Convention of District 22 United Mine Workers of America," 31–32, box 2, folder 26, HCLA 1824, Safety Division Records, United Mine Workers of America Archives, Pennsylvania State University.
4. J. E. Brinley and Arthur Biggs to the Officers and Members of All Local Unions, District 22, July 23, 1951, box 71, folder 23, U-ST; Kendell and Ona Barnett, interview by Eldon and Carole Miller, Hiawatha, November 12, 1993, transcript, box 1, folder 3, CCOH-JWM.
5. Arthur Biggs, "Daily Minutes of the Nineteenth Consecutive Constitutional Convention of District 22, UMWA," February 12–13, 1957, box 90, folder 12, U-ST.
6. Robert Stanley Lowe to Harry Mangus, October 5, 1959, box 98, folder 20, U-PC; Harry Mangus to Thomas Kennedy, December 12, 1961, box 98, folder 27, U-PC.
7. Harry Mangus to John L. Lewis, August 5, 1963, box 168, folder 9, U-PC.
8. Krajcinovic, *From Company Doctors to Managed Care*, 158–61; Mulcahy, *A Social Contract*, 131–33.
9. Harry Mangus to John L. Lewis, August 5, 1963, box 168, folder 9, U-PC; Harry Mangus to Thomas Kennedy, June 29, 1961, box 98, folder 25, U-PC.
10. Mangus to Kennedy, June 29, 1961.

11. Seltzer, *Fire in the Hole*, 80.

12. Ibid., 80–81.

13. Ibid.

14. Frank M. Stevenson to Michael F. Widman, October 16, 1967, box 11, folder 33, U-OD Org. Dept; Frank M. Stevenson, "District 22 UMWA Monthly Report on Organization," September 1968, box 8, folder 16, U-OD; The following items are located in box 13, folder 31, U-OD: Frank M. Stevenson to all Officers and Members of all Local Unions, District 22, October 17, 1967, U-OD; Frank J. Sacco to John T. Kmetz, Nov 1, 1967, U-OD.

15. "Soldier Creek Opts for Non-Union Mine," *SA*, August 1, 1979; "UMWA Set to Organize in Sanpete," *SA*, December 18, 1981; "President Named to Skyline Mine Project," *SA*, February 4, 1981.

16. "Official Election Returns of District 22, UMWA," September 12, 1961, box 98, folder 27, U-PC; Officers of Local 9958 to John L. Lewis, March 5, 1958, box 98, folder 10, U-PC; the following in box 98, folder 25, U-PC: Harry Mangus to Thomas Kennedy, June 29, 1961; Harry Mangus to Thomas Kennedy, December 18, 1961.

17. Arthur Biggs, "Daily Minutes of the Nineteenth Consecutive Constitutional Convention of District 22, UMWA," February 12–13, 1957, box 90, folder 12, U-PC; Eloy Widdison and F. J. Sacco to John L. Lewis, May 15, 1959, box 98, folder 17, U-PC; Frank J. Sacco to Thomas Kennedy, March 19, 1962, box 98, folder 30, U-PC; "Frank Saco Seeks Board Member Post From Sub District 5," *Dragerton Tribune*, August 30, 1949.

18. Frank J. Sacco to the Officers and Members of All Local Unions, District 22, UMWA, Sub-District 2, Utah, October 27, 1964, box 168, folder 9, U-PC.

19. Frank M. Stevenson to George Tilter, July 1, 1966, box 11, folder 33, U-OD; Frank M. Stevenson to John T. Kmetz, October 5, 1966, box 9, folder 9, U-OD; "Kennecott Coal Holdings Under Fire of FTC," *SA*, August 15, 1968.

20. Baker, *Above the Clouds*, 137; the following in box 11, folder 33, U-OD: Frank M. Stevenson and Frank J. Sacco to John T. Kmetz, March 20, 1967; "Labor Agreement," April 10, 1967; Clyde F. Wears to International Union of District 50, June 29, 1967; Frank Sacco to Michael F. Widman, September 29, 1967; Frank J. Sacco to Michael F. Widman, December 2, 1968.

21. Frank J. Sacco, Affidavit, July 31, 1969, box 13, folder 31, U-OD.

22. Frank M. Stevenson, "District 22 UMWA Monthly Report on Organiza-

tion," March 1969, box 8, folder 16, U-OD; The following in box 104, folder 45, U-PC: John T. Kmetz to W. A. Boyle, September 29, 1967; "Special Report on My Contact with Frank Eaquinta, Employee of the Swisher Coal Company, a Non-Union Mine, Located in Consumers, Utah," November 21, 1968.

23. Wayne Baker to Elvin Byrge, October 4, 1969, box 12, folder 1, U-OD; Frank M. Stevenson, Affidavit, November 5, 1969, box 12, folder 3, U-OD; the following in box 11, folder 34, U-OD: Frank M. Stevenson to Michael F. Widman, February 10, 1969; United Mine Workers of America Welfare and Retirement Fund to Mike, February 13, 1969; Charlotte Herzon to Wives of Plateau Employees, February 20, 1969; Frank M. Stevenson and Frank J. Sacco to Plateau Employees, February 19, 1969; Frank M. Stevenson and Frank J. Sacco to Plateau Employees, February 26, 1969; "Notes for Plateau Mining Co. Meeting of Price, Utah," March 2, 1969; Castle Valley Workers' Association to Frank M. Stevenson, undated letter; Jerry Landauer, "Pension Fund Fuss: Critics Say the UMW's Retirement Program Shortchanges Miners," *Wall Street Journal*, December 26, 1968.

24. The following in box 12, folder 8, U-OD: Arthur Biggs to W. A. Boyle, July 19, 1963; Arthur Biggs to W. A. Boyle, October 18 and December 6, 1963.

25. Frank M. Stevenson to Michael F. Widman, January 20, 1969, box 11, folder 34, U-OD; The following in box 12, folder 8, U-OD: Frank M. Stevenson to John and Joe Marinoni, January 7, 1969; Frank J. Sacco to Thomas F. Widman, January 21, 1969; Frank M. Stevenson to Michael F. Widman, January 27, 1969.

26. "Research Department Memorandum Re: Premium Coal Company Soldier Canyon mine," July 3, 1973, box 12, folder 8, U-OD; the following in box 13, folder 21, U-OD: Frank J. Sacco to George Tilter, August 30, 1966; John T. Kmetz to Frank J. Sacco, May 23, 1966; "Southern Utah Fuel Company," *Dun & Bradstreet Report*, April 13, 1967.

27. Jensen v. Eddy, 514 P.2d 1142 (Utah Supreme Court, 1973).

28. John T. Kmetz to W. A. Boyle, June 11, 1967, box 13, folder 30, U-OD.

29. The following in box 13, folder 21, U-OD: Frank J. Sacco to John T. Kmetz, May 16, 1966; John T. Kmetz to Frank J. Sacco, May 23, 1966; Frank J. Sacco to John T. Kmetz, September 26, October 6, November 2, and December 1, 1966.

30. The following in box 13, folder 21, U-OD: John R. Schone to Frank J. Sacco,

September 19, 1966; Frank J. Sacco to John T. Kmetz, September 22, 1966; Frank J. Sacco to George Tilter, September 2, 1966.

31. The following in box 13, folder 21, U-OD: Frank J. Sacco to George Tilter, September 2, 1966; Frank J. Sacco to John T. Kmetz, September 22, October 11, October 27, and November 16, 1966.

32. Frank Sacco to John Kmetz, October 6, 1966, box 13, folder 21, U-OD.

33. The following in box 13, folder 21, U-OD: "Tally of Ballots" United States of America National Labor Relations Board, November 17, 1966; Frank J. Sacco to John T. Kmetz, November 21, 1966; Frank M. Stevenson to Boyd Anderson, November 30, 1966; the following in box 13, folder 30, U-OD: Clyde F. Waers to United Mineworkers of America, District 22, January 17, 1967; James F. Miller, "Intermediate Report, Case No. R-992," State of Utah Labor Relations Board, March 14, 1967.

34. The following in box 13, folder 21, U-OD: Frank J, Sacco, "Statement of Frank J. Sacco, Special Meeting, LU 1485, City Hall, Salina, Utah," February 12, 1967; Frank M. Stevenson, "Charge Against Employer," United States of America National Labor Relations Board, December 1, 1966; "Phone Call from District 22 President Frank M. Stevenson Regarding the Southern Utah Fuel Company," February 3, 1967.

35. The following in box 13, folder 30, U-OD: Frank J. Sacco to John T. Kmetz, December 2 and 15, 1966; Clyde F. Waers to United Mine Workers of America, District 22, January 17, 1967.

36. The following in box 13, folder 21, U-OD: Frank M. Stevenson to Stephen J. Beeley, February 22, 1967; Stephen J. Beeley to Frank M. Stevenson, February 23, 1967; Frank M. Stevenson to W. A. Boyle, March 26, 1967; Frank M. Stevenson to W. A. Boyle, March 30, 1967; Frank M. Stevenson to John T. Kmetz, April 17, 1967; John T. Kmetz to W. A. Boyle, April 20, 1967; Stephen J. Beeley to Frank M. Stevenson, March 2, 1967; Frank M. Stevenson to Stephen J. Beeley, May 2, 1967; John T. Kmetz to Edward L. Carey, May 11, 1967; Frank M. Stevenson to Stephen J. Beeley, May 13, 1967; John T, Kmetz to W. A. Boyle, June 6, 1967; District 22 to W. A. Boyle, June 15, 1967.

37. The following in box 13, folder 30, U-OD; Jensen v. Eddy; Don V. Tibbs to Boyd Anderson, August 23, 1967; Frank M. Stevenson to Don V. Tibbs, September 19, 1967; Don V. Tibbs to Frank M. Stevenson, September 21, 1967; Frank M. Stevenson to Don V. Tibbs, September 25, 1967; Don V. Tibbs to Frank M. Stevenson, September 29, 1967.

38. The following in box 13, folder 21, U-OD: Frank M. Stevenson to Stephen J. Beeley, February 22, 1967; Frank M. Stevenson to James Dickert and Boyd Anderson, March 21, 1967; Frank M. Stevenson to Boyd Anderson, April 27, 1967; Frank M. Stevenson to John T. Kmetz, July 6, 1967; Frank M. Stevenson to Don V. Tibbs, July 31 and September 19, 1967.

39. Frank M. Stevenson to Michael F. Widman, November 16, 1967, box 13, folder 21, U-OD; the following in box 8, folder 16, U-OD: Frank M. Stevenson "District 22 UMWA Monthly Report on Organization," March 1969; Jess M. Vinci to Michael Widman, September 20, 1972.

40. The following in box 13, folder 21, U-OD: Frank M. Stevenson, "Charge Against Employer," United States of America National Labor Relations Board, July 21, 1967; Frank M. Stevenson to Stephen J. Beeley, October 12, 1967.

41. Frank J. Sacco to John T. Kmetz, November 9, 1967, box 13, folder 21, U-OD.

42. Frank M. Stevenson to Michael F. Widman, November 16, 1967, box 13, folder 21, U-OD.

43. The following in box 13, folder 21, U-OD: Frank M. Stevenson to Michael F. Widman, December 21, 1967; Frank M. Stevenson to Stephen J. Beeley, October 24, 1968; Curtis et al. to Frank M. Stevenson, February 18, 1969.

44. Baker, *Above the Clouds*, 78-101, 122–56.

45. Ibid., 136, 151–52, 145, 142; Francis Sperandeo, "Regional Director's Report on Challenged Ballots," April 23, 1969, box 11, folder 34, U-OD.

46. Total workforce numbers fluctuated during this period. In June 1966, eleven of fourteen employees had signed union cards. In January 1967, four out of eleven employees had signed cards. In May 1967, Plateau employed a workforce of ten, and in November 1968, the mine employed twenty-four. Frank J. Sacco to John T. Kmetz, May 3, 1967, box 11, folder 34, U-OD; "Wattis Coal Mine Open House," *Salt Lake Tribune*, March 23, 1967; Frank J. Sacco to W. A. Boyle, November 13, 1968, box 11, folder 33, U-OD.

47. The following in box 11, folder 33, U-OD: "UMWA Authorization for Membership Cards—Signed"; "Charge Against Employer," United States of America National Labor Relations Board, Case No. 27-CA-2240, April 3, 1967; Clyde F. Waers to International Union of District 50, June 29, 1967.

48. A. Wally Sandack, "Appeal to General Counsel Reviewing Actions of 27th Region, Director," October 20, 1969, box 13, folder 31, U-OD.

49. Frank Sacco to Michael F. Widman, September 29, 1967, box 11, folder 33, U-OD.

50. Frank J. Sacco to John T. Kmetz, May 3, 1967, box 11, folder 34, U-OD; the following in box 11, folder 33, U-OD: "Transcript of the Statement of Frank M. Stevenson, President District 22 to John Sayer, Agent for the NLRB," September 29, 1967; "Transcript of the Statement of Frank J. Sacco, Int'l Rep, UMWA to John Sayer, Agent for the NLRB," September 29, 1967.

51. Caswell Silver to the Stockholders of Sundance Oil Company, May 9, 1968, box 12, folder 5, U-OD; the following in box 11, folder 33, U-OD: Y. R. Byrge to Frank Sacco, December 13, 1968; Frank J. Sacco to Michael F. Widman, December 4, 1968.

52. The following in box 11, folder 34, U-OD: Frank J. Sacco to Michael F. Widman, January 21, 1969; Frank M. Stevenson and Frank J. Sacco to Plateau Employees, February 19, 1969; Francis Spernando, "Regional Director's Report on Challenged Ballots and Certification of Representative," April 23, 1969, United States of America National Labor Relations Board; Baker, *Above the Clouds*, 143.

53. Affidavit of Frank M. Stevenson, November 5, 1969, box 12, folder 3, U-OD; the following in box 11, folder 34, U-OD: Frank M. Stevenson and Frank J. Sacco to Thomas F. Widman, May 20, 1969; Wayne Baker to Pete Ardohain, June 26, 1969; the following in box 12, folder 1, U-OD: Wayne Baker to Elvin Byrge, October 4, 1969; Michael F. Widman to W. A. Boyle, December 2, 1969.

54. A. Wally Sandack to Frank M. Stevenson, April 24, 1970, box 13, folder 31, U-OD; the following in box 12, folder 3, U-OD: Frank M. Stevenson, Affidavit, November 5, 1969; A. Wally Sandack, "Appeal to General Counsel Reviewing Actions of 27th Regional Director," February 5, 1970.

55. The following in box 12, folder 3, U-OD: "Petition," June 1, 1970, United States of America National Labor Relations Board; Frank M. Stevenson to Allison E. Mett, July 7, 1970.

56. The following in box 13, folder 31, U-OD: Thomas A. Williams to Michael F. Widman, June 14, 1967; John T. Kmetz to W. A. Boyle, September 29, 1967; Frank M. Stevenson to John T. Kmetz, June 21 and August 7, 1967.

57. Frank M. Stevenson to John T. Kmetz, August 7, 1967, box 13, folder 31, U-OD; the following in box 104, folder 45, U-PC: W. A. Boyle, Memorandum, September 7, 1967; "Minutes of Meeting Between Official Representa-

tives of the UMWA and Colombine," September 12, 1967; John T. Kmetz to W. A. Boyle, September 29, 1967.

58. John T. Kmetz to W. A. Boyle, September 29, 1967; "Swisher Coal Company Employees," November 22, 1968, box 104, folder 45, U-PC; Frank M. Stevenson, "District 22 UMWA Monthly Report on Organization," March 1969, box 8, folder 16, U-OD; the following in box 13, folder 31, U-OD: Frank M. Stevenson to Mr. Ura Swisher, December 5, 1967; John T. Kmetz to W. A. Boyle, January 3, 1968.

59. Frank M. Stevenson to Ura Swisher, July 1, 1969, box 4, folder 39, U-RD; the following in box 13, folder 31, U-OD: "Petition," July 1, 1969, United States of America National Labor Relations Board; Frank J. Sacco, Affidavit, July 31, 1969; Paul R. Schmidt, Affidavit, July 30, 1969.

60. The following in box 13, folder 31, U-OD: Frank M. Stevenson to Michael F. Widman, July 17, 1969; Ura Swisher to Frank M. Stevenson, September 17, 1969; George Fasselin, Affidavit, July 30, 1969.

61. A. Wally Sandack, "Appeal to General Counsel Reviewing Actions of 27th Region, Director," October 20, 1969, box 13, folder 31, U-OD.

62. Ibid.; Irving M. Herman to A. Wally Sandack, April 22, 1970, box 104, folder 45, U-PC; Jess M. Vicini to Michael F. Widman, September 20, 1972, box 8, folder 16, U-OD; the following in box 13, folder 31, U-OD: Irving M. Herman to A. Wally Sandack, September 22, 1970; Francis Sperandeo, "Consolidated Complaint and Notice of Hearing," October 15, 1970, United States of America National Labor Relations Board; Frank M. Stevenson to Michael F. Widman, April 29, 1971.

63. Perry, *Collective Bargaining*, 87.

64. Baker, *Above the Clouds*, 134; "'Coalman' Art Linkletter and Associates Host Barbeque, Mine Tours at Wattis," *SA*, June 1, 1967; the following in box 11, folder 33, U-OD: "Grand Opening of the Plateau Coal Mine, May 27, 1967"; John T. Kmetz to W. A. Boyle, June 6, 1967; W. A. Boyle to John T. Kmetz, July 11, 1967.

65. Henry Allai to Michael F. Widman, September 29, 1969, box 12, folder 1, U-OD; the following in box 11, folder 34, U-OD: S. Lyle Johnson to Frank M. Stevenson, June 19, 1969; Michael F. Widman to Art Linkletter, June 24, 1969; Frank M. Stevenson to W. A. Boyle, September 19, 1969.

66. The following in box 12, folder 1, U-OD: Director of Organization to Henry Allai, September 30, 1969; Frank M. Stevenson to Michael F. Widman,

October 8, 1969; W. A. Boyle to Edward L. Carey, October 15, 1969; Michael F. Widman, Memorandum, October 15, 1969; Michael F. Widman, Memorandum, October 29, 1969.

67. John T. Kmetz to Frank M. Stevenson, June 23, 1967, box 104, folder 45, U-PC; : Frank M. Stevenson to John T. Kmetz, June 21, 1967 and, August 7, 1969, box 13, folder 31, U-OD.

68. W. A. Boyle, Memorandum, September 7, 1967, box 104, folder 45, U-PC.

69. The following in box 13, folder 31, U-OD: "Charge Against Employer," October 14, 1968, United States of America National Labor Relations Board; Frank J. Sacco to Michael F. Widman, November 19, 1968; W. A. Boyle, to Michael F. Widman, November 22, 1968.

70. Frank M. Stevenson to W. A. Boyle, July 13, 1967, box 10, folder 2, U-OD.

71. Frank M. Stevenson to John T. Kmetz, October 12, 1964, box 9, folder 9, U-OD; Jess M. Vicini to Michael Widman, September 20, 1972, box 8, folder 16, U-OD.

72. The following in box 10, folder 2, U-OD: Frank M. Stevenson to John T. Kmetz, January 15, 1967; "Tally of Ballots," June 4, 1970, United States of America National Labor Relations Board; Francis Sperandeo, "Complaint and Notice of Hearing," July 23, 1970, United States of America National Labor Relations Board; Albert A. Metz to S. Lyle Johnson, July 28, 1970.

73. Frank M. Stevenson to Michael F. Widman, March 2, 1971, box 10, folder 2, U-OD.

74. E. R. Phelps to Frank M. Stevenson, January 22, 1971, box 104, folder 3, HCLA 1820, Contract Services, United Mine Workers of America Archives, Pennsylvania State University.

75. Frank M. Stevenson to John T. Kmetz, December 8, 1967, box 13, folder 30, U-OD; John T. Kmetz to President Boyle, January 3, 1968, box 13, folder 31, U-OD; Baker, *Above the Clouds*, 146.

76. The following in box 67, folder 6, MFD: Frank J. Sacco to W. A. Boyle, February 9, September 30, October 1 and 31, and November 30, 1968.

77. The following in box 67, folder 6, MFD: Frank J. Sacco, Report of Meeting at Price District Office, November 27, 1970; Frank J. Sacco to W. A. Boyle, undated letter, ca. December 1970.

78. Frank J. Sacco to Arnold Miller, July 26, 1972, box 92, folder 20, MFD.

79. The following in box 82, folder 10, MFD: "Lignite Contract—Sweetheart Deal," unsigned draft; "Press Release," November 16, 1972.

80. Frank J. Sacco to W. A. Boyle, August 5, 1972, box 67, folder 7, MFD; Michael F. Widman to Frank J. Sacco, July 21, 1972, box 67, folder 9, MFD; Frank J. Sacco to Sylvester Lorenzo, June 16, 1972, box 67, folder 9, MFD; Frank J. Sacco to W. A. Boyle, June 21, 1972, box 67, folder 9, MFD; Nicholas W. Goluba to W. A. Boyle, May 19, 1972; Frank J. Sacco to W. A. Boyle, July 26, 1972, box 92, folder 20, MFD.

CHAPTER 5

Epigraph source: Governor Calvin L. Rampton, *HJ*, January 2, 1975.

1. Hume, *Death in the Mines*, 240–49.

2. "Official UMWA Election Returns," *UMWJ*, January 15, 1970; Hume, *Death in the Mines*; Joseph E. Finley, *The Corrupt Kingdom: The Rise and Fall of the United Mine Workers* (New York: Simon and Schuster, 1972); Clark, *Miners' Fight*, 4–32; Seltzer, *Fire in the Hole*, 108–24; Fox, *United We Stand*, 481–85.

3. "1972 UMWA Election Results," *UMWJ*, January 1, 1973.

4. Mrs. John Henderson to W. A. Boyle, November 8, 1971, box 22, folder 26, HCLA 1827, Health and Retirement Fund Records, United Mine Workers of America Archives, Pennsylvania State University, (hereafter cited as U-HR).

5. J. Lorin Winn to W. A. Boyle, February 22, 1970, box 22, folder 26, U-HR.

6. Julian M. Paiz to United Mine Workers of America, September 13, 1970, box 22, folder 26, U-HR.

7. Clorinda Cordova to W. A. Boyle, September 27, 1972, box 22, folder 26, U-HR.

8. The following in box 22, folder 26, U-HR: Don Logston to W. A. Boyle, January 29, 1971; W. A. Boyle to Don Logston, February 8, 1971.

9. R. H. Tweddell to W. A. Boyle, September 3, 1968, box 4, folder 39, UMWA Research Department Records, United Mine Workers of America Archives, Pennsylvania State University (hereafter cited as U-RD); Mary G. Lopez to W. A. Boyle, September 18, 1971, box 22, folder 26, U-HR.

10. H. Ward to Michael F. Widman, February 13, 1969, box 11, folder 34, U-OD.

11. "UMWA Campaign Committee Organized to Support Election of Tony

Boyle," *Helper (Utah) Journal* (hereafter *HJ*), October 5, 1972; "UMW President Tony Boyle to Visit Oct. 28," *HJ*, October 19, 1972; Advertisement, *HJ*, October 19, 1972; Advertisement, *HJ*, November 16, 1972; Advertisement, *HJ*, November 30, 1972; Advertisement, *HJ*, November 23, 1972.

12. A Greatful Coal Miner's Wife of Darrell Norton, letter to the editor, *SA*, September 28, 1972.

13. "UMWA Welfare Fund Answers Criticisms," *SA*, May 8, 1969; "UMWA Members to Elect International Officers December 9," *SA*, December 4, 1969; "Struggle Brewing for UMWA Presidency," *SA*, September 25, 1969; "Boyle Charges UMWA Victim of 'Journalistic Lynching Bee,'" *SA*, February 19, 1970; "Statement from UMW's Boyle," *SA*, March 12, 1970; "Boyle Was Big Winner in District 22," *SA*, April 12, 1970; "UMW Pension Regulations Effective April 1," *SA*, February 18, 1971; "UMW Leaders Deny Embezzle Charges," *SA*, March 3, 1971; "UMWA to Seek Medicare Coverage for Disabled," *SA*, April 1, 1971; "UMWA Candidate to Be in Carbon County Saturday," *SA*, September 7, 1972; "Is This Any Way to Run a Newspaper?" *SA*, November 23, 1972.

14. "Labor Day Celebration Large Crowd Attends," *SA*, September 10, 1970; "Labor Day—1971," *SA*, September 9, 1971; "Labor Day Celebration on Top," *SA*, August 3, 1972; "Labor Day 1972 in Carbon County," *SA*, September 7, 1972.

15. "Why the Journal Looks Like It Does and Some Other Information," *UMWJ*, July 15, 1972; the following in box 92, folder 21, MFD: Frank J. Sacco to Don Stillman, undated letter, ca. September 1972; "Information for the Candidates on Field Organization, Districts 10, 14, 15, 21, 22, 27."

16. Seltzer, *Fire in the Hole*, 88, 123.

17. The following in box 168, folder 1, U-PC: Steve Kochis to Local 9958, undated letter; Frank J. Sacco to Steve Kochis, May 11, 1964.

18. Frank J. Sacco to W. A. Boyle, undated letter, ca. December 12, 1970, box 67, folder 6, MFD.

19. Frank J. Sacco, "Statement of Frank J. Sacco, Special Meeting, Local 1485, City Hall, Salina, UT," February 12, 1967, box 13, folder 21, U-OD.

20. "Union Man Leaves Post," *SA*, August 3, 1972.

21. Richard J. Jensen, "Rebellion in the United Mine Workers: The Miners for Democracy, 1970–1972" (PhD diss., Indiana University, 1974), 89.

22. John Kuzio to Mike Trbovich, August 1, 1972, box 97, folder 12, MFD; John Kuzio to Mike Trbovich, March 12, 1973, box 99, folder 16, MFD; Carl Norton to UMWA, undated letter, box 99, folder 16, MFD; John Kuzio to Amy, September 12, 1972, box 92, folder 6, MFD; John Kuzio to Ed, August 22, 1972, box 92, folder 6, MFD.

23. "Area UMW Locals Prefer Miller," *SA*, August 10, 1972; "UMWA District 22 Supporting Boyle," *SA*, August 17, 1972; "'Tony' Boyle Leading Nominations," *SA*, August 24, 1972.

24. "Miners for Democracy Rally," *SA*, September 14, 1972.

25. Ibid.; "The Miller Platform," *UMWJ*, July 1, 1972; "Miners for Democracy Rally," *SA*, September 14, 1972; Jensen, "Rebellion in the United Mine Workers," 89.

26. UMWA Member for the Miller Slate, letter to the editor, *SA*, October 19, 1972.

27. "Is This Any Way to Run a Newspaper?," *SA*, November 23, 1972; An Enraged Coal Miner's Wife, letters to the editor, *SA*, September 7 and October 5 and 12, 1972; Don G. Logston, letter to the editor, *SA*, September 21, 1972; A Greatful Coal Miner's Wife, letter to the editor; Concerned Coal Miners of District 22, letter to the editor, *SA*, October 5, 1972; An Enraged Coal Miner's Wife, letter to the editor, *SA*, October 5, 1972; Widow of Mary G. Lopez, letter to the editor *SA*, October 5, 1972; The Enraged Coal Miner's Wife, letter to the editor, *SA*, October 12, 1972; UMWA Member for the Miller Slate, letter to the editor, *SA*, October 19, 1972; A Disgruntled Pensioner, letter to the editor, September 10, 1972, box 97, folder 12, MFD; Don G. Logston and Dick Dallon Larson, letter to the editor, *SA*, October 19, 1972.

28. "UMWA President Boyle Campaigns in Carbon County Coal Fields," *SA*, November 2, 1972; "Platforms Vary in Race for United Mine Workers Presidency," *SA*, November 30, 1972.

29. "1972 UMWA International Election Results," *UMWJ*, January 1, 1973; "Official UMWA Election Results," *UMWJ*, January 15, 1970.

30. Richard Miller and Austin Pearlman to MFD, September 20, 1972, "Information for the Candidates on Field Organization, Districts 10, 11, 14, 15, 21, 22, 27—The Western Districts," box 91, folder 19, MFD.

31. Tim Cogan, "Look What Ya Done for Us," August 18, 1972, box 88, folder 10, MFD; Tim Cogan, "Hot and Cold in District 27," August 10, 1972, box 91, folder 12, MFD.

32. Cogan, "Hot and Cold in District 27."

33. Arnold Miller to John Mix Sr., October 10, 1972, box 92, folder 6, MFD; Don Stillman to Dine Researchers, December 10, 1971, box 105, folder 4, MFD; Jimmy L. Anderson to Miners for Democracy, August 10, 1972, box 92, folder 6, MFD.

34. Arnold Miller to John Mix Sr.; Arnold Miller to Lou Schuster, September 18, 1972, box 92, folder 1, MFD.

35. "Key Contacts," ca. 1972, box 98, folder 9, MFD.

36. Seltzer, *Fire in the Hole*, 129; Nyden, "Rank-and-File Movements," 185.

37. Seltzer, *Fire in the Hole*, 132; Fox, *United We Stand*, 506; Steve Early, *Save Our Unions: Dispatches from a Movement in Distress* (New York: Monthly Review Press, 2013), 30; Cal Winslow, "Overview: The Rebellion from Below, 1965–81," in *Rebel Rank and File: Labor Militancy and Revolt from Below During the Long 1970s*, ed. Aaron Brenner, Robert Brenner, and Cal Winslow (New York: Verso, 2010), 28; Nyden, "Rank-and-File Movements," 185.

38. Clark, *Miners' Fight*, 33–44; Seltzer, *Fire in the Hole*, 131–38; Fox, *United We Stand*, 488–93.

39. Mulcahy, *A Social Contract*, 166–68; Krajcinovic, *From Company Doctors to Managed Care*, 168; Clark, *Miners' Fight*, 54–55; Seltzer, *Fire in the Hole*, 135; Fox, *United We Stand*, 493.

40. "Press Release," May 29, 1969, box 23, folder 32, MFD; Arnold Miller to Melroy Hutchinson, August 12, 1972, box 92, folder 6, MFD; Kim Moody, *Battle Line: The Coal Strike of '78* (Detroit: Sun Press, 1978), 74.

41. "UMWA President Issues Warning about Energy Crisis Stampede," *SA*, April 26, 1973; Charles Sweetland, letter to the editor, *UMWJ*, June 1, 1973; John J. Kuzio, letter to the editor, *SA*, August 9, 1973.

42. "Report Urges Merger of Western Districts," *UMWJ*, February 15, 1973; Everett West, letter to the editor, *UMWJ*, April 15, 1973; Joe Lyons, letter to the editor, *UMWJ*, April 15, 1973; Richard Romero, letter to the editor, *UMWJ*, April 15, 1973; Harold L. Alger, letter to the editor, *SA*, February 15, 1973.

43. Rich Bank and Bernie Anderson to Arnold Miller, August 29, 1973, box 99, folder 9, MFD.

44. Ibid.; Arnold Miller to James Brewer, October 23, 1972, box 92, folder 1, MFD; "Background Information for Trip to District 15," 1973, box 99, folder 9, MFD.

45. Fox, *United We Stand*, 289; "Miller Wins Presidency, Promises Utah Mine Trip," *SA*, December 21, 1972; "Kosec Named to UMWA Board," *SA*, December 28, 1972; "Official Roster of the United Mine Workers of America," *UMWJ*, January 15, 1971.

46. "Stevenson Wins Second Term as UMWA District 22 President," *SA*, December 23, 1965.

47. "Clash Set for District Fund Control," *SA*, March 22, 1973; "UMWA Suit Names Stevenson, Associates for Funds Misuse," *SA*, March 15, 1973; "UMWA Wins First Major Test in Western Organizing Drive," *UMWJ*, June 15, 1975; "Clash Set for Mine District Fund Control," *SA*, March 22, 1973; "Kosec Named to UMWA Board," *SA*, December 28, 1972.

48. "Stevenson Nominated for UMWA Executive Board," *SA*, October 25, 1973; Harold L. Alger, letter to the editor, *SA*, November 1, 1973; Clarice R. Feldman, Memorandum, April 9, 1974, box 177, folder 5, U-PC; "Smith Wins for District UMWA Post," *SA*, January 17, 1974; "UMWA Posts Shift with Resignation," *SA*, February 14, 1974.

49. Fox, *United We Stand*, 490; Frank J. Roybal to Frank M. Stevenson, November 1, 1973, box 177, folder 7, U-PC; the following in box 177, folder 5, U-PC: Frank M. Stevenson to Frank J. Roybal, November 9, 1973; Frank J. Roybal to Frank M. Stevenson, November 15, 1972.

50. The following in box 177, folder 7, U-PC: Frank J. Roybal and Albert G. Urbanik to Arnold Miller, February 8, 1974; Frank J. Roybal to Arnold Miller, November 12, 1973; Local 8003 to Frank M. Stevenson, November 24, 1973; Frank M. Stevenson to Frank J. Roybal, January 3, 1974; Local 8003 to Arnold Miller, January 19, 1974; Edward Hansen, Frank J. Roybal, and Albert G. Urbanik to Arnold Miller, February 8, 1974. The following in box 177, folder 5, U-PC: Arnold Miller to Frank J. Sacco, April 5, 1974; Frank J. Roybal to Arnold Miller, April 16, 1974.

51. "Labor Management Reporting and Disclosure Act of 1959, As Amended," United States Department of Labor, http://www.dol.gov/olms/regs/statutes/lmrda-act.htm; Lichtenstein, *State of the Union*, 162–65; Jefferson Cowie, *Staying Alive: The 1970s and the Last Days of the Working Class* (New York: New Press, 2010), 34, 42; Goldfield, *Decline of Organized Labor*, 32, 106–7; Thomas Geoghegan, *Which Side Are You On?: Trying to Be for Labor When It's Flat on Its Back* (New York: New Press, 1991), 198–99.

52. "UMWA President Slates District 22 Confab Stop," *SA*, August 1, 1974.

53. Aldon J. Anderson, "Order C 74-164," United States District Court for the District of Utah Central Division, July 22, 1975, box 177, folder 8, U-PC; "Court Overturns Stevenson Election," *UMWJ*, August 16, 1975; the following in box 177, folder 7, U-PC: Joseph A. Yablonski, Memorandum, March 15, 1974; John N. Niswander to Arnold Miller, May 13, 1974.

54. "UMW Election Decision Under Appeal in Denver," *SA*, October 9, 1975; "Roybal Unseats Incumbent in UMWA Board Election," *SA*, January 22, 1976; Harrison Combs to Arnold Miller, November 4, 1976, box 177, folder 11, U-PC; "Roybal Takes UMW Post," *SA*, July 29, 1976; "Judge to Hear Proposal to Certify UMWA Election," *SA*, June 22, 1977.

55. "Organizing," Platform of Miners for Democracy, 1972, box 17, folder 7, U-RD.

56. Lynda Ann Ewen, *Which Side Are You On? The Brookside Mine Strike in Harlan County, Kentucky, 1973-1974* (Chicago: Vanguard Books, 1979), 123-31.

57. "Premium Coal Company," 1973, box 12, folder 8, U-OD.

58. "Over 240 Men Laid Off in Carbon Coal Mines," *SA*, April 20, 1972.

59. Jess M. Vicini to Michael F. Widman, September 20, 1971, box 8, folder 16, U-OD; "Soldier Creek Mine Waits Opening," *SA*, June 3, 1976; the following in box 12, folder 8, U-OD: Memo, December 2, 1971; Arthur Biggs to Rick Banks, May 10, 1973; "Notice of Cessation of Operations," June 7, 1973; "Research Department Memorandum Re: Premium Coal Company," July 3, 1973; undated memo, August 1, 1973, box 99, folder 16, ACCN 589, MFD.

60. Matt Witt, "UMWA Wins First Major Test in Western Organizing Drive," *UMWJ*, June 15, 1973.

61. Arnold Miller to Anthony Mascarenas, July 20, 1973, box 99, folder 9, MFD.

62. Rick Bank and Bernie Aronson to Arnold Miller et al., August 29, 1973, box 99, folder 9, MFD.

63. Arnold Miller to Members of District 22, June 3, 1974, box 177, folder 5, U-PC.

64. "Sundance Strike Enters Fourth Month," *UMWJ*, March 1, 1975.

65. Ibid.; "The Strike at Sundance," *UMWJ*, March 1, 1975; "UMWA's Western Strike in 11th Week," *UMWJ*, April 1, 1975; "UMWA Miners Are On Strike

Out West," *UMWJ*, April 16, 1975; "Consol, P&M Yield to UMWA in West; Only Amax, North American Hold Out," *UMWJ*, May 1, 1975; "Miners Back Western Strike With $," *UMWJ*, May 16, 1975; Steve Early, "UMWA Steps Up Support for Amax Strikes as No. American Signs," *UMWJ*, June 16, 1975; Delmar Beck, letter to the editor, *UMWJ*, July 1, 1975; Jesse Gilbert, letter to the editor, *UMWJ*, July 1, 1975; "Support Needed for Western Strikers," *UMWJ*, January 16, 1976; "Contract at Sundance," *UMWJ*, May 16, 1976.

66. Fox, *United We Stand*, 493–94; A. Dudley Gardner and Verla Flores, *Forgotten Frontier: A History of Wyoming Coal Mining* (Boulder, CO: Westview Press, 1989), 212–13; "UMWA's Western Strike in 11th Week," *UMWJ*, April 1, 1975; Victor Henry to Arnold Miller, January 18, 1976, box 177, folder 12, U-PC.

67. Hollie Hopper to All Amax Employees, April 3, 1975, box 177, folder 10, U-PC; Jess M. Vicini to Michael F. Widman, September 20, 1972, box 8, folder 16, U-OD.

68. Arnold Miller to Donald Gibson, December 3, 1975, box 177, folder 9, U-PC.

69. Frank M. Stevenson to Arnold Miller, September 30, 1975, box 177, folder 9, U-PC.

70. H. A. Brownfield to Officers and Members of All Local Unions, District 22, November 20, 1975, box 177, folder 9, U-PC.

71. The following in box 177, folder 12, U-PC: Harold Alger to Arnold Miller, January 7, 1976; Arnold Miller to Harold Alger, January 16, 1976.

72. Arnold Miller to Harold Alger.

73. "Trbovich Suspended by Miller for Refusing Organizing Duty in West," *UMWJ*, April 16, 1976; "Trbovich Reinstated," *UMWJ*, May 16, 1976; Arnold Miller to Karl Kafton, November 26, 1975, box 177, folder 8, U-PC; Steve Galati to Arnold Miller, May 3, 1977, box 177, folder 13, U-PC; the following in box 177, folder 12, U-PC: Frank M. Stevenson to Arnold Miller, June 10, 1975; Arnold Miller to Frank M. Stevenson, June 16, 1976; Frank Roybal Jr. to Arnold Miller, April 28, 1976; Arnold Miller to Frank Roybal Jr., May 11, 1976; Victor Henry to Arnold Miller, January 18, 1976.

74. The following in box 177, folder 12, U-PC: "Report of the Commission on Assignment in Gillette," undated, November 1975; Victor Henry to Arnold

Miller, January 18, 1976; Arnold Miller to Trbovich, February 2, 1976; Trbovich to Miller, February 3, 1976; Victor Henry to Arnold Miller, June 11, 1976.

75. Victor Henry to Arnold Miller, January 18, 1976, box 177, folder 12, U-PC.

76. Fox, *United We Stand*, 425; "Memorial Period Called by UMWA," *SA*, August 15, 1974.

77. "Miners Continue to Back Leader in Work Stoppage; Lewis Found Guilty," *SA*, December 5, 1946; "Lewis Held in Contempt," *SA*, March 13, 1947; Fox, *United We Stand*, 408, 414.

78. Harold Alger to Arnold Miller, June 23, 1975, box 177, folder 8, U-PC; H. A. Brownfield to Arnold Miller, December 7, 1976, box 177, folder 11, U-PC; the following in box 177, folder 12, U-PC: Harold Alger to Arnold Miller, January 7, 1976; Lames L. Jensen to Arnold Miller, January 14, 1976; Harold R. Hansen to Arnold Miller, February 15, 1976.

79. "Sale of Plateau Mining Properties Announced," *SA*, November 4, 1971; "Plateau Mining Secures Land for Coal Preparation Plant," *SA*, October 26, 1972; "Plateau Names New General Sales Head," *SA*, March 22, 1973; "Plateau Mining Company," *SA*, September 13, 1973; "Plateau Completes Growth Plans," *SA*, Energy Supplement, February 14, 1979.

80. "Swisher Coal Purchased by Gen. Exploration Co.," *SA*, September 4, 1975; "Swisher Proposes Reopening of Old Leamaster Mine," *SA*, March 18, 1976; "Swisher Towers," *SA*, June 28, 1978; "Swisher Coal Co.," *SA*, Energy Supplement, February 14, 1979.

81. "Soldier Creek Mine Waits Opening," *SA*, June 3, 1976; "Plants Depend on Soldier Creek Mine," *SA*, Energy Supplement, February 14, 1979.

82. Harold Alger to Arnold Miller, January 7, 1976, box 177, folder 12, U-PC; Harold Alger to Arnold Miller, June 23, 1975, box 177, folder 8, U-PC.

83. The following in box 177, folder 8, U-PC: Harold Alger to Arnold Miller, June 23, 1975; William Preston to Arnold Miller, July 25, 1975.

84. Harold Alger to Arnold Miller, June 23, 1975, box 177, folder 8, U-PC.

85. Arnold Miller to Harold Alger, July 2, 1975, box 177, folder 8, U-PC; Harold R. Hansen to Arnold Miller, February 15, 1976, box 177, folder 12, U-PC.

86. "Firm Renovates Dog Valley Mine," *ECP*, October 2, 1975; "New Mine Facility Dedicated," *ECP*, April 19, 1979; "UMWA Organizing Report," 1976, box 16, folder 35, U-RD.

87. Frank Pugliese, interview by J. J. Blue, in Scoville & Whittle, eds., *Yarns of Carbon and Emery Counties* (North Salt Lake: Dmt Publishing, 2006), 166–67; Robert Trapanier, interview by author, Lehi, July, 2014; Dennis Ardohain and Frank Markosek, interview by author, Price, July 15, 2014; "UMW Loses $9 Million Because of Work Stoppage," *SA*, September 25, 1975; "UMW's Patrick Asks for Union Unity," *SA*, June 17, 1976; "Carbon Unaffected by Coal Strike," *SA*, August 5, 1976; "Work Stoppage Blamed for Liquidation of Pension Fund," *SA*, August 5, 1976; "Equality UMW Goal," *SA*, December 16, 1976.

88. "Western Organizing Report," *UMWJ*, April 1979; Barbara Ekker, "Hanksville," *SA*, November 18, 1978; "Mine to Re-open Near Hanksville," *SA*, September 12, 1979; "Mine Changes Hands," *ECP*, July 22, 1981; "UMWA Organizing Report," 1976, box 16, folder 35, U-RD.

89. Name Withheld, letter to the editor, *SA*, December 21, 1977; John Serfustini, Doug Tullis, and Joe Rolando, "Order Restored After Violence Mars Strike," *SA*, December 10, 1977; John Serfustini, Doug Tullis, and Joe Rolando, "Bomb Threat Halts Coal Strike Hearings," *SA*, December 14, 1977.

90. Harold L. Alger, letter to the editor, *UMWJ*, October 1, 1975; the following in box 177, folder 10, U-PC: Edward E. Shaff to Arnold Miller, undated letter of February or March 1975; Steve Galati to Edward E. Shaff, March 18, 1975; Harold L. Alger to Matt Witt, July 24, 1974.

91. The following items are located in box 177, folder 12, U-PC: Harold Alger to Arnold Miller, December 2, 1975; William Preston to William Savitsky, April 22, 1976; William Preston to Arnold Miller, April 22, 1976; Harold Alger to Arnold Miller, April 26, 1976.

92. Harold Alger to Arnold Miller, April 26, 1976, box 177, folder 12, U-PC.

93. The following in box 177, folder 12, U-PC: "Petition of Local 9958 Miners to Arnold Miller, July 30, 1976"; Harold L. Alger to All Local Unions in District 22, July 30, 1976.

94. "Judge to Hear Proposal to Certify UMWA Election," *SA*, June 22, 1977; Joe Rolando, "Search for Democracy Leads to District Presidency," *SA*, July 6, 1977; "District Reports," *UMWJ*, July 16, 1977; the following in box 177, folder 13, U-PC: Harrison Combs to Arnold Miller, June 27, 1977; "Officers and Employees of District 22, Effective June 29, 1977."

95. Krajcinovic, *From Company Doctors to Managed Care*, 169; "UMWA Chops Health Plan," *SA*, June 29, 1977; Joe Rolando, "UMWA President Vows to Defend Miners," *SA*, April 20, 1977.

96. Joe Rolando, "UMWA Benefit Cuts Rile Local Coal Miners," *SA*, August 27, 1977; William Preston to Arnold Miller, July 30, 1977, box 177, folder 13, U-PC.

97. Taniguchi, *Castle Valley, America*, 265.

98. "Disgruntled Miners Talk of Seceding from UMWA," *SA*, September 14, 1977.

99. "UMWA Finances in Sad State; Reserves Fall to $3 Million," *UMWJ*, November 1977.

100. Victor Henry to Arnold Miller, January 18, 1976, box 177, folder 12, U-PC.

101. "'No Contract, No Work' Idles 'Union' Coal Mines," *SA*, October 7, 1971; "D15 Checklist Pittsburg + Midway Coal (McKinley Mine)," February 23, 1974, box 99, folder 9, MFD.

102. Don Stillman to International Officers, March 27, 1974, box 99, folder 11, MFD.

Chapter 6

Epigraph source: Miners for Democracy, undated press release, December 1972, box 97 folder 12, MFD.

1. Taniguchi, *Castle Valley, America*, 272–73; Daniel J. Curran, *Dead Laws for Dead Men: The Politics of Federal Coal Mine Health and Safety Legislation* (Pittsburgh: University of Pittsburgh Press, 1993), 171–76; Fox, *United We Stand*, 535–36; Chuck Zehnder, "Miners Still Trapped in Wilberg," *SA*, December 21, 1984; "Judge Orders Stop to MSHA Hearings," *SA*, January 25, 1985; Larry W. Davis, "Congress May Look into Wilberg," *SA*, February 27, 1985; Chuck Zehnder, "Blake Testimony Released by MSHA After Hearings," *SA*, April, 10, 1985; Chuck Zehnder, "Final Body Recovery Made at Wilberg," *SA*, December 18, 1985; "Death in the Mines," *UMWJ*, February 1985; Marat Moore, "'Fire in the Intake,'" *UMWJ*, July 1987; "Historic Mining Disasters in Utah," Utah Department of Administrative Services, Division of Archives and Records Service, accessed April 1, 2015, http://archives.utah.gov/research/guides/mining-disasters.html.

2. "Workers Return," *SA*, July 5, 1980.

3. "Walkout Occurs at the Wilberg Mine," *SA*, November 5, 1980; "Mine Strike Continues," *SA*, February 20, 1981; "Miner Causes Emery Walkout," *SA*, March 25, 1981; Don Vetter, "Emery Miners Return to Work," *SA*, February 12, 1982; "Miners Stage Walkout at Wilberg Operation," *SA*, April 14, 1982.

4. Curran, *Dead Laws for Dead Men*, 171–74; Marat Moore, "Chronicle of a Disaster," *UMWJ*, July 1987.

5. "Fire Closes Mine," *SA*, January 4, 1984; "Des-Bee-Dove Mine Lays Off 100 Miners," *SA*, March 23, 1984.

6. Seltzer, *Fire in the Hole*, 163, 165; Clark, *Miners' Fight*, 129–30; Fox, *United We Stand*, 497–98.

7. Panel Discussion, "Seventh National Conference of Women Miners," AppMs 355 Tape 74, Coal Employment Project Records, Video Files, Archives of Appalachia, East Tennessee State University (hereafter cited as: CEP-V).

8. Don Vetter, "Emery Miners Return to Work," *SA*, February 12, 1982; Steve Heide, "Striking Miners Balk at Violence, But . . .," *SA*, February 17, 1982; Dennis Ardohain and Frank Markosek, interview by author, Price, July 15, 2014.

9. "Sabotage at Deer Creek Mine," *ECP*, November 10, 1977; "Mine Belt Vandalism Prompts Reward Offer," *ECP*, November 29, 1979; "Threat Closed Local Mine," *SA*, April 17, 1981; "Mine Bomb Threat Prompts Reward," *SA*, November 6, 1981; "Bomb Threat Empties Valley Camp Mine," *SA*, January 27, 1982; "Bomb Threat Empties Mine," *SA*, April 30, 1982; "Death in the Mines," *UMWJ*, February 1985.

10. "McCulloch Buys Mine," *SA*, January 3, 1974; "AEP Mine Decides on Union," *SA*, August 27, 1980; "First Unit Train Load Slated by Valley Camp," *SA*, February 19, 1976; "'King Coal' Mine Sold to Pennsylvania's Sharon Steel," *SA*, January 28, 1981.

11. Moody, *Battle Line*, 39; Perry, *Collective Bargaining*, 62, 70; Nyden, "Rank-and-File Movements," 189.

12. "'No Contract, No Work' Idles 'Union' Coal Mines," *SA*, October 7, 1971; "Work Continues at Plateau Mine; Pickets Keep Vigil," *SA*, October 14, 1971; "Negotiations Resume on Coal Contract," *SA*, October 28, 1971.

13. "First Week of Strike Peaceful in County," *ECP*, December 15, 1977; Harold L. Alger, letter to the editor, *SA*, October 28, 1971; "Miner Firing Upheld," *SA*, July 25, 1979.

14. Harold L. Alger and Louis Pestotnik Jr., letter to the editor, *SA*, May 6, 1981.

15. Baker, *Above the Clouds*, 150–52; "Plateau Mine; Pickets Keep Vigil," *SA*, October 14, 1971; "Picketing Ends at 2 Non-union Coal Mines," *SA*, October 21, 1971.

16. "Picketing Ends at 2 Non-union Coal Mines"; "Unfair Labor Charges Filed Against UMWA," *SA*, October 28, 1971.

17. Name Withheld, letter to the editor, *SA*, December 21, 1971.

18. "Strike Begins, Passic Calls UHP to Assist at Pickets," *SA*, December 7, 1977; John Serfustini, Doug Tullis, and Joe Rolando, "Order Restored After Violence Mars Strikes," *SA*, December 10, 1977; "Picket Lines Gone," *SA*, December 14, 1977; John Serfustini, "Picket Lines Quiet," *SA*, December 21, 1977; John Serfustini, Doug Tullis, and Joe Rolando, "Bomb Threat Halts Coal Strike Hearing," *SA*, December 14, 1977; John Serfustini and Joe Rolando, "UMW—Nonunion Talks Stall on Night Picket Line," *SA*, December 12, 1977; "Use Reason, Not Illegal Actions to Make UMWA Gains," *SA*, April 8, 1981.

19. "Threat Closed Local Mine," *SA*, April 17, 1981; "Vandals Set Bridge Fire Near Mine," *SA*, April 29, 1981; Robert R. Servatius, letter to the editor, *SA*, April 15, 1981; Scott Lloyd, "Hunter Engineer Shot in Shoulder," *SA*, April 15, 1981.

20. Perry, *Collective Bargaining*, 177; "Miners Kill Proposal," *SA*, April 1, 1981; "Coal Labor Talks Should Be Separate," *SA*, April 29, 1981; Scott Lloyd, "Strike Talks Still Snarled," *SA*, May 6, 1981.

21. "Coal Labor Talks Should Be Separate."

22. Harold L. Alger and Louis Pestotnik Jr., letter to the editor, *SA*, May 6, 1981; Harold L. Alger, letter to the editor, *SA*, May 20, 1981.

23. Perry, *Collective Bargaining*, 61; "Poll Shows Miners Want Local Accord," *SA*, May 13, 1981; "Miners Vote on Agreement," *SA*, September 28, 1984.

24. "Miner President: 'Strike Possible,'" *SA*, September 26, 1984.

25. Bill Zeller, letter to the editor, *SA*, October 17, 1984.

26. Ibid.

27. Alene E. Hansen, letter to the editor, *SA*, October 10, 1984.

28. Harold Alger, letter to the editor, *SA*, October 24, 1984.

29. Michael Dame, "Strike Finally Ends," *SA*, November 2, 1984.

30. Advertisement, "To Miners Who Have Picketed Plateau," *SA*, October 21, 1971; Frank J. Sacco to Michael F. Widman, December 13, 1968, box 11, folder 33, U-OD.

31. Ms. Gene S. Byrge, letter to the editor, *SA*, September 28, 1977.

32. Name Withheld, letter to the editor, *SA*, December 7, 1977; Dave Munden, letter to the editor, *SA*, December 14, 1977; Carol Sue Martinez, letter to the editor, *SA*, January 25, 1978; Iris H. Tatton, letter to the editor, *SA*, February 18, 1978; Name Withheld, letter to the editor, *SA*, March 8, 1978; Sarie Guy, letter to the editor, *SA*, December 13, 1978.

33. Ivana Krajcinovic, *From Company Doctors to Managed Care: The United Mine Workers' Noble Experiment*, Cornell Studies in Industrial & Labor Relations, no. 31 (Ithaca: ILR Press, 1997), 171-72; Sarie Guy, letter to the editor, *SA*, December 13, 1978.

34. "Straight Talk to UMW," *SA*, March 29, 1978; "Miner Firing Upheld," *SA*, July 25, 1979; John Serfustini, "'No Contract, No Work' Miners Insist," *SA*, March 15, 1978.

35. Doug Tullis, "Scrubber Rule Purely Political," *SA*, August 17, 1977.

36. Advertisement, "Soldier Creek Miners," *SA*, July 25, 1979; "Soldier Creek Opts for Non-Union Mine," *SA*, August 1, 1979.

37. "Soldier Creek Opts for Non-Union Mine."

38. Fox, *United We Stand*, 507; Geoghegan, *Which Side Are You On?*, 19.

39. "Soldier Creek Opts for Non-Union Mine"; "Plants Depend on Soldier Creek Mine," *SA*, Energy Supplement, February 14, 1979; Tom Bethell to Clarice Feldman, July 5, 1973, box 12, folder 8, HCLA 1827, U-OD.

40. "Lab Wins Coastal States Contract," *SA*, February 11, 1982; "UMWA Set to Organize in Sanpete," *SA*, December 18, 1981; "President Named to Skyline Mine Project," *SA*, February 4, 1981; "Skyline Delays Project," *SA*, February 24, 1982.

41. "Views of UMWA: Coal—It's Abundant, Available, Affordable," Energy Edition, *SA*, January 26, 1983.

42. Dorothy Sue Cobble, *The Other Women's Movement: Workplace Justice and Social Rights in Modern America* (Princeton: Princeton University Press, 2004), 204; Karen Nussbaum, "Working Women's Insurgency Consciousness," in *The Sex of Class: Women Transforming American Labor*, ed. Dorothy Sue Cobble (Ithaca: ILR Press, 2007), 165; Cowie, *Staying Alive*, 239.

CHAPTER 7

Epigraph source: Mrs. Rosa Sandoval, interview by Chuck Lobato, Katarina

Trujillo, and Margie Archuleta, Dragerton, UT, June 13, 1972, Utah Minorities Number S-46, transcript, AWC-Helper.

1. Fox, *United We Stand*, 27; Herbert Hill, "Myth-Making as Labor History: Herbert Gutman and the United Mine Workers of America," *International Journal of Politics, Culture and Society* 2 no. 2 (Winter 1988): 132–200.

2. Paul John Nyden, "Miners for Democracy: Struggle in the Coal Fields," PhD diss., Columbia University, 1974, 536, 537–38, 578–80, 672–73, 830; Tom Murphy, "Miners Smack Firm with Suit," *SA*, October 31, 1979.

3. "Minstrel Show Promises Real Entertainment," *SA*, November 17, 1938; "Castle Gate," *SA*, March 16, 1939; "Rains," *SA*, March 28, 1939; "Large Audience Attends Shrine Minstrel Show," *SA*, April 10, 1941; "Minstrel Show for Canteen Plan Given Tonight," *SA*, November 30, 1944; "Shriners Staged Successful 'Blackface' Show Saturday," *SA*, March 7, 1946; "Price Junior High Boys Chorus Sets Minstrel Show," *SA*, December 8, 1949; "Lions Ready Stage for Annual Benefit 'Black Face,'" *SA*, April 6, 1950; "Minstrel Show Slated for June 29," *ECP*, June 24, 1971; "Cub Scouts to Provide Minstrel Show," *SA*, March 23, 1972.

4. August, Mary, and William Tapolovec, interview by Nancy Taniguchi, undated, Non-Transcribed Oral History Digital Tape Collection, Western Mining and Railroad Museum, Helper, UT (hereafter cited as DTC-Helper); Willard Craig, interview by Mark Hutchings, June 12, 1976, Castle Gate Oral History Project, Harold B. Lee Library, Brigham Young University, Provo, UT (hereafter cited as CGOHP-HBL); Tommy and May Hilton, interview by John Bluth, May 1974, CGOHP-HBL; Manson E. Huff, interview by D. Mark Hastings, March 6, 1976, CGOHP-HBL.

5. Gomer Peacock, interview by Carol and Kendra Tomsic, Price, February 10, 1973, transcript, box 1A, folder 95.92.12, WMRRM-Helper; Raymond Toson, interview by Madge Tomsic, July 23, 1993, WMRRM-Helper; Joseph Cha, interview by Madge Tomsic, February 26, 1994, WMRRM-Helper; Shefta and Roxella Gordon, interview by Nancy Taniguchi, East Carbon, 1982, transcript, box 1, folder 19, CCOH-JWM; James Gardner, interview by Nancy Taniguchi, Price, April 25, 1982, transcript, box 1, folder 18, CCOH-JWM; Ann and John Spensko, interview by Nancy Taniguchi, May 7, 1982, transcript, box 2, folder 15, CCOH-JWM.

6. Fon and Vernon Lemaster, interview by Tanner Gardner, February 9, 2006, transcript in Scoville and Whittle, *Yarns of Carbon and Emery Counties*, 54.

7. Taniguchi, *Castle Valley, America*, 194–96.

8. Howard Warren Browne, interview by Leslie Kelen, September 14–16, 1983, transcript, box 1, folders 14–15, Blacks in Utah, J. Willard Marriott Library, Salt Lake City, UT.

9. "Population Characteristics for Carbon Shown on Report," *SA*, September 25, 1941.

10. Taniguchi, *Castle Valley, America*, 228.

11. Obituary for Ramon Cisneros, *SA*, March 16, 2006; Obituary for David Ochoa, *SA*, May 24, 2005; Obituary for Mike Gabriella, *SA*, February 17, 2004; Obituary for Lucio Cruz, *SA*, May 20, 2010; Obituary for Eduardo Velasquez, *SA*, July 16, 2002; Obituary for Joe Leyba, *SA*, January 7, 2002; Obituary for Mike Trujillo, *SA*, June 4, 2002; Obituary for Maria Roybal, *SA*, February 5, 2008; Obituary for Juan Escandon, *SA*, September 4, 2007; Obituary for Jessee Arroyo, *SA*, May 30, 2006.

12. "Hispanic Population Up," *SA*, April 17, 1981; Jose Jesus Palacios, interview by Margie Archuleta and Vincent Mayer, Dragerton, June 13, 1972, Utah Minorities Number S-59, transcript, AWC-Helper; Mr. and Mrs. Richard Cordova, interview by Vincent Mayer and Bernice Martinez, Helper, June 1972, Utah Minorities Number S-22, transcript, AWC-Helper.

13. Watt, *History of Carbon County*, 242–43; Jose Jesus Palacio, interview; Mr. and Mrs. Richard Cordova, interview; "Hispanic Population Up."

14. Mrs. Rosa Sandoval, interview by Chuck Lobato, Dragerton, Katarina Trujillo, and Margie Archuleta, June 13, 1972, Utah Minorities Number S-46, transcript, AWC-Helper.

15. Clorinda Cordova, interview by Bernice Martinez and Katrina Trujillo, Helper, June 13, 1972, Utah Minorities Number S-25, transcript, AWC-Helper; Mr. and Mrs. Richard Cordova, interview.

16. Teodolo Anton and Alice Ramos, interview by Kathy Trujillo, Bernice Martinez, and Chuck Lobato, Utah Minorities Number S-60, transcript, AWC-Helper; Jim and Ramona Valdez, interview by author, Price, UT, March 2017.

17. Jim and Ramona Valdez, interview by author, Price, UT, March 2017.

18. Obituary for Joseph Palacios, *Deseret News*, May 3, 1992; "SEUEPA Lifetime Achievement Awards 2007," *SEUEPA News* 4, no. 2 (October 15, 2007): 12, http://www.seuepa.org/uploads/6/5/9/7/6597361/2007_10.pdf.

19. Calvin L. Rampton, "Coal to Shape Utah's Future," *SA*, January 2, 1975.

20. The following in box 2, folder 25, SOCIO records, J. Willard Marriott Library,

Salt Lake City, UT: "Ideology and Description & History of SOCIO," undated; "What is SOCIO?," undated.

21. Taniguchi, *Castle Valley, America*, 245–46; "SOCIO Organization Forms Unit in Price," *SA*, August 29, 1968; "Mexican Club Contributes $30,000 to County Family, Children Support Center," *SA*, November 27, 2008.

22. Mrs. Rosa Sandoval, interview; Clorinda Cordova, interview.

23. "Chicano Studies Program Begins This Year at CEU," *SA*, November 2, 1972; "Chicano Studies Center Begins Operation at CEU," *SA*, November 9, 1972; "Chicano History Portrayed on College Library Wall," *SA*, March 11, 1978; "Chicano Representative Asks Citizens Opinions on Local, National, Issues," *SA*, October 9, 1975; "Woman Resigns from Hispanic Group," *SA*, July 30, 1980; "Chicanos Slate Seminar," *SA*, October 7, 1976; "Racial Rift Bridged in Talks," *SA*, May 21, 1980; "Racial Dispute Eases in Town," *SA*, May 21, 1980; Clorinda Cordova, letter to the editor, *SA*, July 28, 1982; Jim and Ramona Valdez, interview.

24. Mr. and Mrs. Richard Cordova, interview.

25. Jose Jesus Palacios, interview.

26. "The Strike at Sundance," *UMWJ*, March 1, 1975; Robert Dimas, letter to the editor, *UMWJ*, July 15, 1976.

27. "Union Man Leaves Post," *SA*, August 3, 1972; "'Tony' Boyle Leading Nominations," *SA*, August 24, 1972; "UMWA Candidate to Be in Carbon County Saturday," *SA*, September 7, 1973; "1972 UMWA International Election Results," *UMWJ*, January 1, 1973; Frank G. Farliano to Arnold Miller, October 29, 1974, box 177, folder 6, U-PC.

28. Harold L. Alger, letter to the editor, *SA*, November 1, 1973; Obituary for Maria Roybal, *SA*, February 5, 2008; "Roybal Unseats Incumbent in UMWA Board Election," *SA*, January 22, 1976; Roybal to Miller, multiple letters, 1973–1977, box 177, folders 5–13, U-PC.

29. Mrs. Rosa Sandoval, interview; Clorinda Cordova, interview; Mr. and Mrs. Richard Cordova, interview.

30. "Chicanos Honored at Confab," *SA*, October 20, 1979; Joe Roland, "Needy Strikers Get Food," *SA*, January 25, 1978; "Help Planned in Price for Needy Miners," *ECP*, January 26, 1978; "UMWA Organizing Food Bank," *ECP*, April 15, 1981; "UMW Begins Food Giveaway," *SA*, April 17, 1981; Harold Alger, letter to the editor, *SA*, December 2, 1981.

31. Nyden, "Miners for Democracy," 536–37.

32. Ibid., 673, 827, 830; "Trbovich Suspended by Miller for Refusing Organizing Duty in the West," *UMWJ*, April 16–30, 1976; "Trbovich Reinstated," *UMWJ*, May 16–31, 1976.

33. Eric Swenson to Arnold Miller, October 24, 1973, box 99, folder 16, MFD.

34. Frank J. Sacco to W. A. Boyle, undated letter, ca. December 1970, box 67, folder 6, MFD; The following in box 99, folder 16, MFD: Tom Shirley to Arnold Miller, November 7, 1973; Arnold Miller to Eric Swenson, November 19, 1973. "Kayenta Miners Back at Job," May 8, 1975, *Arizona Republic*.

35. Ray Bustos to Arnold Miller, March 10, 1975, box 177, folder 8, U-PC; the following in box 177, folder 11, U-PC: Samuel C. Calloway to Thomas J. Starks, October 8, 1974; Harold Alger to Arnold Miller, May 20, 1976.

36. Bustos to Miller, March 10, 1975.

37. Ray Bustos to Arnold Miller, March 17, 1975, box 177, folder 8, U-PC; Harold Alger to Arnold Miller, August 11, 1976, box 177, folder 11, U-PC. From 1974 to 1977, nineteen pieces of correspondence addressing the lampman issue appear in box 177, folders 5 and 8–11.

38. Harold Alger to Arnold Miller, undated letter, box 177, folder 11, U-PC.

39. The following in box 177, folder 8, U-PC: John Woodrum to Steve Galati, June 6, 1976; John Woodrum to Harold Alger, June 18, 1975.

40. "New UMWA Officers," *SA*, July 6, 1977; "Patterson Gets District 22 Support," *SA*, June 18, 1977.

41. Clark, *Miner's Fight*, 94–99, 101–5, 107–12, 175; Seltzer, *Fire in the Hole*, 142–43; Fox, *United We Stand*, 508–10; "Patterson Gets District Support," *SA*, June 18, 1977.

42. Nyden, "Miners for Democracy," 858; "Geneva Miners Strike, Local President Suspended," *SA*, September 18, 1975; "Geneva Strike: Miners, Widows Man Pickets," *SA*, October 2, 1975; "Restraining Order: 15 E. Carbonites Barred from Picketing," *SA*, October 9, 1975; "A Parade for Animals and Kids, Too," *SA*, September 9, 1981.

43. SOCIO Newsletter, September 1984 to May 1985, box 10, folder 15, SOCIO; "Membership: Price Carbon Chapter," 1985, box 8, folder 8, SOCIO.

44. Jorge Iber, *Hispanics in the Mormon Zion: 1912–1999* (College Station: Texas A&M University Press, 2000), 110–14.

45. "Minority Women & Employment SOCIO Program Proposal," ca. 1981, box 114, folder 1, SOCIO.

46. James E. Peterson, "Utah Women in Economic Crisis: A Report from the Governor's Task Force on Integrating Women into the Workforce," June 1984, 2, 6, box 114, folder 6, SOCIO.

47. Orlando Rivera, interview by Donald Stauss, Salt Lake City, Spanish-Speaking Peoples in Utah Oral Histories, box 2, folder 55, J. Willard Marriott Library, Salt Lake City, UT.

48. Robert Nieves, interview by Leslie Kelen, April 19, 1985, box 4, folder 1, Hispanic Oral Histories, J. Willard Marriott Library, Salt Lake City, UT; "Minority Women & Employment SOCIO Program Proposal," ca. 1981, box 114, folder 1, SOCIO.

49. Taniguchi, *Castle Valley, America*, 281; "Co Op Miners," *ECP*, June 28, 2005; Corey Bluemel, "Co-Op Rally Draws Crowd," *ECP*, December 23, 2003; "Coop Miners Picket to Mark Anniversary of Election," *ECP*, January 3, 2006; Patsy Stoddard, "Co-Op Miners Celebrate with Victory after Long Struggle," *ECP*; "Stakes Are High in Co-Op Strike," *The Militant*, December 29, 2003.

50. "Group Seeks Town Status," *ECP*, July 10, 1980; Utah Energy Office, *Utah Energy Developments*, 65; F. R. Jabanbani, *2000 Annual Review and Forecast of Utah Coal Production and Distribution* (Salt Lake City: Utah Department of Natural Resources, 2001).

51. Tom Murphy, "Miners Smack Firm with Suit," *SA*, October 31, 1979; "Utah Coal Miners Receive Messages of Solidarity with Unionizing Struggle," *The Militant*, November 2, 2004.

52. Murphy, "Miners Smack Firm with Suit"; "Utah Coal Miners Receive Messages."

53. "Co-Op Miners in Utah Win Back Their Jobs," *UMWJ*, July–August 2004.

54. "Co-Op Miners' Strike: A Pivotal Battle for Workers," *UMWJ*, January–February 2004; "Co-Op Miners Stand Strong," *UMWJ*, January–February 2005.

55. Arva Smith, "Lady Miners to Hold National Conference," *SA*, May 27, 1985; Arva Smith, "Women Miners Hold Conference in Price," *SA*, June 26, 1985; "Women Miners Hold First Western Conference," *UMWJ*, August 1985.

56. Panel Discussion, "Seventh National Conference of Women Miners," AppMs 355, Tape 73, CEP-V.

57. Advertisement, CEU Supplement, *SA*, September 14, 1983; Advertisement, Energy Edition, *SA*, January 18, 1984; "Utah's Great Coal Resource and the People Who Mine It," Energy Edition, *SA*, February 10, 1982; "Retired Miners," *SA*, June 6, 1984; "Retired Miners," *SA*, March 6, 1985; "Retired Miners," *SA*, October 16, 1985; "Wilberg Monument Dedicated," December 20, 1985.

Chapter 8

Epigraph source: Carolyn A. Booker to CEP, undated letter ca. May 1979, box 80, folder 9b, CEP-S.

1. "Wedding Party Reaches All-Time High at UP&L," *ECP*, July 21, 1982; Obituary for Sherri Crofts Williams.

2. "Decision on Dress Code Still Hanging in the Hair," *ECP*, March 28, 1972.

3. "E.C.H.S. Dress Code," *ECP*, May 9, 1974.

4. Robert Finney, "Easy to Get Mad When War Hits Near," *SA*, June 24, 1971.

5. "Planned Parenthood Group Plans Carbon County Chapter," *HJ*, September 16, 1971; "School Dress Code Okay," *HJ*, September 14, 1972; "Emery Dress Code," *ECP*, April 4, 1974; "Price Woman Begins UP&L Apprenticeship," *ECP*, April 8, 1976; "Women Give Reasons They Flag Vehicles," *HJ*, June 6, 1974; "Woman Becomes Lawyer," *SA*, December 10, 1980; "First Girl Tests Helper Ball Players," *HJ*, August 6, 1975; "Myths Shattered as Woman Wins Derby," *SA*, July 15, 1981.

6. Brenda Brock, "After the Storm," in *Women in the Mines: Stories of Life and Work*, ed. Marat Moore (New York: Twayne Publishers, 1996), 150-51.

7. "Castle Gate," *SA*, March 16, 1939; the following from box 96, folder 9, U-PC: A. H. DeCroo to John L. Lewis, November 6, 1944; Alfred Carey to A. H. DeCroo, October 30, 1944.

8. "District 22 UMW Office Picketed; Officials Ignore Picket Line," *Rock Springs Daily Rocket*, July 28, 1951; Ann Jelaco, letter to the editor, *SA*, August 1951.

9. The following in box 97, folder 10, U-PC: Mary Butkovich to John L. Lewis, October 19 and November 2, 1951; John Kmetz to Thomas Kennedy, October 17, 1951.

10. "The Coal Mining Job," *UMWJ*, April 15, 1972; "Should Women Be Coal Miners?" *UMWJ*, May 15, 1973; Bill Looney, "First Women Get Jobs

Underground," *UMWJ*, January 15, 1974; Pam Schube, letter to the editor, *UMWJ*, June 16, 1974; "Coal Mining Is Our Life," *UMWJ*, March 1976, 16–31; Jonalee Mills, letter to the editor, *UMWJ*, October 1976; Carol Brittain, letter to the editor, *UMWJ*, October 1976.

11. Ann Byerley, undated letter, box 80, folder 9c, CEP Subject Files, Archives of Appalachia, East Tennessee State University (hereafter CEP-S); Laura Mandery, "An Underground Survival Guide for Women," undated, box 46, folder 26, CEP–Information Request Files, Archives of Appalachia, East Tennessee State University (hereafter CEP-I); "Different but Equal: Special Hygiene Problems in the Mines," *Coal Mining Women's Support Team News* (hereafter cited as *CMWSTN*), July 1983.

12. Dennis Ardohain and Frank Markosek, interview; "Women Miners Still Fighting for Acceptance, Fair Wages," *SA*, December 8, 1982; Shaunna L. Scott, *Two Sides to Everything: The Cultural Construction of Class Consciousness in Harlan County, Kentucky*, SUNY Series in Oral Public History, ed. Michael Frisch (Albany: State University of New York Press, 1995), 94; Randall Norris and Jean-Philippe Cypress, *Women of Coal* (Lexington: University Press of Kentucky, 1996), 70; Dona G. Gearhart, "'Surely a Wench Can Choose Her Own Work!': Women Coal Miners in Paonia, Colorado, 1976–1987" (PhD diss., University of Nevada, 1996), 186; Carletta Savage, "Re-gendering Coal: Female Miners and Male Supervisors," *Appalachian Journal* 27, no. 3 (Spring 2000): 237–38; Suzanne E. Tallichet, "Gendered Relations in the Mines and the Division of Labor Underground," *Gender and Society* 9, no. 4 (December 1995): 701, 705; Suzanne E. Tallichet, *Daughters of the Mountain: Women Coal Miners in Central Appalachia* (University Park: Pennsylvania State University Press, 2006), 83–87.

13. Rebecca Ann Montoya Bragdon, "Beneath a Balanced Rock: Hardscrabble Miners' Widows and Their Families Search for Justice" (PhD diss., University of North Carolina–Greensboro, 2004), 101; "CEP Releases Sexual Harassment Study Results," *CMWSTN*, April 1981.

14. Evan Turner, "The Impacts Associated with Energy Developments in Carbon and Emery Counties, Utah, Part I: Economic and Demographic Impacts" (Provo, UT: Brigham Young University, Center for Business and Economic Research, 1975), 26; Donna C. Davidson, "Overview of the Boomtown Phenomenon and Its Effect on Women and Minorities," in State Advisory Committees to the U.S. Commission on Civil Rights in the Rocky Mountain Region, *Energy Resource Development: Implications for Women and Minorities in the Intermountain West*, edited by Roger C. Wade and

Jeanne Stibman (Washington, DC: U.S. Government Printing Office, 1979), 91. For an overview of the energy boom in Carbon and Emery Counties, see Edward A. Geary, *A History of Emery County*, Utah Centennial County History Series (Salt Lake City: Emery County Commission, 1996), 366–400.

15. Shirley Haycock, interview by Lee Bennett, Price, May 16, 2013, transcript, Statewide Oral History Project, Abandoned Mines Reclamation Program, Utah Division of Oil, Gas, and Mining (hereafter UT-DOGM), https://fs.ogm.utah.gov/PUB/MINES/AMR_Related/miningHistory/Haycockfinal.pdf; "Lady Miner at Work Near Helper," *HJ*, December 10, 1975; Richard Shaw, "1973: Oil Embargo Hits Country Hard," *SA*, September 27, 2011.

16. Elizabeth Hanson, "Women Take First Step into Mine," *SA*, May, 8, 1975; Arva Smith, "Mining Job Not Glamorous," *Deseret News*, July 1978; Joe Rolando, "Woman Miner Digs Her Work," *SA*, March 17, 1977; Joyce Skidmore, "Women Find Jobs in Mines," *SA*, July 18, 1979; "Walkin' the Belt Line," *SA*, February 19, 1982.

17. Shirley Haycock, interview; Duane Preston, interview by author, Carbondale, August 19, 2014.

18. Hanson, "Women Take First Step into Mine"; Rolando, "Woman Miner Digs Her Work"; Arva Smith, "Mining Job Not Glamorous," *Deseret News*, July 1978; Joy Huitt, "For the Future," in Marat Moore, *Women in the Mines: Stories of Life and Work* (New York: Twayne Publishers, 1996), 223–24.

19. Betty Jean Hall, "Women Miners Can Dig It, Too," box 1, folder 7, CEP-S.

20. Ibid.

21. Ibid.

22. Martha Tabor, "Women in Coal: Employment Patterns," *Off Our Backs* 10, no. 40 (April 1980): 10.

23. Huitt, "For the Future"; "Coal Companies Pay Settlement," *SA*, December 5, 1979; "Women in Coal," 10; "Coal Companies Pay Settlement," *SA*, December 5, 1979; "Fact Sheet: 3,825 Women Have Begun Underground Coal Mining Careers Since 1973," box 25, folder 2, CEP Conferences and Workshop Files, Archives of Appalachia, East Tennessee State University (hereafter cited as CEP-CW).

24. "Minutes of Planning Meeting for a Conference of Women Coal Miners," Jan 27–28, 1979, box 1, folder 8, CEP Correspondence Files, Archives of Appalachia, East Tennessee State University (hereafter cited as CEP-C);

"Future Directions for the Coal Employment Project: Recommendations for Future Action," undated, 1984, box 80, folder 8, CEP-S.

25. "Women Miners to Meet," *SA*, January 28, 1981; "Women Organize for Mining Work," *SA*, February 4, 1981.

26. Connie White to Ms. Debra Monsoor, July 20, 1979, box 1, folder 10, CEP-C; Arva Smith, "Women Coal Miners Organize Support Group in Helper," *Deseret News*, ca. February 1981.

27. Smith, "Women Coal Miners Organize Support Group"; Scott, *Two Sides to Everything*, 89; Savage, "Re-gendering Coal," 235; Jessica Smith Rolston, *Mining Coal and Undermining Gender: Rhythms of Work and Family in the American West* (New Brunswick, NJ: Rutgers University Press, 2014), 9, 18–19; Ruth Milkman, "Two Worlds of Unionism: Women and the New Labor Movement," in Cobble, *The Sex of Class*, 63–80; Nussbaum, "Working Women's Insurgent Consciousness," 159–76; Cobble, *The Other Women's Movement*, 3, 192–93; Martha Taylor, "First National Women Coal Miners' Conference," *Off Our Backs* 9, no. 8 (August–September 1979): 20–21.

28. Irene Pritchett to Joyce Dukes, March 7, 1981, box 80, folder 9b, CEP-S.

29. Thomas F. Connors to Ms. Millie Walters, July 19, 1978, box 1, folder 4, CEP-C.

30. Glen Zumwalt, interview by Lee Bennett, Leeds, December 11, 2014, transcript, UT-DOGM, https://fs.ogm.utah.gov/PUB/MINES/AMR_Related/miningHistory/Zumwaltfinal.pdf.

31. The following from box 1, folder 8, CEP-C: Betty Jean Hall to Ms. Laurie Castleberry, May 25, 1979; Connie White to Jane Datisman, May 8, 1979; "Support Team News: Utah," *CMWSTN*, May 1981.

32. Moore, *Women in the Mines*, 226–27.

33. Joyce Dukes to Joy Huitt, March 25, 1982, box 80, folder 9b, CEP-S.

34. John Banovics, "Speech for Women's Coal Mining Conference, June 21 & 22, 1985, Price, UT," box 25, folder 4, CEP-CW.

35. Richard L. Trumka, "Statement of Support," box 55, folder 5, CEP-S.

36. "Portrait of a Woman Miner: Joy Huitt," *CMWSTN*, November 1982; Betty Jean Hall to Ann Byerley, May 7, 1981, box 47, folder 2, CEP-I; "Portrait of a Woman Miner: Gene Byrge of Utah," *CMWSTN*, December 1986; Elnora Clark, letter to the editor, *CMWSTN*, December 1980; "Portrait of a Woman

Miner: Wanda Carrier Lankford," *CMWSTN*, August 1983; "Portrait of a Woman Miner: Rita Miller," *CMWSTN*, ca. 1983.

37. "Portrait of a Lady Miner: Fay Lee," *CMWSTN*, Feburary 1981; Fay Lee Martin, interview by Lee Bennett, Spring Glen, April 3, 2014, transcript, UT-DOGM.

38. "Women Miners Schedule Conference in Illinois," *SA*, May 13, 1981; "Women Miners Meet," *SA*, January 26, 1983; "Lady Miners to Attend Confab," *SA*, June 22, 1983; "Price to Host Women Miners in 1985," *SA*, July 4, 1984; "A Book for Pregnant Miners," *SA*, August 25, 1982; Undated Memorandum, ca. October 1984, box 41, folder 30b, CEP Personnel Records, Archives of Appalachia, East Tennessee State University (hereafter CEP-P); "Support Team News: Utah," *CMWSTN*, December-January 1985; Joy Huitt, interview by Lee Bennett, Price, May 16, 2013, transcript, UT-DOGM.

39. Joy Huitt to Joyce Dukes, October 18, 1981, box 41, folder 30a, CEP-P; "Support Team News: Utah," *CMWSTN*, January 1983; Joy Huitt to Betty Jean Hall, November 14, 1984, box 41, folder 30b, CEP-P.

40. Martha Tabor, "Women in Coal, Employment Patterns," *Off Our Backs* 10, no. 4 (April 1980): 10; Nancy MacLean, "The Hidden History of Affirmative Action: Working Women's Struggles in the 1970s and the Gender of Class," *Feminist Studies* 25, no. 1 (Spring 1999): 63; "Write Now to Help Win Parental Leave," *UMWJ*, September 1986; "Women Miners' Conference Focuses on Negotiations, Parental Leave," *UMWJ*, September 1987; "Family Leave Helps All of Us," *UMWJ*, November 1987.

41. "Film to Aid Lady Miners," *SA*, May 13, 1983; "Lady Miners Show Film," *SA*, June 6, 1984; Fay Lee, letter to the editor, *SA*, June 3, 1981.

42. "Island Creek Agrees to Hire More Women," *UMWJ*, November 1977; "Women Miners in West Virginia File Suit Against Consolidation," *UMWJ*, August 1981; "Union Sponsors Women's Conference, First in History of the UMWA," *UMWJ*, November 1979; "Couple Meets, Weds in UMWA Coal Mine," *UMWJ*, October 16, 1981; Arva Smith, "Women Miners Hold Conference in Price," *SA*, June 26, 1985; "Labor Day," *SA*, September 5, 1984; *Harlan County USA*, directed by Barbara Kopple (Cabin Creek Films, 1977), DVD (The Criterion Collection, 2006).

43. "Organizing Support Groups," *CMWSTN*, June 1981.

44. Emile Loring to Betty Jean Hall, March 16, 1982, box 57, folder 14, CEP-S; "Support Team News: Arizona," *CMWSTN*, December 1981; Joy Huitt, "Progress

Report November 1985–December 1985," box 41, folder 1, CEP-P; Betty Jean Hall to Sylvia B. Gonzales, June 13, 1987, box 75, folder 20, CEP-S.

45. E. Michelle Smith to Mike Dalpaiz, September 23, 1983, box 20, folder 30, CEP Chronological Files, Archives of Appalachia, East Tennessee State University (hereafter CEP-CHR); E. Michelle Smith to CEP, February 1, 1984, box 21, folder 1, CEP-CHR; E. Michelle Smith to Staff, Progress Report, Week of August 28, 1983, box 20, folder 29, CEP-CHR; "Support Team News: Colorado," *CMWSTN*, April 1985.

46. Utah Energy Office, *Utah Energy Developments*, 44–81; Tom Eblen, "High Pay Lures Women to Dangers of Coal Mining: Workers Fight Barriers Besides Discrimination," *Atlanta Journal Constitution*, December 30, 1984.

47. Moore, *Women in the Mines*, xxiii, 139.

48. Tape 073, VHS, Seventh National Conference of Women Miners, CEP Records, Archives of Appalachia, East Tennessee State University.

49. Betty Jean Hall to David Freeman, June 21, 1978, box 1, folder 4, CEP Correspondence Files; Betty Jean Hall, interview by KRCL, Salt Lake City, January 27, 1981, box 101, tape 52, CEP; Mary Anne to Staff, January 3, 1983, box 75, folder 24, CEP-S.

50. Moore, *Women in the Mines*, 232.

51. Donald Huitt, "Joy Huitt: Secretary–treasurer, District 22, UMW, Utah," box 42, folder 1, CEP-P; Donald Huitt, "The Other Side of the Portrait Story: Joy Huitt of Utah Pt 2," *CMWSTN*, July 1986.

52. Barbara Rusmore to June Rostan, September 8, 1986, box 80, folder 9a, CEP-S.

53. "Utah," *CMWSTN*, October 22, 1984; Lady Miners of Utah Newsletter, Spring 1987, box 47, folder 9, CEP Infromation Request Files; "Utah," *CMWSTN*, January–February 1988; "Support Team News: Utah," *CMWSTN*, Summer 1989; Gene Byrge, draft letter, ca. 1988, box 47, folder 3, CEP-I; Glenda Cloward to Betty Jean Hall, undated letter, ca. October 1987, box 80, folder 9a, CEP-S.

54. E. Michelle Smith to CEP, March 12, 1983, box 20, folder 28, CEP-CHR; E. Michelle Smith to CEP, November 7, 1983, box 20, folder 34, CEP-CHR.

55. E. Michelle Smith to CEP Staff, "Progress Report for the Week of November 7, 1983," December 21, 1983, box 20, folder 34, CEP-CHR; "Nancy P. Burnett to Ms. Debbie Paize," January 10, 1985, box 80, folder 9b, CEP-S.

56. Agnes K. Pierce to Equal Employment Opportunity Commission, March 21, 1985, box 21, folder 7a, CEP-CHR.

57. "Portrait of a Woman Miner: Aggie Pierce," *CMWSTN*, July 1985; "Support Team News: Utah," *CMWSTN*, April 1985; Rose S. Hurtado, "Support Team News: Utah," *CMWSTN*, January 1988.

58. "Women Miners Hire New Director, Relocate National Office," *CMWSTN*, November–December 1988.

Chapter 9

Epigraph source: Robert Nieves, interview by Leslie Kelen, Salt Lake City, April 19, 1985, Hispanic Oral Histories, J. Willard Marriott Library, Salt Lake City, UT.

1. "Brennan Speaks on Coal Manpower Crisis," *UMWJ*, July 15, 1970; Paul J. Nyden, "Rank-and-File Movements in the United Mine Workers of America: Early 1960s–Early 1980s," in Brenner, Brenner, and Winslow, *Rebel Rank and File*, 176, 180.

2. Seltzer, *Fire in the Hole*, 136; Fox, *United We Stand*, 461.

3. "George Tilter Talks about the Old Days and a 'Generation Gap,'" *UMWJ*, April 15, 1969; "What've You Done for Me Lately? Well, Here Are Just a Few Things," *UMWJ*, May 15, 1971.

4. Joseph P. Brennan to Sue Richards, May 9, 1967, box 1, folder 36, U-HR.

5. Ibid., September 23, 1969, box 1, folder 36, U-RD.

6. "Mike Ross Talks about the Life Style of the Coal Miner," *UMWJ*, July 1, 1970.

7. Marsha Nye Wice, "Revolution in the Mines: An Analysis of the Miners' Revolt of 1969–1970," (PhD diss., University of Illinois at Urbana-Champaign, 1973), 58, 163, 182; Jensen, "Rebellion in the United Mine Workers," 36, 78–79, 100, 146; Nyden, "Miners for Democracy," 562–63; Fox, *United We Stand*, 461–62.

8. Nyden, "Miners for Democracy," 563; Seltzer, *Fire in the Hole*, 112; Clark, *Miners' Fight*, 30.

9. Seltzer, *Fire in the Hole*, 89–90, 105; Fox, *United We Stand*, 465.

10. "Union Man Leaves Post," *SA*, August 3, 1972; Joe Rolando, "Search for Democracy Leads to District Presidency," *SA*, July 6, 1977.

11. "Communication Channels Should Open Up," *SA*, March 26, 1980.

12. Statistics extrapolated from Powell, *Utah History Encyclopedia*, 432–33; Utah Geological Survey (UGS), *Table 2.9*; "Average Emery County Worker Made $1,452 per Month in 1977, Report Says," *ECP*, April 27, 1978; "Labor Force Statistics from the Current Population Survey," United States Department of Labor, Bureau of Labor Statistics, accessed February 15, 2015, http://data.bls.gov/timeseries/LNU04000000?years_option=all_years&periods_option=specific_periods&periods=Annual+Data; Don Vetter, "Mines Make Carbon 2nd Richest in State," *SA*, July 3, 1981; "Student Survey Released," *SA*, March 26, 1980.

13. John S. Gilmore, "Boom Towns May Hinder Energy Resource Development," *Science* 191, no. 4227 (February 13, 1976): 537; Thomas Greider and Richard S. Krannich, "Neighboring Patterns, Social Support, and Rapid Growth: A Comparison Analysis From Three Western Communities," *Sociological Perspectives* 28, no. 1 (January 1985): 51, 66; William R. Freudenburg, "The Density of Acquaintanceship: An Overlooked Variable in Community Research?," *American Journal of Sociology* 92, no. 1 (July 1986): 39, 43; Michael D. Smith, Richard S. Krannich, and Lori M. Hunter, "Growth, Decline, Stability, and Disruption: A Longitudinal Analysis of Social Well-Being in Four Western Rural Communities," *Rural Sociology* 66, no. 3 (2001): 428, 443.

14. Laurie Castleberry, "Coal Brains," *CMWSTN*, January 1981.

15. Robert Trapanier, interview.

16. Ibid.

17. Justin Lowe, "Hiawatha," *SA*, June 29, 1970; Justin Lowe, "Hiawatha," *SA*, November 12, 1970; Judy Martin, "Hiawatha," *SA*, September 13, 1973; Judy Martin, "Hiawatha," *SA*, December 20, 1973; Judy Martin, "Hiawatha," February 27, 1973; Judy Martin, "Hiawatha," *SA*, December 11, 1975.

18. Judy Martin, "Hiawatha," *SA*, October 4, 1973; "Coal Mine Vacation Schedule," *SA*, June 24, 1976; "Area Coal Miners' Vacations Set for July, August," *SA*, June 28, 1978; Judy Martin, "Hiawatha," *SA*, May 15, 1975; Judy Martin, "Hiawatha," *SA*, November 6, 1975.

19. Ralph and Louise Fossat, interview by Nancy Taniguichi, Price, May 4, 1982, CCOH-JWM.

20. John Mahleres, interview by Madge Tomsic, February 28, 1996, DTC-Helper.

21. "Rains," *News Advocate*, July 5, 1917; "Anglers Await Season," *SA*, June 2, 1979; Helen Lacko, "Selling Like Hotcakes," *SA*, October 21, 1978; "Boggy Bottom 4-Wheelers," *SA*, September 29, 1982; Joe F. Roland Jr., "At the River Hills: Motorcyclists Need Nerves of Steel," *SA*, August 17, 1972; "Here Are the Results of Sunday's Motocross Schedules," *SA*, September 16, 1976; Gordon Lambourne, "Local Bikers Enjoy Moto-Cross Club," *SA*, June 20, 1979; "Sunday Boating," *SA*, July 3, 1975; "Gas Available at Lake Powell," *SA*, May 9, 1979; Don Vetter, "Past Still Lives in Coal Town," *SA*, June 24, 1986.

22. TV Section, *SA*, July 26, 1976; Steve Hide, "VCR Movie Clubs Bring Theater into Your Home," *SA*, November 26, 1982; Advertisement *SA*, August 18, 1979; Kosuye Okura, interview by Nancy Taniguchi, January 8, 1989, box 2, folder 8, CCOH-JWM; Tom Murphy, "Hi-Spot 'Restaurant' Sold," *SA*, May 28, 1980; "Main Street Metamorphosis Hoped For," *SA*, July 16, 1980; Advertisement, *SA*, September 17, 1980; Advertisement, *SA*, July 29, 1981; Advertisement, *SA*, January 27, 1984; Allen Palmer, "Redevelopment Worries City," *SA*, May 29, 1981; Don Vetter, "City Organizes to Upgrade the Downtown," *SA*, September 3, 1980.

23. Wice, "Revolution in the Mines," 182; Jensen, "Rebellion in the United Mine Workers," 78–79; Nyden, "Miners for Democracy," 672, 884–85; John Bradford, letter to the editor, and Larry Cari, letter to the editor, *UMWJ*, June 16–30, 1975.

24. Fox, *United We Stand*, 508.

25. Clark, *Miners' Fight*, 69–73.

26. Ibid., 116.

27. Barry Sheppard, *The Party: The Socialist Workers Party, 1960–1988: Volume 2: Interregnum, Decline, and Collapse, 1972–1988: A Political Memoir* (Berkeley: Minuteman Press, 2012), 123, 139.

28. "Socialists to Celebrate New Office Opening," *SA*, June 2, 1982; "Socialist Workers Open Price Office," *SA*, June 9, 1982; "Socialists Schedule Forum on Saturday," *SA*, May 4, 1983; "Socialist Party Candidate Meets with Local Support," *SA*, April 18, 1984; "Community News," *SA*, April 27, 1984.

29. Sheppard, *The Party*, 271–73.

30. "Joe Geiser: A Socialist Coal Miner for Mayor of Price," 1985, box 80, folder 9a, CEP-S; "Company Greed Killed Coal Miners in Utah," *The Militant*, January 11, 1985.

31. Glenda Cloward to CEP, undated letter, February 1986, box 75, folder 38, CEP-S; June Rostan to Cecelia Moriarity, May 13, 1985, box 80, folder 9b, CEP-S; "Support Team News: Utah," *Coal Mining Women's Support Team News*, May 1987, box 82, folder 36, CEP-S; Obituary for Joseph Louis Geiser IV, *SA*, July 14, 2011.

32. Clark, *Miners' Fight*, 71; H. Wool and J. B. Ostbo, "Labor Relations Outlook for Bituminous Coal Mining" (New York: Electric Power Research Institute, 1980), box 27, folder 4, U-HR.

33. Clark, *Miners' Fight*, 68; Seltzer, *Fire in the Hole*, 89.

34. Seltzer, *Fire in the Hole*, 136.

35. Geoghegan, *Which Side Are You On?*, 30.

36. Dean Julian, letter to the editor, *SA*, February 8, 1978.

37. Joe Rolando, "UMWA Benefit Cuts Rile Local Coal Miners," *SA*, August 27, 1977; Hughes to Miller, September 15, 1977, box 177, folder 13, U-PC; Tom Owings, Harvey Pinegar, Nephi R. Poecker, and Dwight Hughes, letter to the editor, *ECP*, September 15, 1977.

38. "Disgruntled Miners Talk of Seceding from UMW," *SA*, September 14, 1977; "New Contract Proposition Shouted Down," *ECP*, September 22, 1977; "Rally Reaction," *SA*, September 24, 1977; Bill Jones, letter to the editor, *SA*, September 28, 1977; Harold Alger, letter to the editor, *SA*, September 21, 1977; Anonymous, letter to the editor, *SA*, September 28, 1977.

39. Joe Rolando, "Pensioners Still Loyal to UMW," *SA*, February 8, 1978.

40. Harold Alger, letter to the editor, *SA*, May 6, 1981; "Poll Shows Miners Want Local Accord," *SA*, May 13, 1981; "EMC Breaks from 'Eastern Negotiators,'" *ECP*, April 29, 1981.

41. Gordon Lambourne, "Carter Commission on Coal Visits Carbon County Miners," *SA*, May 30, 1979; Remo Spigarelli, interview by Nancy Taniguchi, May 5, 1982, transcript, box 2, folder 16, CCOH-JWM; Ann and John Spensko, interview by Nancy Taniguchi, May 7, 1982, transcript, box 2, folder 15, CCOH-JWM; Louis Pestotnick Jr., interview by Nancy Taniguchi, May 5, 1982, transcript, box 2, folder 10, CCOH-JWM; Frank Pugliese, interview by J. J. Blue, March 13, 2006, DTC-Helper.

42. Phil Sparks, "Like Our Fathers Before Us," *UMWJ*, December 1, 1975; Mike Hall, "Major Organizing Driving Getting Underway," *UMWJ*, August 1980.

43. "District 15 Checklist Pittsburgh + Midway Coal," February 23, 1974, box 99, folder 9, MFD.

44. Cyprus Coal Company, "Plateau Mining Co.," ca. 1985, 8, Plateau box, WMRRM-Helper.

45. Glen Zumwalt, interview by Lee Bennett, Leeds, UT, December 11, 2014, transcript, UT-DOGM.

46. Mrs. John A. Sullivan to Arnold Miller, July 18, 1972, box 92, folder 1, MFD.

47. Zumwalt, interview.

48. Ibid.

Epilogue

Epigraph source: Brittney Hall, "Reflections on a 4-Year Labor Strike," *Daily Kos*, February 26, 2006, http://www.dailykos.com/story/2006/2/26/190122/-.

1. V. M. Johnson, "The Union–Non-Union Problem in Bituminous Coal," March 31, 1960, box 1, folder 38, UMWA Research Department.

2. Perry, *Collective Bargaining*, 61, 65, 1, 17.

3. Ibid., 71; Early, *Save Our Unions*, 30.

4. Lichtenstein, *State of the Union*, ix–x, x, xiii; Goldfield, *Decline of Organized Labor*, 185–87; H. Craig Petersen and Keith Lumsden, "The Effect of Right-to-Work Laws on Unionization in the United States," *Journal of Political Economy* 83, no. 6 (December 1975): 1237–48; William J. Moore and Robert J. Newman, "The Effects of Right-to-Work Laws: A Review of the Literature," *Industrial and Labor Relations Review* 38, no. 4 (July 1985): 571–85; Benjamin Collins, "Right to Work Laws: Legislative Background and Empirical Research," *Congressional Research Service*, January 6, 2014, https://fas.org/sgp/crs/misc/R42575.pdf; Dennis Ardohain and Frank Markosek, interview by author, Price, July 15, 2014; Lawrence Richards, *Union Free America: Workers and Antiunion Culture* (Urbana: University of Illinois Press, 2008), 5; Thomas Borstelmann, *The 1970s: A New Global History* (Oxfordshire: Princeton University Press, 2012), 4, 12, 134.

5. DJS to Harry Patrick, Ed James, and Art Biggs, August 3, 1973, box 99, folder 9, MFD; Foley, *Front Porch Politics*.

6. "Strike Won't Solve Problem," *SA*, September 21, 1977; Cecil S. Henry to Arnold Miller, December 15, 1977, box 177, folder 13, U-PC.

7. Advertisement, *SA*, November 30, 1972; H. A. Brownfield and Andrew J. Smith, "Joint Report of Officers," August 1974, box 177, folder 5, U-PC; Arnold Miller to H. A. Brownfield, June 30, 1976, box 177, folder 12, U-PC; Local 1854 to UMWA, February 13, 1975; box 177, folder 9, U-PC.

8. Brownfield and Smith, "Joint Report of Officers."

9. James Morgan to John L. Lewis, February 18, 1946, box 96, folder 14, U-PC.

10. "Strike Won't Solve Problem," *SA*, September 21, 1977.

11. Houston Martin to Thomas Kennedy, March 10, 1949, box 96, folder, 40, U-PC.

12. "Use Reason, Not Illegal Action to Make UMWA Gains," *SA*, April 8, 1981; Dennis Ardohain and Frank Markosek, interview; Mathew Collin, "Who's to Blame for Coal Slump?" *SA*, October 26, 1983.

13. B. Jenne Hall, "Reflections on a Four-Year Labor Strike," *Daily Kos*, February 26, 2006, http://www.dailykos.com/stories/2006/2/26/190122/-.

14. Moody and Woodward, *Battle Line*, 87.

15. Ibid., 141.

16. Aaron Vaughn, "Possible Plans to Reopen Crandall Canyon Mine," Fox 13 Salt Lake City, August 3, 2012, http://fox13now.com/2012/08/03/possible-plans-to-reopen-mining-operation-in-crandall-canyon/; Mike Gorrell, "Bob Murray Lays Off 102 Utah Miners in Response to Obama Win," *Salt Lake Tribune*, November 10, 2012; Editorial Board, "Black Lung, Incurable and Fatal, Stalks Coal Miners Anew," *New York Times*, December 24, 2016.

17. Patsy Stoddard, "PacifiCorp/Energy West/Rocky Mtn. Power Updates," *ECP*, February 4, 2014; "Two Local Power Plants Recognized for Operational Excellence," *SA*, August 22, 2017.

18. Trenton Willson, "Is Coal Worth Fighting For?" *ECP*, August 18, 2015.

19. Doris H. Quinn, letter to the editor, *ECP*, March 5, 2013; Mel Coonrod, letter to the editor, *SA*, July 21, 2016.

20. John Serfustini, "Carbon Caucuses Go for Cruz, Sanders," *SA*, March 23, 2016; Renee Banasky, "Democratic Party Hopefuls Support Gradual Transition from Fossil Fuels," *SA*, June 15, 2017.

21. Geoghegan, *Which Side Are You On?*, 202, 91, 323–25, 333.

22. Ibid., 197, 200, 201; Early, *Save Our Unions*, 30, 24; Seltzer, *Fire in the Hole*, 147.

23. Geoghegan, *Which Side Are You On?*, 278, 276, 57; Thomas Geoghegan, *Only One Thing Can Save Us* (New York: New Press, 2014), 32.

24. Geoghegan, *Only One Thing Can Save Us*, 65.

25. Ibid.

26. "Straight Talk to UMW," *SA*, March 29, 1978; Geoghegan, *Only One Thing Can Save Us*, 216.

27. Geoghegan, *Only One Thing Can Save Us*, 73–74.

28. Ibid., 137.

INDEX

Note: Page numbers followed by *f* and *t* refer to figures and tables respectively.

African Americans in Utah: areas of residence in Carbon and Emery Counties, 203; employment in coke ovens, 203; and segregation, 205; wartime work in mines, 203, 205

Alger, Harold L.: and Amax unionization efforts, 163, 165, 171–72; and contract negotiations, 185–86, 191*f*; and District 22 election of 1973, 152; and District 22 election of 1977, 169, 169*f*; and east-west tensions in UMWA, 271–72; and grievance procedures, 150, 214–15; and revolt against District 22 ineffectiveness, 168; and unionization efforts, 166; on Welfare and Pension Fund, 188–92

Allai, Henry, 87, 88, 95, 141

Allen Mine, 148

Amax Coal: unionization efforts at, 147, 161–65, 171–72, 279; women miners at, 238–39

American Coal Company: anti-UMWA movement at, 170, 271–72; merger with Castle Valley Mining, 127–29; unionization of, *xxxiv*

American Electric Power Company, 180

American Federation of Labot (AFL), 16, 17

American Fuel Company: as nonunion coal producer, 62; and UMWA organizing in 1940s–50s, 65, 68, 79*f*

American Mining Congress convention (1958), Lewis at, 83

American New Left, mine activism in 1970s, 266–67

antiunion activism: in contract negotiations of 1971, 190*f*, 191*f*, 192–93; in contract negotiations of 1977, 193

antiunion miners: in 1960s–70s, 102, 112; high unemployment and, *xxxii*, *xxxv*, *xlviii*, 106; as minority in Utah in 1970s, 278; modern skepticism about value of unions and, *xxviii–xxix*; range of concerns about UMWA, in 1970s,

xxxv–xxxvi; UMWA organizing failures and, 156, 164, 165, 167, 278, 281–82
antiunion strategies of coal operators: in 1940s–50s, 62–64, 68, 80–81, 82, 96; in 1960s–70s, 102–4, 107, 113–15, 117–22, 125, 132; firings and layoffs of union activists as, 14, 25, 60, 74–75, 77, 85, 113, 114, 118, 119–20, 125, 216, 221, 265*f*, 278, 282; hiring from diverse geographical areas as, 274–75; provoking of wildcat strikes as, 265; screening of employees to weed out union activists, *xxxv*, 274; small mine entrepreneurs and, *xxxii*
Appalachia, challenges to UMWA in (1950s), *xxxviii–xxxix*
Arizona: CEP chapter in, 246; support for MFD in, 147; UMWA success in, *xxxiv*
Aronson, Bernie, 158–60
ash content, and cost of coal processing, *xxv*
Atlas Resources, 167
authoritarianism of UMWA leadership: anonymous *Salt Lake Telegram* expose of, 92–94; Boyle and, 95; bureaucratization, and decline in accountability and transparency, 84, 96; and erosion of democracy, 84, 94–95, 96; installation of provisional division governments as tool in, 32, 84, 94, 95; Lewis's controlling leadership and, 32–33, 95; and loss of local autonomy, 94, 95, 145; and suppression or removal of dissenters, 93, 94, 96. *See also* democracy challenges to union leadership
autonomy for districts, reformers' support for, 143, 145
autonomy for locals: decline of, under centralized bureaucracy, 94, 95, 145; Edmundson's movement in support of, 92

Baker, Wayne: antiunionism of, *xxxv*, 101*f*, 108–9, 117–20, 139, 192; and contract strike of 1971, 182; sale of Plateau Mining, 165; and union negotiations, 129, 130
Bank, Rich, 150–51, 158–60
BCOA. *See* Bituminous Coal Operators Association
Bear Coal: and Miller administration, 151; reduced-royalty contract for, 129; underbidding by nonunion mines, 102
Beaver Creek mine, 259–60
Belina mine, women miners in, 232
Belle Ayr mine, unionization efforts at, 161–65, 173, 215
benefits packages: of modern miners, as product of UMWA work, 7; in nonunion mines, as inoculation against union organizing, 102, 104, 109, 110, 119, 122, 173, 197, 273–74; won by UMWA, 7–8. *See also* Welfare and Retirement Fund
Biggs, Arthur, 64*f*; and bureaucratization of union, 94; and decline of democracy in UMWA, 94–95; and District election of 1949, 90–91; and efforts to organize small mines, in 1940s–50s, 62–63, 64, 66, 68, 80; election to IEB, 88; firing of District 22 secretaries, 229; lobbying by, 15; and organizing in

1960s, 109–10; organizing under Miller administration (1973), 154, 157; rank-and-file dissatisfaction with, 151
Big Horn Coal Company: efforts to remove UWMA, 74–76; settlement in gender discrimination lawsuit, 236; as threat to underground mining jobs, 70; UMWA organizing at, 64, 70, 72–74
Bituminous Coal Operators Association (BCOA): and contract negotiations after 1950, 57; decline of, 185, 186, 272; east-west rift in union solidarity and, 185; and mechanization, support of, *xxxvii–xxxviii*. *See also* National Bituminous Coal Wage Agreement
Black Lung Disease: compensation for, UMWA's belated support for, *xli*; increased coal dust from mechanization and, *xli*; renewed modern outbreaks of, 284; and union activism for health and safety regulations, *xxvii*; wildcat strikes for compensation (1969), *xliii*, 270, 283
Black Mesa mine, 129, 147, 157, 214, 279
Blankenship v. Boyle (1972), *xliii*, 138*f*
Blue Flame Coal Company, 80
Bonacci, Frank: and CIO founding, 17; and NMU, efforts to counter inroads in Utah by, 21; and Roosevelt Recession of 1937–38, 33; and small mines, efforts to unionize, 28; as state legislator, 203; and UMWA efforts to force small mines' compliance with safety regulations, 30–31

Book Cliff mine, 56
Boyle, R. J. "Dick," 131
Boyle, W. A. "Tony," 138*f*; annual income from union presidency, 148; and assassination of Yablonski, 134–35; and authoritarianism in UMWA, 95; callous attitude toward miner fatalities, *xli*; and complaints about denial of pension benefits, 137–39; corruption of, *xlii–xliii*; and declining influence of UMWA, sweetheart deals in response to, *xli–xlii*, *xlii*, 104, 129; election loss to MFD (1972), *xliii*, 136, 140, 141, 146, 256–57; and election of 1969, 134, 140, 141; hiding of union decline, 133; lack of charisma, *xlii*; as Lewis's successor, 94–95, 133, 142; miners' reluctance to remove from office, 140; opposition to rank-and-file activism, 124–25, 130; racial and ethnic minorities, unresponsiveness to, 201; rank-and-file anger with, *xli–xlii*, 257; sources on, *xlii–xliii*; and strip miners, organizing of, 76; *Sun Advocate* criticisms of, 141; suppression of unflattering news reports, 124, 126; top–down organizing strategy of, 124–27; and violence in union organizing, 105
Boys Markets ruling (1970), 265
Braztah Corporation: as mine-owning conglomerate, 179*f*, 180, 259; wildcat strikes, 1968–1985, 268*f*
Brinley, J. E., 35, 64*f*, 84–85, 90–91, 102
Browne, Howard, 3–5, 8, 152
Brownfield, H. A. "Dell," 95, 162–63, 168–69, 171, 214, 279–80

Bureau of Mines, and UMWA efforts to force small mines' compliance with safety regulations, 30
Burlington Northern Railroad, Gillette-Orin line, 194
business unionism, criticisms of, *xxix*, 283
Butkovich, Mary, 228*f*, 229–31
Byerley, Ann, 237, 241, 242
Byrge, Elvin, 119, 120
Byrge, Gene, 239, 241–42, 250

Carbon County: and coal boom of 1970s, *xxxiv*, 257–58; and cultural changes of 1970s, 226; economic blows of 1980s–90s, 218–19; school dress code debate (1972), 226–27; SOCIO chapter in, 210; Trump's 2016 victory in, 284, 285; turn to Republican majority in 2008, *xxv*; UMWA strength in 1970s, 99; World War II fatalities, mines *vs.* soldiers, 46
Carbon County Central Labor Union, 16
Carbon County Industrial Union Council, 35–36
Carbon County Miner (NMU newspaper), 19
Carbon County Miners Executive Council, union abolition of, 87
Carbon Fuel mine: explosion in (1963), *xl–xli*, *xl–xli*, 5; purchase by Braztah conglomerate, 180
Carey, Alfred, 25, 34, 36, 229
Carleon mine, 28
Carter administration commitment to coal, *xlvi*, 236
Castleberry, Laurie, 238–39, 258
Castle Dale, museum in, *xxiv*

Castle Gate: coal-fired power plant in, 106*f*; founding of, 8; Mormon's union support in, *xxxiv*; relocation of, 261; as still existing in 1971, 261
Castle Gate mine, 11*f*; abuse of workers, before unionization, 11, 13, 14–15; closing of, 156; closing of No. 3 mine, in Roosevelt Recession of 1937–38, 31; mechanization and, 58; miners' complaints about ineffective organizers, 139; protests against union dues, 90; purchase by large conglomerate, 178*f*, 180; unionization, improved safety and wages due to, 15
Castle Valley Mining Company, *xxxiv*, 100, 101*f*, 126–29
Castle Valley Workers' Association (CVWA), 108, 118–19
CEP. *See* Coal Employment Project
CEU. *See* College of Eastern Utah
Change to Win federation (Service Employees International Union), 222
Chavez, Caesar, 144*f*, 216
Chicana women, work and daycare issues for, 216–17
Chicano Conference on Equal Opportunity (1971), 209*f*
Chicano miners: activism of, 215–16, 245*f*; demands for equal opportunity by, *xliv*; as UMWA organizers and administrators, 216; and UMWA reforms, *xxxiv–xxxv*
Chicano movement: decline of, 219–20; shift to Emery County, 218; and SOCIO, 207; in Utah *vs.* other states, 207–8
Chicanos: support for union reform,

211; and union politics, 211–12. *See also* Hispanics
Chicano studies program, College of Eastern Utah, 210
Christensen, Howard, 111–12, 116
Civilian Conservation Corp, purchases of nonunion coal, 31
Civil Rights Commission, US, report on increased job qualifications in coal boom towns, 233
civil rights movement: advances by 1980s, 217; Coal Employment Project and, 227, 239; Co-op mine strike and, 220, 282; and union movement, 202, 202*f*, 206, 218–19, 220, 245*f*; women miners and, *xliv*, 222–23, 231–32, 247–48, 250–52. *See also* Chicano movement; Coal Employment Project (CEP); women miners
Clark, Elnora, 237, 242
Clean Air Act of 1970, coal sulfur-content provisions, *xxxiii*; division of eastern and western miners' interests by, 193–94
Clear Creek (town), as still existing in 1971, 261
Clear Creek mine: miners' complaints about lack of viable alternative to Lewis, 36–37; purchase by conglomerate, 180; sexual harassment at, 251
closed shop clause, addition to UMWA contract, in 1933, 26
coal: competition from other energy sources, in 1940s–50s, 51–52, 54, 57; conversion to cleaner fuels, discussion of, in 1950s, 51; economic importance in twentieth century, *xxi–xxii*

coal boom of 1970s, *xxxiii*, 153–54, 158–59, 159*f*; impact on Carbon and Emery counties, *xxxiv*, *xlvi–xlvii*, 257–58; and surfacing mining's outproduction of underground mining, *xxxiii–xxxiv*; and unrest in growing mines, 267, 268*f*. *See also* younger miners' entering mining after 1970
"Coal Brains" (Castleberry), 258
Coal Creek Coal Company, UMWA efforts to organize at, 76–80
coal demand, decline, in Roosevelt Recession of 1937–38, 31
coal demand decline, after 1982: and job losses, *xlvii*; and UMWA decline, 197, 277, 282
coal demand decline, postwar: and bureaucratization of UMWA, 84; and decline in members' influence over union officials, 86–88; and declining power of wildcat strikes, 85–86; and defensive posture of UMWA, 86; and economic distress of miners, 89, 90; and fears of union overreach, 52; and financial pressure on mines, 83; and growing corruption of UMWA, 60–62, 90–91; and layoffs of older workers, 59–60; and union calls for three-day work week, 54; and union efforts to save money, 87–89; and union fees, as increasing burden, 89–90; and weakening of union power, 58, 60, 81–83
coal demand decline in twenty-first century: and community survival as issue, 284–85; and health and pension funds' insolvency, *xxvii*; and mine closures, 221

coal demand rise: in early 1980s, and Utah's expectations for boom, *xlvi*; in World War I, 9, 10; in World War II, 45–47, 50

coal demand rise in 1960s–70s, *xxxiii*, *xxxix*, 133; and hiring of young miners, 253, 257; and increased union power, 149, 154; and rapid growth in Carbon and Emery Counties, 257–58. *See also* younger miners' entering mining after 1970

coal deposits in Rocky Mountain region, formation of, *xxxiii*

coal dust: and Black Lung disease, *xli*; danger of combustion, measures to control, 6; increase with mechanization, *xli*, *xlf*; lag in US laws on, *xli*; measures to reduce, 6

Coal Employment Project (CEP): advocacy for women's employment in coal mines, 235–37; annual national conferences, 237, 238; consultant hired to evaluate, 249–50; disbanding of, 252; expansion to women outside mining, 249–50; founding of, 234; internal conflict in, 252; leaders of, 241–42; legal aggressiveness, members' concerns about, 250–51; legal victories by, 234–35, 236; mission drift in, 249–50; newsletter of, 237, 246; optimism about coal mining growth, 236; records of, as source, *xlv*; rising unemployment as damper on, 247, 248, 252; self-identification as labor and civil rights organization, 239; sexual harassment study by, 232; and statewide support networks for women, 236–37; and UMWA, relations with, 238, 239–40; varying types of state organizations, 246. *See also* National Conference of Women Coal Miners

coal extraction, conventional methods of, 3–4. *See also* mechanization of mining

coal industry: boom-and-bust cycles characteristic of, *xxvi*, 7; incomplete unionization, as opening for inevitable union decline, 276–77. *See also* coal operators

coal industry in Utah: boom despite globalization, *xxxii*; and historical tourism, *xxiv*; locations of, 8; production, 1969, 99; production 1925–1955, 49*t*; production in World War II, 45–47, 50

Coalition of Labor Union Women: LMU and, 244; media interest in, 231

coal miners: drop in media age in 1960s–70s, 253; laid-off miners, UMWA denial of financial assistance to, 86; of older generation, group living of, 261–62, 263; pride in work, 6; superstitions of, 4; turn to nonunion employers, 278; in UMWA, age distributions, 1967–75, 255*f*; wages, in first UMWA contract, 23; willingness to accept risk, 6. *See also* minority miners in UMWA; unemployed miners

coal miners' economic plight: importance of public awareness about, *xxvi*; politicians' failure to address, *xxvi*; and potential for political change, *xxvii*

Coal Miners' Health Act of 2017, *xxvii*

coal miners in Utah: aging of, and increased conservatism, 275; average annual pay, 7; average daily workforce, 1968–1985, 268f; complaints about UMWA, in 1930s–40s, 35–36; critical role of, 170–71; number employed, 1925–1955, 49t; racial and ethic composition before 1942, 203; relative independence within UMWA, 32, 35; wartime influx of African Americans and ethnic Mexicans, 47, 203, 205; wildcat strikes by company, 1968–1985, 268f

Coal Miners' Political Action Committee, 168

Coal Mine Safety Act of 1969: cost of compliance with, 154–56; effectiveness of, 155–56; and reduction of deaths and injuries, 263f

Coal Mining Women's Support Team News, 238

coal operators: cooperation with UMWA founding, reasons for, 18–19; exploitation and abuse of miners before unionization, *xxii*, 10–14; reduction of exploitation and abuse after unionization, 14–15; reluctance to spark strike in declining coal markets of 1950s, 86; resistance to postwar coal production cuts, 54; retaliation against UMWA organizing in 1960s–70s, *xxxix–xl*; right to manage, *vs.* miners' right to safe management, 44–45; screening out of prounion job applicants, *xxxv*, 274; and wildcat strikes, lawsuits to stop, 270–71. *See also* antiunion strategies of coal operators; firings, unwarranted; nonunion mines; punishments, unwarranted; work assignments, punitive

coal operators' aligned interests with unions in 1930s: in enforcement of Code of Fair Competition, 29; in stabilizing mining industry, 18

coal operators' aligned interests with unions in 1950s: to address nonunion competition, 106–7; and need for production stability, 57

Coal Queen, 17, 229, 246

Coalville mine, 28

Coastal States: purchase of SUFCO, 111; and Skyline mine, 196

Code of Fair Competition, 29

Cogan, Tim, 146–47

coked coal, use in steel industry, 6

Cole, George, 34–35

collaborative management: as European model for unions, 288; need for in US, 288; UMWA national contract as turn from, 281, 283–84

collective bargaining in US: legal expertise needed for, *xxix*; limitations of Lewis's model for, *xxxvii*; need for alternative to, 283, 287; need for government-level reforms in, 283, 287; unique complexity of, *xxix*. *See also* unions in United States

College of Eastern Utah (CEU), Chicano studies program at, 210

Colombo, Frank V., 84, 120, 125, 130

Colorado: CEP branch in, 246–47; support for MFD in, 147–48; underground coal mining in 1970s, 151

Colorado Fuel and Iron, 148

Colorado Westmoreland mine, 246–47

Columbia, as steel company town, 9
Columbia mine: abuse of miners before unionization, 14; as steel company mine, 45, 46
communism, postwar fear of, as tool used against unions, 53
communities, coal-mining: bonds of tragedy and loss binding, 6; boom-and-bust cycles characteristic of, *xxvi*; invisibility to general public, *xxiii*; modern decay of, *xxiii–xxiv*; survival of, as issue in twenty-first century, 284–85; turn to tourism, *xxvi*
company-based unions, as antiunion strategy, 102, 108, 112, 118–19, 121, 132, 221
company stores, exploitation of miners, before unionization, 14
company towns, 9*f*; closing of, and scattering of miners' homes, 261–62; company-sponsored entertainment in, 261; establishment of, 8–9; ethnic and racial divides in, 10; exploitative rents in, before unionization, 14; as sites for union organization, 9–10; small number remaining by 1971, 260–61
Condie, Malcolm, 66, 67, 74, 75, 77
Congress of Industrial Organizations (CIO): and business's postwar effort to curb union power, 53; early organizing successes, 17; founding of, *xxxii*, 8, 17; and industry regulation model of unions, 283–84; postwar unionization efforts in South (Operation Dixie), 53
Consolidated Coal Company, *xxxix*, *xli*, 236
Consumers (town), 9, 261

Consumers mine: closing of, in Roosevelt Recession of 1937–38, 31; NMU strike at (1933), 20–22
continuous mining machines, and productivity increases, 56*f*, 57, 119, 260
contract negotiations: emphasis on stability, 1950–1973, 57; and parental leave issue, 244
contract negotiations in 1935, 26
contract negotiations in 1937, 26
contract negotiations in 1939, 26–27
contract negotiations in 1950, UMWA turn to focus on stability in, 56–57
contract negotiations in 1958: accommodation of hard-pressed producers in, 83; and protective-wage clause, 83
contract negotiations in 1968, 125–26
contract negotiations in 1971, antiunion activism in, 190*f*, 191*f*, 192–93
contract negotiations in 1974, 149–50
contract negotiations in 1977: antiunion activism in, 193; rank-and-file activism in, 170; wildcat strike fines as issue in, 271
contract negotiations in 1981, and development of east-west rift, 185–86
contract negotiations in 1984, 186–92; interim contracts signed in, 186; royalty-based contributions to Welfare and Pension Fund as issue in, 187–92; and selective strikes against companies not signing interim agreements, 186–92, 281
contract(s) with UMWA: early willingness to negotiate with companies individually, 280–81; ratification

by rank-and-file vote as platform of MFD, 143
contract(s) with UMWA, national one-size-fits-all approach to: as bargaining liability, 76, 104–5, 280–81; return to selective strikes (1984) as recognition of flaws in, 281; as turn from workplace control model to industry regulation model, 281, 283–84, 289. *See also* National Bituminous Coal Wage Agreement
contract(s) with UMWA, sweetheart agreements with coal operators, 131; miners' anger at, 129, 131; as necessary in competitive environment of 1960s–70s, 129, 131–32; as slippery slope, 131; and underfunding of Welfare and Retirement Fund, 129
Co-op mine: abuse of miners at, 220–21, 284; closure to avoid unionization, 221, 282; Mormon ownership of, 103; racial and immigrant justice elements in strike at, 282; Socialist Workers Party activists and, 267; UMWA organizing at, 219*f*, 220, 221, 222, 282
Cordova, Clorinda, 137, 206, 210, 212, 216
Cordova, Richard, 205, 206, 211–12, 222, 245*f*
corruption in UMWA: Boyle's inner circle and, *xlii–xliii*; MFD exposure of, 141, 142, 213; as obstacle to organizing, 107, 153–54; postwar growth of, 60–62, 90–91; sources on, *xlii–xliii*; violent struggles over unionization and, 105–6

Crandall Canyon mine disaster, 284
cultural changes of 1970s, 226
CVWA. *See* Castle Valley Workers' Association
Cyprus Minerals Corporation, 273

Dalrymple, William, 60, 67–69, 76–80, 78*f*
dangers of mining: in conventional extraction, 4; as driver of conflict in industry, 5; mine collapse as, 4–5; and miner militancy, 10. *See also* fatalities; mine disasters
Davis, Mike, *xxix*, *xxx*, 52–53
death and hardship funds, elimination in union cutbacks, 89
Decker Coal Company: organizing efforts at, 131, 282; settlement of gender discrimination lawsuit, 236
Deer Creek coal mine: closing of, *xxiv–xxv*, 278; as Emery Mining property, 187; growth in 1970s, *xxxiv*, 128*f*, 129; labor unrest in 1970s, 267; as last UMWA mine in Utah, *xxiv*, *xxv*, 278; Socialist Workers Party activists in, 266, 267; UMWA organizing efforts at, 28–29; unionization efforts at, 62, 69, 127; as UP&L-owned, 174; women miners at, 233, 234, 242–43
Defense Plant Corporation: loans to United States Steel, 45–46; and wartime housing for Utah miners, 46
democracy challenges to union leadership (1940s–50s): anonymous *Salt Lake Telegram* expose of union authoritarianism, 92–94;

in District 22, 86–87; District 22 election of 1949 and, 90–91; Edmonson's autonomy movement and, 92; limited organization of, 92

democracy challenges to union leadership (1960s–70s), *xlii–xliii*; autonomy for districts, reformers' support for, 143, 145; district and International officers' undermining of, *xliii–xliv*; growing scholarly interest in, 282; isolation from other unions, 283; lawsuits, *xliii*; UMWA policies in 1950s–60s as root of, *xxxvii–xlii*; wildcat strikes and, *xliii*. *See also* Miller, Arnold; Miners for Democracy (MFD) movement

Democratic Party: and election of 1946, 53; and labor law reform, need for movement to demand action on, 287–88; lack of support for union law reforms, 283; primary election of 2016, in Carbon County, 285; US unions as product of New Deal policies of, 288; Utah's turn from, in 2016 election, 284–86

demographic changes, and decline of Utah miners unions, *xxxiv–xxxv*

Denver & Rio Grande Western Railroad (D&RGW): transition to diesel trains, 51–52; Utah Fuel as subsidiary of, 8

Des-Bee-Dove mine: as Emery Mining property, 187; fire at (1983), 177; labor unrest in 1970s, 267; as nonunion mine, 100, 107; unionization efforts at, *xxxiv*, 101*f*; as UP&L-owned, 174; younger miners' organizing against UMWA, 271–72

Deseret-Beehive mine. *See* Des-Bee-Dove mine

Dickert, James, 111, 114

diesel fuel, competition with coal, 51

Dine Researcher, 147

Dirty Devil strip mine, 167

Disabled Miners and Widows of West Virginia, complaints about pension fund benefits, 109, 140, 257

dissension within UMWA: anti-UMWA movement in District 22 (1977), 271–72; different perspectives of rank-and-file *vs.* leadership as source of, 26; failures in organizing and, 163–64, 166, 172; historians' de-emphasis of, *xxx–xxxi*; large number of, in long 1970s, *xxx*; by racial and gender minorities, *xxxi*; rank-and-file anger at Boyle, *xli–xlii*, 257; rank-and-file anger with international level in 1960s, 103–4; revolt against District 22 ineffectiveness of (1976), 168–69; sources on, *xxxi*; value of frank history of, *xxx–xxxi*; Welfare and Retirement Fund problems and, 51, 104, 107, 108–9, 136–39, 143, 145, 169–70, 193, 257. *See also* east-west rift in solidarity; Miners for Democracy (MFD) movement; solidarity among miners

District 10 of UMWA, support for MFD in, 146

District 12 of UMWA, Edmundson's autonomy movement and, 92

District 15 of UMWA, support for MFD in, 147–48

District 22 of UMWA: administrative structure, in 1930s, 34; and anticipated boom of 1980s, *xlvi*; and anti-UMWA movement (1977), 170, 171*f*, 271–72; autonomy of, 94; challenges to, by Mormon investors, 103; Coal Miners Political Action Committee, 162; convention of 1944, Edmonson's autonomy movement and, 92; convention of 1948, 89; convention of 1953, 63*f*, 86; convention of 1957, 64–65; convention of 1973 (constitutional convention), 152; daunting issues facing reformers in, 136; decline of rank-and-file miners' power within, 87–88; and Deer Creek mine closure, *xxv*; delays in union reforms in, 136; and east-west rift in union solidarity (1981), 185; efforts to organize small mines, in 1940s, 62–69, 95–96; and election obstacles to challengers, 88, 136, 152; election of 1945, controversy surrounding, 86; and election of 1949, members' activism in overturning, 90–91; election of 1961, 107; election of 1972, 211; election of 1973, contesting of, 152–53; election of 1977, reform ticket elected in, 169, 169*f*, 215; election of 1986, 246; enlarged, Miller's effort to create, 150–51; erosion of democracy in, 94–95; firing of secretaries in Rock Springs office, 228*f*, 229–31; first women district officers, 242*f*, 246; isolation of rank-and-file from activities of, 64, 103; and Labor Department, over-reliance on, 168; leadership of, as older men (1970), 256*f*; locals, ca. 1983, 305–6; locals, historic, 307; miners' belief in right to oversee work of, 86–87; miners' complaints about District salaries, 35; miners' letters of complaint to International president, 136–39; and nonunion home heating coal, necessity of using, 166; officers' difficulty of returning to mines after term, 34–35; officers eliminated with shrinking budgets, 88; organizing campaigns after 1985, 282; Price offices, construction of, *xlvi*; rank-and-file anger with, in 1960s, 103–4; reports to rank-and-file members, curtailment of, in 1940s–50s, 87; restrictive nominating procedures, and MFD reform delays, 136, 152; revolt against ineffectiveness of (1976), 168–69; size of, as obstacle to union operations, 34, 67; states included in, *xxxiii*; and Sunnyside mine explosion, resistance to miners' strike following, 41; support for MFD in, 147; support for MFD in election of 1972, 143–46; support for UMWA western organizing efforts, 165, 167

District 27 of UMWA, support for MFD in, 146–47

District 50 of UMWA: Baker and, 130; as catch-all union for non-coal-mine workers, 63–64, 83–84; Edmundson as regional director of, 92; and LDS retail businesses, 103; and Mountain States Machinery Company, 101*f*; UMWA secretaries as members of, 229

District 450, 117

district autonomy, as platform of MFD, 143, 145, 152
district officers: precarious careers of, 34–35; roles of, in 1930s, 33
Dog Valley mine, unionization efforts at, 167
Dragerton, 42f; construction of, 46; as steel company town, 9, 46
Dragerton Hospital, protests against, 84
Dragerton mine, relative postwar prosperity as steel company mine, 46
Dukes, Joyce, 237, 239
Dunlop v. District 22 United Mine Workers of America (1975), 153

East Carbon, as still existing in 1971, 261
East Carbon-Sunnyside: as center of union power, 46; decay of, *xxiii–xxiv*; lost mining jobs, modern landfill jobs as poor replacement for, 219; museum in, *xxiv*
East Tennessee Research Corporation, 235
east-west rift in solidarity: and anti-UMWA organizing, 271–72; Clean Air Act coal sulfur-content provisions and, 193–94; development of, *xliv*, 185–86
eight-hour workday, 23
Eisenhower administration, lack of support for unions, 106
election, UMWA, in 1969: Boyle campaign and, 134, 140, 141; Yablonski challenge to Boyle in, 134
election, UMWA, in 1972: Boyle campaign and, 140, 141; district autonomy as issue in, 143, 145; intimidation tactics of Boyle supporters, 146–47; Miller defeat of Boyle in, *xliii*, 136, 146, 256–57; pension fund abuses as issue in, 143, 145; support for Miller and MFD in, 143–48
elections, US: of 1946, Republican capture of Congress, 53; of 2016, miners' discontent and, *xxv–xxvi*, 284–86
elections in District 22. *See* District 22 of UMWA
electricity generation. *See* power plants
EMC. *See* Emery Mining Corporation
Emery County: and coal boom of 1970s, *xxxiv*, *xlvi–xlvii*, 257–58; and cultural changes of 1970s, 226; Mexican American population in, 219; mining jobs remaining in, 219; school dress code debate (1972), 226–27; shift of Chicano activism to, 218; shift of UMWA activism to, 218; and strikes of 1949, 54; Trump's 2016 victory in, 284, 285; UMWA growth in 1960s–70s, 129; UMWA organizing in 1960s–70s, 100; UMWA strength in 1970s, 99; union organizing in 1960s–70s, *xxxiv*; and World War II fatalities of miners *vs.* soldiers, 46
Emery County Progress, *xxv*, 179, 226
Emery Mining Corporation (EMC): contract negotiations in 1984, 187–92, 189f, 243–44; cost of Welfare and Pension Fund to, 187; firing of wildcat strikers, 177; highly efficient operations of, 187; mines operated by, 174, 187; pursuit of

separate contract (1981), 185–86, 272; and Welfare and Pension Fund, special contract adjusting payments to, 192; wildcat strikes, 1968–1985, 267, 268*f*

employment for miners: high pay as incentive for, 6; importance of retaining, *xxvi–xxvii*; lack of viable alternatives to, *xxvi*; losses after 1982, *xlvii*; mechanization and, *xxxii*, *xxxviii*, *xlvii*, 57, 253; in mid-twentieth century, *xxi*; in Utah, 1925–1955, 49*t*. *See also* unemployment

environmentalists' view of coal, *vs.* miners', *xxvi–xxvii*

environmental regulations, Utah residents' fear of economic impact from, 284–86

equipment for mining, forcing miners to buy: provisions on, in first UMWA contract, 23; before unionization, 13

European-style healthcare, US need for, 281

European-style unions: *vs.* legal constraints of US unions, 283; need for US emulation of, 288

Executive Order 11246, 235

exploitation and abuse of miners before unionization, *xxii*, 10–14; reduction of, with unionization, 14–15

Family and Medical Leave Act of 1993, 244

fatalities: annual number of, in 1960s, *xli*; Boyle's callous attitude toward, *xli*; as inevitable, 6; Miners' Memorial Project, 5–6; notable mine explosions of twentieth century, 5; number in US, in 1963, *xlf*; number in Utah, 1925–1955, 49*t*; number in Utah, since 1884, 5–6; reduction in US, 1950–1978, 263*f*; at Sunnyside mine explosion (May, 1945), 40; types of injuries, 6; in Wilberg coal mine explosion (1984), 175*f*, 176; World War II production increases and, 46–47

federal mine inspectors, and small mines' compliance with safety regulations, 30

financial pressures on UMWA: leaderships' hiding of, 129–30, 133; and necessity of sweetheart deals to attract operators, 129, 131–32; Welfare and Retirement Fund and, *xxvii*, 89, 129, 169–70, 193, 277–78, 279–80

firings, unwarranted: to discourage union activism, 14, 25, 60, 74–75, 77, 85, 113, 114, 118, 119–20, 125, 216, 221, 265*f*, 278, 282; prohibition of, in UMWA contract, 7, 8; as retaliation for lawsuits, 250–51; before unionization, 10–11, 14–15

Florin, Terry, 222

Fontecchio, Nicholas, 21, 22

Fox, Frank: on Carbon County Miners Executive Council, 87; and District election of 1949, 90–91; and rank-and-file criticisms of District officers, 86; and strip mines, efforts to close, 76; union organizing efforts, 63–64, 65, 67–69

GCWA. *See* Gordon Creek Workers Association

Gebo mine: closing of, in Roosevelt

Recession of 1937–38, 31; miners anger at union benefits cutbacks, 89–90; and union fees, 88–89
gender discrimination lawsuits against coal mines, success of, 236
gender roles: national desire for change in, 226; women in traditionally male jobs, in 1970s, 227. *see also* women
General Exploration Company, 165
generational shift. *See* younger miners' entering mining after 1970
Geneva Steel: firing of union activists, 216; Utah miners employed by, 46; wartime recruiting of miners, 205; and World War II production, 46
Geoghegan, Thomas, 195, 270–71, 286–88
Gilded Age, exploitation of miners in, *xxii*
globalization, Utah's coal industry boom despite, *xxxii*
Gordon Creek mine, reopening of, *xxxiv*
Gordon Creek Workers Association (GCWA), 101*f*, 121, 122
government-level reform: failed efforts at, 283; as key to union recovery, 283, 287
Governor's Task Force of Integrating Women into the Workforce, 217
Great Depression: and coal demand, drop in, 18; and coal operators' incentives to support unionizing, 18; and legalization of unions, *xxiii*; mine closings in, 27; miners' financial struggles in, 27–28
Great National Corporation, 157
Green River, museum in, *xxiv*

Green River Mutual Improvement Association, 203
grievance procedure: in contract of 1974, 149–50; in first UMWA contract, 24–25; miners' right to, under UMWA contract, 7–8, 43*f*; types of grievances, in 1930s, 24
grievance procedure, ineffective: as drain on union morale, 230; as obstacle to union organizing, 215, 264–65

Hall, Betty Jean, 235, 237, 248, 252
Hanford Engineering Works, and Manhattan Project, 70
Hardscrabble mine, 28, 76
hardship funds, elimination of, with union cutbacks, 89
Harlan County, USA (1976 film), 154, 244
healthcare system: as benefit won by UMWA, 7–8; Coal Miners' Health Act of 2017 and, *xxvii*; criticisms of, 108–9; eligibility cutbacks in 1960s, 104; European-style, potential to reverse UMWA decline, 281; insolvency, with coal industry decline, *xxvii*; unprecedented gains in postwar period, 50. *See also* Welfare and Retirement Fund
Heiner mine, 28
Helper: African American community in, 203; Labor Day parades in 1970s, 99; museum in, *xxiv*; union organization in 1930s–40s, 15, 19
Helper Journal, 141
Hiawatha: decay of, *xxiv*; founding of, 9; Mormon's union support in, *xxxiv*; as still existing in 1971, 261; UMWA organizing in, 68

Hiawatha mine: closing of, 221, 252; layoffs at, 252; mechanization and, 58; purchase by conglomerate, 180; wildcat strike at, 1955, 85; wildcat strikes at, 1968–1985, 268f; women miners at, 233, 234, 245f, 246, 251–52

Hilton, Tommy, 13, 14

Hispanics: miners, support for union, 272; population in Carbon County, 205–6. *See also* Chicano; Mexicans, ethnic

historians of unions: de-emphasis of conflict within union ranks, *xxx–xxxi*; focus on strip mining as cause of UMWA decline, 195–96; growing interest in reform efforts of 1970s, 282; role in reversing UMWA decline, 288, 289; and simplistic "good *vs.* evil" view of union struggle, *xxx, xxxi*

historical tourism, increase in, *xxiv*

Hormel meatpackers' strike (1985), *xxix*

Horse Canyon mine: Chicano support for union reform at, 211; closing of, 219; and contract negotiations in 1981, 185; mechanization and, 58; as steel company mine, 46; support for MFD at, 211; wartime hiring of inexperienced miners at, 47; wildcat strikes at, 85

Huitt, Joy: background of, 241; on bias against female miners, 234; as first woman District 22 officer, 242f, 246, 248–49; and Lady Miners of Utah, 237; on mining as career, 233–34; on nonunion women miners, problems faced by, 239; on sexual harassment of female miners, 234

Hunter power plant, *xxf*; and environmental regulation, 284–85; marriage atop (1982), 224–26; mines supplying coal to, *xxxiv*, 174; opening of, 127–29

Huntington (town), 68, 128f

Huntington Coal Co., resistance to unionization, 29

Huntington power plant, 128f; and environmental regulation, 284–85; mines supplying coal to, *xxiv, xxxiv*, 174, 278; opening of, 127–29

iconography of coal, photographs in, 224

Independent Coal and Coke, 4f, 83, 86

Independent Union of Southern Union Fuel Company, 112

Indianhead mine, 157

individualism, rise of, 278; and younger miners' entering mining after 1970, 261–63

industrial democracy, need to consider future of, *xxvii*, 288

International Brotherhood of Electrical Workers: draining of support from UMWA, 22–23; percent of US bituminous coal industry represented by, 155t

International Brotherhood of Teamsters, draining of support from UMWA, 22–23

International Construction Workers Union, percent of US bituminous coal industry represented by, 155t

International convention of UMWA, 1948, 87–88, 89

International convention of UMWA, 1973, 144f, 149, 216

International convention of UMWA, 1976, 231
International convention of UMWA, 1983, 244
International Executive Board (IEB): control of information given to members, 129–30; dismantling of rank-and-file power by, 87; District 22 revolt against ineffectiveness of, 168–69; efforts to organize small mines in 1940s, 64; election process for, 33, 88; functions of, 33; Hispanic representatives on, 212; Miller's purge of Boyle appointees to, 151–52; and organizing of western coal operators under Miller, 164; and parental leave, support for, 244; on women in mines, 229
International Labor Defense Fund, 19
International level of UMWA: officers and roles, in 1930s, 33–34; rank-and-file anger with, in 1960s, 103–4
International Union of Operation Engineers: and Big Horn Coal, struggle with UMWA to represent, 72–73, 75; draining of support from UMWA, 22–23, 150, 157–58; percent of US bituminous coal industry represented by, 155*t*; UMWA truce with (1973), 158
Interstate 70, and historical tourism, *xxiv*

Jelaco, Ann, 229–31
Jensen, Richard, 143–45, 256
Jones, Bill, 143, 169, 169*f*, 195, 271

Kaiser, Henry, 46

Kaiser Steel: Chicano support for union reform at, 211; discrimination complaint at, 214–15; Hispanics in workforce of, 205–6, 210–11, 212; longwall mining, introduction of, 207; loss of local autonomy, 95; Mexican American managers at, 207; miners' fear of filing grievances at, 60; miners of, *xlvf*; miners' support for Amax unionization efforts, 163; Utah miners employed by, 46; wartime recruiting of miners, 205; wildcat strikes, 1968–1985, 268*f*; women miners at, 233, 238; and World War II production, 46
Kayenta mine, 214
Kenilworth, decay of, *xxiv*
Kenilworth mine, 4*f*; closing of, 156; explosion in (1945), 5; mechanization and, 58; union corruption in 1950s, 90; wildcat strikes at, 85
Kennecott Copper, 102, 108
Kennedy, John F., *xxvi*
Kennedy, Thomas, 35, 37, 90, 94, 124
Kingston family, 220, 221
Kirby mine, unionization efforts at, 122–23
Kmetz, John T., 88, 95, 111, 120
Knight-Ideal mine: antiunionism of miners at, 81–82; hiring of former miners from, by antiunion operators, *xxxv*, 108–9, 118, 121; unionization efforts at, 108
Ku Klux Klan in Utah, 204
Kuzio, John, 142–43, 147, 166–67

Labor Day celebrations: in 1930s, 16*f*, 17; in 1970s, 99, 100*f*, 141; in 1972, 141, 142; in 1981, 244; in 1984,

245*f*, 246; Chicano participation in, 216; Cordova as UMWA activities chairman for, 212; meaning of, in 1930s, 17; and UMWA Coal Queen, 17, 229, 246

Labor Department: as ineffective partner in UMWA unionization efforts, 168, 171; and members' revolt against District 22 ineffectiveness, 169; UMWA leaders' overreliance on, 168

Labor Law Reform Act of 1978, 283

labor laws: reform of, as key to union recovery, 283, 287–88; as unfavorable to unions, 163

Labor-Management Reporting and Disclosure Act of 1959 (Landrum-Griffin Act), 152

ladies' auxiliaries: of National Miners Union, 227–29; of unions, purposes of, 227

ladies' auxiliary of UMWA, 225*f*, 227–29

Lady Miners of Utah (LMU), 240*f*; founding of, 237; functions of, 243; hosting of CEP national conference, 243–44; and Labor Day celebrations, 243, 244; leadership of, 242–43; longevity of, 246; move to employment outside mining, 250; social events by, 244; Socialist activists in, 267; social justice activism by, 244; support for UMWA miners and events, 243–44; and women's demands for equal opportunity, *xlv*, 222–23

Landrum-Griffin Act. *See* Labor-Management Reporting and Disclosure Act of 1959

Latuda, 9

Latuda miners, concerns about automation, 38

Lee, Faye, 237, 242–43, 245*f*

legal defenses of union rights, as time consuming and expensive, 102

legal jeopardy of illegal strikes, costs to union, 103, 150, 163, 265–66, 270–71

legal restrictions on unions: critics' failure to acknowledge, *xxxi*; as obstacle to union organizing, 105–6; sources on, *xxix*; Taft-Hartley Act and, 53, 102–3; in United States *vs.* Europe, 283; Wagner Act and, 18

Lemaster, 203–4

Lewis, A. D., 30

Lewis, John L.: Alinsky biography of, *xxi–xxii*; at American Mining Congress convention (1958), 83; and authoritarian rule in UMWA, 32–33, 95; and Big Horn Coal unionization, 74; commitment to free enterprise, consequences of, 54; and contract negotiations, 56–57, 82–83; and contract strikes, 1945–1950, 50; and declining market for coal in 1940s, need to accommodate operators in, 83; and divisions within early labor movements, 20; on efforts to organize small mines in 1940s, 66, 67–68; emphasis on contract adherence over miner autonomy, 33; and illegal strike at Sego (1940), 25–26; isolationism of 1940s, 37; lack of viable alternative to, as focus of miners' discontent, 36–37; and layoffs of older workers before retirement, 59–60; limitations of collective bargaining model of, *xxxvii*; and local UMWA officers, 35; and mechanization, support for, *xxxvii–xxxviii*, 57; miners' gratitude for wartime activism of, 48; miners' support for, *xlii*; and National Bituminous Coal Wage Agreement, negotiation of, *xxxvii*; and NMU, efforts to counter inroads in Utah by, 21; and Pension Fund establishment, 50; on poor condition in mining communities, 3; prioritization of union operators' profitability, 104; promotion of family and followers in UMWA, 32; resignation as president of CIO, 37; and strip mines, efforts to organize, 72, 76; success in raising workers' standard of living, *xxxviii*; and Sunnyside mine explosion (May, 1945), 41, 43; support for Willkie, and loss of miners' support, 36–37; and UMWA financial irregularities, 37; and union democracy reform efforts, 92, 93–94; and union elections, control of, 88; and Utah union organizing, 18; and violence in union organizing, 105; and wartime pay and benefit increases, authorization of strikes for, 47–48; and Welfare and Retirement Fund establishment, 165; and World War II, return to prominence in, 38

Linkletter, Art, 124

Lion Coal Company, 117

Little Standard Mine, abuse of miners, before unionization, 13

LMU. See Lady Miners of Utah

locals, UMWA: of District 22, 305–7; role of, in 1930s, 33

lodges, ethnic, 206–7

Logston, Don, 137–39, 145–46

longwall system: and job losses, *xlvii*; and productivity increases, *xli*, 174, 204*f*, 207, 260, *xlvf*

Love, George H., *xxxvii*, 56, 57

Madrigal, James, 123*f*, 207

Madrigal, Paul, 207, 245*f*, 256*f*

Mangus, Harry, 63*f*; defeat in 1961 district election, 34, 107; on importance of Welfare and Retirement Fund, 104; on internal union decay, 99; and Mormon challenge to UMWA, 103; on obstacles to organizing, 81, 82, 104; on rank-and-file unrest in 1960s, 103–4; and union organizing, 68; and Welfare and Retirement Fund cutbacks, 109

Manhattan Project, at Hanford Engineering Works, 70

mantrips, 3, 12*f*, 260

Maple Creek mine, UMWA organizing at, 28

Marinoni family, 101*f*, 109–11, 154, 156, 194

Martin, Houston: on burden of UMWA fees, 90; and Carbon County Miners' Executive Council, 87; and District election of 1949, 90–91; on multiple contracts types in District 22, 280–81; removal from District 22 presidency, 91; and UMWA organizing, 65, 67, 68, 69, 77

McAlpine Coal Company, 76

McArthur, Shirl, *xxxiv*, 100, 126, 127

McCulloch Oil Corporation, 180, 261

McKinley mine, unionization efforts at, 173, 272

McPhie, William, 34, 41, 50, 86

mechanization of mining: and coal dust increases, *xli*, *xlf*; continuous mining machines and, 56*f*, 57, 119, 260; as economic necessity, 57; and increased productivity, *xl*, *xli*, 56*f*, 57, 119, 174, 204*f*, 207, 260, *xlvf*; and job gains in 1980s, *xxxii*; and job losses, *xxxii*, *xxxviii*, *xlvii*, 57, 253; larger mines' relative stability during, 58; Lewis's support for, *xxxvii*–*xxxviii*, 57; and masking of audible danger signs, *xli*; and nonunion mines, good wages and safety records at, 173; and pay increases for remaining workers, 57; at Plateau Mining Co., 119; and reduction in size of mining crews, 260; and small unionized mines, demise of, 58; UMWA acceptance of, *xxxvii*–*xxxviii*, 57; and undermining of miner solidarity, *xli*. See also longwall system

Megeath mine, closing of, 31

memorial periods, as UMWA strategy, 165

Mexicans, ethnic: discrimination against, 206, 210, 219–20; in Emery County, 219; Mexican lodge in Helper, 206–7; small numbers in Utah, and greater acceptance, 207–8; and SOCIO, 207; in UMWA administration, 207; undocumented, hiring by nonunion mines, 219–21; and union work as opportunity for equal wages, 210–11; wartime work in Utah mines, 47, 203, 205; work as miners, 207, 220

MFD. *See* Miners for Democracy (MFD) movement

Mid-Continent Coal and Coke Company, 132

The Militant (SWP newspaper), 267

Miller, Arnold, 144*f*; and anti-UMWA movement (1977), 170; Boyle allies' smears of, 140; and complex politics of UMWA, 213–14; and contract for 1974, gains and lost opportunities in, 149–50; cutting of union officials' salaries, 148; daunting workload of, 215; decline in support, 168, 170, 172, 215; and District 22 issues, 136; and District 22 revolt (1976), 168; and district autonomy, support for, 152; election defeat of Boyle (1972), *xliii*, 136, 146, 256–57; enlarged District 22, effort to create, 150–51; formidable obstacles as president, 172, 173; Health and Pension Funds as intractable problem for, 279; and International Union of Operation Engineers, truce with, 158; on labor laws, 163; lack of administration experience, 212–13; Left's criticism of, 282; lukewarm Western support for, 150; and miners' fear of change, 140; on mine safety, 174; and minority members' complaints, 213, 214, 215; and operators' royalty payments, failure to raise, 172; platform of, 143; purge of Boyle IEB appointees, 151–52; and rank-and-file right to vote on contract, 149; reforms initiated by,

148–49; retirement of, *xlvi*; rewriting of UMWA constitution, 149; selection as MFD candidate, 212; and strip mining, opposition to, 150, 173, 272–73; struggle against entrenched UMWA enemies, 213; support for, in election of 1972, 143–48; and UMWA organizing, *xliv*, 154, 157–58, 160, 163–64, 172, 197; and wildcat strikes, efforts to reduce, 170, 172. *See also* Miners for Democracy (MFD) movement; UMWA organizing under Miller (1970s)

Miller, Rita, 242, 242*f*, 246, 249, 250

mine disasters: Carbon Fuel mine explosion (1963), *xl–xli*, *xl–xli*, 5; Crandall Canyon mind disaster, 284; deaths of women in, 224; Kenilworth mine explosion (1945), 5; Peerless Mine explosion (1930), 5; Sunnyside mine explosion (1952), 84. *See also* fatalities; Sunnyside mine explosion (1945); Wilberg mine, explosion at (1984)

miners. *See* coal miners

Miners for Democracy (MFD) movement: building of support from scratch, 257; Chicano support for, 211; dismantling of, after election of 1972, *xliii*, 148; and election of 1972, defeat of Boyle in, *xliii*, 136, 146, 256–57, 274; election to District 22 top offices (1977), *xliv*; founding of, 136; growing scholarly interest in, 282; impact of, as unclear, 171; increased scholarly interest in, *xxx–xxxi*; minority miners' support for, 201; platform of, 143, 153–54; problems with contract negotiations, *xliv*; racial discrimination in, 212; as response to desperate situation, 278–79; revelation of UMWA corruption, 141; revelation of Welfare and Retirement Fund shortfalls, 109; role of younger *vs.* older miners in, 257; on strip mining, 147; support for, in election of 1972, 143–48; and *United Mine Workers Journal*, 109, 141, 148–49; Wheeling conference (1972), 212; wildcat strikes called by, 270; women miners' support of, 244. *See also* democracy challenges to union leadership (1960s–70s); Miller, Arnold

Miners' Pension Protection Act, *xxvii*

Miners'-Right-to-Strike Committee, 266

The Miners' Voice, 135*f*, 147

mining, range of jobs in, 6–7

minority miners in UMWA: activist groups in union activism of 1980s, 222–23; complaints about discriminatory union treatment, 213–15; increased representation in union offices, 222; struggle for equal treatment, 201; support for MFD, 201, 211; and unions as vehicle for interracial, democratic cooperation, 202. *See also* Chicano miners; Mexicans, ethnic; Navajo miners

Moab, turn to tourism, *xxvi*

Mohrland, founding of, 9

Mohrland mine: abuse of miners, before unionization, 13; closing of, in Roosevelt Recession of 1937–38, 31

Montana, union weakness in 1970s, 146
Morgan, James: and founding of CIO, 16; and illegal strike at Sego (1940), 25–26; and strip miners, efforts to organize, 72–74; and strip mining, efforts to discourage, 70–71, 72; and union organizing at small mines, in 1940s, 66; on union organizing in economic downturns, 32
Mormon Church, and Deseret-Beehive mine, 100
Mormons: discrimination against early European migrants, 222; investors, challenges to UMWA, 103; as prounion, *xxxiv*; and UMWA politics, 107
Mountain States Machinery Company, 101*f*, 117
Ms. Foundation, 235
Murray, Richard, 25, 68, 69, 76, 93–94
Mutual, founding of, 9
Mutual mine: NMU organizing in 1930s, 20; wildcat strikes at, 28

National (town), founding of, 9
National Bituminous Coal Wage Agreement (NBCWA): for 1945, no-strike clause in, 44; for 1974, gains and lost opportunities in, 149–50; for 1978, and operators' right to fire illegally striking workers, 177, 178–79; benefits under, in 1960s, 112–13; democracy movement's protests against, *xliii*; growth of document over time, 23; and inadequacy of one-size-fits-all approach, 76, 104–5, 280–81, 289; initial agreement, protections and benefits won in, 23–24; miners' right to vote on, under Miller, 149; negotiation of, *xxxvii*; nonunion miners' resentment of, *xxxviii*; as perceived attack on small nonunion mines, *xxxviii*; production disparities and, *xli*; small mines' objections to, 114–15. *See also* contract negotiations
National Coal Policy Conference, creation of, 83
National Conference of Women Coal Miners, 239–41, 240*f*; Seventh (Price, 1985), 222, 241*f*, 244, 247
National Industrial Recovery Act of 1933, 18, 22, 288
National Labor-Management Conference (1945), 52–53
National Labor Relations Act, employers' ability to discourage unions despite, 32
National Labor Relations Board (NLRB): and firing of striking workers, 182; proemployer bias of, *xxix*; and protective-wage clause, 83; sources on, *xxix*; and UMWA unionization efforts, 113, 114, 115, 117, 118, 120, 122, 125, 132
National mine: closing of, in Roosevelt Recession of 1937–38, 31; NMU strike at (1933), 20–22
National Miners' Union (NMU): as communist-led, 10; early organizing success in Carbon County, 19, 20–21, 20*f*, 21*f*; founding of, 18; march to protest leaders' arrest, 21*f*, 22; miner strikes of 1933, 10; radicalism of, and loss of support to UMWA, 18, 22–23; strikes of

1933, 20–22; UMWA efforts to undermine, 21–22. *See also Carbon County Miner* (NMU newspaper)

National Recovery Administration: and Code of Fair Competition, failure to enforce, 29; and union grievance procedure, 24

National War Labor Board, and miner wages in World War II, 47, 48

natural gas, competition with coal, 51

Navajo miners: complaints about UMWA discrimination, 213–14; support for union, 272; unionization of, *xxxiv*; and union work as opportunity for equal wages, 211; women as, 246

Navajo strip mine, 157–58

NBCWA. *See* National Bituminous Coal Wage Agreement

neoliberal consensus, historians' role in replacing, 288

New Deal: lessons of, 287; and unions' rise, *xxiii*, 37–38, 202–3

Nieves, Robert, 218, 253

NMU. *See* National Miners' Union

nonunion mines: abuses by, 284; antiunion sentiment at, *xxxv*, *xl*–*xli*, 81–82, 101*f*, 108–9, 117–20, 139, 192, 196, 278; challenges to UMWA, in 1950s, *xxxix*; company-based unions to inoculate against, 102, 108, 112, 118–19, 121, 132, 221; competition from, and UMWA sweetheart deals to attract operators, 129; denial of jobs to union-friendly miners, 274; establishment of significant presence in 1960s–70s, 104, 106; expansion of in 1970s, as concern in District 22, 165–66; good wages and safety records of many in Utah, 284; high productivity of, *xxxiv*; improved wages and benefits to inoculate against union organizing, 102, 104, 109, 110, 119, 122, 167, 173, 197, 273–74; improvements in working conditions, and decline in union support, *xxxvi*, *xl*; miners' increasing turn to, 278; National Bituminous Coal Wage Agreement as perceived attack on, *xxxviii*; UMWA efforts to block from Utah, 107; wages after 1979, as equal or better than union salaries, 220; women miners at, 238–39. *See also* antiunion strategies of coal operators; small mines, nonunion; UMWA organizing

North American Coal, 156, 157

Nugget Coal and Timber Company, antiunion strategies at, 103

Nugget mine, and company unions, 102

Nyden, Paul, 212, 256, 257

Occupational Health and Safety Act of 1970, as product of union activism, *xxvii*

oil, competition with coal, 51–52

oil shale, short-lived replacement of mining jobs by, 275

Only One Thing Can Save Us (Geoghegan), 287–88

OPEC oil embargo, and resurgence of coal, *xxxiii*

Operation Dixie, 53

Orchard Valley mine, 247

Organization for Community, Integrity, and Opportunity. *See* SOCIO

organizing of unions. *See* UMWA organizing

overtime work: as cheaper for operators than hiring new miners, 178; compulsory, before unionization, 13

Oviatt, Rose, 233, 234

Pacific Northwest, support for MFD in, 146

Pacific Power & Light, resistance to UMWA organizing, 82

Palacios, Joe, 205, 207, 210–11

Palacios brothers, 207

parental leave, UMWA support for, 244

Park City, turn to tourism, *xxvi*

Patrick, Harry, 144*f*; and election of 1972, 136, 143–45, 148, 215

pay: average, for Utah miner, 7; and equal pay for minority workers, 210–11; high, as incentive for becoming miner, 6; increase with mechanization, 57; losses of, in strikes, 50–51, 195; at modern coal-fired power plants, *xx*; in nonunion mines. as equal or better than union salaries after 1979, 220; operators' cheating miners out of, before unionization, 11, 12–13; protections for, in first UMWA contract, 23; standardization of, in first UWMA contract, 23; of union leadership, as issue in 1972 union election, 143; for women miners, *vs.* other available employment, 232–33. *See also* National Bituminous Coal Wage Agreement (NBCWA)

Peabody Coal Company: discounted Fund royalty payments for, as practical necessity, 129; lawsuits to stop wildcat strikes, 270–71; and nonunion development work, 100; unionization efforts at, 127, 157; and wildcat strike by Navajo miners, 214

Pecorelli, Malio, 64*f*; on coal market decline in 1950s, 81; devotion to Lewis's leadership, 94; loss of IEB seat, 35, 88, 123; and UMWA organizing efforts, 102, 124

Peerless, founding of, 9

Peerless Mine: explosion in (1930), 5; illegal miners' strike, in World War II, 10; working conditions in, 3–5

Pension Fund. *See* Welfare and Retirement Fund

pensions for management at mining companies, as frequently lost, 103

Pestotnik, Louis, Jr., 11, 169, 169*f*, 185–86, 256*f*, 272

Peter Kiewitz & Sons Construction Company, 70, 71, 282

Peterson, Orwel, 26–27, 30–31

Phelps-Dodge copper strike (1983), *xxix*

Pierce, Agnes "Aggie," 233, 234, 251–52

pillars, pulling of, 3–5

Pilling, Bud, 125–26, 126*f*

Pittston Coal Company, unionization efforts at, 165

Planned Parenthood, Carbon County office, 226

Plateau Mining Company: company union at (CVWA), 108, 118–19; and contract negotiations of 1971,

190*f*, 191*f*, 192–93; formation of, 118; growth after fending off unionization, 123, 165; high wages at, to fend off union organizing, 273; hiring of antiunion minors at, *xxxv*; intimidation of union supporters at, 118–19; mechanization by, 119; and miners' bitterness over failed organizing effort, 167; as nonunion, 117; picketing of, in 1971 contract strike, 180, 181*f*, 182; picketing of, in 1977 contract strike, 182–84, 184*f*; purchase by United Nuclear Corporation, 165; purge of prounion employees, 119–20; takeover of old mining towns, 261; and UMWA blocking of nonunion coal, 107; UMWA picketing of opening of, 123*f*, 124; UMWA's timid response to management tactics, 120; underbidding of union mines, 102; unionization efforts at, 100, 101*f*, 108, 117–20, 124–25, 130, 139; women miners at, 239. *See also* Wattis mine

Pleasant Valley railroad, 8

pollution from coal-fired power plants: London deaths from (1952), *xxi*; in West, *xx*

postwar decline in coal demand: and bureaucratization of UMWA, 84; and decline in members' influence over union officials, 86–88; and declining power of wildcat strikes, 85–86; and defensive posture of UMWA, 86; and economic distress of miners, 89, 90; and fear of union overreach, 52; and financial pressure on mines, 83; and growing corruption of UMWA, 60–62, 90–91; and layoffs of older workers, 59–60; and union calls for three-day work week, 54; and union efforts to save money, 87–89; and union fees, as increasing burden, 89–90; and weakening of union power, 58, 60, 81–83

postwar period: business's effort to curb union power, 52–53; challenges faced by unions in, 52–54; contract strikes, 1945–1950, 50; as era of transition, 50; inflation in, 53; and reintegration of returning troops, 52; strike increase in many industries, 52; unprecedented union gains in, 50

Powder River Basin, connection to national rail networks, 194

power plants, modern coal-fired: Clean Air Act and, 193–94; construction near fuel sources ("coal-by-wire"), *xx*, *xxxiii*, *xxxix*, 106*f*; high-paying jobs at, *xx*; long term coal contracts preferred by, 193–94; as perceived future of coal demand, in 1970s, 193; and pollution in West, *xx*; visibility in flat Western landscape, *xix–xx*, *xxf*

power plants in mid-twentieth century, location near urban centers, *xxi*

Premium Coal Company: closing of, 154–55; number of employees, 154; underbidding of union mines, 102; unionization efforts at, 100, 108, 129, 154–56

President's Commission on Coal, 272

press, on miners' wartime strikes, 47, 48

408 | INDEX

Preston, William, 166, 170
Price: as center of Utah's coal industry, 8; decay of, *xxiv*; Labor Day parades in, 16*f*, 99; memorial to miners killed since 1884, 5–6; museum in, *xxiv*; NMU march to protest leaders' arrest (1933), 21*f*, 22; residential and occupational integration in, 202*f*; segregation in, 205; union organization in 1930s–40s, by workers other than miners, 15
Price, Danny, 108, 109, 119
Price River Coal: wildcat strikes, 1968–1985, 268*f*; women miners at, 234, 237
productivity: balance between safety and, 6–7; mechanization and, *xl, xli,* 56*f,* 57, 119, 174, 204*f,* 207, 260, *xlvf*
Professional Air Traffic Controllers Organization strike (1981), *xxix*
profits from coal industry, and increased class stratification, *xxii*
Progressive Mine Workers: efforts to drain support from UMWA, 22–23; percent of US bituminous coal industry represented by, 155*t*
protective-wage clause in UMWA contract for 1958, 83
Provo, steel smelter at, 46
punishments, unwarranted: prohibition on, in UMWA contract, 7; before unionization, 11. *See also* firings, unwarranted; work assignments, punitive

race and ethnicity: of Carbon County residents, 205–6; of miners in Utah, 203, 205; wartime influx of African Americans and ethnic Mexicans, 47, 203, 205
racial and ethnic discrimination: ethnic Mexicans' experiences of, 206, 210, 219–20; at Kaiser (1970s), UMWA's weak response to, 214–15; in Miners for Democracy movement, 212; in UMWA, 212–13, 222; UMWA resolution against at founding convention, 201; and union work as opportunity for equal wages, 210–11
racial attitudes of Utah miners: in 1970s–80s, 203; Ku Klux Klan activity, 204; lynchings, 204–5; minstrel shows, 1938–1970, 203
Radalj, Tony, 31, 35–36
Rains, founding of, 9
Rains Mine, 12, 90
Rampton, Calvin, 99, 107, 134, 207, 208, 210
rank-and-file members of UMWA: declining power of, in 1940s–50s, 86–88; different perspective from union officers, as frequent source of friction, 26; rebellions of long 1970s, historians' de-emphasis of, *xxx*
Reconstruction Finance Corporation, 27
recreation of miners, younger miners' individualistic forms of, 262–63
redistribution of wealth, redistribution of power necessary for, 287
Reliance mine, 86, 92
Republican Party: control of Congress after 1946 election, 53; and postwar restrictions on unions, 53
right-to-work laws, costs to unions of, *xxix*

right-to-work rhetoric of antiunion miners, 278
roads, development, and mines' ability to hire commuter miners, 275
Roche, Josephine, 37, 56–57
Rock Springs Daily Rocket, 36, 230
Rocky Mountain Fuel Company, 37
Rocky Mountain Power, *xxiv–xxv*
Roncco mine, 82
room-and-pillar mining method, in Soldier Creek–Soldier Canyon Mine, 55*f*
Roosevelt, Franklin D.: and Lewis's endorsement of Willkie, 36–37; and unions, support of, 18, 22, 288
Roosevelt Recession of 1937–38: mine closings in, 31–32; and mine unionization efforts, 31
Rosebud Sales Corporation, 157
Ross, John, 28, 30, 34–35
Ross, Mike, 254–56
Roybal, Frank Jr., 216, 251
Roybal, Frank Sr., 123*f*; and district election of 1973, 152–53, 168, 211; and district election of 1977, 169, 169*f*; as IEB member, 169; and Stevenson, 130; support for Boyle administration, 142

Sacco, Frank J., 64*f*, 123*f*; background of, 107–8; on benefits of union contract, 112–13; break with Boyle administration, 130–32; conflict with Stevenson, 130, 152; exposure of union corruption, 142, 213; on MFD revelations to miners, 141; Miller appointment as IEB member, 152; on miners' fear of filing complaints, 60; and organizing in 1960s–70s, 100, 108–9, 111–14, 120–21, 125–26; organizing under Miller administration (1973), 154, 157, 171, 278; on rank-and-file's lack of information, 59; resignation of, 132, 142; on Stevenson's poor performance, 130; support for Boyle administration, 141–42; and sweetheart deals, exposure of, 131; transfer to District 15, 132; turn to MFD organizing, *xliii*, 132, 142–43
safety: balance between productivity and, 6–7; coal dust, control of, 6; improvements in, after unionization, 15; maintaining roof integrity, 7; mechanization and, 173; modern nonunion mines' good record in Utah, 284; relative safety of strip mining, and diminished need for unions, 195; rock dusting of flammable walls, 40; wildcat strikes to address, in 1930s and 40s, 24–26. *See also* fatalities; mine disasters
safety committees: grievance procedure and, 24; introduction in first UMWA contract, 15, 23; power and limitations of, 23–24
safety regulations, UMWA efforts to force small mines' compliance with, 30–31
Salina mine, unionization efforts at, 28, 69, 139
Salt Lake Telegram, expose of union authoritarianism published in, 92–93
Salt Lake Tribune, 37, 202*f*
Savage Brothers trucking firm, 174
Save Our Cumberland Mountains, 235

Seagull mine, 61*f*
Sego Mine, illegal miners' strike (1940), 10, 25–26
self-organization of workers, modern lack of, *xxix*
Seltzer, Curtis, *xxxi*, *xlii*, 105, 141, 270
seniority protections: coal operators' objections to, 114; need for contractual definition of, 23; strikes against violations of, in 1940s–50s, 85–86; UMWA introduction of, 14–15; and women's job losses in 1980s, 247
Service Employees International Union, 222
Sevier County, UMWA strength in 1970s, 99
Sevier Valley Coal Company, UMWA organizing at, 28
sex discrimination by federal contractors, Executive Order prohibiting, 235
Sharon Steel Company, 180
Sherman Antitrust Act, UMWA and, *xxxix*
Skyline mine: hiring from diverse geographical areas, as antiunion strategy, 274–75; pay at, as antiunion strategy, 273–74; screening of workers to avoid union sympathizers, 274; unionization efforts at, 196–97
small mines, nonunion: coal production in Carbon and Emery counties, in 1945, 62; Code of Fair Competition, failure to observe, 29; exemption from safety regulations before 1970, *xxxviii*; fluctuations in workforce size, 31; and heavy burden of union fees, 88–89; interest in unionization, as sporadic, 110–11; miners' use of unionization threat in negotiations, 111; National Bituminous Coal Wage Agreement as perceived attack on, *xxxviii*; number of, 31; opposition to one-size-fits-all UMWA contracts, 104–5; resistance to unionization, 28; as threat to union gains, 105, 111; UMWA efforts to enforce mining standards on, 29–31; union-avoidance strategies of, *xxxii*. *See also* UMWA organizing at small mines
Smith, Andrew J., 152, 169, 279–80
social inequality, political danger of, *xxvii*
Socialist Workers Party (SWP): mine activism of 1970s, 266–67; remnant still in operation, 267
Sociedad Mexicana de Cuauhtemoc, 206–7
SOCIO (Spanish-Speaking Organization for Community, Integrity, and Opportunity): acceptance into Utah society, 207–8; activities and activism of, 208–10, 209*f*, 211–12, 216–17, 218; in Carbon County, 210; and Chicano demands for equal opportunity, *xlv*; conflict between multiple roles of, 217–18; disbanding of, 216; founding of, 207; in Labor Day parade (1984), 216; membership in 1980s, 216
Soldier Canyon Mine, unionization efforts at, 100, 101*f*, 108, 109–11
Soldier Creek mine, 110*f*; and contract strike of 1977–1978, 181–82; mining methods, 196; picketing

of, in 1977 contract strike, 183, 183*f*, 184; reopening in 1970s, *xxxiv*, 165–66, 194; sale to California Portland Cement, 165, 194; unionization efforts at, 167, 194–96

Soldier Creek–Soldier Canyon Mine, room-and-pillar method in, 55*f*

solidarity among miners: introduction of women miners and, 227; mechanization and, *xli*. *See also* dissension within UMWA

solidarity among miners, east-west rift in: and anti-UMWA organizing, 271–72; Clean Air Act coal sulfur-content provisions and, 193–94; development of, in 1981 contract negotiations, 185–86

Southern Labor Union, percent of US bituminous coal industry represented by, 155*t*

Southern Utah Fuel Company (SUFCO), 100, 111; mine, unionization efforts at, 101*f*; and pay rates designed to fend off unionization, 273–74; women miners at, 238

Southern Utah Fuel Company mine (near Salina Canyon): retaliations against union organizers, 116–17; strike at, 115–16; unionization efforts at, 111–17

Spanish-Speaking Organization for Community, Integrity, and Opportunity. *See* SOCIO

Spring Canyon: African Americans in, 203; Depression-era struggles in, 27; founding of, 9; student strike in (1939), 15–16

Spring Canyon mine: miners' complaints about District salaries, 35; miners concerns about automation, 38; NMU strike at (1933), 20–22; purchase by Braztah conglomerate, 180; wildcat strike, in World War II, 10; and younger miners of 1970s, 259

Spring Glen, NMU organizing in 1930s, 19

Standardville: decay of, *xxiv*; Depression-era struggles in, 27–28; founding of, 9

Standardville miners: concerns about automation, 38; opposition to Lewis's support of Willkie, 36–37

Stansbury mine, 164

Star Point Coal Company, UMWA organizing efforts at, 80

State Chicano Unity Conferences, 211–12

steel industry: use of coal in, 6; in Utah, company towns, 8–9

steel industry, captive mines of: fewer postwar layoffs at, 54, 205; stronger economic viability of, 83

Steel Workers Fight Back movement, *xxx*

Stevenson, Frank M., 63*f*, 123*f*; accusations of corruption against, 145; Baker on, 117–18; conflict with Sacco, 130, 152; and contract strike of 1971, 182; and District 22 election of 1973, 152–53; effectiveness as union official, 171; fielding of miners' complaints by, 139; and financial irregularities at Local 9958, 95; firing by Miller, 151–52; MFD challenger for IEB seat in 1972, 211; and minority members' complaints, 214; misuse of funds by, 130; and nonunion mines, efforts to block, 107; on obstacles to organizing, 102; and organizing in 1960s–70s, 35, 100, 104, 109, 113–18, 120–23, 124–25, 127, 129; organizing under Miller, 162, 215; Sacco's criticism of, 130; support for Boyle administration, 141, 142

strikes: during contract negotiations, lack of, 1951–1971, 57; costs to union, 25; customers' preference for stable nonunion coal sources and, 197; frequency of, damage to UMWA western recruitment efforts, 167; high cost to miners, 50–51; increasing rancor of, with decline in UMWA influence, 197; miners' suffering in, 193; pay lost in, as obstacle to unionization efforts, 195; picketing of non-union operations, as illegal under Taft-Hartley, 103; prohibition on, in first UMWA contract, 24–25; and public resentment of unions, xl, 47, 48, 50, 52; small number before World War II, 25–26; threat of, as negotiating tool in 1930s, 25; in UMWA organizing efforts in 1960s–70s, 115–16; UMWA reluctance to use, in organizing of 1960s, 124–25; and weakening of consumers' faith in coal, 51

strikes in 1968, contract strike, 125–26

strikes in 1970s–80s, declining effectiveness of, 177–85; and increasing length and divisiveness of strikes, 182, 273; judicial suppression of pickets and, 184; mine ownership by large conglomerates and, 179–80, 179*f*; operators' right to fire wildcat strikers and, 177, 178–79, 182; and turn to violence and threats, 179, 181–85, 183*f*; and violence, erosion of public sympathy by, 179, 185; weakening of union power through, 182

strikes in 1971, contract strike, 180, 181*f*, 182

strikes in 1974, contract strike, 149–50, 180, 211

strikes in 1977–78, contract strikes, 170, 180–84, 183*f*, 193

strikes in 1980s, union defeats in, *xxix*

strikes in 1981, contract strike, 184–85

strikes in 1984, selective contract strikes against companies not signing interim agreements, 186–92

strikes in 1939, contract strike, 26–27

strikes in 1940s: benefits won in, 7–8, 50; contract strike, 1949, 54–56; contract strikes, 1945–1950, 50; fines for, 50–51; and union power, *xxiii*; violence against nonunion producers during, 54–56, 80

strikes, illegal (wildcat): 1901–1933, 10; in 1930s, to address safety, 24–25; in 1940s, 25–26; 1945–1956, 84–86; in 1950s, declining effectiveness of, 85; in 1970s, decreasing ineffectiveness of, 177, 178–79, 265, 265*f*, 267; in 1970s, heavy union legal fees and fines for, 150, 163, 265–66, 270–71; in 1970s, nationwide spread of August strikes, 270–71; anti-injunction strikes of 1975–76, 265; black-lung strike of 1969, *xliii*, 270, 283; company-specific conditions as cause of, 267, 268*f*; costs to union, 103,

150, 163, 265–66, 270–71; damage to Health and Retirement Funds from, 265; employers' right to sue union for, under Taft-Hartley, 103; under first UMWA contract, 24–25; inadequate grievance resolution as catalyst for, 265; ineffectiveness of, by 1980s, 177*f*; mandays lost to, 1965–1979, 264*f*, 270; by MFD, 270; Miller's efforts to reduce, 170, 172; by Navajo miners (1975), 214; operators' provoking of, as strategy, 265; operators' right to fire, after 1978 contract, 177, 178–79, 182; over Wilberg mine safety violations, 176, 177*f*, 178–79; as potential strategy in organizing western mines, 165; reasons for, 1968–1985, 269*f*, 270, 272; reasons for, in eastern *vs.* western mines, 270; Sunnyside mine explosion and, 40–45; Supreme Court ruling on fines for, 265; UMWA history of bearing fines for, 165; and Welfare and Pension Fund shortfalls, 170

strip mines, 69–74; and decline of UMWA influence, 195–96; discounted Fund royalty payments for, as practical necessity, 129, 131–32; larger and cheaper output *vs.* underground mines, *xxxiii–xxxiv*, 70; low cost of coal produced by, 161*f*; MFD view on, 147; Miller's opposition to, 150, 173, 272–73; miners' resentment of royalty payments to health and retirement funds, 273; nonunion, increase in 1970s, 168; one-size-fits-all contract as problem for, 76, 280–81; percentage of national coal production (1980), 277; postwar rise of, 70; and potential for massive job losses in mining, *xxxiv*, 71; rapid growth in West, 160*f*, 162; relative safety of, and diminished need for unions, 195; UMWA efforts to close, 70–72; Utah geography as barrier to, 76; Utah restrictions on, *xxxiv*; in West, epicenter of, 168; in Wyoming, women miners in, 237–38

strip mines, UMWA organizing at, *xxxiv*, 70, 72–74, 157–58; and appropriate contract, difficulty of developing, 76, 280; importance to UMWA, 160, 160*f*; under Miller (1970s), 160–65; obstacles to, 72–73, 76; struggles once established, 74–76; successes, 74

Stump Flat Coal Company, and UMWA efforts to force small mines' compliance with safety regulations, 30–31

"Sub-bituminous and Lignite Agreement" (1968), 131–32

SUFCO. *See* Southern Utah Fuel Company

sulfur content: and cost of coal processing, *xxv*; legal restrictions on, and District 22 producers, *xxxiii*

Sun Advocate (Price newspaper): on 1949 contract strikes, 54; antiunion letters in (1977), 193; on contract negotiations of 1971, 190*f*, 191*f*; on contract negotiations of 1981, 185; criticisms of Boyle administration, 141; editorial questioning UMWA (1945), 52; and election of 1972, 144*f*; on

European-style unions, 288; on Labor Day celebration of 1937, 17; on mechanization costs for small mines, 58; minstrel shows advertised in, 203; and rank-and-file knowledge of UMWA organizing, 64; Sacco's letter of resignation in, 142; on secretaries' picketing of District 22 offices, 230; and Socialist Workers Party events, 266; SOCIO members' letters to, 210; and Soldier Creek mine unionization effort, 195; Statehood Day celebration, 1975, 208; on UMWA Pension Fund, financial trouble of, 280; on UMWA reputation, 167; Utah Fuel antistrike ad in, 44; on Vietnam War, 226; on Wilberg mine strikes, 177f, 179

Sundance Mine, 157, 211

Sundance Oil Company, 119

Sunnyside: ca. 1950s, 42f; founding of, 8; large African American community in, 203; as still existing in 1971, 261

Sunnyside mine, 61f; closings of, 219; continuous mining machine at, 56f; explosion at (1952), 84; Kaiser leasing of, in World War II, 46; Kaiser postwar purchase of, 46; known flammable gas issue in, 46; loss of local autonomy, 95; mechanization and, 58; metallurgical coal in, 8–9; miners' criticisms of Kennedy, 94; relative postwar prosperity as steel company mine, 46; union corruption in 1950s, 90; wartime hiring of inexperienced miners at, 47; wildcat strikes, 1945–1952, 84–86

Sunnyside mine explosion (1945), 5, 39–40; finding of company negligence in, 41; miners' safety-related strikes following, 40–45; number killed in, 40, 46; and struggle for control of workplace, 44–45

Sun Valley mine: closing of, 123; debts of, 115; unionization efforts at, 101f, 111–15

supervisors, ineligibility for union membership, under Taft-Hartley Act, 102–3

Supreme Court, *Boys Markets* ruling (1970), 265

Susie mine, closing of, 31

Sweet mine, closing of, 58

Sweets, founding of, 9

Sweets mine: illegal miners' strike (1940), 25; miners' complaints about District salaries, 35; NMU strike at (1933), 20–22; protests against union dues, 90

Swisher, Ura, *xxxv*, 101f, 108, 120–22, 259–60

Swisher Coal: company-based union at (GCWA), 121, 122; growth after fending off unionization, 123, 165; and miners' bitterness over failed organizing effort, 167; picketing of, in 1971 contract strike, 180; purchase by General Exploration Company, 165; takeover of old mining towns, 261; and UMWA blocking of nonunion coal, 107; underbidding of union mines, 102; unionization efforts at, 120–22, 125–26, 139, 272

Swisher mine: picketing of, in 1977 contract strike, 183, 183f; unionization efforts at, 100, 101f, 108–9,

130

SWP. *See* Socialist Workers Party

Taft-Hartley Act, crippling of union organizing by, 53, 102–3

T and K Coal Company, 35

Teamsters for a Democratic Union, *xxx*

Tennessee Valley Authority (TVA) coal contracts: and federal laws on sex discrimination, 235; undercutting of UMWA by, 105

Thayn, Alonzo, 108–9, 121–22

Tibbs, Don V., 114, 115, 183–84

Trail Mountain mine, and contract strikes of 1977–1978, 181

Trbovich, Mike, 136, 144*f*, 163, 164, 213

Truck mines. *See* small mines

Truman, Harry S.: and atomic bombing of Japan, 52; and election of 1946, 53; and National Labor-Management Conference (1945), 52–53; and postwar inflation, 53; and UMWA contract negotiations in 1950, 56

Trumka, Richard: and contract negotiations for 1984, 186, 281; on women miners, 240–41

Trump, Donald: 2016 victory in Carbon and Emery Counties, 284, 285; and potential revival of mining jobs, 285, 286; and Utah progressive tradition, 286

Twelve Mile Coal Company, UMWA organizing at, 28

UMWA (United Mine Workers of America): administrative structure, in 1930s, 33–34; anticipated boom of 1980s, *xlvi–xlvii*; antidiscrimination resolution passed at founding convention, 201; benefits won by, 7; bureaucratization of, and decline in accountability and transparency, 84, 96; and Carbon County Central Labor Union, 16; challenges to, in 1950's Appalachia, *xxxviii–xxxix*; control over districts, 32, 84, 94, 95; current membership, 277–78; decline of rank-and-file miners' power within, 86–88; difficult position of, in 1980s, *xxxvi*; drop in membership since 1980, 277–78; image of strength in 1970s, 99; importance in union movement, *xxxii*; International staff turmoil in 1970s, *xliv*; miners' sense of relief under protections of, 14–15; as model for unionization in other industries, 8; and nonunion western coal, as threat, *xlv*, 105, 111; officers' postwar distancing from rank-and-file members, 60; organization of workers outside coal industry, 63–64, 83–84; peak influence in 1940s, 38; percentage of miners represented by (1980), 277; percentage of tonnage represented by (1980), 277; percentage of US bituminous coal industry represented by, 155*t*; policies in 1950s–60s, as root of internal democracy challenges of 1970s, *xxxvii–xlii*; relations with CEP, 238, 239–40; strong worker support in early twentieth century, *xxii*; unique features of US unions as source of obstacles faced by, 38;

and women miners, integration into, 239–41

UMWA decline: since 1980s, as ongoing, 197, 277; as catalyst for further decline, 197; collapse of miners' support, reasons for, *xxxii–xxxvi*; constraints on growth after 1970s, *xxix*; cost of Welfare and Retirement Fund as factor in, 277–78; generational conflict after 1970 and, 272; high miner unemployment and, *xxxii, xxxv, xlviii*, 106; historians' focus on strip mining as cause of, 195–96; historical context necessary for, 8; inevitability of, with incomplete coal industry unionization, 276–77; interacting factors driving, *xxxiv–xxxv*, 132–33; and last union mine in Utah, *xxiv–xxv*, 278; limitations of UMWA model and, 8; and miners' turn to nonunion employers, 278; and organizing failures as blow to reputation, 156, 164, 165, 167, 278, 281–82; postwar weakening of power and, 60; rise of strip mining and, 277; as surprising, 8. *See also* unions' decline

UMWA decline reversal, strategies for: European-style healthcare as, 281; European-style unions as, 288; Johnson on, 277; need for alternative to collective bargaining in, 287; need for focus on government reform rather than individual companies, 283, 287; role of historical narrative in, 288, 289; role of rank-and-file democracy in, 286–87

UMWA dues and fees: as heavy burden on small mines, 88–89; protests against, with declining benefits, 89–90. *See also* Welfare and Retirement Fund

UMWA founding, 7; coal operators' cooperation with, 18–19; ease of, before government involvement, 18; radicalism of competing NMU and, 18, 22–23

UMWA leadership: factionalism in, effect on members, 215; isolation from rank-and-file miners, 135*f*; pay and benefits of, as issue in 1972 union election, 143. *See also* authoritarianism of UMWA leadership; democracy challenges to union leadership

UMWA organizing: in 2003–2005, 219*f*, 220, 221; after 1980, as difficult uphill battle, 282; cooperation with civil rights activists, in twenty-first century, 220, 245*f*; difficulty of, in economic downturns, 33; ethnic division as factor in, *xliv–xlv*; failures as fuel for antiunion sentiment, 156, 164, 165, 167, 278, 281–82; failures in 1970s–80s, reasons for, *xxxii–xxxvi, xlii*; and firing of organizers and sympathizers, 14, 25, 60, 74–75, 77, 85, 113, 114, 118, 125, 216, 221, 265*f*, 278, 282; ineffective grievance procedure as obstacle to, 215, 264–65; initial success in 1930s, reasons for, 17–19; Miller's criticisms of, 154; modern costs of, as prohibitive, *xxix*; and need to sell younger miners on union, 253, 254, 263–64; one-size-fits-all contract as obstacle to, 76, 104–5, 280–81,

289; plans to organize in west, in 1980s, *xlvi*; pressure on organizers to obfuscate union problems, 129–30; provisions protecting organizers in first UMWA contract, 23; relative ease of, before 1960s, 8; systemic constraints on, 283; Taft-Hartley Act's crippling of, 53, 102–3; taint of fund-driven motives as obstacle to, 279–80; in twenty-first century, 222; unlikely success of, in any scenario, 277; younger miners' lack of union identification and, *xxxv*, 253, 254, 259–60, 264, 272. *See also* strip mines, UMWA organizing at

UMWA organizing at small mines, in 1930s, 26–27, 28–29, 31–32

UMWA organizing at small mines, in 1940s, 62–69, 78*f*, 95–96; conflicts between organizers and, 68–69; and difficulty getting contracts, 62, 65, 68, 69; District 22's distraction with other projects, 63–64; and issue of suitable union contract, 61*f*; leaflet used in, 78*f*; miners' minimal interest in, 65; motives for, 62; obstacles to, 66–69, 76–77, 79*f*; operators' strategies to undercut, 62–64, 68, 96; rank-and-files' lack of information on, 64–65; seasonal mine workers and, 66–67; small successes in, 65

UMWA organizing at small mines, in 1950s, 77–82; and difficulty getting contracts, 77, 81, 82; failure to stem rise of nonunion mines, 104, 106; obstacles to, 81–83, 105–6; operators' strategies to undercut, 80–81, 82; and risks to miners supporting union, 81; Taft-Hartley Act and, 103; violence in, 105–6

UMWA organizing at small mines in 1960s–70s, *xxxix*, 100–102, 101*f*, 111–18; antiunion miners and, 108; and bitterness of miners caught in failed unionization efforts, 133; class antagonisms and, 107; coal operators' opposition to, *xxxix*, 100; cost of Welfare and Retirement Fund as liability in, 117; cuts to Welfare and Retirement Fund as liability in, 108–9; factors in miners' resistance to, 112; and flaws in UMWA model, 104–5; ineffectiveness of, and miners' withdrawal, 116–17, 120, 122; initial successes of, *xxxix*; long-term effects of failures in, 123–24; multiple factors in failures of, 132–33; National Labor Relations Board as ineffective ally in, 113, 114, 115, 117, 118, 120, 122, 125, 132; obstacles to, 102–3; and operators' delaying tactics, 113–14, 115, 117, 127; operators' opposition to, 117–18; operators' strategies against, 102–4, 107, 113–15, 117–22, 118, 125, 132; poor UMWA strategy and, 132; purges of prounion employees, 119–20; rank-and-file complaints about, 139; reluctance to use rank-and-file activism in, 124–26, 130; strikes in, 115–16, 117; Taft-Hartley Act and, 102–3; and top-down organizing strategy, limited success of, 124–27; UMWA corruption as obstacle to, 107; UMWA internal conflict and, 103–4; UMWA lack of tenacity and, 122–23; and undercutting of prices by small mines, 102; and union turn to defensive posture, 129; and worker intimidation, 118–19

UMWA organizing under Miller (1970s), 153–68, 157f; and anti-unionism, ascendancy of, 196; difficulty in getting signed contracts, 171; dissatisfaction among UMWA miners as obstacle to, 158–60; failure to mobilize sufficient pressure in, 172; few options available for, 282; growth of western production and, 153–54, 158–60, 159f; IEB budget cuts as obstacle for, 167; Labor Department as ineffective partner in, 168, 171; lack of communication with rank-and-file members about, 166; and lack of substantial benefits to offer nonunion miners, 172–73, 195, 196–97, 281; Left's criticism of, 282; limits of legal options in, 171–72; miners' aversion to UMWA corruption and, 153–54; potential alternative strategies for, 165, 172; as priority, 153–54; problems faced by, 166–68; rapid growth in nonunion strip mines and, 157–58; and strip mine organizing, importance of, 160, 160f; and strip mine organizing, poor success in, 160–65; struggle to find working formula for, 278; successes in, 157; unlikeliness of success in, in any scenario, 277; Welfare and Pension Fund cuts as obstacle for, 170; and Western Surface Agreement, 160–61, 162

UMWA organizing under Miller, failures in, 194–97; as beginning of long decline, 197; as product of factors beyond union control, 282; reputation damage from, 156, 164, 165, 167, 278, 281–82; strip mines and, 161–65; union factionalism spurred by, 163–64, 166, 172

undocumented migrants: hiring by nonunion mines, 219–21; UMWA efforts to organize, 221–22

unemployed miners: laid-off, UMWA denial of financial assistance to, 86; large pool available for work, 1950–1970, 253; UMWA payments to, 156

unemployment, high: in 1950s, 86, 89; and collapse of worker support for unions, *xxxii*, *xxxv*, *xlviii*, 106; as damper on Coal Employment Project, 247, 248, 252; and decline in number of women miners, 252; and decrease in union leverage, 177–78, 186; and defensive posture of UMWA, 86; as issue in 2016 election, 285–86; job looses 1950–1970, 253; in late 1970s–80s, 177–78, 186, 274–75; and miners' inability to find other work, 275; and operators' denial of work to union sympathizers, 81, 82, 274. *See also* employment for miners

union membership (private sector), in 2015, *xxxvii*

union organizing: in Carbon County, in 1930s–40s, by workers other than miners, 15–16, 17; growth of, in World War II, 38; simplicity of, before government involvement,

18; in US bituminous coal industry, by union and mine type, 155*t*. *See also* UMWA organizing

Union Pacific Coal Company, Wright's secret agreement with, 91

unions: accomplishments of twentieth century, *xxvii*; American model of, as source of UMWA decline, 38; company-based, as operators' alternative to UMWA, 102, 108, 112, 118–19. 121, 132, 221; failed efforts at revival of, *xxviii–xxix*; legalization of, *xxiii*; legalization of, and greater complexity of organizing, 18; and lifting of workers into middle class, *xxvii*; long struggle for recognition, *xxii*; for miners, development of, *xxii*; rise of, and unique New Deal environment, *xxiii*, 37–38; running as profit-based business, *xxix*, 283; strong worker support in mid-twentieth century, *xxiii*; as vehicle for interracial, democratic cooperation, 202; as vehicle for marginalized citizens to exercise democratic power, 203

unions' decline: economic and political consequences of, *xxxi*; need for frank exploration of, *xxx–xxxii*; role of rank-and-file rebellions in, *xxx*; union sins and inadequacies as factor in, *xxviii*; unions' transformation and, *xxxvii*; as unmatched in other industrialized countries, *xxix–xxx*. *See also* UMWA decline

unions in United States: as alternative to welfare state, 288; constraints on, *vs.* European-style unions, 283; flawed structure of, 38; need for emulation of European-style unions, 288; as product of New Deal government action, 288. *See also* collective bargaining in US

United Autoworkers, rank-and-file unrest in, *xxxi*

United Mine Workers Journal: Boyle's control of, 124, 126; on Co-op mine unionization efforts, 221, 282; Miners for Democracy as court-ordered half editor of, 109, 141; on postwar decline in coal demand, 54; reforms under Miller administration, 148–49; and revolt against District 22 ineffectiveness, 168; *Sun Advocate* criticisms of, 141; on UMWA reputation, 167; on UMWA western recruitment, 160–61; on women miners, introduction of, 231; on young miners' lack of interest in union, 264

United Mine Workers of America. *See* UMWA

United Nuclear Corporation, 165

United States Fuel, 14

United Steelworkers, and Steel Workers Fight Back movement, *xxx*

uranium mining, short-lived replacement of mining jobs by, 275

US Steel: wildcat strikes at mines of, 1968–1985, 268*f*; and World War II production, 45–46

Utah: last UMWA mine in, *xxiv*, *xxv*, 278; miner layoffs in 1980s, 247; minority ombudsman position, creation of, 208; Policy Advisory Council on Spanish Speaking Affairs, 210; projected job increases in

1980s, 247, 248; UMWA strength in 1970s, 99
Utah Coal Operators' Association, 85
Utah coal production: 1925–1955, 49*t*; in 1969, 99; in World War II, 45–47, 50
Utah Fuel: company towns of, 8; as subsidiary of Denver & Rio Grande Western Railroad, 8; and Sunnyside mine explosion, 40–45
Utah Industrial Commission: and Sunnyside mine explosion (1945), 41; and UMWA efforts to force small mines' compliance with safety regulations, 30
Utah International, 157
Utah Labor Relations Board, and unionization efforts, 113
Utah Power & Light (UP&L): Castle Gate power plant, *xxxix*, 106*f*; Castle Valley Mining, purchase of, 126–27; hiring of female electrical worker (1976), 227; Huntington power plant, 128*f*; and UMWA blocking of nonunion coal, 107. *See also* Hunter power plant; Huntington power plant
Utah residents: fear of environmental regulations' impact on jobs, 284–86; perception of government as anticoal, 285; turn from Democratic Party in 2016 election, *xxv–xxvi*, 284–86
Utility Workers of America, 155*t*

Vail mine, unionization of, 31
Valley Camp Coal, 180
Vietnam War, Utah views on, 226
violence against nonunion producers: in strike of 1940s, 54–56, 80; in strike of 1956, 80
violence in strikes of 1970s–80s, 179, 181–85, 183*f*; and erosion of public sympathy, 179, 185
violence in union organizing, 120; moral effect on union leaders, 105–6
violent union disputes, as primarily defensive confrontations, *xxii–xxiii*

wages. *see* pay
Wagner Act (1935), 18
Wagon-Truck mines. *See* small mines
Wall Street Journal, 109, 139
Walters, Sherri, 224–26
War Manpower Commission, and Sunnyside mine explosion (May, 1945), 41
Washington State, collapse of coal industry in, 146
Wattis: closing of, 261; Depression-era struggles in, 27; founding of, 9
Wattis mine: miners' complaints about UMWA financial irregularities, 37; miners' protests against union dues, 90; reopening under Plateau Mining Company, *xxxiv*, 117
wealth inequality, political danger of, *xxvii*
Welfare and Retirement Fund: breakup into separate company funds (1978), 170, 193; changes to, as politically difficult, 277; chronic underfunding of, 89; control of union members through, 35; eligibility requirements for, 50, 51; establishment of, 7–8, 50; imperfections in coverage, 51, 89; importance to union attractiveness,

104; introduction of deductibles, controversy caused by, 169–70, 193; and layoffs of older workers before retirement, 59–60; as less attractive to younger miners, 109–10; Miners for Democracy revelation of shortfalls in, 109; miners' gratitude to Lewis for, 50; Miners' Pension Protection Act and, *xxvii*; nonunion operators' company-based replacements for, 102, 104, 109, 110, 119, 122; opaque management of, as source of miner's resentment, 51; resentment caused by breakup of, 193; Roche as trustee of, 56–57; as selling point in unionization, 112–13; separation into four Health and Retirement Funds, 149; strike necessary to win, 165; sweetheart deals allowing reduced producer payments to, as necessary in competitive environment of 1960s–70s, 129, 131–32; underfunding of, rank-and-file outrage at, 129; union concessions on, at Deer Creek mine, *xxv*; union prioritization of union operators' profitability over, 104. *See also Blankenship v. Boyle* (1972); healthcare system

Welfare and Retirement Fund, cost of: as factor in union decline, 277–78; and insolvency with coal industry decline, *xxvii*; to operators, as issue in contract negotiations in 1984, 187–92; to operators, as obstacle to securing UMWA contracts, 117, 120, 156, 162, 173; to union members, as obstacle to union organizing, 80, 173, 272

Welfare and Retirement Fund, cuts in eligibility or benefits: as liability in organizing efforts, 108–9, 281–82; members' anger at, 104, 107, 108–9, 257

Welfare and Retirement Fund, denial of benefits by, 51, 89; fund managers' perspective on, 139–40; as issue in union election of 1972, 143, 145; members' complaints about, 136–39

Welfare and Retirement Fund, royalty-based funding of, 50; royalty increase in 1950 contract, 56–57; royalty increase in 1956 contract, 80; as untenable system, 279–80

welfare state: unions in US as alternative to, 288; weakness in US, as factor in union weakness, 283

Wellington, union organization in 1930s–40s, by workers other than miners, 15

western coal production: in 1969, 153; growth potential for, 153–54

Western European coal mines, postwar nationalization of, 54

Western Surface Agreement, 160–61, 162

West Ridge mine, 284

West Virginia, wildcat strikes for Black Lung Disease compensation, *xliii*

Wilberg mine: advanced longwall equipment at, 174; efforts to unionize, in 1960s, 127; as Emery Mining property, 187; explosion at (1984), 174–77, 175*f*, 224, 243–44; growth in 1970s, *xxxiv*; labor unrest in 1970s, 267; multiple known safety violations at, 176–77; So-

cialist Workers Party activists in, 266; wildcat strikes over safety violations at, 176, 177*f*, 178–79
Williams, Jim, 224–26
Willow Creek Coal Company mine, UMWA organizing at, 28
Winton mine, Edmundson's autonomy movement and, 92
women: Chicana, work and daycare issues for, 216–17; complex relationship with UMWA, 231; economically independent, increasing numbers in 1980s, 225–26; and gender stereotypes, 217; mine work in World War II, 229; and school dress code debate, Carbon and Emery counties (1972), 226–27; UMWA secretaries' picketing against unjustified firing, 228*f*, 229–31. *see also* gender roles
women miners: activism for separate bathrooms and showers, 234; collapse of mine employment and, 252; collective action by, 237; concerns about husband-stealing by, 232; court judgments requiring hiring of, 236; deaths in mine disasters, 224; deemphasis of sexual differences by, 237–38; demands for equal opportunity by, *xliv*, 222–23; discrimination against, 247–48; eventual acceptance of, 243; first in Utah, 233; first women district officers in District 22, 242*f*, 246; hiring of, in 1970s–80s, 248; history of, in British coal mines, 252; introduction in 1970s, 227, 231; job losses in 1980s and, 247; legal actions by, backlash against, 250–52; linking of work to care of families, 233–34; male miners' contesting of presence, 227, 231, 233, 234, 242–43; miners' wives' criticisms of, 232; at nonunion mines, 238–39; obstacles faced by, 231–32; pay, *vs.* other available employment, 232–33; as politically active, 252; range of political views in, 237; and sexual harassment, 232, 234, 251; small number initially hired, 233; support for MFD, 244; undermining of male miners' mystique by, 227; *United Mine Workers Journal* on, 231; unrecorded stories of, 234; and work requiring physical strength, 232; during World War II, 229; in Wyoming strip mines, 237–38. *See also* Coal Employment Project (CEP); Coal Mining Women's Support Team; Lady Miners of Utah; National Conference of Women Coal Miners
women miners, and UMWA: initial resistance of, 234; integration into, 239–41, 244; opposition to women's outside activism by, 238; reforms at, *xxxiv–xxxv*
work assignments, punitive: to intimidate prounion miners, 119; prohibition of, as UMWA benefit, 7, 23; before unionization, 11–12; wildcat strikes to protest, 85
workers' standard of living: decline since 1970s, *xxxi*; Lewis's success in raising, *xxxviii*; ongoing importance of unions to, 284, 287–88; UMWA postwar activism and, 58
World War I, demand for coal in, 9, 10, 18

World War II: abrupt end of, and economic anxiety, 52; coal production increases in Utah, 45–47, 50; and hiring of inexperienced miners, 47; importance of coal in, *xxi*; increased miner injuries in, 46–47; industrial expansion, and rise in union recognition, 38; influx of African American and Mexican miners during, 47, 203, 205; miners' dissatisfaction with pay *vs.* defense plant workers, 47; miners' strikes for pay and benefit increases, 47–48; steel production increases, and growth of Utah coal mining, 45–46; strikes by Utah miners during, 48–50; women's work in mines during, 229

Wright, Virgil: and District election of 1949, 90–91; secret agreement with Union Pacific Coal, 91; on small mine organizing, 28, 66–67

Wyoming: and strip mining, early resistance to, 70–71; support for MFD in, 147; women miners in, 237–38; World War II coal production, 50

Yablonski, Joseph A. "Jock": assassination of, 134–36; bid for union presidency, *xliii*, 256–57; and investigation of Local 9958 corruption, 95; platform of, 149

Yablonski, Joseph "Chip," 143–45, 148, 212, 244

Yablonski, Ken, 212

younger miners' entering mining after 1970: boom in coal demand and, 257; characteristics of, 254–56; and destabilization of union power, 254; difficulty of assimilating into existing communities, 258–59; and dramatic drop in average miner age, 253, 255*f*; high absentee rate among, 272; and increase in injuries through inexperience, 263*f*; individualism of, 261–63; and labor unrest in growing mines, 267; little interest in unions, 254, 259–60, 264, 272; and MFD movement, 257; number of, 257; organizing against UMWA by, 271–72; risky behaviors by, 272; and UMWA decline, 272; UMWA's need to sell union to, 253, 254, 263–64; as unattached to UMWA through family ties, *xxxv*, 253, 254